taste of home

Home Style
COOKING

taste of home
BOOKS

REIMAN MEDIA GROUP, INC. • GREENDALE, WI

taste of home Reader's Digest

EDITORIAL

Editor-in-Chief: Catherine Cassidy
Creative Director: Howard Greenberg
Editorial Services Manager: Kerri Balliet

Managing Editor, Print and Digital Books: Mark Hagen
Associate Creative Director: Edwin Robles Jr.

Editor: Janet Briggs
Associate Editor: Christine Rukavena
Art Director: Jessie Sharon
Layout Designer: Catherine Fletcher
Editorial Production Manager: Dena Ahlers
Copy Chief: Deb Warlaumont Mulvey
Copy Editor: Alysse Gear
Content Operations Manager: Colleen King
Contributing Copy Editor: Valerie Phillips
Executive Assistant: Marie Brannon

Chief Food Editor: Karen Berner
Food Editor: Peggy Woodward, RD
Associate Food Editor: Krista Lanphier
Associate Editor/Food Content: Annie Rundle
Recipe Editors: Mary King; Jenni Sharp, RD; Irene Yeh

Test Kitchen and Food Styling Manager: Sarah Thompson
Test Kitchen Cooks: Alicia Rooker, RD (lead); Holly Johnson; Jimmy Cababa
Prep Cooks: Matthew Hass (lead), Nicole Spohrleder, Lauren Knoelke
Food Stylists: Kathryn Conrad (senior), Shannon Roum, Leah Rekau
Grocery Coordinator: Molly McCowan

Photo Director: Dan Bishop
Photographers: Dan Roberts, Grace Natoli Sheldon, Jim Wieland
Set Styling Manager: Stephanie Marchese
Set Stylists: Melissa Haberman, Dee Dee Jacq

BUSINESS

Vice President, Publisher: Jan Studin, jan_studin@rd.com

General Manager, Taste of Home Cooking Schools: Erin Puariea

Vice President, Brand Marketing: Jennifer Smith
Vice President, Circulation and Continuity Marketing: Dave Fiegel

READER'S DIGEST NORTH AMERICA
Vice President, Business Development: Jonathan Bigham
President, Books and Home Entertaining: Harold Clarke
Chief Financial Officer: Howard Halligan
VP, General Manager, Reader's Digest Media: Marilynn Jacobs
Chief Marketing Officer: Renee Jordan
Vice President, Chief Sales Officer: Mark Josephson
General Manager, Milwaukee: Frank Quigley
Vice President, Chief Content Officer: Liz Vaccariello

THE READER'S DIGEST ASSOCIATION, INC.
President and Chief Executive Officer: Robert E. Guth

For other Taste of Home books and products,
visit us at **tasteofhome.com.**

For more Reader's Digest products and information,
visit **rd.com** (in the United States) or see **rd.ca** (in Canada).

Pictured on front cover: Carribbean Jerk Chicken, page 138; Sweet Potato Minestrone, page 75; Mushroom-Spinach Bake, page 19; Ginger Plum Tart, page 266.

Pictured on back cover: Beef & Veggie Stew, page 160; Jeweled Buffet Ham, page 209; Chocolate Strawberry Truffle Brownies, page 243; Freezer Raspberry Sauce, page 296.

Pictured on spine: Grandma's Dill Pickles, page 282.

CONTENTS

f **LIKE US**
facebook.com/tasteofhome

VISIT OUR BLOG
loveandhomemaderecipes.com

E-MAIL US
bookeditors@tasteofhome.com

TWEET US
@tasteofhome

SHOP WITH US
shoptasteofhome.com

FOLLOW US
pinterest.com/taste_of_home

SHARE A RECIPE
tasteofhome.com/submit

VISIT
tasteofhome.com
FOR MORE!

Grab a Plate and Make Yourself *at Home!*

Country cooks know how to appeal to family and friends with flavorful, from-scratch recipes...and now they're sharing their best dishes with you! Pull up a seat and dig into a hearty favorite because there's old-fashioned goodness in the 420 recipes found in Home Style Cooking from *Taste of Home.*

Home Style Cooking is all about satisfying meals that taste as wonderful as they look. It's about turning everyday ingredients into **comfort foods that'll keep your family at the table and asking for seconds.** It's about stick-to-your-ribs specialties that come together easily with ingredients you likely already have on hand. And that's just what you'll find in this collection of down-home dinners, breads, sides, desserts and more! In fact, Home Style Cooking will make your kitchen the most popular room of the house.

As you page through this book you'll find everything from **Sunday suppers,** such as Caramelized Onion Chuck Roast, to special-occasion fare, like Jeweled Buffet Ham. You'll also discover **treats that indulge anyone's sweet tooth.** Just consider Caramel-Pecan Cheesecake Pie the next time you need to round out a meal. A home style collection just wouldn't be complete without **eye-opening breakfasts** such as Baked Eggs with Cheddar and Bacon. There's even a **special chapter** of **jams, jellies, pickles and relishes!**

For a true taste of country life, each chapter offers **a first-person account of a home cook's life** in the fresh air, complete with wide-open spaces and beautiful scenery. From running a tearoom to crafting prize-winning cheeses, these ladies enjoy rich lives, and they're happy to share them with you. Meet **April Silbaugh** on the next page, a city dweller turned country girl...and loving it!

Whether you live in the heartland or in a big town...whether you operate a farm of your own or merely long for the simple goodness of country living, you're sure to enjoy preparing and sharing the delicious dishes found in Home Style Cooking. After all, when it comes to feeding our families satisfying, wholesome foods, we're truly all home style cooks at heart.

Country at the Heart

Getting away from it all brought us home.

BY APRIL SILBAUGH

Moving to our 50 isolated acres in the rugged hills of Wyoming has been both challenging and magical. Neither my husband, Derek, nor I grew up in the country—but little miracles happen every day that reassure us this is where we're meant to be.

After selling our house in town, our family of four lived in a camper on our land while we had a 36- by 70-foot storage building erected. The plan was to live there for six months, until we could build our house. But many unexpected costs—including drilling a 1,000-foot well and putting in a road—delayed us. That storage building was home sweet home for nearly five years.

We went from a four bedroom, three-bath house to a one-room structure with a single bathroom and a resident family of mice. Our teenage son, Weston, and daughter, Savannah, shared a partitioned loft. A woodstove was our only heat source when it got down to 40 below.

The kids, who were used to walking two blocks to school, now had an hour-long bus ride. If it was too snowy for me to drive them to the bus stop, they'd snowshoe with their dad 3½ miles to the highway. Derek would pile everyone into the vehicle we left parked there when heavy snow was predicted, take the kids to school and drive another hour to his job.

Love Conquers All

There was a lot of complaining at first, but the siren song of country life was louder. We instantly fell in love with our land—sledding, hiking in the canyon and sleeping under the stars. Weston found a great snowboarding hill. Savannah likes picking colorful wildflowers. Our playground is as big as all outdoors.

Nature's embrace is my favorite thing about rural life, like the feel of chickadee feet on my shoulder as I tote seed to the feeder, or the sound of mockingbirds singing. The country is a year-round classroom. So far I've learned to do everything from raising chicks and growing tomatoes to maneuvering the ATV to round up our horses and donkey from the pasture.

Our land is also my creative sanctuary. I've started a jewelry-making business, Sunny Fields Pottery. Creating clay beads is a great outlet on a winter evening. I joined a writers' group and began to work on a memoir about our first year here. I'm hoping other families considering a move to the country will read it, laugh and cry with us, and catch the pioneer spirit.

Here to Stay

People often ask me if I had known then what I know now, would I move to the country again?

Above, from left: April with her husband, Derek, their children, Weston and Savannah (also shown with horse), and goldendoodle, Lila; samples of April's jewelry; and April creating pieces.

Today, looking out the window of the house we just finished building, I see Derek barbecuing on the front porch and our kids playing volleyball.

Last year, I'm proud to say, I canned 50 jars of homegrown tomatoes. We get fresh eggs from our henhouse, and our guinea fowl patrol the grounds regularly for grasshoppers and ticks.

Rocky as it was, that first year out here produced some of my best memories: sitting around the small table by the woodstove playing cards; snowdrifts swaddling us in pure silence; Savannah smiling, with a fistful of dewy flowers in her hand. I will always treasure those things. Facing challenges together has cemented us as a family. And somehow, the rough times have made everything about living in the country look better and brighter to us now.

Yes. I would do it all over again in a heartbeat.

Morning Meals

Golden pancakes drizzled with maple syrup, fluffy eggs, a side of crispy bacon and a lightly dusted fresh doughnut...these eye-opening breakfasts can be a reality! Let the classic fare that follows pull you from your slumber and give you plenty to dream about all day long!

Dutch Baby Tropicale

(recipe on page 33)

"A simple but impressive breakfast, a Dutch baby is a cross between a pancake, souffle and omelet. The eggy batter puffs up golden brown."

—CINDY RAPPUHN STARTUP, WASHINGTON

Fines Herbes & Mushroom Omelets Deluxe

The subtle blend of fine herbs doesn't overtake other flavors in these omelets—it enhances them. Garnish with extra herbs or shredded Asiago cheese for a special breakfast, lunch or dinner.

—LEE LOCKWOOD MAYBROOK, NEW YORK

PREP: 30 MINUTES **COOK:** 15 MINUTES
MAKES: 4 SERVINGS

- 1 **pound sliced baby portobello mushrooms**
- 2 **tablespoons butter**
- ¼ **cup white wine**
- 1 **teaspoon each minced fresh parsley, tarragon and chives**
- ½ **teaspoon dried chervil**
- ⅛ **teaspoon salt**
- ⅛ **teaspoon pepper**

ASIAGO SAUCE
- 2 **tablespoons butter**
- 2 **tablespoons all-purpose flour**
- 1 **cup 2% milk**
- ¼ **cup shredded Asiago cheese**
- ¼ **teaspoon salt**

OMELETS
- 4 **teaspoons butter, divided**
- 8 **eggs**
- ½ **cup water**
  Additional minced fresh herbs, optional

Home Style COOKING NOTES

1. In a large skillet, saute mushrooms in butter until tender. Add wine, stirring to loosen browned bits from pan. Stir in the herbs, salt and pepper. Remove from the heat; set aside.

2. In a small saucepan, melt butter; stir in flour until smooth. Gradually add milk. Bring to a boil; cook and stir for 1-2 minutes or until thickened. Stir in cheese and salt. Keep warm.

3. In a small nonstick skillet, melt 1 teaspoon butter over medium-high heat. Whisk eggs and water until blended. Add ⅔ cup egg mixture to skillet (mixture should set immediately at edges).

4. As eggs set, push cooked edges toward the center, letting uncooked portion flow underneath. When the eggs are set, spoon ½ cup mushroom mixture on one side; fold other side over filling. Slide omelet onto a plate; top with ¼ cup sauce. Sprinkle with additional herbs if desired. Repeat.

Baked Eggs with Cheddar and Bacon

These little treats are super easy to make and perfect for a special breakfast. They're also very nice for a casual dinner. The smoky cheese and bacon elevate eggs to another level!

—CATHERINE WILKINSON DEWEY, ARIZONA

PREP/TOTAL TIME: 25 MINUTES **MAKES:** 4 SERVINGS

- 4 **eggs**
- 4 **tablespoons fat-free milk, divided**
- 2 **tablespoons shredded smoked cheddar cheese**
- 2 **teaspoons minced fresh parsley**
- ¼ **teaspoon salt**
- ⅛ **teaspoon pepper**
- 2 **bacon strips**

1. Coat four 4-oz. ramekins with cooking spray; break an egg into each dish. Spoon 1 tablespoon milk over each egg. Combine the cheese, parsley, salt and pepper; sprinkle over tops.

2. Bake, uncovered, at 325° for 12-15 minutes or until whites are completely set and yolks begin to thicken but are not firm.

3. Meanwhile, in a small skillet, cook bacon over medium heat until crisp. Remove to paper towels to drain. Crumble bacon and sprinkle over eggs.

Spinach & Bacon Hash Brown Quiche

With a crust of crispy hash browns and a rich, creamy filling studded with spinach and bacon, this cheesy quiche is comfort food at its most satisfying. Delicious for breakfast, lunch or supper!

—SONYA LABBE WEST HOLLYWOOD, CALIFORNIA

PREP: 25 MINUTES
BAKE: 25 MINUTES + STANDING
MAKES: 6 SERVINGS

- 3 **cups frozen shredded hash brown potatoes, thawed**
- ¼ **cup butter, melted**
- 6 **bacon strips, diced**
- 1 **small onion, chopped**
- 3 **eggs**
- 1 **cup half-and-half cream**
- ¼ **teaspoon salt**
- ⅛ **teaspoon pepper**
- 2 **cups chopped fresh spinach**
- ⅔ **cup shredded part-skim mozzarella cheese**
- ⅓ **cup shredded Swiss cheese**

1. Press hash browns between paper towels to remove excess moisture; toss with butter. Press onto the bottom and up the sides of a 9-in. pie plate. Bake at 425° for 20-25 minutes or until edges are browned.

2. Meanwhile, in a large skillet, cook the bacon and onion over medium heat until bacon is crisp. Remove to paper towels to drain. In a large bowl, combine eggs, cream, salt and pepper. Stir in the spinach, cheeses and bacon mixture; pour into crust.

3. Bake at 350° for 25-30 minutes or until a knife inserted near the center comes out clean. Let stand for 10 minutes before cutting.

Griddle Corn Cakes

This is a downsized version of a recipe that belonged to my husband's mother and has been in their family for over 80 years. I have been making them since my husband and I got married more than 30 years ago.

— **MYRNA GERSON**
STATEN ISLAND, NEW YORK

PREP/TOTAL TIME: 20 MINUTES
MAKES: 2 SERVINGS

- ¾ **cup all-purpose flour**
- 2 **tablespoons sugar**
- ½ **teaspoon baking powder**
- ¼ **teaspoon salt**
- 1 **egg**
- 1 **can (8¼ ounces) cream-style corn**
- 3 **tablespoons 2% milk**
- ½ **teaspoon vanilla extract**

1. In a small bowl, combine the flour, sugar, baking powder and salt. Combine the egg, corn, milk and vanilla; stir into dry ingredients just until moistened.

2. Drop batter by ¼ cupfuls onto a hot nonstick griddle. Cook for 4-5 minutes on each side or until golden brown.

Potato Crust Quiche

My husband and I have lived in four different states, and we've grown potatoes in every one of them. I mostly make this dish for family, but company loves it, too. It's almost a meal in itself—all you need to add is a salad.

— **NANCY SMITH** SCOTTSDALE, ARIZONA

PREP: 20 MINUTES **BAKE:** 35 MINUTES **MAKES:** 8 SERVINGS

CRUST
- 4 **cups coarsely shredded uncooked potatoes (about 4 large)**
- ½ **cup chopped onion**
- 1 **egg, lightly beaten**
- 1 **cup all-purpose flour**
- ½ **teaspoon salt**

FILLING
- 1½ **cups (6 ounces) shredded Colby cheese, divided**
- ½ **cup chopped onion**
- 1½ **cups cubed fully cooked ham**
- 1½ **cups fresh broccoli florets**
- 3 **eggs, lightly beaten**
- 1 **cup half-and-half cream**
- ½ **teaspoon salt**
  Dash ground nutmeg
  Paprika

1. In a large bowl, combine crust ingredients; press into a well-greased 10-in. deep-dish pie plate. Bake at 400° for 20 minutes.

2. Remove from oven; reduce heat to 350°. Add 1 cup cheese, onion, ham and broccoli to pastry crust. Whisk the eggs, cream, salt and nutmeg; pour over broccoli. Sprinkle with paprika.

3. Bake for 35-40 minutes or until a knife inserted near the center comes out clean. Sprinkle with remaining cheese. Let stand for 5 minutes before serving.

Blueberry Waffles

These light, tender homemade waffles are just bursting with juicy blueberries. They're topped with blueberry sauce, too!

—DEVYN WEAKLEY HOWARD, KANSAS

PREP: 20 MINUTES **COOK:** 5 MINUTES/BATCH **MAKES:** 12 WAFFLES (1⅓ CUPS SAUCE)

2 cups all-purpose flour
2¼ teaspoons baking powder
½ teaspoon salt
1⅔ cups milk
3 eggs, separated
¼ cup butter, melted
⅔ cup fresh or frozen blueberries

SAUCE

1½ cups fresh or frozen blueberries
½ cup orange juice, divided
3 tablespoons honey
1 tablespoon cornstarch

1. In a large bowl, combine the flour, baking powder and salt. Whisk the milk, egg yolks and butter; stir into dry ingredients just until moistened. Fold in blueberries.

2. In a small bowl, beat egg whites until stiff peaks form; fold into batter.

3. Bake in a preheated waffle iron according to the manufacturer's directions until golden brown.

4. Meanwhile, in a small saucepan, combine the blueberries, ¼ cup orange juice and honey. Bring to a boil. Combine cornstarch and remaining orange juice until smooth; gradually stir into berry mixture. Bring to a boil; cook and stir for 2 minutes or until thickened. Serve warm with waffles.

Editor's Note: *If using frozen blueberries, use without thawing to avoid discoloring the batter.*

Berry-Topped Puff Pancake

Impressive to look at and even better to taste, my gorgeous pancake is surprisingly simple to make.

—MARIE COSENZA CORTLANDT MANOR, NEW YORK

PREP: 20 MINUTES **BAKE:** 15 MINUTES **MAKES:** 4 SERVINGS

- 2 **tablespoons butter**
- 2 **eggs**
- ½ **cup 2% milk**
- ½ **cup all-purpose flour**
- 2 **tablespoons sugar**
- ¼ **teaspoon salt**

TOPPING

- ⅓ **cup sugar**
- 1 **tablespoon cornstarch**
- ½ **cup orange juice**
- 2 **teaspoons orange liqueur**
- 1 **cup sliced fresh strawberries**
- 1 **cup fresh blueberries**
- 1 **cup fresh raspberries**
  Confectioners' sugar, optional

1. Place butter in a 9-in. pie plate. Place in a 425° oven for 4-5 minutes or until melted. Meanwhile, in a large bowl, whisk eggs and milk. In another bowl, combine the flour, sugar and salt. Whisk into egg mixture until blended. Pour into prepared pie plate. Bake for 14-16 minutes or until sides are crisp and golden brown.

2. Meanwhile, in a small saucepan, combine sugar and cornstarch. Gradually stir in orange juice and liqueur. Bring to a boil over medium heat, stirring constantly. Cook and stir 1-2 minutes longer or until thickened. Remove from the heat.

3. Spoon berries over pancake and drizzle with sauce. Dust with confectioners' sugar if desired.

Swedish Doughnuts

One day, my father got a hankering for doughnuts and asked me to make some for him. I ended up trying these. Dad—and everyone else—loved the results. They come out so golden and plump.

—LISA BATES DUNHAM, QUEBEC

PREP: 20 MINUTES + CHILLING **COOK:** 5 MINUTES/BATCH
MAKES: ABOUT 2½ DOZEN

- 2 **eggs**
- 1 **cup sugar**
- 2 **cups cold mashed potatoes (mashed with milk and butter)**
- ¾ **cup buttermilk**
- 2 **tablespoons butter, melted**
- 1 **teaspoon vanilla or almond extract**
- 4½ **cups all-purpose flour**
- 4 **teaspoons baking powder**
- 1 **teaspoon baking soda**
- 1 **teaspoon salt**
- 2 **teaspoons ground nutmeg**
- ⅛ **teaspoon ground ginger**
   Oil for deep-fat frying
   Additional sugar, optional

1. In a large bowl, beat eggs and sugar. Add the potatoes, buttermilk, butter and vanilla. Combine the flour, baking powder, baking soda, salt, nutmeg and ginger; gradually add to egg mixture and mix well. Cover and refrigerate for 1-2 hours.
2. Turn onto a lightly floured surface; roll to ½-in. thickness. Cut with a floured 2½-in. doughnut cutter. In an electric skillet or deep-fat fryer, heat oil to 375°.
3. Fry doughnuts, a few at a time, until golden brown on both sides, about 2 minutes. Drain on paper towels. Roll warm doughnuts in sugar if desired.

Granola with Apricots and Ginger

This crunchy granola is a favorite of guests at my bed and breakfast. You can serve it with milk and over yogurt and ice cream.

—EVA AMUSO CHESHIRE, MASSACHUSETTS

PREP: 15 MINUTES **BAKE:** 40 MINUTES + COOLING
MAKES: 8 CUPS

- 4 **cups old-fashioned oats**
- 1½ **cups unblanched almonds**
- 1 **cup sunflower kernels**
- ½ **cup flaxseed**
- ½ **cup packed brown sugar**
- 1 **teaspoon ground cinnamon**
- ½ **teaspoon salt**
- ¼ **cup canola oil**
- ¼ **cup honey**
- 1 **teaspoon vanilla extract**
- 1 **cup chopped dried apricots**
- ½ **cup crystallized ginger, finely chopped**

1. In a large bowl, combine the first seven ingredients; set aside. In a small saucepan, combine oil and honey. Cook and stir over medium heat for 2-3 minutes or until heated through. Remove from the heat; stir in vanilla. Pour over oat mixture and toss to coat.
2. Transfer to a greased 15-in. x 10-in. x 1-in. baking pan. Bake at 300° for 40-45 minutes or until golden brown, stirring every 10 minutes. Cool on a wire rack. Add apricots and ginger. Store in an airtight container.

Home Style COOKING NOTES

Farmer's Country Breakfast

When we're camping, we eat a late breakfast, so this hearty combination of sausage, hash browns and eggs is just right.

—**BONNIE ROBERTS** NEWAYGO, MICHIGAN

PREP/TOTAL TIME: 30 MINUTES **MAKES:** 4 SERVINGS

   6   **eggs**
   ⅓   **cup 2% milk**
   ½   **teaspoon dried parsley flakes**
   ¼   **teaspoon salt**
   6   **ounces bulk pork sausage**
   1½ **cups frozen cubed hash brown potatoes, thawed**
   ¼   **cup chopped onion**
   1   **cup (4 ounces) shredded cheddar cheese**

1. Whisk the eggs, milk, parsley and salt; set aside. In a large skillet, cook sausage over medium heat until no longer pink; remove and drain. In the same skillet, cook potatoes and onion for 5-7 minutes or until tender. Return sausage to the pan.
2. Add egg mixture; cook and stir until almost set. Sprinkle with cheese. Cover and cook for 1-2 minutes or until cheese is melted.

Orange Ricotta Pancakes

These popular pancakes are likely to spark a craving. For a different twist, switch the citrus ingredient to lime or lemon juice.

—**BREHAN KOHL** ANCHORAGE, ALASKA

PREP/TOTAL TIME: 30 MINUTES
MAKES: 12 PANCAKES

   1½ **cups all-purpose flour**
   3   **tablespoons sugar**
   1½ **teaspoons baking powder**
   ½   **teaspoon baking soda**
   ¼   **teaspoon salt**
   1   **egg**
   1   **cup part-skim ricotta cheese**
   ¾   **cup 2% milk**
   ½   **cup orange juice**
   ¼   **cup butter, melted**
   ½   **teaspoon grated orange peel**
   ½   **teaspoon vanilla extract**
       Maple syrup and confectioners' sugar

1. In a small bowl, combine the flour, sugar, baking powder, baking soda and salt. In another bowl, whisk the egg, cheese, milk, orange juice, butter, orange peel and vanilla. Stir into dry ingredients just until moistened.
2. Pour batter by ¼ cupfuls onto a greased hot griddle; turn when bubbles form on top. Cook until the second side is golden brown. Serve with maple syrup and confectioners' sugar.

Breakfast Sausage Patties

Buttermilk is the secret ingredient that keeps these savory pork patties moist, while a blend of seasonings create a distinctive flavor.

—HARVEY KEENEY
MANDAN, NORTH DAKOTA

PREP: 30 MINUTES
COOK: 10 MINUTES/BATCH
MAKES: 21 SAUSAGE PATTIES

  ¾ **cup buttermilk**
 2¼ **teaspoons kosher salt**
 1½ **teaspoons rubbed sage**
 1½ **teaspoons brown sugar**
 1½ **teaspoons pepper**
  ¾ **teaspoon dried marjoram**
  ¾ **teaspoon dried savory**
  ¾ **teaspoon cayenne pepper**
  ¼ **teaspoon ground nutmeg**
 2½ **pounds ground pork**

1. In a large bowl, combine buttermilk and seasonings. Crumble the pork over the mixture; mix well. Shape into twenty-one 3-in. patties.
2. In a large skillet coated with cooking spray, cook the patties in batches over medium heat for 5-6 minutes on each side or until meat is no longer pink. Drain if necessary on paper towels.

Home Style COOKING NOTES

Tomato Herb Frittata

Fresh herbs and garlic really add to the flavor of this hearty, savory and filling breakfast. Every slice is brimming with cheesy eggs and bright tomatoes.

—CANDY SUMMERHILL ALEXANDER, ARKANSAS

PREP: 20 MINUTES **BAKE:** 15 MINUTES **MAKES:** 6 SERVINGS

  9 **eggs**
 1¼ **cups (5 ounces) shredded part-skim mozzarella cheese, divided**
  ½ **cup 2% milk**
  1 **tablespoon minced fresh basil or 1 teaspoon dried basil**
  1 **tablespoon minced fresh oregano or 1 teaspoon dried oregano**
  1 **teaspoon minced fresh thyme or ¼ teaspoon dried thyme**
  ½ **teaspoon salt**
  ¼ **teaspoon pepper**
 1½ **cups grape tomatoes**
  2 **tablespoons olive oil**
  2 **garlic cloves, minced**
     Thinly sliced fresh basil, optional

1. In a small bowl, whisk the eggs, ¾ cup cheese, milk, herbs, salt and pepper; set aside.
2. In a 10-in. ovenproof skillet, saute the tomatoes in oil until tender. Add the garlic; cook 1 minute longer. Pour the egg mixture into pan; sprinkle with the remaining cheese.
3. Bake at 400° for 12-15 minutes or until eggs are completely set. Let stand for 5 minutes. Cut into wedges. Garnish with sliced basil if desired.

Broccoli Brunch Skillet

Whether for brunch, lunch or dinner, this recipe is always a people pleaser.

—FRANCES ROWLEY
BARTLESVILLE, OKLAHOMA

PREP: 15 MINUTES **COOK:** 20 MINUTES
MAKES: 6 SERVINGS

- 6 **fresh broccoli spears**
- 6 **slices part-skim mozzarella cheese**
- 6 **thin slices fully cooked ham**
- 1 **tablespoon butter**
- 6 **eggs**
- ⅓ **cup water**
  Coarsely ground pepper, optional

1. In a small saucepan, bring 1 in. of water and broccoli to a boil. Reduce heat; cover and simmer for 5-8 minutes or until broccoli is crisp-tender; drain.

2. Place one cheese slice over one ham slice and wrap around one broccoli spear. Secure with a toothpick. Repeat five times. Melt butter in a 9-in. skillet. Arrange ham rolls in a spoke pattern.

3. In a large bowl, beat the eggs and water; pour over ham rolls. Cook over medium-low heat for 10 minutes; as eggs set, lift edges, letting uncooked portion flow underneath. Cover and cook 2-3 minutes longer or until the eggs are completely set. Sprinkle with pepper if desired. Carefully remove toothpicks; cut into wedges.

Home Style COOKING NOTES

Brunch Pizza

Whenever I entertain guests, this zippy pizza always boosts my cooking confidence— people really love it! It also makes a tantalizing late-night snack when you're in the middle of a good movie. Just rename it Movie Pizza when you serve it!

—JANELLE LEE APPLETON, WISCONSIN

PREP: 15 MINUTES **BAKE:** 25 MINUTES **MAKES:** 6-8 SERVINGS

- 1 **pound bulk pork sausage**
- 1 **tube (8 ounces) refrigerated crescent rolls**
- 1 **cup frozen shredded hash browns**
- 1 **cup (4 ounces) shredded cheddar cheese**
- 5 **eggs**
- ¼ **cup milk**
- ½ **teaspoon salt**
- ¼ **teaspoon pepper**
- 2 **tablespoons grated Parmesan cheese**

1. Cook and crumble the sausage; drain and set aside. Separate the crescent roll dough into eight triangles and place on an ungreased 12-in. round pizza pan with points toward center. Press over the bottom and up the sides to form a crust; seal the perforations. Spoon sausage over crust; sprinkle with the hash browns and cheddar cheese.

2. In a bowl, beat eggs, milk, salt and pepper; pour over cheese. Sprinkle with Parmesan. Bake at 375° for 25-30 minutes or until crust is golden.

Breakfast Enchiladas

Draped in gooey cheese and a savory sauce, these enchiladas are a popular option at any holiday brunch. Chorizo gives the hearty filling a Southwestern punch.

—TAHNIA FOX TRENTON, MICHIGAN

PREP: 25 MIN. **BAKE:** 25 MINUTES **MAKES:** 8 SERVINGS

- ½ **pound uncooked chorizo or spicy pork sausage**
- 1 **small onion, finely chopped**
- ½ **medium green pepper, finely chopped**
- 2 **teaspoons butter**
- 6 **eggs, beaten**
- ¾ **cup shredded cheddar cheese, divided**
- ¾ **cup shredded pepper jack cheese, divided**
- 2 **cans (10 ounces each) enchilada sauce, divided**
- 8 **flour tortillas (8 inches), room temperature**
- 1 **green onion, finely chopped**

1. Crumble chorizo into a large skillet; add onion and green pepper. Cook over medium heat for 6-8 minutes or until sausage is fully cooked; drain.

2. In another skillet, heat butter over medium heat. Add eggs; cook and stir until almost set. Remove from the heat; stir in the chorizo mixture and ⅓ cup of each cheese.

3. Spread ½ cup enchilada sauce into a greased 13-in. x 9-in. baking dish. Spread 2 tablespoons enchilada sauce over each tortilla; place 2 tablespoons of egg mixture down the center. Roll up and place seam side down in prepared dish.

4. Pour the remaining enchilada sauce over the top; sprinkle with remaining cheeses.

5. Bake, uncovered, at 350° for 25-30 minutes or until heated through. Sprinkle with green onion.

Brunch Beignets

Enjoy breakfast the New Orleans way with these warm, crispy bites. Topped with powdered sugar, they're heavenly!

—LOIS RUTHERFORD ELKTON, FLORIDA

PREP: 20 MINUTES **COOK:** 5 MINUTES/BATCH **MAKES:** ABOUT 2 DOZEN

2 **eggs, separated**
1 **cup all-purpose flour**
1 **teaspoon baking powder**
⅛ **teaspoon salt**
½ **cup sugar**
¼ **cup water**
1 **tablespoon butter, melted**
2 **teaspoons grated lemon peel**
1 **teaspoon vanilla extract**
1 **teaspoon brandy, optional**
   Oil for deep-fat frying
   Confectioners' sugar

1. Place egg whites in a small bowl; let stand at room temperature for 30 minutes.

2. Meanwhile, in a large bowl, combine the flour, baking powder and salt. Combine the egg yolks, sugar, water, butter, lemon peel, vanilla and brandy if desired; stir into dry ingredients just until combined. Beat egg whites on medium speed until soft peaks form; fold into batter.

3. In an electric skillet or deep-fat fryer, heat oil to 375°. Drop batter by teaspoonfuls, a few at a time, into hot oil. Fry until golden brown, about 1½ minutes on each side. Drain on paper towels. Dust with confectioners' sugar. Serve warm.

Mushroom-Spinach Bake

With a pretty spinach layer and a golden-brown top, this airy souffle is a holiday staple at our house. It makes a delicious entree for brunch.

—FREDERICK HILLIARD CHARLESTON, WEST VIRGINIA

PREP: 30 MINUTES **BAKE:** 20 MINUTES **MAKES:** 6 SERVINGS

- 3 **tablespoons plus 1½ teaspoons butter**
- ½ **cup all-purpose flour**
- 2 **cups 2% milk**
- 4 **eggs, lightly beaten**
- 1 **cup (4 ounces) shredded Gruyere or Swiss cheese**
- ½ **teaspoon salt**
- ⅛ **teaspoon pepper**
  Dash ground nutmeg

MUSHROOM SPINACH FILLING
- 2 **cups sliced baby portobello mushrooms**
- 1 **tablespoon chopped shallot**
- 1 **tablespoon butter**
- 1 **teaspoon white truffle oil, optional**
- 1 **package (10 ounces) frozen chopped spinach, thawed and squeezed dry**
- 1 **tablespoon all-purpose flour**
- ⅛ **teaspoon salt**
- ⅛ **teaspoon pepper**
- ¼ **cup heavy whipping cream**
- ⅓ **cup shredded Gruyere or Swiss cheese**

1. In a large saucepan, melt butter. Stir in flour until smooth; gradually add milk. Bring to a boil; cook and stir for 1-2 minutes or until thickened.

2. Stir a small amount of hot mixture into eggs. Return all to the pan, stirring constantly. Stir in cheese, salt, pepper and nutmeg; set aside.

3. For filling, in a large skillet, saute the mushrooms and shallot in butter and oil if desired until tender. Add the spinach; cook 1 minute longer. Stir in flour, salt and pepper until blended. Gradually add the cream; heat through (do not boil).

4. Pour half of the egg mixture into a greased 8-in. square baking dish. Top with filling and remaining egg mixture. Sprinkle with cheese. Bake at 400° for 20-25 minutes or until a knife inserted near the center comes out clean.

Bacon Potato Waffles

I like to garnish these great waffles with sour cream and chives, or even a simple cheese sauce. My mother liked to sprinkle them with a touch of sugar.

—LAURA FALL-SUTTON BUHL, IDAHO

PREP: 20 MINUTES **COOK:** 5 MINUTES/BATCH
MAKES: 12 WAFFLES

- 1 **cup all-purpose flour**
- 2 **tablespoons sugar**
- 2 **teaspoons baking powder**
- ½ **teaspoon salt**
- 2 **eggs**
- 1½ **cups mashed potatoes (with added milk and butter)**
- 1 **cup 2% milk**
- 5 **tablespoons canola oil**
- ¼ **cup finely chopped onion**
- 3 **bacon strips, cooked and crumbled**
  Maple syrup or chunky applesauce
  Additional crumbled cooked bacon, optional

1. In a large bowl, combine the flour, sugar, baking powder and salt. In another bowl, whisk the eggs, mashed potatoes, milk and oil. Stir into dry ingredients just until moistened. Fold in onion and bacon.

2. Bake in a preheated waffle iron according to manufacturer's directions until golden brown. Serve with syrup or applesauce. Sprinkle with additional bacon if desired.

Italian Sausage & Egg Croissants

Wake up your taste buds with breakfast sandwiches featuring spicy sausage, fluffy egg, fresh, juicy tomato and creamy avocado piled high on a flaky croissant.

—EMORY DOTY JASPER, GEORGIA

PREP: 25 MINUTES **COOK:** 15 MINUTES
MAKES: 8 SERVINGS

- 1 cup (4 ounces) crumbled blue cheese
- 1 jalapeno pepper, seeded and minced
- 1 teaspoon each dried basil, oregano and parsley flakes
- 1 pound bulk Italian sausage
- 8 eggs
- 3 tablespoons 2% milk
- ⅛ teaspoon salt
- ⅛ teaspoon pepper
- 3 tablespoons butter
- ½ cup mayonnaise
- 8 croissants, split
- 8 slices tomato
- 1 medium ripe avocado, peeled and sliced

1. In a large bowl, combine cheese, jalapeno and herbs. Crumble sausage over mixture and mix well. Shape into eight patties.

2. In a large nonstick skillet over medium heat, cook patties for 4-5 minutes on each side or until no longer pink. Set aside and keep warm.

3. Whisk the eggs, milk, salt and pepper. In another large nonstick skillet, melt half of the butter over medium-high heat. Add half of the egg mixture to the skillet (mixture should set immediately at edges).

4. As eggs set, push cooked edges toward the center, letting uncooked portion flow underneath. Cover and cook 1-2 minutes longer or until top is set. Slide eggs onto a plate; cut into four wedges. Repeat with remaining butter and egg mixture.

5. Spread mayonnaise over croissants; top with sausage patties, eggs, tomato and avocado.

Editor's Note: *Wear disposable gloves when cutting hot peppers; the oils can burn skin. Avoid touching your face.*

Buttermilk Pancakes

You just can't beat a basic buttermilk pancake for a down-home hearty breakfast. Pair it with sausage and fresh fruit for a mouthwatering morning meal.

—BETTY ABREY IMPERIAL, SASKATCHEWAN

PREP: 10 MINUTES **COOK:** 5 MINUTES/BATCH **MAKES:** 2½ DOZEN

- 4 cups all-purpose flour
- ¼ cup sugar
- 2 teaspoons baking soda
- 2 teaspoons salt
- 1½ teaspoons baking powder
- 4 eggs
- 4 cups buttermilk

1. In a large bowl, combine the flour, sugar, baking soda, salt and baking powder. In another bowl, whisk the eggs and buttermilk until blended; stir into dry ingredients just until moistened.

2. Pour batter by ¼ cupfuls onto a lightly greased hot griddle; turn when bubbles form on top. Cook until second side is golden brown.

Ham & Asparagus Puff Pancake

Turn any morning into a special occasion by serving this fluffy and flavorful puff pancake filled with hearty ham and tender asparagus.

—**TASTE OF HOME COOKING SCHOOL**

PREP/TOTAL TIME: 30 MINUTES **MAKES:** 6-8 SERVINGS

- ¼ **cup butter, cubed**
- 1 **cup all-purpose flour**
- 4 **eggs**
- 1 **cup milk**
- ¼ **teaspoon salt**
- ⅛ **teaspoon white pepper**

FILLING

- ¾ **pound (1½ cups) chopped fully cooked ham**
- ½ **pound fresh asparagus spears, trimmed and cut into 1-inch pieces**
- 3 **tablespoons butter**
- 2 **tablespoons all-purpose flour**
- ¾ **cup milk**
- ¼ **cup sour cream**
- 1 **teaspoon lemon juice**
- ¼ **teaspoon hot pepper sauce**
- ½ **cup shredded cheddar cheese**

1. Place the butter in a 10-in. ovenproof skillet; place in a 425° oven for 3-4 minutes or until melted. In a bowl, beat the flour, eggs, milk, salt and pepper until smooth. Pour the mixture into prepared skillet. Bake at 425° for 22-25 minutes or until puffed and golden brown.

2. Meanwhile, in a saucepan over medium-high heat, cook ham and asparagus in melted butter for 5 minutes, stirring occasionally. Stir in flour until blended. Gradually stir in milk. Bring to a boil; cook and stir for 3 minutes. Reduce heat; stir in sour cream, lemon juice and pepper sauce.

3. Spoon into center of puff pancake. Sprinkle with cheese. Cut into wedges; serve immediately.

Michigan Fruit Baked Oatmeal

Whole-grain oatmeal is a delicious way to start every day. For a change, swap chunks of Granny Smith apples for the dried fruit. Leftovers warm well in the microwave.

—**JEANETTE KASS** RAVENNA, MICHIGAN

PREP: 15 MINUTES **BAKE:** 45 MINUTES
MAKES: 2 SERVINGS

- 1 **cup old-fashioned oats**
- ¼ **cup dried cranberries or cherries**
- 1 **tablespoon brown sugar**
- 2 **cups fat-free milk**
- ½ **cup chunky applesauce**
- ¼ **teaspoon almond extract**
- 2 **tablespoons sliced almonds**
  Optional toppings: vanilla yogurt and additional dried cranberries and sliced almonds

1. In a large bowl, combine the first six ingredients. Transfer to a 3-cup baking dish coated with cooking spray; sprinkle with almonds.

2. Bake, uncovered, at 350° for 45-50 minutes or until set. Serve with the toppings if desired.

HOME STYLE tip

66 In order to keep asparagus fresh longer, I place the cut stems in a container of cold water—similar to flowers in a vase. I keep the asparagus in the refrigerator, changing the water at least once every 3 days. 99

—**MARY S.**
COUNCIL BLUFFS, IOWA

Chicken 'n' Ham Frittata

Because my family is busy, Sunday is a time we gather for brunch to discuss plans for the upcoming week over servings of this hearty egg dish. It's colorful and special enough to prepare for holiday get-togethers, too.

—RUTH ALLEN HEBRON, KENTUCKY

PREP: 15 MINUTES **BAKE:** 25 MINUTES
MAKES: 6 SERVINGS

- ½ cup chopped green onions
- 2 garlic cloves, minced
- 2 tablespoons canola oil
- 1¼ cups chopped yellow summer squash
- 1 cup chopped zucchini
- ½ cup chopped sweet yellow pepper
- ½ cup chopped sweet red pepper
- 1 teaspoon minced fresh gingerroot
- 2 cups cubed cooked chicken breast
- 1 cup chopped deli ham
- 6 eggs
- ¾ cup mayonnaise
- ¼ teaspoon prepared horseradish
- ¼ teaspoon pepper
- 1 cup (4 ounces) shredded Monterey Jack cheese

1. In a large ovenproof skillet, saute the onions and garlic in oil for 1 minute. Add the yellow squash, zucchini, peppers and ginger; cook and stir for 8 minutes or until vegetables are crisp-tender. Add the chicken and ham; cook 1 minute longer or until heated through. Remove from the heat.

2. In a large bowl, whisk the eggs, mayonnaise, horseradish and pepper until blended. Pour into skillet.

3. Bake, uncovered, at 350° for 25-30 minutes or until eggs are completely set. Sprinkle with cheese; cover and let stand for 5 minutes or until the cheese is melted.

Chocolate Chip Pancakes

This recipe is a favorite of mine to make for special occasions like birthday or holidays. To make it extra special, serve the pancakes with berries and whipped cream.

—LORI DANIELS BEVERLY, WEST VIRGINIA

PREP: 20 MINUTES **COOK:** 20 MINUTES
MAKES: 16 PANCAKES (1 CUP WHIPPED CREAM)

- ½ cup heavy whipping cream
- 1 tablespoon confectioners' sugar
- ½ teaspoon vanilla extract

BATTER

- 1½ cups all-purpose flour
- 3 tablespoons sugar
- 1 teaspoon baking powder
- ½ teaspoon baking soda
- ¼ teaspoon salt
- 2 eggs
- 1 cup milk
- 1 cup (8 ounces) sour cream
- ¼ cup butter, melted
- ½ cup miniature semisweet chocolate chips

1. In a small bowl, beat the cream, confectioners' sugar and vanilla until stiff peaks form. Cover and refrigerate until serving.

2. In a large bowl, combine the flour, sugar, baking powder, baking soda and salt. In another bowl, whisk the eggs, milk, sour cream and butter until blended; stir into dry ingredients just until moistened. Fold in chocolate chips.

3. Pour the batter by ¼ cupfuls onto a lightly greased hot griddle; turn when bubbles form on the top. Cook until second side is golden brown. Serve with whipped cream.

Artichoke & Spinach Eggs Benedict

This rich breakfast classic stars fresh artichokes. It's bound to make everyone at your table feel like an honored guest.

—**LORI WIESE** HUMBOLDT, MINNESOTA

PREP: 40 MINUTES **COOK:** 5 MINUTES **MAKES:** 4 SERVINGS

- 1 **envelope hollandaise sauce mix**
- 4 **medium artichokes**
- 4 **eggs**
- 1 **tablespoon chopped green onion**
- 2 **tablespoons butter**
- 2 **tablespoons all-purpose flour**
- 1 **cup half-and-half cream**
- 1 **package (10 ounces) frozen chopped spinach, thawed and squeezed dry**
- 2 **teaspoons lemon juice**
- ⅛ **teaspoon salt**
- ⅛ **teaspoon pepper**
- 3 **tablespoons shredded Parmesan cheese Paprika**

1. Prepare sauce mix according to package directions. Set aside and keep warm.

2. Using a sharp knife, cut stems from artichokes. Remove and discard outer leaves, leaving each artichoke bottom exposed. Cut off tops ½ in. above artichoke bottoms and discard. With a grapefruit spoon, carefully remove the fuzzy centers and discard. Place artichoke bottoms in a large saucepan; add 1 in. of water. Bring to a boil. Reduce heat; cover and simmer for 15-20 minutes or until tender.

3. Place 2-3 in. of water in a large skillet with high sides. Bring to a boil; reduce heat and simmer gently. Break cold eggs, one at a time, into a custard cup or saucer. Holding the cup close to the surface of the water, slip each egg into water. Cook, uncovered, until whites are completely set and yolks are still soft, about 4 minutes.

4. Meanwhile, in a large skillet, saute green onion in butter until tender. Stir in flour until blended; gradually add cream. Bring to a boil; cook and stir for 1-2 minutes or until thickened. Add the spinach, lemon juice, salt and pepper; heat through. Remove from the heat; stir in cheese until melted.

5. With a slotted spoon, lift each egg out of the water. On each artichoke bottom, place ⅓ cup spinach mixture, a poached egg and ⅓ cup sauce. Sprinkle with paprika. Serve immediately.

Pear-Blueberry Granola

Oatmeal fans will love this dish. Although the pears, blueberries and granola make a beautiful breakfast, it also makes a nutritious dessert when served with vanilla ice cream.

—LISA WORKMAN BOONES MILL, VIRGINIA

PREP: 15 MINUTES **COOK:** 3 HOURS **MAKES:** 10 SERVINGS

- 5 **medium pears, peeled and thinly sliced**
- 2 **cups fresh or frozen unsweetened blueberries**
- ½ **cup packed brown sugar**
- ⅓ **cup apple cider or unsweetend apple juice**
- 1 **tablespoon all-purpose flour**
- 1 **tablespoon lemon juice**
- 2 **teaspoons ground cinnamon**

- 2 **tablespoons butter**
- 3 **cups granola without raisins**

1. In a 4-qt. slow cooker, combine the first seven ingredients. Dot with the butter. Sprinkle the granola over top. Cover and cook on low for 3-4 hours or until fruit is tender.

Brie and Prosciutto Tart

After our two children were born, my husband and I cut down on restaurant hopping. We replaced it with relaxing meals at home and an every-weekend brunch where I can experiment. My prize-wining tart stars on many of my Sunday buffets.

—AMY TONG ANAHEIM, CALIFORNIA

PREP: 30 MINUTES + COOLING **BAKE:** 30 MINUTES **MAKES:** 12 SERVINGS

- ½ cup finely chopped pecans
- 1½ cups all-purpose flour
- 2 teaspoons sugar
- ½ cup cold butter, cubed
- 1 egg yolk
- 1 tablespoon water
- 1 teaspoon Dijon mustard

FILLING

- 3 shallots, thinly sliced
- 1 tablespoon olive oil
- 2 cups fresh baby spinach
- 4 thin slices prosciutto or deli ham
- 3 eggs
- ⅔ cup 2% milk
- ¼ teaspoon salt
- ⅛ teaspoon pepper
- ⅛ teaspoon ground nutmeg
- ⅛ teaspoon crushed red pepper flakes
- 4 ounces Brie cheese, rind removed and cubed
- ¼ teaspoon minced fresh thyme

1. In a food processor, process pecans until finely chopped. Add flour and sugar; cover and pulse until blended. Add butter; cover and pulse until mixture resembles coarse crumbs. Combine the egg yolk, water and mustard. While processing, gradually add egg yolk mixture until dough forms a ball.

2. Press onto the bottom and up the sides of an ungreased 14-in. x 4-in. fluted tart pan with removable bottom or a 9-in. round fluted tart pan with removable bottom. Bake at 350° for 18-22 minutes or until crust is lightly browned. Cool on a wire rack.

3. In a large skillet, saute shallots in oil until tender. Add spinach; cook 1-2 minutes longer or until wilted. Remove and set aside to cool.

4. Meanwhile, in the same skillet, cook prosciutto over medium heat until slightly crisp. Remove to paper towels; drain. In a large bowl, whisk the eggs, milk, salt, pepper, nutmeg and pepper flakes. Spoon spinach mixture into crust; pour egg mixture over top. Top with the prosciutto and cheese.

5. Bake for 30-35 minutes or until a knife inserted near the center comes out clean. Sprinkle with thyme. Serve warm.

Home Style COOKING NOTES

Sausage Cranberry Pancakes

Hearty sausage and dried cranberries enhance every bite of these puffy pancakes. Just add maple syrup for a festive holiday breakfast.

—DEBBIE REID CLEARWATER, FLORIDA

PREP: 25 MINUTES **COOK:** 5 MINUTES/BATCH
MAKES: 24 PANCAKES

- 1 pound bulk pork sausage
- ⅓ cup dried cranberries
- ⅓ cup orange juice
- 1½ cups all-purpose flour
- 3 tablespoons baking powder
- ¼ teaspoon salt
- 1 egg
- 1½ cups 2% milk
- 3 tablespoons maple syrup
- 1 tablespoon canola oil
- 2 teaspoons grated orange peel
  Additional maple syrup

1. In a large skillet, cook sausage over medium heat until no longer pink; drain.

2. Meanwhile, place cranberries in a small bowl. Cover with orange juice; let stand for 5 minutes.

3. Drain cranberries, reserving juice. In a large bowl, combine the flour, baking powder and salt. In another bowl, whisk egg, milk, maple syrup, oil and orange peel; add to dry ingredients just until moistened. Stir in the cranberries, sausage and reserved juice.

4. Pour batter by ¼ cupfuls onto a greased hot griddle; turn when bubbles form on top. Cook until the second side is golden brown. Serve with syrup.

Home Style COOKING NOTES

Potato & Bacon Frittata

This filling frittata is so versatile. You can serve it with pesto or fresh salsa, and it's tasty with almost any type of cheese.

—MARIELA PETROSKI HELENA, MONTANA

PREP: 30 MINUTES **BAKE:** 20 MINUTES + STANDING **MAKES:** 8 SERVINGS

- 10 eggs
- ¼ cup minced fresh parsley
- 3 tablespoons 2% milk
- ¼ teaspoon salt
- ⅛ teaspoon pepper
- 8 bacon strips, chopped
- 2 medium potatoes, peeled and thinly sliced
- 2 green onions, finely chopped
- 4 fresh sage leaves, thinly sliced
- 1 cup (4 ounces) shredded pepper jack cheese
- 2 plum tomatoes, sliced

1. In a large bowl, whisk the eggs, parsley, milk, salt and pepper; set aside. In a 10-in. ovenproof skillet, cook bacon over medium heat until partially cooked but not crisp.

2. Add the potatoes, onions and sage; cook until potatoes are tender. Reduce heat; sprinkle with cheese. Top with egg mixture and tomato slices.

3. Bake, uncovered, at 400° for 20-25 minutes or until eggs are completely set. Let stand for 15 minutes. Cut into wedges.

Baked Long Johns

No one will ever guess how much lighter these scrumptious long johns glazed with rich chocolate are than the fried ones you buy!

—NICKI LAZORIK MELLEN, WISCONSIN

PREP: 15 MIN **BAKE:** 20 MINUTES + COOLING **MAKES:** 8 SERVINGS

- 2 cups all-purpose flour
- ½ cup sugar
- 2 teaspoons baking powder
- ½ teaspoon salt
- ¼ teaspoon ground cinnamon
- 2 eggs
- ¾ cup fat-free milk
- 1 tablespoon butter, melted
- 1 teaspoon vanilla extract

GLAZE
- ¾ cup semisweet chocolate chips
- 1 tablespoon butter
- 4½ teaspoons fat-free milk

1. In a small bowl, combine the flour, sugar, baking powder, salt and cinnamon. In another bowl, whisk the eggs, milk, butter and vanilla. Stir into dry ingredients just until moistened.

2. Transfer to eight 4½-in. x 2½-in. x 1½-in. loaf pans coated with cooking spray. Bake at 325° for 18-22 minutes or until golden brown. Immediately remove from pans to a wire rack to cool completely.

3. In a microwave, melt chocolate chips and butter. Add milk; stir until smooth. Dip tops of doughnuts in glaze. Return to wire rack; let stand until set.

Veggie Couscous Quiche

Tomato, green onions and broccoli bring pretty color to this sunrise specialty. It also gets an interesting taste twist from a bit of nutmeg.

—JULIE KIRKPATRICK
BILLINGS, MONTANA

PREP: 25 MINUTES
BAKE: 50 MINUTES + STANDING
MAKES: 6 SERVINGS

- 1 egg
- ½ teaspoon onion salt
- 2 cups cooked couscous, cooled
- ¼ cup shredded Swiss cheese

FILLING
- 4 eggs
- 1 cup half-and-half cream
- 4 cups frozen broccoli florets, thawed
- 1 can (6 ounces) sliced mushrooms, drained
- 1 cup (4 ounces) shredded Swiss cheese, divided
- ¼ teaspoon ground nutmeg
- 1 plum tomato, finely chopped
- 2 green onions, chopped

1. In a large bowl, whisk egg and onion salt. Add couscous and cheese; stir until blended. Press onto the bottom and up the sides of a greased 9-in. deep-dish pie plate. Bake at 350° for 5 minutes.

2. For filling, in a large bowl, whisk eggs and cream. Stir in the broccoli, mushrooms, ½ cup cheese and nutmeg. Pour into crust. Bake for 45-55 minutes or until a knife inserted near the center comes out clean.

3. Sprinkle with tomato, onions and remaining cheese. Bake 3-5 minutes longer or until cheese is melted. Let stand for 10 minutes before cutting.

Apple Sausage Puffs

I love serving these tender little puffs when I entertain during the holiday season. No one is able to resist them, and I need just four basic ingredients to prepare the simple recipe.

—VERONICA JOHNSON
JEFFERSON CITY, MISSOURI

PREP/TOTAL TIME: 25 MINUTES
MAKES: 2 DOZEN

- 1 **pound bulk pork sausage**
- 1 **medium apple, finely chopped**
- 3 **ounces cream cheese, softened**
- 3 **tubes (8 ounces each) refrigerated crescent rolls**

1. In a large skillet, cook sausage and apple over medium heat until meat is no longer pink; drain. Stir in cream cheese.
2. Unroll one tube of the crescent dough; separate into eight triangles. Place 1 tablespoon filling on the long side of each triangle. Roll up starting with a long side; pinch seams to seal.
3. Place point side down 2 in. apart on a greased baking sheet. Repeat with remaining crescent dough and filling. Bake at 375° for 10-12 minutes or until golden brown. Serve warm.

Home Style COOKING NOTES

Breakfast Custard

With a side of warmed ham and whole wheat toast, this custard makes for an uncommon and satisfying breakfast.

—ARLENE BENDER MARTIN, NORTH DAKOTA

PREP/TOTAL TIME: 25 MINUTES **MAKES:** 4 SERVINGS

- 4 **eggs, lightly beaten**
- 2 **tablespoons butter, melted**
- 1 **cup milk**
- 1 **teaspoon cornstarch**
- ⅛ **teaspoon baking powder**
- ¼ **teaspoon salt**
  Dash pepper
- ½ **cup shredded cheddar cheese**

1. In a large bowl, whisk the first seven ingredients. Stir in cheese. Pour into four buttered 4-oz. custard cups.
2. Place cups in a baking pan. Fill pan with boiling water to a depth of 1 in. Bake, uncovered, at 425° for 15-20 minutes or until a knife inserted near the center comes out clean.

Pumpkin Pancakes with Apple Cider Compote

For an out-of-the-ordinary breakfast on fall or winter mornings, try these spiced pumpkin pancakes. The accompanying compote made with apple pie filling is the crowning touch.

—MARGE MITCHELL PORTLAND, OREGON

PREP: 25 MINUTES **COOK:** 10 MINUTES/BATCH **MAKES:** 14 PANCAKES (5 CUPS COMPOTE)

1 cup sugar
2 tablespoons cornstarch
½ teaspoon ground cinnamon
2 cups apple cider or juice
2 tablespoons orange juice
1 can (21 ounces) apple pie filling
2 tablespoons butter

PANCAKES

1 cup old-fashioned oats
1¼ cups all-purpose flour
2 tablespoons brown sugar
2 teaspoons baking powder
1 teaspoon pumpkin pie spice
1 teaspoon ground cinnamon
¼ teaspoon salt
1 egg
1½ cups milk
1 cup canned pumpkin
3 tablespoons maple syrup
2 tablespoons canola oil
1 cup chopped pecans, toasted, divided

1. In a large saucepan, combine the sugar, cornstarch and cinnamon. Stir in cider and orange juice until smooth. Bring to a boil; cook and stir for 2 minutes or until thickened. Stir in pie filling and butter. Remove from the heat; set aside and keep warm.

2. For pancakes, place oats in a food processor; cover and process until ground. Transfer to a large bowl; add the flour, brown sugar, baking powder, pie spice, cinnamon and salt. In another bowl, whisk the egg, milk, pumpkin, syrup and oil. Stir into dry ingredients just until moistened; fold in ½ cup pecans.

3. Pour batter by ¼ cupfuls onto a hot griddle; flatten with the back of a spoon. Turn when the undersides are browned; cook until the second sides are golden brown. Serve with compote and remaining pecans. Store leftover compote in the refrigerator.

Editor's Note: *Leftover compote may be served with hot cereal or vanilla ice cream. It's also a tasty condiment for pork chops.*

Scrambled Egg Spinach Casserole

Here's a fantastic make-ahead casserole that's ideal for company. Nutmeg is a wonderfully unexpected complement to the sausage, spinach and mild feta.

—LISA SPEER PALM BEACH, FLORIDA

PREP: 40 MINUTES + CHILLING **BAKE:** 45 MINUTES + STANDING **MAKES:** 8 SERVINGS

2	**tablespoons butter**
2	**tablespoons all-purpose flour**
½	**teaspoon ground nutmeg**
⅛	**teaspoon plus ½ teaspoon salt, divided**
⅛	**teaspoon plus ¼ teaspoon pepper, divided**
2	**cups 2% milk**
½	**pound bulk Italian sausage**
½	**cup chopped sweet onion**
12	**eggs**
3	**tablespoons half-and-half cream**
1	**package (10 ounces) frozen chopped spinach, thawed and squeezed dry**
1½	**cups (6 ounces) crumbled feta cheese**

TOPPING

¾	**cup soft bread crumbs**
1	**tablespoon butter, melted**
2	**tablespoons grated Parmesan cheese**
¼	**teaspoon paprika**

1. In a small saucepan, melt butter. Stir in the flour, nutmeg and ⅛ teaspoon each salt and pepper until smooth; gradually add milk. Bring to a boil; cook and stir for 2 minutes or until thickened. Remove from the heat; cool completely.

2. Meanwhile, in a large skillet, cook the sausage, onion and remaining salt and pepper over medium heat until meat is no longer pink; drain. Transfer to a greased 13-in. x 9-in. baking dish; set aside.

3. In a large bowl, whisk the eggs and cream. Stir in the spinach, feta and cooled white sauce. Pour over sausage mixture. Cover and refrigerate overnight.

4. Remove from the refrigerator 30 minutes before baking. For topping, toss bread crumbs and melted butter; sprinkle over casserole. Top with Parmesan cheese and paprika.

5. Bake, uncovered, at 350° for 45-50 minutes or until a knife inserted near the center comes out clean. Let stand for 10 minutes before serving.

Pumpkin-Cranberry Cake Doughnuts

Pumpkin and cranberry really say holiday in these moist, spiced-filled doughnuts. They are so good...try not to eat them all in one sitting.

—CAROLYN COPE ALLSTON, MARYLAND

PREP: 40 MINUTES **COOK:** 5 MINUTES **MAKES:** 1½ DOZEN

- 3 tablespoons butter, softened
- 1 cup sugar
- 2 eggs
- 1 teaspoon vanilla extract
- 3½ cups all-purpose flour
- 2 teaspoons baking powder
- 1 teaspoon salt
- 1 teaspoon ground cinnamon
- ½ teaspoon baking soda
- ½ teaspoon ground ginger
- ¼ teaspoon ground cloves
- ⅛ teaspoon ground nutmeg
- 1 cup canned pumpkin
- ½ cup buttermilk
- 2 cups fresh or frozen cranberries, coarsely chopped
  Oil for deep-fat frying

SPICED SUGAR
- 1 cup sugar
- ¾ teaspoon ground cinnamon
- ¼ teaspoon ground ginger
- ⅛ teaspoon ground cloves
  Dash ground nutmeg

1. In a large bowl, beat butter and sugar until crumbly, about 2 minutes. Add eggs, one at a time, beating well after each addition. Beat in the vanilla.

2. Combine the flour, baking powder, salt, cinnamon, baking soda, ginger, cloves and nutmeg. Combine pumpkin and buttermilk. Add flour mixture to the creamed mixture alternately with buttermilk mixture, beating well after each addition. Stir in cranberries. Cover and refrigerate overnight.

3. Turn onto a lightly floured surface; roll to ½-in. thickness. Cut with a floured 2½-in. doughnut cutter. Reroll scraps.

4. In an electric skillet or deep fryer, heat oil to 375°. Fry doughnuts, a few at a time, until golden brown on both sides. Drain on paper towels. In a shallow bowl, combine the sugar, cinnamon, ginger, cloves and nutmeg; roll warm doughnuts in mixture.

Home Style COOKING NOTES

Poultry *in* Motion

When eggs are fresh & hens are pampered.

BY CINDY RAPPUHN

Chickens roam at home on the range at the author's farm near Sultan, Washington.

Raising free-range chickens is good for the environment, the hens and their eggs. Brent, my husband, and I are the third generation to farm his family's land in the Skykomish River Valley in Washington. First and foremost, we consider ourselves grass farmers. The animals we raise—hogs, cattle and poultry—are our primary helpers in keeping our soil and sod healthy and prolific.

We play a sort of musical chairs with livestock in our pastures. Pigs are strategically placed in areas we want deeply tilled and rid of weeds. We use cattle as lawn mowers; they eat the paddock grasses to a reasonable length so it can be easily gleaned later by our poultry. We keep our chicken flock to 1,000 and ducks to around 150.

The poultry do a great job eliminating insects and fertilizing the soil. When the time is right, they hop into their nesting boxes and lay wonderful delicious and nutritious eggs—what a bonus!

The eggs our hens lay have bright-orange yolks, thanks to a diet of grasses, legumes and clover plants rich in vitamins A, D and E. The protein-heavy whites stand up nice and tall, and look bright and beautiful on the plate.

Customers and chefs tell us our eggs are tasty and excellent for baking and cooking. Believe it or not, when my parents moved to the country in my high school years, they had to buy supermarket eggs for me until I grew accustomed to the rich flavor and striking hue of our precious farm eggs. Now I'd have a hard time eating anything else.

We take pride in how we care for the hens. They are kept on pasture from April until November, in grass paddocks with space to roam. For shelter, they have portable, open-ended hoop houses with roosts and nesting boxes inside, and electrified netting all around to protect them from predators. The houses are on skids, so we use a tractor to move them to a new patch of pasture every three days or so. That way, no one spot becomes overused.

In winter, the hens stay in more permanent greenhouses, out of the cold, wet wind. And we increase their rations of grain-based chicken feed. Egg production goes down from the peak season, when each hen lays five eggs per week. This chilly break gives our chickens a chance to rejuvenate for spring—kind of a vacation for them.

For us, this is a family business, and all our children are involved. Our son David, 21, helps with construction and tractor work. Anna, 18, assists with chicks and egg collection. They both balance farm chores with college. Our youngest, Robert, 15, pitches in with egg washing and grading, and staffing our farmers market booth.

We feel immeasurably blessed to be caretakers of a small, rewarding family farm. And we'd recommend it to anyone willing to be a hard worker and a perennial student.

You'd be amazed what you can learn from a chicken!

Cindy tends to her grass-fed chickens with help from son David.

from Cindy's kitchen

Dutch Baby Tropicale

A simple but impressive breakfast, a Dutch baby is a cross between a pancake, souffle and omelet. The eggy batter puffs up golden brown.

—**CINDY RAPPUHN** STARTUP, WASHINGTON

PREP: 15 MINUTES **BAKE:** 20 MINUTES **MAKES:** 8 SERVINGS

- 5 **eggs**
- 1 **cup 2% milk**
- 1 **cup all-purpose flour**
- ⅓ **cup butter, cubed**

FILLING

- 3 **tablespoons butter**
- 2 **large bananas, sliced**
- 1 **medium papaya, peeled and sliced**
  Lime wedges, optional

1. In a blender, combine the eggs, milk and flour; cover and process just until smooth. Place cubed butter in an ungreased 13-in. x 9-in. baking dish. Place in a 425° oven for 5 minutes or until melted.

2. Pour batter into hot dish. Bake, uncovered, for 20 minutes or until puffy and golden brown.

3. Meanwhile, for filling, melt butter in a large skillet. Add bananas and papaya. Cook over medium heat until tender, stirring frequently. Spoon into Dutch baby. Serve immediately with lime wedges.

Beating EGGS

LIGHTLY BEATEN
Beat the egg with a fork until the yolk and white are combined.

LEMON-COLORED
Beat the egg with an electric mixer on high for about 5 minutes. The volume of the beaten eggs will increase, the texture will go from liquid to thick and foamy, and the color will be light yellow.

THICK AND PALE YELLOW
Beat eggs and sugar with an electric mixer on high speed for about 7-8 minutes or until mixture has thickened and turned a very pale yellow. Mixture will fall in ribbons from a spoon.

SOFT PEAKS
Beat egg whites with an electric mixer on medium speed until they are thick and white. To test for soft peaks, lift the beaters from the whites— the egg white peaks should curl down. For best results, make sure the bowl and beaters are free from oil and the egg whites contain no specks of yolk. Both will prevent the whites from reaching full volume.

STIFF PEAKS
Continue beating the egg whites after they have reached the soft-peak stage with an electric mixer on high speed until the volume increases more and they are thicker. To test for stiff peaks, lift the beaters from the whites—the egg white peaks should stand straight up, and if you tilt the bowl, the whites should not slide around.

Finger Foods

Having a casual get-together or movie night with your family? An assortment of delectable nibbles will turn an ordinary evening into something special. Saucy meatballs, crunchy nut mix, melty warm dips and savory bites are guaranteed to rally the group and make everyone smile.

Curried Tropical Nut Mix
(recipe on page 46)

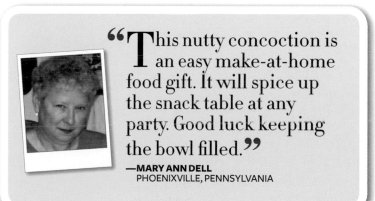

"This nutty concoction is an easy make-at-home food gift. It will spice up the snack table at any party. Good luck keeping the bowl filled.**"**

—MARY ANN DELL
PHOENIXVILLE, PENNSYLVANIA

Zippy Shrimp Skewers

These flavorful skewers deliver a mouthwatering kick with minimal effort. Fix them for your next party and watch them disappear.

—JALAYNE LUCKETT MARION, ILLINOIS

PREP: 10 MINUTES + MARINATING
GRILL: 5 MINUTES **MAKES:** 6 SERVINGS

- 2 tablespoons brown sugar
- 2 teaspoons cider vinegar
- 1½ teaspoons canola oil
- 1 teaspoon chili powder
- ½ teaspoon salt
- ½ teaspoon paprika
- ¼ teaspoon hot pepper sauce
- ¾ pound uncooked medium shrimp, peeled and deveined

1. In a large resealable plastic bag, combine the first seven ingredients; add shrimp. Seal bag and turn to coat; refrigerate for 2-4 hours.
2. Drain and discard marinade. Thread shrimp onto six metal or soaked wooden skewers. Using long-handled tongs, moisten a paper towel with cooking oil and lightly coat the grill rack. Grill, uncovered, over medium heat or broil 4 in. from the heat for 2-3 minutes on each side or until shrimp turn pink.

Cranberry Cream Cheese Spread

This festive dip is a snap to make, taking only 10 minutes from start to finish. Thanks to its hint of sweetness, both kids and adults will gobble it up.

—FRANKIE ROBINSON LOCKHART, TEXAS

PREP/TOTAL TIME: 10 MINUTES
MAKES: 1½ CUPS

- 1 package (8 ounces) reduced-fat cream cheese
- ½ cup dried cranberries, chopped
- ½ cup chopped dried apricots
- 1 teaspoon grated orange peel
  Assorted crackers

1. In a bowl, beat the cream cheese, cranberries, apricots and orange peel until blended. Chill until serving. Serve with crackers.

Three-Cheese Fondue

I got this easy recipe from my daughter, who lives in France. It's become my go-to fondue, and I make it often for our family.

—BETTY MANGAS TOLEDO, OHIO

PREP/TOTAL TIME: 30 MINUTES **MAKES:** 4 CUPS

- ½ pound each Emmentaler, Gruyere and Jarlsberg cheeses, shredded
- 2 tablespoons cornstarch, divided
- 4 teaspoons cherry brandy
- 2 cups dry white wine
- ⅛ teaspoon ground nutmeg
- ⅛ teaspoon paprika
  Dash cayenne pepper
  Cubed French bread baguette, boiled red potatoes and/or tiny whole pickles

1. In a large bowl, combine cheeses and 1 tablespoon cornstarch. In a small bowl, combine remaining cornstarch with cherry brandy; set aside. In a large saucepan, heat wine over medium heat until bubbles form around sides of pan.
2. Reduce heat to medium-low; add a handful of cheese mixture. Stir constantly, using a figure-eight motion, until almost completely melted. Continue adding cheese, one handful at a time, allowing the cheese to almost completely melt between additions.
3. Stir brandy mixture; gradually stir into the cheese mixture. Add spices; cook and stir until mixture is thickened and smooth.
4. Transfer to a fondue pot and keep warm. Serve with bread cubes, potatoes and/or pickles.

Strawberry Brunch Bruschetta

Try this sweet bruschetta for a brunch or indulgent weekend breakfast. The goat cheese, fresh herbs and strawberries are light and refreshing.

—JOHANNA HAUER KENNEBUNK, MAINE

PREP/TOTAL TIME: 30 MINUTES **MAKES:** 1½ DOZEN

- 3 **tablespoons olive oil**
- 1 **teaspoon minced fresh thyme or ¼ teaspoon dried thyme**
- 1 **teaspoon minced fresh rosemary or ¼ teaspoon dried rosemary, crushed**
- ¼ **teaspoon salt**
- ¼ **teaspoon pepper**
- 24 **slices French bread baguette (½ inch thick)**
- ½ **pound fresh goat cheese**
- 2 **cups chopped fresh strawberries**
- 2 **cups fresh arugula or fresh baby spinach, chopped**

1. In a small bowl, combine the first five ingredients. Place bread on ungreased baking sheets; brush with oil mixture.

2. Broil 3-4 in. from the heat for 1-2 minutes or until lightly browned. Spread with goat cheese. Broil 2-3 minutes longer or until cheese begins to melt.

3. In a small bowl, combine strawberries and arugula; layer over cheese.

Artichoke-Cheese French Bread

You'll love this amazing French bread appetizer. The creamy artichoke mixture is heaped on top of lightly toasted bread and then sprinkled with cheddar.

—BECKY GRONDAHL
FOOTHILL RANCH, CALIFORNIA

PREP: 20 MINUTES **BAKE:** 25 MINUTES
MAKES: 16 SERVINGS

- 1 **loaf (1 pound) unsliced French bread**
- 3 **jars (6½ ounces each) marinated quartered artichoke hearts, drained**
- 1½ **cups (6 ounces) shredded pepper jack cheese**
- 1 **cup (8 ounces) sour cream**
- 1 **can (4 ounces) chopped green chilies**
- 2 **garlic cloves, minced**
- 2 **cups (8 ounces) shredded cheddar cheese, divided**

1. Cut the bread in half lengthwise; carefully hollow out top and bottom of loaf, leaving ½-in. shells. Cube removed bread; set aside.

2. In a large bowl, combine artichokes, pepper jack cheese, sour cream, green chilies, garlic and 1 cup cheddar cheese. Add bread cubes and toss to coat. Spoon filling into bread shells; sprinkle with remaining cheddar cheese.

3. Place bread on an ungreased baking sheet. Cover with foil. Bake at 350° for 15 minutes. Remove the foil; bake 10-15 minutes longer or until heated through. Slice and serve warm.

Goat Cheese Wontons

Tangy goat cheese and fresh herbs shine through in every bite of these crispy bundles.

—CARLA DEVELDER MISHAWAKA, INDIANA

PREP/TOTAL TIME: 30 MINUTES
MAKES: 16 WONTONS

- 1 cup crumbled goat cheese
- 1 teaspoon each minced fresh basil, parsley and chives
- 1 garlic clove, minced
  Dash salt and pepper
- 1 egg, beaten
- 1 tablespoon water
- 16 wonton wrappers
  Oil for deep-fat frying

1. In a small bowl, combine the cheese, herbs, garlic, salt and pepper. Beat egg and water.
2. Place 1 tablespoon cheese mixture in the center of a wonton wrapper. (Keep remaining wrappers covered with a damp paper towel until ready to use.) Fold bottom corner over filling. Fold sides toward center over filling. Moisten remaining corner with egg; roll up tightly to seal.
3. In an electric skillet or deep-fat fryer, heat oil to 375°. Fry wontons, a few at a time, for 30-60 seconds on each side or until golden brown. Drain on paper towels.

Zippy Peach Spread

Don't think twice about the ingredient pairings. This creamy spread is absolutely addictive!

—LAURIE HICKS TROY, MONTANA

PREP/TOTAL TIME: 10 MINUTES
MAKES: 10 SERVINGS

- 1 package (8 ounces) cream cheese, softened
- ⅔ cup peach preserves
- 1½ teaspoons prepared horseradish
- 1½ teaspoons ground mustard
- ¼ teaspoon white pepper
  Assorted crackers

1. Place cream cheese on a serving plate. In a bowl, combine the preserves, horseradish, mustard and pepper; pour over cream cheese. Serve with crackers.

Corn Salsa

My colorful salsa is a hit with family and friends. It's an easy accompaniment to an outdoor cookout and adds a kick of flavor to whatever's on the grill.

—SHIRLEY GLAAB HATTIESBURG, MISSISSIPPI

PREP: 20 MINUTES + CHILLING **MAKES:** 5 CUPS

- 3 cups frozen corn, thawed
- 1 can (15 ounces) black beans, rinsed and drained
- 5 green onions, thinly sliced
- 1 medium sweet red pepper, finely chopped
- 1 jalapeno pepper, finely chopped
- ⅓ cup rice vinegar
- 1 tablespoon olive oil
- 1 tablespoon Dijon mustard
- ½ teaspoon salt
- ¼ to ½ teaspoon hot pepper sauce
- ¼ teaspoon pepper
  Dash cayenne pepper
- ⅔ cup minced fresh cilantro

1. In a large bowl, combine the first five ingredients. In another bowl, whisk the vinegar, oil, mustard, salt, pepper sauce, pepper and cayenne. Stir in cilantro. Drizzle over corn mixture and toss to coat.
2. Chill until serving. Serve with your favorite snack chips or grilled meats.

Editor's Note: *Wear disposable gloves when cutting hot peppers; the oils can burn skin. Avoid touching your face.*

Curried Chicken Balls Appetizer

Guests love these little chicken bites, which get some of their zip from curry. The savory snacks work well for any occasion, big or small.

—JUDY SLOTTER ALPHARETTA, GEORGIA

PREP: 20 MINUTES + CHILLING **MAKES:** ABOUT 5 DOZEN APPETIZERS

- 2 packages (3 ounces each) cream cheese, softened
- 2 tablespoons orange marmalade
- 2 teaspoons curry powder
- ¾ teaspoon salt
- ¼ teaspoon pepper
- 3 cups finely chopped cooked chicken
- 3 tablespoons finely chopped green onion
- 3 tablespoons finely chopped celery
- 1 cup finely chopped almonds, toasted

1. In a large bowl, beat the first five ingredients until well blended. Stir in the chicken, onion and celery.

2. Shape into 1-in. balls; roll in almonds. Cover and chill until firm (can refrigerate up to 2 days).

Warm Chicken Fiesta Dip

This crowd-pleasing dip is always a success, whether I follow the recipe as is or substitute shredded pork and stir in chopped fresh mushrooms.

—SHANNON ARTHUR PICKERINGTON, OHIO

PREP: 25 MINUTES **BAKE:** 25 MINUTES
MAKES: 8 CUPS

- 1 medium green pepper, chopped
- 1 medium onion, chopped
- 1 tablespoon olive oil
- ½ teaspoon chili powder
- ¼ teaspoon salt
- ¼ teaspoon pepper
- ¼ teaspoon ground cumin
- 1 package (8 ounces) cream cheese, softened
- 1 can (10¾ ounces) condensed cream of chicken soup, undiluted
- 1 can (10 ounces) diced tomatoes and green chilies, undrained
- 1 jalapeno pepper, finely chopped
- 4 cups shredded rotisserie chicken
- 2 cups (8 ounces) shredded Mexican cheese blend, divided
- 1 green onion, thinly sliced
  Tortilla or corn chips

1. In a large skillet, saute green pepper and onion in oil until tender. Add the chili powder, salt, pepper and cumin; cook 1 minute longer. Remove from the heat and set aside.

2. In a large bowl, beat cream cheese until smooth. Add the soup, tomatoes and jalapeno. Stir in the chicken, 1 cup cheese blend and green pepper mixture. Transfer dip to a greased 11-in. x 7-in. baking dish. Sprinkle with green onion and remaining cheese blend.

3. Bake dip, uncovered, at 350° for 25-30 minutes or until bubbly. Let stand for 5 minutes. Serve with chips.

Editor's Note: *Wear disposable gloves when cutting hot peppers; the oils can burn skin. Avoid touching your face.*

Crab-Stuffed Mushrooms

Mushroom caps plump with crabmeat make a wonderful appetizer for entertaining. Try the recipe as a light entree, too, served on salad greens.

—TONYA FARMER IOWA CITY, IOWA

PREP: 25 MINUTES **BAKE:** 15 MINUTES
MAKES: 2½ DOZEN

- 1 medium tomato, seeded and diced
- ½ cup soft bread crumbs
- 2 tablespoons mayonnaise
- 1 tablespoon minced fresh parsley
- 1 garlic clove, minced
- ¼ teaspoon salt
  Dash cayenne pepper
- 1 can (6 ounces) crabmeat, drained, flaked and cartilage removed
- 30 medium fresh mushrooms
- 1 tablespoon olive oil
- ¼ cup shredded Parmesan cheese

1. In a bowl, combine the first seven ingredients. Fold in crabmeat; set aside.
2. Remove and discard mushroom stems. Brush inside of mushroom caps with oil. Spoon 1-2 teaspoons of crab mixture into each cap; sprinkle with Parmesan cheese.
3. Place in a 15-in. x 10-in. x 1-in. baking pan coated with cooking spray. Bake at 400° for 15-20 minutes or until mushrooms are tender and filling is lightly browned. Serve warm.

Home Style COOKING NOTES

Barbecued Meatballs

This dish is one of my favorites to take to potlucks. Everybody loves the thick, sweet barbecue sauce, and it's so simple to make.

—GWEN GOSS GARDEN CITY, KANSAS

PREP: 20 MINUTES **BAKE:** 30 MINUTES **MAKES:** 6 SERVINGS

- 1 cup quick-cooking oats
- 1 egg
- ⅓ cup evaporated milk
- ¾ teaspoon chili powder
- ¾ teaspoon salt
- ¼ teaspoon pepper
- ⅛ teaspoon garlic powder
- 1½ pounds ground pork
- 1 cup ketchup
- ¾ cup packed brown sugar
- 2½ teaspoons liquid smoke, optional
- ½ teaspoon lemon juice

1. In a large bowl, combine the first seven ingredients. Crumble pork over mixture and mix well. Shape into 2-in. balls. Place meatballs on a greased rack in a shallow baking pan. Bake, uncovered, at 375° for 20-25 minutes or until a thermometer reads 160°. Drain on paper towels. Transfer to an ungreased 2-qt. baking dish.
2. Meanwhile, in a saucepan, combine ketchup, brown sugar, liquid smoke if desired and lemon juice; cook and stir until brown sugar is dissolved. Pour over meatballs. Bake, uncovered, at 375° for 10-15 minutes longer or until heated through.

Spicy Breaded Chicken Wings

Everyone really loves these spicy chicken wings! They taste just like fried chicken but they're baked, and they are wonderful even without the dipping sauce. You can also make them with bags of drumettes instead of whole wings.
—BARBARA WHITE KATY, TEXAS

PREP: 25 MINUTES **BAKE:** 25 MINUTES **MAKES:** 6 SERVINGS

1 **egg**
1 **tablespoon water**
⅔ **cup dry bread crumbs**
1 **teaspoon onion powder**
1 **teaspoon dried basil**
1 **teaspoon cayenne pepper**
½ **teaspoon garlic salt**
½ **teaspoon paprika**
10 **whole chicken wings**
DIPPING SAUCE
2 **tablespoons ketchup**
2 **tablespoons honey**
1 **tablespoon Worcestershire sauce**
½ **teaspoon hot pepper sauce**

1. In a shallow bowl, beat egg and water. In another shallow bowl, combine the bread crumbs, onion powder, basil, cayenne, garlic salt and paprika.
2. Cut chicken wings into three sections; discard wing tip sections. Dip chicken wings into egg mixture, then coat with crumb mixture. Place in a greased 15-in. x 10-in. x 1-in. baking pan. Bake at 425° for 25-30 minutes or until juices run clear, turning every 10 minutes.
3. In a small bowl, combine the sauce ingredients. Serve with chicken wings.

Broiled Tomato-Mozzarella Dip

You'll love the savory Italian flavor of this dip topped with plenty of mozzarella cheese. Don't be surprised if party guests wipe the plate clean!

—**CONNIE BARSZCZ** ELMVALE, ONTARIO

PREP: 35 MINUTES **BROIL:** 5 MINUTES **MAKES:** 5 CUPS

1	medium onion, finely chopped
2	tablespoons olive oil
1	can (28 ounces) diced tomatoes, drained
½	cup dry red wine or chicken broth
1	tablespoon dried basil
1	tablespoon fennel seed, crushed
1	tablespoon dried oregano
3	garlic cloves, minced
2	teaspoons sugar
½	teaspoon crushed red pepper flakes
½	teaspoon salt
2	cartons (8 ounces each) fresh mozzarella cheese pearls, drained
	Toasted sliced Italian bread

1. In a large saucepan, saute onion in oil until tender. Stir in the tomatoes, wine, basil, fennel, oregano, garlic, sugar, pepper flakes and salt. Bring to a boil. Reduce heat; cover and simmer for 10 minutes.

2. Uncover and cook 10-15 minutes longer or until thickened. Transfer mixture to a 10-in. baking dish; sprinkle with cheese.

3. Broil 6 in. from the heat 3-5 minutes or until cheese is golden brown. Serve with toasted bread.

Microwave Potato Chips

Is it possible to make golden, crispy homemade potato chips in the microwave? We had our doubts, but this recipe quickly put them to rest.
—TASTE OF HOME TEST KITCHEN

PREP: 10 MINUTES **COOK:** 10 MINUTES/BATCH
MAKES: 5 SERVINGS

- 3 **medium red potatoes**
- ¼ **cup olive oil**
- 1 **teaspoon salt**
  Curry powder

1. Layer three paper towels on a microwave-safe plate; set aside.
2. Scrub potatoes and cut into ¹⁄₁₆-in.-thick slices. Brush slices on both sides with olive oil and lightly sprinkle with salt and curry. Arrange on prepared plate (do not overlap).
3. Microwave on high for 3 minutes; turn and microwave 2-3 minutes longer or until chips are dry and brittle. Repeat with remaining potatoes, oil and seasonings. Let chips cool for at least 1 minute before serving. Store in an airtight container.

Cumin Crunch Potato Chips: *Substitute garlic powder and ground cumin for the curry powder.*

Nice & Spiced Potato Chips: *Substitute chili powder and ground chipotle pepper for the curry powder.*

Editor's Note: *This recipe was tested in a 1,100-watt microwave.*

Prosciutto-Wrapped Asparagus with Raspberry Sauce

What a delightful way to kick off a summer party! This upscale appetizer will make guests feel pampered. With only four ingredients, it's incredibly easy to make, and absolutely yummy.
—NOELLE MYERS GRAND FORKS, NORTH DAKOTA

PREP/TOTAL TIME: 30 MINUTES **MAKES:** 16 APPETIZERS

- ⅓ **pound thinly sliced prosciutto or deli ham**
- 16 **fresh asparagus spears, trimmed**
- ½ **cup seedless raspberry jam**
- 2 **tablespoons balsamic vinegar**

1. Cut prosciutto slices in half. Wrap a prosciutto piece around each asparagus spear; secure ends with toothpicks. Moisten a paper towel with cooking oil; using long-handled tongs, lightly coat the grill rack.
2. Grill asparagus, covered, over medium heat for 6-8 minutes or until the prosciutto is crisp, turning once. Discard toothpicks.
3. In a small microwave-safe bowl, microwave jam and vinegar on high for 15-20 seconds or until jam is melted. Serve with asparagus.

> **HOME STYLE tip**
>
> 66 To revive limp asparagus spears, cut ¼ inch from the bottom of each spear. Place spears in a glass of ice water; cover with a plastic bag and refrigerate for 2 hours. The spears will crisp right up. 99
>
> **—ARLENE J.**
> MARBLE FALLS, TEXAS

Mash yolks with a fork. Add remaining filling ingredients; mix well. Spoon filling into a pastry bag fitted with a #20 decorating tip. Pipe filling into egg white halves.

Smokin' Hot Deviled Eggs

Nearly everybody loves deviled eggs, and this variation has a nice kick. You can't go wrong bringing these to a party or potluck.

—**JAN ROBERTS** SAN PEDRO, CALIFORNIA

PREP/TOTAL TIME: 20 MINUTES **MAKES:** 2 DOZEN

- 12 **hard-cooked eggs**
- ½ **cup mayonnaise**
- 3 **chipotle peppers in adobo sauce, finely chopped**
- 1 **tablespoon capers, drained**
- 1 **tablespoon stone-ground mustard**
- ¼ **teaspoon salt**
- ¼ **teaspoon white pepper**
  Minced fresh cilantro

1. Cut eggs in half lengthwise. Remove yolks; set whites aside. In a small bowl, mash yolks. Add the mayonnaise, chipotle peppers, capers, mustard, salt and white pepper; mix well. Stuff or pipe into egg whites. Refrigerate until serving. Sprinkle with cilantro.

Strawberry Fruit Dip

Fresh fruit tastes even better served with a strawberry-flavored dip! I turn to this recipe for just about every family gathering.

—**DAWN BRANDT** KALKASKA, MICHIGAN

PREP/TOTAL TIME: 5 MINUTES **MAKES:** 2½ CUPS

- 1 **package (8 ounces) cream cheese, softened**
- ¾ **cup (6 ounces) strawberry yogurt**
- 1 **package (10 ounces) frozen sweetened sliced strawberries, thawed**
  Assorted fresh fruit

1. In a small bowl, beat the cream cheese and yogurt until blended. Add the strawberries. Serve with fresh fruit. Cover and refrigerate any leftovers.

Party Crab Puffs

I received this recipe years ago from my grandmother, who taught me the importance of experimenting and being creative in the kitchen. My friends request these little puffs at every gathering.

—**JEAN BEVILACQUA** RHODODENDRON, OREGON

PREP: 45 MINUTES **BAKE:** 20 MINUTES/BATCH **MAKES:** 8 DOZEN

- 1 **cup water**
- ½ **cup butter, cubed**
- ¼ **teaspoon salt**
- 1 **cup all-purpose flour**
- 4 **eggs**

FILLING

- 4 **hard-cooked eggs, finely chopped**
- 1 **can (6 ounces) lump crabmeat, drained**
- 4 **ounces cream cheese, softened**
- ¼ **cup mayonnaise**
- 2 **tablespoons finely chopped onion**
- 2 **tablespoons prepared horseradish, drained**
  Minced fresh parsley, optional

1. In a large saucepan, bring the water, butter and salt to a boil. Add flour all at once and stir until a smooth ball forms. Remove from the heat; let stand for 5 minutes. Add eggs, one at a time, beating well after each addition. Continue beating until mixture is smooth and shiny.

2. Drop by teaspoonfuls 2 in. apart onto greased baking sheets. Bake at 400° for 18-22 minutes or until golden brown. Remove to a wire rack. Immediately split puffs open; remove tops and set aside. Discard soft dough from inside. Cool puffs.

3. In a large bowl, combine the filling ingredients. Just before serving, spoon 1 teaspoonful filling into each puff; sprinkle with parsley if desired. Replace tops.

Maple-Pecan Snack Mix

This is perfect when I need something portable for my kids to put in a bag to eat on the go. We love blueberry pancakes, and this recipe incorporates some of that great flavor in a handy, healthy treat.

—**JACKIE GREGSTON** HALLSVILLE, TEXAS

PREP/TOTAL TIME: 20 MINUTES
MAKES: 9 CUPS

- 5 **cups Honey Nut Chex**
- 1 **cup granola without raisins**
- 1 **cup chopped pecans, toasted**
- ¼ **cup butter, cubed**
- ¼ **cup brown sugar**
- ¼ **cup maple syrup**
- 1 **package (3½ ounces) dried blueberries**
- ¾ **cup semisweet chocolate chips, optional**

1. In a large microwave-safe bowl, combine the cereal, granola and pecans; set aside. In a small microwave-safe bowl, combine butter, brown sugar and syrup. Microwave on high for 2 minutes, stirring once. Pour over cereal mixture; toss to coat.

2. Microwave on high for 4 minutes, stirring every minute. Spread onto waxed paper; cool for 5 minutes. Sprinkle with blueberries and chocolate chips. Store in an airtight container.

Editor's Note: *This recipe was tested in a 1,100-watt microwave.*

Home Style COOKING NOTES

Hot Ham & Cheese Slices

My recipe has everything partygoers want in an appetizer. Get ready to wow everyone with these unique treats.

—PAT STEVENS GRANBURY, TEXAS

PREP: 15 MINUTES **BAKE:** 20 MINUTES
MAKES: 8 SERVINGS

- 1 **cup sliced fresh mushrooms**
- 1 **small sweet red pepper, chopped**
- 2 **green onions, chopped**
- 2 **tablespoons butter**
- 1 **package (17.3 ounces) frozen puff pastry, thawed**
- ½ **pound thinly sliced deli ham**
- ½ **pound sliced Swiss cheese**

1. In a large skillet, saute mushrooms, pepper and onions in butter until tender. Set aside.

2. Unfold pastry. Layer the ham, cheese and mushroom mixture off-center on each sheet of pastry. Fold pastry over filling; pinch seams to seal.

3. Place in a greased 15-in. x 10-in. x 1-in. baking pan. Bake at 400° for 18-22 minutes or until golden brown. Let stand for 5 minutes. Cut each with a serrated knife into 4 slices.

Home Style COOKING NOTES

Curried Tropical Nut Mix

This nutty concoction is an easy make-at-home food gift. It will spice up the snack table at any party. Good luck keeping the bowl filled.

—MARY ANN DELL PHOENIXVILLE, PENNSYLVANIA

PREP: 20 MINUTES + COOLING **MAKES:** 7½ CUPS

- 2 **tablespoons curry powder**
- 1 **tablespoon butter**
- 1 **tablespoon olive oil**
- 1 **teaspoon ground cumin**
- ½ **teaspoon cayenne pepper**
- 2 **cups salted roasted almonds**
- 2 **cups salted cashew halves**
- 2 **cups salted peanuts**
- 1 **cup flaked coconut**
- ½ **cup dried mangoes, chopped**

1. In a large microwave-safe bowl, combine the first five ingredients. Microwave, uncovered, on high for 30 seconds. Add the almonds, cashews, peanuts and coconut; toss to coat.

2. Cook, uncovered, 5-6 minutes longer or until lightly browned, stirring after each minute. Add mangoes. Spread onto waxed paper to cool. Store in an airtight container.

Editor's Note: *This recipe was tested in a 1,100-watt microwave.*

Crispy Grilled Zucchini with Marinara

You don't need a deep-fat fryer to make crispy snacks. Let your indoor grill do the work! Try this marinara over ziti or bow tie pasta for a delicious side dish, too.

—STEVE FOY KIRKWOOD, MISSOURI

PREP: 15 MINUTES **COOK:** 5 MINUTES/BATCH **MAKES:** 2 DOZEN (2⅓ CUPS SAUCE)

- 1 can (14½ ounces) diced tomatoes with basil, oregano and garlic, undrained
- 1 can (6 ounces) tomato paste
- ½ cup water
- 2 teaspoons sugar
- ¼ teaspoon salt
- ¼ teaspoon dried basil
- ¼ teaspoon dried oregano
- 1 egg
- ⅓ cup prepared Italian salad dressing
- 1 cup Italian-style panko (Japanese) bread crumbs
- 2 medium zucchini, cut diagonally into ¼-inch slices

1. In a large saucepan, combine first seven ingredients. Bring to a boil. Reduce heat; simmer, uncovered, for 5-10 minutes or until thickened, stirring occasionally.
2. Meanwhile, in a shallow bowl, whisk egg and salad dressing. Place bread crumbs in another shallow bowl. Dip zucchini slices in egg mixture, then coat with bread crumbs. Cook on an indoor grill for 2-3 minutes or until golden brown. Serve with marinara.

Calla Lily Tea Sandwiches

Your appetizer tray will bloom with beauty when you include these novel lily-shaped sandwiches. The tasty filling will delight guests at your next luncheon or shower.

—LEANN WILLIAMS BEAVERTON, OREGON

PREP: 40 MINUTES + CHILLING **MAKES:** 1½ DOZEN

¼ cup mayonnaise
1 teaspoon grated onion
¼ teaspoon dried tarragon
⅛ teaspoon pepper
1 can (4½ ounces) chunk white chicken, drained
1 celery rib, finely chopped
18 slices white bread, crusts removed
2 tablespoons butter, softened
1 tablespoon minced fresh parsley
18 pieces (1 inch each) julienned carrot

1. In a large bowl, combine the first four ingredients; stir in chicken and celery; set aside. With a rolling pin, flatten each slice of bread to ⅛-in. thickness; cut into 2½-in. squares. Spread with butter. Roll up into a funnel shape, overlapping the two adjacent sides; secure with a toothpick.

2. Spoon about 1 teaspoon chicken filling into each sandwich. Cover with plastic wrap; refrigerate for 1 hour.

3. Remove the toothpicks. Sprinkle sandwiches with parsley. Insert a carrot piece into the filling of each sandwich.

Artichoke & Mushroom Toasts

I like to greet guests with oven-fresh appetizers. Crunchy bread slices are topped with mushrooms, artichokes and a blend of cheeses.

—NANCY MUELLER HIGHLANDS RANCH, COLORADO

PREP: 30 MINUTES **BAKE:** 5 MINUTES **MAKES:** 3 DOZEN

- 36 slices French bread baguette (½ inch thick)
- 3 tablespoons olive oil, divided
- ½ pound sliced fresh mushrooms
- ½ pound sliced baby portobello mushrooms
- ½ teaspoon Italian seasoning
- 2 tablespoons butter
- 6 garlic cloves, minced
- 1 jar (7½ ounces) marinated quartered artichoke hearts, drained
- ⅓ cup mayonnaise
- 1 tablespoon shredded Parmesan cheese
- 2 cups (8 ounces) shredded Swiss cheese

1. Place bread on baking sheets; brush with 2 tablespoons oil. Broil 4-6 in. from heat for 1-2 minutes or until lightly toasted.

2. In a large skillet, saute mushrooms with Italian seasoning in butter and remaining oil until tender. Add garlic; cook 1 minute longer. Remove from the heat and set aside.

3. Place artichokes in a food processor; cover and process until finely chopped. Add mayonnaise and Parmesan cheese; cover and process until blended. Spread over toast slices; top with mushrooms and sprinkle with Swiss cheese.

4. Bake at 350° for 4-6 minutes or until cheese is melted.

To Make Ahead: *Prep the toasts earlier in the day and store on baking sheets in the refrigerator. Sprinkle with Swiss cheese just before baking.*

Classic Hummus

We love hummus, and this version is really amazing. We pair hummus with fresh veggies for a meal or snack.

—MONICA AND DAVID EICHLER LAWRENCE, KANSAS

PREP: 20 MINUTES + SOAKING
COOK: 25 MINUTES + CHILLING **MAKES:** 2½ CUPS

- 1 cup dried garbanzo beans
- 1 medium onion, quartered
- 1 bay leaf
- 4 cups water
- ¼ cup minced fresh parsley
- ¼ cup lemon juice
- ¼ cup tahini
- 4 to 6 garlic cloves, minced
- 1 teaspoon ground cumin
- ¾ teaspoon salt
- ⅛ teaspoon cayenne pepper
- ¼ cup olive oil
  Assorted fresh vegetables

1. Sort beans and rinse in cold water. Place beans in a large bowl; add water to cover by 2 in. Cover and let stand overnight.

2. Drain and rinse beans, discarding liquid. Transfer beans to a pressure cooker; add the onion, bay leaf and 4 cups water.

3. Close cover securely according to the manufacturer's directions. Bring cooker to full pressure over high heat. Reduce heat to medium-high and cook for 12 minutes. (Pressure regulator should maintain a slow, steady rocking motion or release of steam; adjust heat if needed.)

4. Remove from the heat; allow pressure to drop on its own. Immediately cool according to manufacturer's directions until pressure is completely reduced. Drain bean mixture, reserving ½ cup cooking liquid. Discard onion and bay leaf.

5. Place the beans, parsley, lemon juice, tahini, garlic, cumin, salt and cayenne in a food processor; cover and process until smooth. While processing, gradually add oil in a steady stream. Add enough reserved cooking liquid to achieve desired consistency.

6. Cover and refrigerate for at least 1 hour. Serve with vegetables.

Three-Cheese Nachos

I received the recipe for these tasty nachos from a co-worker a few years back. They're fun to serve as party appetizers or as the main course at a casual dinner with family.

—CARI HINZ EAU CLAIRE, WISCONSIN

PREP/TOTAL TIME: 25 MINUTES
MAKES: 10-12 SERVINGS

- 2 **packages (one 8 ounces, one 3 ounces) cream cheese, softened**
- 1 **can (4 ounces) chopped green chilies**
- 3 **tablespoons chopped onion**
- 2 **garlic cloves, minced**
- 1 **tablespoon canned chopped jalapeno pepper**
- 1½ **teaspoons ground cumin**
- 1½ **teaspoons chili powder**
- 2 **cups cubed cooked chicken**
- 2 **cups (8 ounces) shredded Monterey Jack cheese, divided**
- 1 **package (14 ounces) pita bread (6 inches)**
- 1 **cup (4 ounces) shredded cheddar cheese**
  Salsa, optional

1. In a large bowl, beat the cream cheese, chilies, onion, garlic, jalapeno, cumin and chili powder until smooth. Stir in chicken and 1 cup Monterey Jack cheese.

2. Split each pita into two circles. Spread ¼ cup of chicken mixture on each circle; place on ungreased baking sheets.

3. Bake at 400° for 5-10 minutes. Combine the cheddar cheese and remaining Monterey Jack; sprinkle over circles. Bake 5 minutes longer or until cheese is melted. Cut into wedges and serve with salsa if desired.

Home Style COOKING NOTES

Creamy Wasabi Spread

Sesame seeds create an attractive coating for this easy cracker spread. Be sure to watch when you're toasting them; they burn easily. You'll find rice crackers in the ethnic food aisle. You can use any flavor, but the wasabi ones are great.

—TAMMIE BALON BOYCE, VIRGINIA

PREP/TOTAL TIME: 10 MINUTES **MAKES:** 8 SERVINGS

- 1 **package (8 ounces) cream cheese**
- ¼ **cup prepared wasabi**
- 2 **tablespoons sesame seeds, toasted**
- 2 **tablespoons soy sauce**
  Rice crackers

1. Place cream cheese on a cutting board; split into two layers. Spread wasabi over bottom half; replace top layer.

2. Press both sides into sesame seeds. Place on a shallow serving plate; pour soy sauce around cheese. Serve with crackers.

Chicken Salad in Baskets

When I first made these cute little cups, they were a big hit. Now my husband often asks me to fix them for meetings and parties.

—**GWENDOLYN FAE TRAPP** STRONGSVILLE, OHIO

PREP: 15 MINUTES **BAKE:** 15 MINUTES + CHILLING **MAKES:** 20 APPETIZERS

- 1 **cup diced cooked chicken**
- 3 **bacon strips, cooked and crumbled**
- ⅓ **cup chopped mushrooms**
- 2 **tablespoons chopped pecans**
- 2 **tablespoons diced peeled apple**
- ¼ **cup mayonnaise**
- ⅛ **teaspoon salt**
   Dash pepper
- 20 **slices bread**
- 6 **tablespoons butter, melted**
- 2 **tablespoons minced fresh parsley**

1. In a small bowl, combine the first five ingredients. Combine the mayonnaise, salt and pepper; add to chicken mixture and stir to coat. Cover and refrigerate until serving.

2. Cut each slice of bread with a 3-in. round cookie cutter; brush both sides with butter. Press into ungreased mini muffin cups. Bake at 350° for 11-13 minutes or until golden brown and crisp.

3. Cool for 3 minutes before removing from the pans to wire racks to cool completely. Spoon 1 tablespoonful chicken salad into each bread basket. Cover and refrigerate for up to 2 hours. Just before serving, sprinkle with parsley.

Tuscan Sun-Dried Tomato Jam

Tomato jam? Oh, yeah. My simple recipe tastes positively gourmet. The jam's robust flavor complements just about anything. Spread a cracker with cream cheese, then top with jam...yummy!

—**BARBIE MILLER** OAKDALE, MINNESOTA

PREP: 15 MINUTES **COOK:** 55 MINUTES
MAKES: 1½ CUPS

- 1 **jar (7 ounces) oil-packed sun-dried tomatoes**
- ½ **medium onion, thinly sliced**
- 1 **garlic clove, minced**
- 1 **cup water**
- ½ **cup chicken stock**
- ¼ **cup red wine vinegar**
- 1 **tablespoon sugar**
- 1 **teaspoon dried basil**
- ½ **teaspoon salt**
- ½ **teaspoon pepper**

1. Drain the tomatoes, reserving 1 tablespoon of the oil. Finely chop tomatoes. In a large saucepan, saute tomatoes and onion in reserved oil until onion is tender. Add garlic; cook 1 minute longer.

2. Stir in the water, stock, vinegar, sugar, basil, salt and pepper. Bring to a boil. Reduce heat; cover and simmer for 30 minutes. Uncover; simmer for 15-20 minutes or until liquid has evaporated and mixture is the consistency of jam.

HOME STYLE tip

66As the name indicates, sun-dried tomatoes have been dried to remove most of their water content, producing a chewy, intensely flavored tomato product.**99**

—**TASTE OF HOME TEST KITCHEN**

Baked Onion Cheese Dip

This sweet onion dip gets a nice kick from an added cup of pepper jack cheese. It's fun to serve with an assortment of crackers and breadsticks.

—BONNIE HAWKINS ELKHORN, WISCONSIN

PREP/TOTAL TIME: 30 MINUTES **MAKES:** 3 CUPS

2 cups (8 ounces) shredded cheddar cheese
1 cup (4 ounces) shredded pepper jack cheese
4 ounces cream cheese, cubed
½ cup mayonnaise
¼ teaspoon dried thyme
2 cups chopped sweet onions, divided
   Assorted crackers

1. In a food processor, combine the cheeses, mayonnaise, thyme and 1 cup onions; cover and process until blended. Stir in remaining onions.
2. Transfer to a greased 3-cup baking dish. Bake, uncovered, at 375° for 20-25 minutes or until bubbly. Serve with crackers.

1. Unfold puff pastry; cut into 1-in. squares. Place on parchment paper-lined baking sheets. Whisk egg and water; brush over squares. Sprinkle with poppy seeds. Bake at 400° for 8-10 minutes or until golden brown.
2. In a small bowl, combine the cream cheese, sherry and liquid smoke if desired; stir in pecans and onion.
3. Split each square horizontally; spread with ¾ teaspoon of the cream cheese mixture. Replace tops.

Honey-Barbecue Chicken Wings

The slightly sweet barbecue flavor in this sauce provides mass appeal. Most people have a hard time eating just one or two!
—TASTE OF HOME TEST KITCHEN

PREP: 20 MINUTES **COOK:** 10 MINUTES/BATCH
MAKES: 2 DOZEN

- 2½ pounds whole chicken wings
- ½ cup reduced-sodium soy sauce
- ½ cup barbecue sauce
- ⅓ cup honey
- 1 cup all-purpose flour
- 2 teaspoons salt
- 2 teaspoons paprika
- ¼ teaspoon pepper
  Oil for deep-fat frying

1. Cut wings into three sections; discard wing tip sections. In a small saucepan, combine the soy sauce, barbecue sauce and honey. Bring to a boil; cook until the liquid is reduced to about 1 cup.
2. Meanwhile, in a large resealable plastic bag, combine the flour, salt, paprika and pepper. Add wings a few at a time, and shake to coat.
3. In an electric skillet or deep fryer, heat oil to 375°. Fry wings, a few at a time, for 3-4 minutes on each side or until no longer pink. Drain on paper towels. Transfer wings to a large bowl; add sauce and toss to coat. Serve immediately.

Editor's Note: *Uncooked chicken wing sections (wingettes) may be substituted for whole chicken wings.*

Smoky Pecan Puffs

Guests will never guess how easy it was for you to make these pretty puffs. For a more festive look, cut the pastry with a small star cutter.
—AWYNNE THURSTENSON SILOAM SPRINGS, ARKANSAS

PREP: 30 MINUTES **BAKE:** 10 MINUTES **MAKES:** 81 APPETIZERS

- 1 sheet frozen puff pastry, thawed
- 1 egg
- 1 tablespoon water
- 1 tablespoon poppy seeds
- 1 package (8 ounces) cream cheese, softened
- 2 tablespoons sherry
- ½ teaspoon liquid smoke, optional
- ¼ cup finely chopped pecans
- 1 tablespoon finely chopped onion

Creamy Feta Spinach Dip

Garlic and feta make a powerfully tasty pair in this addictive dip. I first tried it at a party and had to drag myself away from the bowl!

—ELISSA ARMBRUSTER
MEDFORD, NEW JERSEY

PREP: 15 MINUTES + CHILLING
MAKES: 2 CUPS

- 1 cup (8 ounces) fat-free plain yogurt
- ¾ cup crumbled feta cheese
- 2 ounces reduced-fat cream cheese, cubed
- ¼ cup reduced-fat sour cream
- 1 garlic clove, minced
- 1½ cups finely chopped fresh spinach
- 1 teaspoon dill weed
- ⅛ teaspoon pepper
  Fresh vegetables and/or sliced bread

1. Line a strainer with four layers of cheesecloth or one coffee filter; place over a bowl. Place yogurt in prepared strainer; cover yogurt with edges of cheesecloth. Refrigerate for 2 hours or until yogurt has thickened to the consistency of whipped cream.

2. Transfer yogurt to a food processor (discard liquid from bowl). Add the feta cheese, cream cheese, sour cream and garlic; cover and process until smooth.

3. Transfer to a small bowl. Stir in the spinach, dill and pepper. Cover and refrigerate until chilled. Serve with vegetables and/or bread.

Home Style COOKING NOTES

Brie-Apple Pastry Bites

Just pop one of these tasty morsels into your mouth for a tangy burst of flavor. If you prefer, make half with just apples and walnuts and the rest with cranberries and walnuts.

—JUDIE THURSTENSON COLCORD, OKLAHOMA

PREP: 30 MINUTES **BAKE:** 15 MINUTES **MAKES:** 4 DOZEN

- 1 package (17.3 ounces) frozen puff pastry, thawed
- 1 round (8 ounces) Brie cheese, cut into ½-inch cubes
- 1 medium apple, chopped
- ⅔ cup sliced almonds
- ½ cup chopped walnuts
- ¼ cup dried cranberries
  Ground nutmeg

1. Unfold puff pastry; cut each sheet into 24 squares. Gently press squares onto the bottoms of 48 greased miniature muffin cups.

2. Combine the cheese, apple, nuts and cranberries; spoon into cups. Bake at 375° for 12-15 minutes or until cheese is melted. Sprinkle with nutmeg.

Chicken Nuggets with Apricot Sauce

Satisfying a hungry crowd is easy with these baked morsels. The bite-sized pieces of chicken are served with a simple but incredible sauce made from apricot preserves and mustard.

—MICHELLE KRZMARCZICK REDONDO BEACH, CALIFORNIA

PREP: 25 MINUTES **BAKE:** 10 MINUTES **MAKES:** 2 DOZEN (1 CUP SAUCE)

1 cup buttermilk, divided
1 pound boneless skinless chicken breasts, cut into 1-inch cubes
¾ cup all-purpose flour
1 cup crushed cornflakes
½ teaspoon onion powder
½ teaspoon garlic salt
¼ teaspoon salt
¼ teaspoon dried oregano
⅛ teaspoon pepper
2 eggs
1 cup apricot preserves
2 tablespoons prepared mustard

1. Pour ½ cup buttermilk into a large resealable plastic bag; add chicken. Seal bag and turn to coat. Place flour in another resealable plastic bag. In a third bag, combine the cornflakes, onion powder, garlic salt, salt, oregano and pepper. In a shallow bowl, whisk eggs and remaining buttermilk.

2. Drain chicken; add to flour and shake to coat. Coat with egg mixture, then add to cornflake mixture and shake to coat. Arrange chicken in a greased 15-in. x 10-in. x 1-in. baking pan.

3. Bake at 350° for 10-15 minutes or until juices run clear. In a small bowl, combine apricot preserves and mustard. Serve with chicken.

Apricot Turkey Pinwheels

I created these unique pinwheels for a football game snack, using ingredients I had on hand. They were a huge hit, and so quick and easy to prepare.

—MELANIE FOSTER BLAINE, MINNESOTA

PREP/TOTAL TIME: 30 MINUTES **MAKES:** 16 PINWHEELS

1 **sheet frozen puff pastry, thawed**
¼ **cup apricot preserves**
½ **teaspoon ground mustard**
½ **cup shredded Monterey Jack cheese**
¼ **pound sliced deli turkey**

1. Unfold pastry; layer with preserves, mustard, cheese and turkey. Roll up jelly-roll style. Cut into 16 slices. Place cut side down on a baking sheet.
2. Bake at 400° for 15-20 minutes or until golden brown.

Caramelized Onion Tart

I've been delighted with the Vidalia onions of Georgia ever since moving here more than 35 years ago. In this savory appetizer pizza, they really get a chance to shine! Don't be afraid of the amount of garlic in the recipe. Roasting mellows its flavor.

—CAROL JORDAN LAWRENCEVILLE, GEORGIA

PREP: 50 MINUTES + COOLING **BAKE:** 25 MINUTES + STANDING **MAKES:** 16 SERVINGS

- 1 whole garlic bulb
- 3 tablespoons olive oil, divided
- 2 pounds sweet onions, sliced
- 1 tablespoon balsamic vinegar
- 1½ cups all-purpose flour
- ¾ cup cold butter, cubed
- ¼ teaspoon salt

FILLING

- 10 ounces fresh goat cheese
- 3 eggs
- 1 teaspoon minced fresh parsley
- ½ teaspoon salt
- ¼ teaspoon coarsely ground pepper
- ¾ cup shredded Parmesan cheese, divided
- 1 cup minced fresh basil

1. Remove papery outer skin from garlic (do not peel or separate cloves). Cut top off garlic bulb. Brush with 1 tablespoon oil. Wrap bulb in heavy duty foil. Bake at 425° for 30-35 minutes or until softened.

2. Meanwhile, in a large skillet, cook onions and vinegar in remaining oil over medium heat for 15-20 minutes or until onions are golden brown, stirring frequently. Set aside.

3. Cool the garlic for 10-15 minutes. Squeeze softened garlic into a food processor; add the flour, butter and salt. Cover and process until mixture resembles coarse crumbs. Press onto the bottom and up the sides of an ungreased 11-in. fluted tart pan with a removable bottom. Bake at 350° for 15 minutes.

4. In a food processor, combine the goat cheese, eggs, parsley, salt and pepper; cover and process until blended. Sprinkle ½ cup Parmesan cheese into crust; top with basil. Spread goat cheese mixture into crust.

5. Arrange onions over top; sprinkle with remaining Parmesan cheese. Bake for 25-30 minutes or until set.

Home Style COOKING NOTES

Herbed Havarti in Pastry

At holiday cocktail parties, I love surprising guests with this impressive Havarti baked inside puff pastry. The wrapped cheese is seasoned with herbs and served alongside crackers and fruit.

—DARCI TRUAX COUPEVILLE, WASHINGTON

PREP: 15 MINUTES **BAKE:** 20 MINUTES
MAKES: 16 SERVINGS

- ½ **cup dried parsley flakes**
- 1 **teaspoon dried thyme**
- 1 **teaspoon dried rosemary, crushed**
- ½ **teaspoon dried oregano**
- 2 **tablespoons Dijon mustard**
- 2 **blocks (8 ounces each) dill Havarti cheese**
- 1 **sheet frozen puff pastry, thawed**
- 1 **egg, beaten**
  Coarse salt, optional
  Assorted crackers and fresh fruit

1. In a shallow bowl, combine the parsley, thyme, rosemary and oregano. Spread mustard over cheese blocks; roll in herbs to coat.

2. On a lightly floured surface, roll pastry to about 13 in. long (or long enough to fit cheese blocks end to end). Place cheese on pastry and fold pastry around cheese; trim excess dough. Pinch edges to seal. Place seam side down on an ungreased baking sheet.

3. Brush pastry with egg. With floured cutters, cut decorative shapes from dough scraps if desired; arrange over the top and brush with egg. Sprinkle with salt if desired. Bake at 375° for 20-25 minutes or until puffed and golden brown. Serve warm with crackers and fruit.

Smoked Gouda & Bacon Potatoes

A hearty, special appetizer you'll need to eat with a fork! Creme fraiche gives these bites a decadent flavor.

—CHERYL PERRY HERTFORD, NORTH CAROLINA

PREP: 50 MINUTES **BAKE:** 10 MINUTES
MAKES: 2½ DOZEN (2 CUPS SAUCE)

- 2 **whole garlic bulbs**
- 1 **tablespoon olive oil**

- 15 **small red potatoes, halved**
- 15 **bacon strips**
- 2 **cups (8 ounces) shredded smoked Gouda cheese**
- 1 **teaspoon coarsely ground pepper**
- 2 **cups crème fraiche or sour cream**
- ¼ **cup fresh cilantro leaves**

1. Remove papery outer skin from garlic (do not peel or separate cloves). Cut tops off garlic bulbs. Brush with oil. Wrap each bulb in heavy-duty foil. Bake at 425° for 30-35 minutes or until softened. Cool for 10-15 minutes.

2. Meanwhile, place potatoes in a large saucepan; cover with water. Bring to a boil. Reduce heat; cover and simmer for 8-10 minutes or just until tender. Cut bacon strips in half widthwise. In a large skillet, cook bacon over medium heat until partially cooked but not crisp. Remove bacon to paper towels to drain; keep warm.

3. Place a tablespoonful of cheese on the cut side of a potato half. Wrap with a half-strip of bacon and secure with a toothpick. Place on an ungreased baking sheet. Repeat. Sprinkle appetizers with pepper. Bake at 375° for 10-15 minutes or until bacon is crisp.

4. For sauce, squeeze softened garlic into a food processor. Add crème fraiche and cilantro; cover and process until blended. Serve with potatoes.

Chickaritos

I created this recipe when our son grew fond of a fast-food restaurant's burritos. My version substitutes chicken for the beef and omits the frying. It's been a big hit with our whole family!

—NANCY COATES ORO VALLEY, ARIZONA

PREP: 30 MINUTES **BAKE:** 20 MINUTES **MAKES:** 1½ DOZEN

3 **cups finely chopped cooked chicken**
1½ **cups (6 ounces) shredded sharp cheddar cheese**
1 **can (4 ounces) chopped green chilies**
4 **green onions, finely chopped**
1 **teaspoon hot pepper sauce**
1 **teaspoon garlic salt**
¼ **teaspoon paprika**
¼ **teaspoon ground cumin**
¼ **teaspoon pepper**
1 **package (17.3 ounces) frozen puff pastry, thawed**
  Guacamole
  Salsa

1. In a large bowl, combine the chicken, cheese, chilies, onions, pepper sauce and seasonings. Refrigerate until serving.

2. Remove half of the pastry from the refrigerator. On a lightly floured surface, roll to a 12-in. x 9-in. rectangle. Cut into nine small rectangles. Place about 2 tablespoons of filling across the center of each rectangle. Wet edges of pastry with water and roll pastry around filling. Crimp ends with a fork to seal. Repeat with remaining pastry and filling.

3. Place seam side down on a lightly greased baking sheet. Refrigerate until ready to heat. Bake at 425° for 20-25 minutes or until golden brown. Serve warm with salsa and guacamole.

Gorgonzola & Cranberry Cheese Ball

A cheese ball is a classic appetizer to take to any gathering, and it's so easy to make. Studded with tangy dried cranberries, this version is always a hit.

—KATHY HAHN POLLOCK PINES, CALIFORNIA

PREP: 15 MINUTES + CHILLING **MAKES:** 2 CUPS

1 package (8 ounces) cream cheese, softened
1 cup (4 ounces) crumbled Gorgonzola cheese
1 cup dried cranberries
2 tablespoons each finely chopped onion, celery, green pepper and sweet red pepper
¼ teaspoon hot pepper sauce
¾ cup chopped pecans
   Assorted crackers

1. In a small bowl, combine the cheeses. Stir in the cranberries, vegetables and pepper sauce. Shape mixture into a ball; wrap in plastic wrap. Refrigerate for 1 hour or until firm. Roll the cheese ball in pecans. Serve with crackers.

Berry Interesting!

BY JUDITH KRALL-RUSSO

Cranberries claim a colorful past.

Perhaps no fruit has played such an important role in the history of America as the tiny ruby-colored cranberry.

Native Americans used cranberries as an all-purpose ingredient—a source of food, medicine and dye, and even a bartering tool. They mixed cranberries with dried meat or fish and melted fat to make pemmican—the original "power bar"—and combined them with corn and beans into succotash.

The Pilgrims and other early settlers also depended on wild cranberries for nutrition, venturing into bogs and marshes to pick them. Today, we only need visit the grocery or farmers market to add their pleasing tartness to garnishes, entrees, beverages and baked treats. This historic berry packs one powerful punch!

PHOTOGRAPHY BY Paul Russo

Judith Krall-Russo from Edison, New Jersey, is a food historian, author and expert on the fruits of her native New Jersey, including cranberries.

Juicy Cranberry Facts

- The cranberry is one of only a handful of commercially grown fruits that are native to North America.
- About 1,000 growers in North America provide most of the world's cranberries.
- Other common names include bear berry (bears love them), bounce berry (fresh ones bounce when dropped) and crane berry (the blossom resembles the head of a sandhill crane).
- The leading cranberry-producing states are Wisconsin, Massachusetts and New Jersey.
- Cranberries don't grow in water, but are raised in sandy bogs or marshes.
- Cranberry plants may live as long as 150 years.
- The Lenni-Lenape Indians of New Jersey called the cranberry *pakim*, meaning "noisy berry"— probably inspired by the popping sound the berry makes during cooking or when eaten raw.
- Some Native American tribes used cranberries as a symbol of peace.
- Commercial cultivation began in the early 1800s. Before that, wild cranberries were so prized that it was illegal to pick them before harvest season.
- In Colonial times, ships were stocked with barrels of cranberries to protect sailors against scurvy.
- Cranberries can be harvested wet or dry. In a wet harvest, bogs are flooded and the berries shaken loose with special machinery, then gathered when they float to the surface. In a dry harvest, a mechanical picker rakes berries off the vines.
- The fresh cranberries used in cooking and baking are usually harvested dry.

Soups & Sandwiches

It's true. Whether you live in a bustling city or the scenic country, a steaming bowl of soup paired with a delicious sandwich is comfort food that can't be beat. The selection that follows will have you headed for the kitchen to bring together a fabulously satisfying lunch or dinner.

Simply Elegant Tomato Soup

(recipe on page 77)

"If you've only had tomato soup from a can, you're going to be blown away when you try this. It's velvety, creamy and just so good."

—HEIDI BLANKEN
SEDRO-WOOLLEY, WASHINGTON

Cream of Chicken Noodle Soup

When we were at a restaurant, my husband remarked that I could make a better soup than they could. A challenge! We began discussing what we'd add and take out, and soon came up with this comforting soup.

—**DONNIE KINGMAN** SAN JACINTO, CALIFORNIA

PREP: 30 MINUTES **COOK:** 50 MINUTES
MAKES: 8 SERVINGS (2 QUARTS)

- 2 medium onions
- 2 celery ribs
- 4 cups water
- 3 boneless skinless chicken breast halves (6 ounces each)
- 1½ teaspoons salt
- ¼ teaspoon pepper
- 2 tablespoons butter
- 1 can (14½ ounces) chicken broth
- 1 large carrot, chopped
- 1 medium potato, peeled and chopped
- 2 teaspoons chicken bouillon granules
- 1½ teaspoons dried basil
- 2 cups uncooked wide egg noodles
- 1¾ cups milk, divided
- ⅓ cup all-purpose flour

Home Style COOKING NOTES

1. Chop one onion and one celery rib; set aside. Cut remaining onion and celery into chunks; place in a Dutch oven. Add the water, chicken, salt and pepper. Bring to a boil. Reduce heat; cover and simmer for 25-30 minutes or until a thermometer reads 170°. Remove chicken and strain broth; set both aside.

2. In the same pan, saute chopped onion and celery in butter until tender. Add the canned broth, carrot, potato, bouillon, basil and reserved broth. Bring to a boil. Reduce heat; cover and simmer for 20-30 minutes or until vegetables are tender.

3. Add noodles. Return to a boil; cook for 6-8 minutes or until noodles are tender. Cut chicken into chunks; add to soup. Stir in 1¼ cups milk; heat through.

4. Combine flour and remaining milk until smooth; add to soup, stirring constantly. Bring to a boil; cook and stir for 2 minutes or until thickened.

Grilled Veggie Tortilla Wraps

The tasty tortillas, stuffed with cream cheese and marinated veggies, will have everyone singing their praises.

—MARTA NORTHCUTT LEBANON, TENNESSEE

PREP: 20 MINUTES + MARINATING **GRILL:** 10 MINUTES **MAKES:** 4 SERVINGS

- 3 **tablespoons red wine vinegar**
- 3 **tablespoons olive oil**
- 1 **teaspoon lemon-pepper seasoning**
- 1 **garlic clove, minced**
- ½ **teaspoon dried oregano**
- ½ **teaspoon dried basil**
- 2 **medium zucchini, cut lengthwise into ¼-inch slices**
- 1 **medium yellow summer squash, cut lengthwise into ¼-inch slices**
- 1 **medium sweet red pepper, cut into strips**
- 4 **ounces cream cheese, softened**
- 1 **tablespoon prepared pesto**
- 4 **whole wheat tortillas (8 inches), warmed**

1. In a large resealable plastic bag, combine the first six ingredients; add zucchini, yellow squash and red pepper. Seal bag and turn to coat; refrigerate overnight, turning once.

2. In a small bowl, combine cream cheese and pesto; set aside. Drain and discard marinade. Place vegetables in a grill basket or disposable foil pan with slits cut in the bottom. Grill, covered, over medium-high heat for 3-4 minutes on each side or until tender.

3. Spread reserved pesto cream cheese over tortillas; top with vegetables. Fold sides over filling. Serve immediately.

Vegetable Beef Barley Soup

Seasoned beef and a host of fresh vegetables make this slow cooker soup taste just like Grandma's. Serve with a loaf of fresh bread and dinner is done!

—TARA MCDONALD KANSAS CITY, MISSOURI

PREP: 45 MINUTES **COOK:** 7 HOURS
MAKES: 8 SERVINGS (2¾ QUARTS)

- 1 **teaspoon seasoned salt**
- 1 **teaspoon onion powder**
- 1 **teaspoon garlic powder**
- 1½ **pounds beef stew meat, cut into 1-inch cubes**
- 2 **tablespoons canola oil**
- 3 **cups water**
- 3 **medium potatoes, peeled and diced**
- 1 **cup sliced fresh carrots**
- 1 **cup chopped celery**
- ½ **cup chopped onion**
- 1 **teaspoon beef bouillon granules**
- 1 **can (15¼ ounces) whole kernel corn, drained**
- 1 **can (14½ ounces) diced tomatoes, undrained**
- 1 **can (8½ ounces) peas, drained**
- 1 **cup tomato juice**
- ¾ **cup medium pearl barley**
- ½ **teaspoon salt**
- ¼ **teaspoon pepper**

1. In a large resealable plastic bag, combine the seasoned salt, onion powder and garlic powder. Add beef and toss to coat. In a large skillet, brown beef in oil until the meat is no longer pink; drain.

2. Transfer to a 5- or 6-qt. slow cooker. Add the water, potatoes, carrots, celery, onion and bouillon. Cover and cook on low for 5-6 hours or until meat and vegetables are almost tender.

3. Add the corn, tomatoes, peas, tomato juice, barley, salt and pepper; cover and cook 2 hours longer or until the barley is tender.

Polynesian Ham Sandwiches

The sweetness of the brown sugar and pineapple combined with the tanginess of the Dijon mustard are a perfect match in this tasty sandwich filling.

—JACKIE SMULSKI LYONS, ILLINOIS

PREP: 20 MINUTES **COOK:** 3 HOURS
MAKES: 12 SERVINGS

- 2 **pounds fully cooked ham, finely chopped**
- 1 **can (20 ounces) crushed pineapple, undrained**
- ¾ **cup packed brown sugar**
- ⅓ **cup chopped green pepper**
- ¼ **cup Dijon mustard**
- 1 **green onion, chopped**
- 1 **tablespoon dried minced onion**
- 12 **hamburger buns or kaiser rolls, split**

1. In a 3-qt. slow cooker, combine the first seven ingredients. Cover and cook on low for 3-4 hours or until heated through. Using a slotted spoon, place ½ cup on each bun.

Turkey Sandwiches with Red Pepper Hummus

This turkey sandwich from comes alive with roasted red pepper hummus. Cook it right on the grill or with a panini maker. Mouthwatering!

—TASTE OF HOME TEST KITCHEN

PREP: 20 MINUTES + CHILLING **COOK:** 5 MINUTES **MAKES:** 4 SERVINGS

- ⅓ **cup mayonnaise**
- 1 **tablespoon lime juice**
- 1 **can (15 ounces) garbanzo beans or chickpeas, rinsed and drained**
- ¼ **cup chopped roasted sweet red peppers, drained**
- 2 **garlic cloves, peeled**
- ½ **teaspoon chili powder**
- ¼ **teaspoon ground cumin**
- 2 **tablespoons butter, softened**
- 8 **slices rye bread**
- 4 **slices Muenster cheese**
- 8 **thin slices cooked turkey**
- 1 **small red onion, sliced**
- 2 **medium tomatoes, sliced**

1. For hummus, combine the first seven ingredients in a blender; cover and process until smooth. Transfer to a small bowl; cover and refrigerate for 1 hour.
2. Spread butter on one side of each slice of bread; spread hummus on the other side. Place four slices buttered side down on a griddle. Layer with cheese, turkey, onion, tomatoes and remaining bread, hummus side down. Toast for 2-3 minutes on each side or until bread is lightly browned and cheese is melted.

Wild Rice and Ham Chowder

The rich and soothing flavor of this chowder appeals to everyone who tries it. I got the recipe many years ago from my younger sister.

—ELMA FRIESEN WINNIPEG, MANITOBA

PREP: 10 MINUTES **COOK:** 40 MINUTES **MAKES:** 8-10 SERVINGS (2¾ QUARTS)

½ cup chopped onion
¼ cup butter, cubed
2 garlic cloves, minced
6 tablespoons all-purpose flour
½ teaspoon salt
¼ teaspoon pepper
4 cups chicken broth
1½ cups cubed peeled potatoes
½ cup chopped carrot
1 bay leaf
½ teaspoon dried thyme
¼ teaspoon ground nutmeg
3 cups cooked wild rice
2½ cups cubed fully cooked ham

2 cups half-and-half cream
1 can (15¼ ounces) whole kernel corn, drained
    Minced fresh parsley

1. In a Dutch oven, over medium heat, saute onion in butter until tender. Add garlic; cook 1 minute longer. Stir in the flour, salt and pepper until blended. Gradually add broth. Bring to a boil. Cook and stir for 2 minutes or until thickened and bubbly.

2. Add the potatoes, carrot, bay leaf, thyme and nutmeg; return to a boil. Reduce heat; cover and simmer for 30 minutes or until vegetables are tender. Stir in the rice, ham, cream and corn; heat through (do not boil). Discard bay leaf. Garnish with parsley.

Cream of Vegetable Soup

Several people told me that my vegetable soup is the best soup that they'd ever had. The biggest compliment I ever received, though, came from my 93-year old grandfather. He usually eats as few vegetables as possible—but he asked for a second bowlful!

—MARY PARKER COPPERAS COVE, TEXAS

PREP/TOTAL TIME: 25 MINUTES **MAKES:** 8-10 SERVINGS (ABOUT 3 QUARTS)

- **1 medium onion, chopped**
- **¾ cup butter**
- **½ cup all-purpose flour**
- **3 cans (10½ ounces each) condensed chicken broth, undiluted, or 4 cups chicken broth**
- **2 cups milk**
- **2 cups half-and-half cream**
- **1 teaspoon dried basil**
- **½ teaspoon salt**
- **½ teaspoon pepper**
- **¼ teaspoon garlic powder**
- **5 cups chopped leftover cooked mixed vegetables (such as broccoli, carrots and cauliflower)**

1. In a Dutch oven, saute onion in butter until tender. Add flour; stir until blended. Gradually add broth. Bring to a boil. Cook and stir for 2 minutes or until thickened.
2. Stir in the milk, cream and seasonings. Add the vegetables; cook gently until heated through.

- ¼ cup cider vinegar
- 2 tablespoons hot pepper sauce
- 1 tablespoon Worcestershire sauce
- 1 teaspoon ground cumin
- 1 boneless pork shoulder butt roast (3 to 4 pounds)
- 8 kaiser rolls, split

1. In a large skillet, saute onions in oil until tender. Add the garlic, pepper flakes and pepper; cook 1 minute longer. Stir in the tomatoes, brown sugar, vinegar, hot pepper sauce, Worcestershire and cumin. Cook over medium heat until sugar is dissolved and heated through.

2. Cut roast in half. Place in a 5-qt. slow cooker; pour sauce over the top. Cover and cook on low for 10-12 hours or until the meat is tender. Remove the roast; cool slightly. Skim fat from cooking juices. Shred meat with two forks and return to the slow cooker. Heat through. With a slotted spoon, spoon ¾ cup meat mixture onto each roll.

HOME STYLE tip

Remove cooked meat from pan with a slotted spoon if necessary. Reserve cooking liquid if called for. Place meat in a shallow pan. With two forks, pull meat into thin shreds. Return shredded meat to the pan to warm, or use as recipe directs.

Pulled BBQ Pork

After years of vacationing on the North Carolina coast, I became hooked on their pork barbecue. The version I developed is a favorite at potluck dinners.

—JOSEPH SARNOSKI WEST CHESTER, PENNSYLVANIA

PREP: 15 MINUTES **COOK:** 10 HOURS **MAKES:** 8 SERVINGS

- 2 medium onions, finely chopped
- 1 tablespoon canola oil
- 6 garlic cloves, minced
- 1 teaspoon crushed red pepper flakes
- 1 teaspoon pepper
- 1 can (14½ ounces) diced tomatoes, undrained
- ¼ cup packed brown sugar

Golden Squash Soup

I served this soup last Thanksgiving and received rave reviews—even people who don't usually like squash enjoyed its hearty flavor. To dress it up, I sometimes top it with a dollop of yogurt.

—NANCY MCFADYEN
SMITHS FALLS, ONTARIO

PREP/TOTAL TIME: 30 MINUTES
MAKES: 6-8 SERVINGS (2 QUARTS)

- 3 cups coarsely chopped onion
- 2 tablespoons canola oil
- ¼ teaspoon ground nutmeg
- ¼ teaspoon ground cinnamon
- ¼ teaspoon dried thyme
- 2 bay leaves
- 1½ cups water
- 2 celery ribs, chopped
- 1 medium carrot, chopped
- 2 cups mashed cooked butternut squash, divided
- 1½ cups tomato juice, divided
- 1 cup apple juice, divided
- 1 cup orange juice, divided
  Salt and pepper to taste

1. In a large saucepan, saute onion in oil with nutmeg, cinnamon, thyme and bay leaves until onion is tender. Stir in the water, celery and carrot; cover and simmer until carrot is tender. Discard bay leaves.

2. In a blender, place half of the squash and half of the tomato, apple and orange juices; add half of the vegetable mixture. Puree; return to pan. Repeat with the remaining squash, juices and vegetable mixture; return to pan. Add salt and pepper. Heat through.

Mango Chicken Wraps

These easy wraps are my go-to recipe when I want to make an exciting sandwich my family will love. The spiced chicken strips taste amazing with the tangy mango sauce.

—JAN WARREN-RUCKER CLEMMONS, NORTH CAROLINA

PREP: 30 MINUTES **GRILL:** 10 MINUTES **MAKES:** 5 SERVINGS

- 1½ cups chopped peeled mangoes
- ¼ cup chopped red onion
- 1 jalapeno pepper, seeded and chopped
- 2 tablespoons lime juice
- 1 teaspoon honey
- ¼ cup fresh cilantro leaves
- 2 packages (6 ounces each) ready-to-use grilled chicken breast strips
- 1½ teaspoons ground cumin
- ¾ teaspoon garlic powder
- ¾ teaspoon chili powder
- ⅛ teaspoon cayenne pepper
  Dash dried oregano
- 4 teaspoons olive oil
- 5 whole wheat tortillas (8 inches)
- ¾ cup shredded Monterey Jack cheese
- 1 small sweet red pepper, julienned
- ¾ cup chopped tomatoes
- 1 cup torn leaf lettuce

1. In a food processor, combine the mangoes, onion, jalapeno, lime juice and honey. Cover and process until pureed. Stir in cilantro; set aside.

2. In a large skillet, saute the chicken, cumin, garlic powder, chili powder, cayenne and oregano in oil until heated through. Spread mango sauce over tortillas. Layer with chicken, cheese, red pepper, tomatoes and lettuce; roll up.

Editor's Note: *Wear disposable gloves when cutting hot peppers; the oils can burn skin. Avoid touching your face.*

Cilantro Bean Burgers

Seasoned with cilantro and cumin, bean patties make a tempting alternative to beef burgers. Jazz them up with a little salsa or guacamole—or both!

—DOROTHY ANDREWS GRAFTON, WISCONSIN

PREP: 15 MINUTES + CHILLING **COOK:** 10 MINUTES **MAKES:** 2 SERVINGS

½ cup canned pinto beans, rinsed and drained
½ cup canned black beans, rinsed and drained
¼ cup shredded carrots
1 tablespoon minced fresh cilantro
¾ teaspoon dried minced onion
¾ teaspoon lime juice
1 small garlic clove, minced
¼ teaspoon ground cumin
⅛ teaspoon salt
⅛ teaspoon pepper
¼ cup soft bread crumbs
2 tablespoons egg substitute

1½ teaspoons cornmeal
1½ teaspoons canola oil
   Salsa, guacamole and tortilla chips, optional

1. In a food processor, combine the first 10 ingredients; cover and pulse until blended. Stir in bread crumbs and egg substitute; refrigerate for 30 minutes.

2. Shape bean mixture into two patties; sprinkle each side with cornmeal. In a large nonstick skillet, cook patties in oil for 4-5 minutes on each side or until lightly browned. Serve with salsa, guacamole and tortilla chips if desired.

Turkey Sloppy Joes

The chili sauce and ground turkey that are used to make these sloppy joes creates a deliciously unique flavor. The avocado adds a special touch to the sandwiches.

—NICHOLE JONES PLEASANT GROVE, UTAH

PREP: 35 MINUTES **COOK:** 4 HOURS
MAKES: 8 SERVINGS

- 1½ pounds lean ground turkey
- 2 medium onions, finely chopped
- 4 garlic cloves, minced
- 1 jar (12 ounces) chili sauce
- 1 jalapeno pepper, seeded and chopped
- 1 tablespoon Worcestershire sauce
- 2 teaspoons dried oregano
- 1 teaspoon ground cumin
- 1 teaspoon paprika
- ½ teaspoon salt
- ½ teaspoon pepper
- 2 cups (8 ounces) shredded Monterey Jack cheese
- 8 onion rolls, split
- 2 medium ripe avocados, peeled and thinly sliced

1. In a large skillet coated with cooking spray, cook the turkey, onions and garlic over medium heat until meat is no longer pink; drain.

2. Transfer to a 1½-qt. slow cooker. Stir in the chili sauce, jalapeno, Worcestershire sauce, oregano, cumin, paprika, salt and pepper. Cover and cook on low for 4-5 hours or until heated through. Just before serving, stir in cheese. Serve on rolls topped with avocado.

Editor's Note: *Wear disposable gloves when cutting hot peppers; the oils can burn skin. Avoid touching your face.*

Home Style COOKING NOTES

Versatile Ham and Corn Chowder

I like to experiment with recipes to shake up the flavors. I sometimes omit the bacon and butter in this soup, and have used canned corn and creamed corn with good results. We like to eat this chowder with big, soft hot pretzels instead of crackers.

—SHARON ROSE BRAND STAYTON, OREGON

PREP: 20 MINUTES **COOK:** 25 MINUTES **MAKES:** 10-12 SERVINGS (3 QUARTS)

- 8 bacon strips, cut into 1-inch pieces
- 1 medium onion, finely chopped
- 1 cup sliced celery
- ½ cup diced green pepper
- 3 cups cubed peeled potatoes (about 3 medium)
- 3 cups chicken broth
- 4 cups whole milk, divided
- 4 cups fresh or frozen whole kernel corn, divided
- 2 cups cubed fully cooked ham
- 2 tablespoons butter
- 3 tablespoons minced fresh parsley
- 1 teaspoon salt
- ⅛ teaspoon pepper
- ⅛ teaspoon hot pepper sauce, optional

1. In a large saucepan, cook bacon over medium heat until crisp. Using a slotted spoon, remove bacon to paper towel to drain, reserving ¼ cup drippings in pan. Saute the onion, celery and green pepper in drippings for 5 minutes. Add potatoes and broth. Reduce heat; cover and simmer for 10 minutes.

2. Place ½ cup milk and 2 cups corn in a blender; cover and process until pureed. Pour into saucepan. Add ham and remaining corn; simmer for 10 minutes or until vegetables are tender. Stir in the butter, parsley, salt, pepper, pepper sauce if desired and remaining milk; heat through. Garnish with bacon.

Philly Burger

The creamy cheese mixture on top of these juicy hamburgers, coupled with the crunchy french-fried onions, makes this recipe a cookout sensation. Serve the burgers with cool potato salad and a fruit salad and dinner is done!

—MARJORIE CAREY ALAMOSA, COLORADO

PREP/TOTAL TIME: 30 MINUTES **MAKES:** 4 BURGERS

- 2 **tablespoons Worcestershire sauce, divided**
- 4 **teaspoons Dijon mustard, divided**
- 1 **can (2.8 ounces) french-fried onions, divided**
- 1 **pound ground beef**
- 1 **package (3 ounces) cream cheese, softened**
- 1 **jar (2.5 ounces) sliced mushrooms, drained**
- 1 **teaspoon dried parsley flakes**
- 4 **Kaiser rolls**

1. In a large bowl, combine 1 tablespoon Worcestershire sauce, 3 teaspoons mustard and half the onions. Crumble beef over mixture; mix well. Form into four patties.

2. Grill, covered, over medium heat or broil 4 in. from the heat for 6-9 minutes on each side or until a thermometer reads 160° and juices run clear.

3. Meanwhile, in small bowl, combine the cream cheese, remaining Worcestershire sauce mixture, mushrooms and parsley. Spread the cheese mixture on cooked patties; top with reserved onions. Grill or broil 30 seconds longer or until the onions are crisp-tender. Serve on Kaiser rolls.

Potato Soup with Sausage

My great-grandmother passed on this soup and her family's been enjoying it for generations. In the 1880s, it was a popular meal after a hard day in the field—hearty to satisfy the most ravenous appetite and delicious, too!

—DOROTHY ALTHAUSE
MAGALIA, CALIFORNIA

PREP: 10 MINUTES **COOK:** 45 MINUTES
MAKES: 6 SERVINGS

- 1 **pound pork sausage links, cut into ¼-inch slices**
- 1 **cup sliced celery**
- ½ **cup chopped onion**
- ½ **teaspoon dried thyme**
- ½ **teaspoon salt**
- 2 **tablespoons all-purpose flour**
- 1 **can (14½ ounces) chicken broth**
- ½ **cup water**
- 4 **medium potatoes, peeled and diced (about 4 cups)**
- 1 **cup milk**
- 1 **cup sliced green beans, partially cooked**
   Minced fresh parsley

1. In a heavy saucepan, brown sausage over medium heat. Remove sausage to paper towels to drain. Drain skillet, reserving 1 tablespoon drippings. Saute the celery, onion, thyme and salt in the reserved drippings until celery is tender. Stir in flour until blended. Gradually add broth and water, stirring until the mixture comes to a boil.

2. Add potatoes; cover and simmer for 25 minutes or until potatoes are tender. Remove from the heat; cool.

3. In blender, cover and process 2 cups soup mixture until smooth; return to pan. Add the milk, beans and sausage; heat through. Garnish with parsley.

Creamy Asparagus Soup

After trying several different recipes for asparagus soup, I put together the best ingredients from each for my favorite version. This soup is great year-round and adds an elegant touch to special-occasion meals.

—PAT STEVENS GRANBURY, TEXAS

PREP/TOTAL TIME: 30 MINUTES
MAKES: 6 SERVINGS

  2 **medium leeks (white portion only), sliced**
12 **green onions, chopped**
  2 **tablespoons olive oil**
  1 **tablespoon butter**
2½ **pounds fresh asparagus, cut into 1-inch pieces**
  4 **cups chicken broth**
  1 **cup half-and-half cream**
  ½ **teaspoon salt**
  ⅛ **teaspoon pepper**

1. In a large saucepan, saute leeks and onions in oil and butter until tender. Add the asparagus and broth. Bring to a boil. Reduce heat; simmer, uncovered, until vegetables are tender. Remove from the heat. Set aside 1 cup of asparagus pieces.

2. In a blender, process the remaining asparagus mixture in batches until smooth; return to pan. Stir in cream, salt and pepper. Cook over low heat until heated through (do not boil). Top with reserved asparagus pieces.

Home Style COOKING NOTES

Shredded Pork Barbecue

Pork shoulder roast is rubbed with seasonings and grilled, creating a crispy exterior that's lip-smacking good! The meat is moist by itself but can also be topped with your favorite barbecue sauce.

—AMANDA MCLEMORE MARYVILLE, TENNESSEE

PREP: 15 MINUTES **GRILL:** 3½ HOURS + STANDING **MAKES:** 16 SERVINGS

1½ **teaspoons each white pepper, paprika and black pepper**
  1 **teaspoon each onion powder, garlic powder and cayenne pepper**
  1 **teaspoon dried thyme**
  ½ **teaspoon salt**
  1 **boneless pork shoulder roast (4 to 5 pounds)**
16 **hard rolls, split**
    Barbecue sauce, optional

1. Combine seasonings; rub over roast. Prepare grill for indirect heat, using a drip pan with 1 in. of water. Grill roast, covered, over medium-low heat for 3½ to 4 hours or until meat is tender.

2. When cool enough to handle, shred meat with two forks. Spoon ½ cup onto each bun; serve with barbecue sauce if desired.

Sweet Potato Minestrone

The pleasing taste of sweet potatoes in this soup is sure to make this recipe a keeper! My daughters love the comforting flavor, and I love that it's high in beta-carotene and other nutrients.

—HELEN VAIL GLENSIDE, PENNSYLVANIA

PREP: 15 MINUTES **COOK:** 20 MINUTES **MAKES:** 14 SERVINGS (ABOUT 3½ QUARTS)

4 cans (14½ ounces each) reduced-sodium beef or vegetable broth
3 cups water
2 medium sweet potatoes, peeled and cubed
1 medium onion, chopped
4 garlic cloves, minced
2 teaspoons Italian seasoning
6 cups shredded cabbage
1 package (7 ounces) small pasta shells
2 cups frozen peas

1. In a stockpot, combine the broth, water, sweet potatoes, onion, garlic and Italian seasoning; bring to a boil. Reduce heat; cover and simmer for 10 minutes.

2. Return to a boil. Add the cabbage, pasta and peas; cook for 8-10 minutes or until the pasta and vegetables are tender.

Breaded Buffalo Chicken Sandwiches

Topped with melted mozzarella cheese and a spicy sauce, these breaded chicken breasts make fantastic sandwiches. Try them whenever you're short on time but need a satisfying dinner.

—TRACY BOLEWARE COVINGTON, LOUISIANA

PREP/TOTAL TIME: 30 MINUTES **MAKES:** 2 SERVINGS

2   **boneless skinless chicken breast halves (4 ounces each)**
¼   **teaspoon salt**
⅛   **teaspoon garlic powder**
⅛   **teaspoon pepper**
¼   **cup seasoned bread crumbs**
2   **tablespoons all-purpose flour**
1   **tablespoon canola oil**
2   **slices mozzarella cheese**
3   **tablespoons butter**
1   **teaspoon cornstarch**
¼   **to ½ teaspoon hot pepper sauce**
2   **sandwich buns, split**
   Blue cheese or ranch salad dressing

1. Sprinkle chicken with salt, garlic powder and pepper. In a large resealable plastic bag, combine bread crumbs and flour. Add chicken and shake to coat. In a skillet over medium heat, brown chicken in oil. Reduce heat; cover and cook for 10 minutes or until the juices run clear.

2. Place cheese over the chicken; cover and cook for 1 minute or until the cheese is melted. In a small saucepan over medium heat, melt the butter; whisk in cornstarch and hot pepper sauce until smooth. Bring to a gentle boil, whisking constantly for 1 minute or until thickened. Drizzle over chicken. Serve on buns with blue cheese or ranch dressing.

Simply Elegant Tomato Soup

If you've only had tomato soup from a can, you're going to be blown away when you try this. It's velvety, creamy and just so good!

—HEIDI BLANKEN SEDRO-WOOLLEY, WASHINGTON

PREP: 25 MINUTES **COOK:** 20 MINUTES **MAKES:** 4 SERVINGS

- 4 **pounds tomatoes (about 10 medium)**
- 1 **tablespoon butter**
- 3 **tablespoons minced chives, divided**
- 1 **teaspoon salt**
- ½ **teaspoon pepper**
- 2 **cups half-and-half cream**

1. In a large saucepan, bring 8 cups water to a boil. Using a slotted spoon, place tomatoes, one at a time, in boiling water for 30-60 seconds. Remove each tomato and immediately plunge in ice water. Peel and quarter tomatoes; remove seeds.

2. In another large saucepan, melt butter. Add tomatoes, 2 tablespoons chives, salt and pepper. Bring to a boil. Reduce heat; simmer, uncovered, for 6-7 minutes or until tender, stirring occasionally. Remove from the heat. Cool slightly.

3. In a blender, process soup until blended. Return to the pan. Stir in cream; heat through (do not boil). Sprinkle each serving with remaining chives.

Turkey Burgers with Blueberry BBQ Sauce

I concocted this entree after researching the nutritional benefits of blueberries. The fruity sauce complements the poultry patties.

—LORI MERRICK DANVERS, ILLINOIS

PREP/TOTAL TIME: 30 MINUTES
MAKES: 4 SERVINGS

- ¼ **cup chopped onion**
- 1 **garlic clove, minced**
- 1 **teaspoon olive oil**
- 2 **cups fresh or frozen blueberries, thawed**
- 2 **tablespoons brown sugar**
- 1 **chipotle pepper in adobo sauce, chopped**
- 2 **tablespoons red wine vinegar**
- 1 **tablespoon Dijon mustard**
- 1 **tablespoon Worcestershire sauce**

BURGERS

- 1 **pound lean ground turkey**
- ½ **teaspoon salt**
- ½ **teaspoon pepper**
- 1 **cup sliced fresh mushrooms**
- 4 **slices reduced-fat provolone cheese**
- 4 **whole wheat hamburger buns, split**
- ½ **cup fresh baby spinach**

1. In a large skillet, cook onion and garlic in oil over medium heat until tender. Stir in the blueberries, brown sugar, pepper, vinegar, mustard and Worcestershire sauce. Cook and stir until thickened, about 10 minutes. Cool slightly. Transfer to a food processor; cover and process until smooth.

2. Shape turkey into four patties; sprinkle with salt and pepper. Place mushrooms on a double thickness of heavy-duty foil (about 12 in. square). Fold foil around mushrooms and seal tightly.

3. Grill burgers and mushroom packet, covered, over medium heat for 5-7 minutes on each side or until a meat thermometer inserted into the burgers reads 165° and juices run clear. Top burgers with cheese; cover and grill 1-2 minutes longer or until cheese is melted.

4. Place buns, cut side down, on grill for 1-2 minutes or until toasted. Serve burgers on buns with mushrooms, spinach and blueberry sauce.

Editor's Note: *Wear disposable gloves when cutting hot peppers; the oils can burn skin. Avoid touching your face.*

Swiss Pear Sandwiches

I'm always on the lookout for a quick meal that'll fit the lifestyle of a very busy retired couple, and this recipe really fills the bill. It uses the microwave, so you don't need to dirty a pan. Also, any kind of nuts will work in this pleasant-tasting sandwich.

—**JANET AKEY** PRESQUE ISLE, WISCONSIN

PREP/TOTAL TIME: 10 MINUTES
MAKES: 2 SERVINGS

- 4 **slices whole wheat bread**
- 4 **teaspoons honey mustard**
- 4 **slices (¾ ounce each) reduced-fat Swiss cheese**
- 1 **large pear, sliced**
- 2 **slices red onion**
- 2 **tablespoons chopped pecans**

1. Spread two slices of bread with mustard. Layer each with the cheese, pear and onion slices and pecans; top with remaining cheese and bread.

2. Place the sandwiches on a microwave-safe plate. Cover and microwave on high for 20-30 seconds or until the cheese is melted.

Pasta Bean Soup

My family loves this soup during our cold New England winters. This one is very thick and hearty.

—**BEVERLY BALLARO** LYNNFIELD, MASSACHUSETTS

PREP: 10 MINUTES **COOK:** 25 MINUTES
MAKES: 6 SERVINGS

- 1 **large onion, chopped**
- 1 **large carrot, chopped**
- 1 **celery rib, chopped**
- 2 **tablespoons olive oil**
- 3 **garlic cloves, minced**
- 4 **cups vegetable or chicken broth**
- ¾ **cup uncooked small pasta shells**
- 2 **teaspoons sugar**
- 1½ **teaspoons Italian seasoning**
- ¼ **teaspoon crushed red pepper flakes**

- 2 **cans (15 ounces each) white kidney or cannellini beans, rinsed and drained**
- 1 **can (28 ounces) crushed tomatoes**
- 3 **tablespoons grated Parmesan cheese**

1. In a Dutch oven, saute the onion, carrot and celery in oil until crisp-tender. Add garlic; saute 1 minute longer. Add the broth, pasta, sugar, Italian seasoning and pepper flakes.

2. Bring to a boil. Reduce heat; simmer, uncovered, for 15 minutes or until pasta is tender. Add the beans and tomatoes; simmer, uncovered, for 5 minutes. Garnish with Parmesan cheese.

Easy Black-Eyed Pea Soup

This recipe is simple, delicious and can be made in very little time. Once you try it, it will become one of your favorite light meals—or favorite meals ever!

—ERIN WALSTEAD ORANGE, CALIFORNIA

PREP: 15 MINUTES **COOK:** 20 MINUTES
MAKES: 6 SERVINGS

>   3 bacon strips, diced
>   1 medium onion, finely chopped
>   1 garlic clove, minced
>   2 cans (14½ ounces each) beef broth
>   1 can (10 ounces) diced tomatoes and green chilies, undrained
>   ¼ teaspoon salt
>   ¼ teaspoon pepper
>   2 cans (15½ ounces each) black-eyed peas, rinsed and drained

1. In a large saucepan, cook bacon over medium heat until crisp. Using a slotted spoon, remove to paper towels to drain.
2. In the drippings, saute onion until tender. Add garlic; cook 1 minute longer. Stir in the broth, tomatoes, salt and pepper. Bring to a boil. Stir in black-eyed peas and bacon; heat through.

Curried Olive Egg Salad

Accessorizing a humble egg salad sandwich with olives, curry powder and celery seed really bumps up the flavor of lunch.

—ANITA DOYLE DODGEVILLE, WISCONSIN

PREP/TOTAL TIME: 15 MINUTES **MAKES:** 4 SERVINGS

>   6 hard-cooked eggs, chopped
>   ½ cup reduced-fat mayonnaise
>   ⅓ cup chopped sweet onion
>   ¼ cup chopped pimiento-stuffed olives
>   ½ teaspoon celery seed
>   ½ teaspoon curry powder
>   ¼ teaspoon sugar
>   ¼ teaspoon pepper
>   ⅛ teaspoon salt
>   8 pita pocket halves
>   8 lettuce leaves

1. In a large bowl, combine the first nine ingredients. Line pita halves with lettuce; fill each with ¼ cup egg salad.

HOME STYLE tip

❝For special flavor in any bean soup, I always drop in a cored unpeeled apple during cooking and remove it before serving.**❞**

—JUANITA E.
BLANCHESTER, OHIO

Grilled Cheese & Pepper Sandwiches

This is a tasty sandwich to make for one or two. It's a nice twist on traditional grilled cheese. It's filling and especially good with rye bread!

—ARLINE HOFLAND
DEER LODGE, MONTANA

PREP/TOTAL TIME: 20 MINUTES
MAKES: 2 SERVINGS

- 4 slices rye bread with caraway seeds
- 2 tablespoons butter, softened, divided
- ½ cup chopped onion
- ½ cup chopped green pepper
- ½ cup chopped sweet red pepper
- 2 teaspoons chopped seeded jalapeno pepper
- 2 tablespoons olive oil
- ¾ cup shredded Monterey Jack cheese

1. Butter one side of each slice of bread with ½ teaspoon butter; set aside. In a small skillet, saute onion and peppers in oil until tender. Spoon onto two buttered bread slices; top with cheese and remaining bread. Spread outsides of sandwiches with remaining butter.
2. In a large skillet, toast sandwiches for 3 minutes on each side or until golden brown.
Editor's Note: *Wear disposable gloves when cutting hot peppers; the oils can burn skin. Avoid touching your face.*

Home Style COOKING NOTES

Fried Green Tomato BLTs

You might call this Southern-inspired sandwich comfort food taken to the next level. The chipotle mayonnaise adds a delicious kick, while the peppered bacon really punches up the flavor.

—NEILLA ROE KINGSTON, WASHINGTON

PREP/TOTAL TIME: 20 MINUTES **MAKES:** 8 SERVINGS

- 1 package thick-sliced peppered bacon strips (24 ounces)
- 1 cup all-purpose flour
- 1 cup cornmeal
- 4½ teaspoons seafood seasoning
- 1 teaspoon pepper
- ⅛ teaspoon salt
- 1 cup buttermilk
- 8 medium green tomatoes, cut into ¼-inch slices
-     Oil for deep-fat frying
- 16 slices Texas toast
- ½ cup reduced-fat chipotle mayonnaise
- 8 Boston lettuce leaves

1. In a large skillet, cook bacon over medium heat until crisp. Remove to paper towels to drain. In a small shallow bowl, combine the flour, cornmeal, seafood seasoning, pepper and salt. Place buttermilk and flour mixture in separate shallow bowls. Dip tomatoes in buttermilk, then coat with flour mixture.
2. In an electric skillet or deep fryer, heat oil to 375°. Fry tomatoes, a few slices at a time, for 1 minute on each side or until golden brown. Drain on paper towels.
3. Serve tomatoes on Texas toast with mayonnaise, bacon and lettuce.

Hearty Bean Soup

My hearty soup is a real crowd-pleaser served with fresh corn bread. No one can believe how quickly it comes together.

—NELDA CAMERON CLEVELAND, TEXAS

PREP/TOTAL TIME: 30 MINUTES **MAKES:** 10 SERVINGS (2½ QUARTS)

- 1 **large onion, chopped**
- ½ **cup chopped green pepper**
- 2 **tablespoons butter**
- 2 **garlic cloves, minced**
- 2 **cans (15½ ounces each) great northern beans, rinsed and drained**
- 2 **cans (15 ounces each) pinto beans, rinsed and drained**
- 2 **cans (11½ ounces each) condensed bean with bacon soup, undiluted**
- 2 **cups diced fully cooked ham**
- 2 **cups water**
- 2 **tablespoons canned diced jalapeno peppers**

1. In a small skillet, saute onion and green pepper in butter for 3 minutes. Add the garlic; cook 1 minute longer. Transfer vegetables to a Dutch oven or stockpot. Stir in the remaining ingredients. Cover and cook over medium-low heat for 20 minutes or until heated through, stirring occasionally.

Asparagus Chowder

While my soup's good with fresh asparagus, it can also be prepared with frozen or canned. I like to blanch and freeze asparagus in portions just right for the recipe. This way, I can make our favorite chowder all year.

—SHIRLEY BEACHUM SHELBY, MICHIGAN

PREP: 10 MINUTES **COOK:** 30 MINUTES **MAKES:** ABOUT 2½ QUARTS

2	**medium onions, chopped**
2	**cups chopped celery**
¼	**cup butter**
1	**garlic clove, minced**
½	**cup all-purpose flour**
1	**large potato, peeled and cut into ½-inch cubes**
4	**cups milk**
4	**cups chicken broth**
½	**teaspoon dried thyme**
½	**teaspoon dried marjoram**
4	**cups chopped fresh asparagus, cooked and drained**
	Salt and pepper to taste

Sliced almonds
Shredded cheddar cheese
Chopped fresh tomato

1. In a Dutch oven, saute onions and celery in butter until tender. Add garlic; cook 1 minute longer. Stir in flour. Add the potato, milk, broth and herbs; cook over low heat, stirring occasionally until the potato is tender and soup is thickened, about 20-30 minutes.

2. Add the asparagus, salt and pepper; heat through. To serve, sprinkle with the almonds, cheese and chopped tomato.

Turkey Salad Croissants

I created this creamy, crunchy salad for a small tea party I had one midwinter afternoon. It's a great way to use up some of that leftover holiday turkey when friends drop by.

—KAREN JANTZ NEW PLYMOUTH, IDAHO

PREP/TOTAL TIME: 30 MINUTES **MAKES:** 8 SERVINGS

- 4 **cups cubed cooked turkey breast**
- 1 **can (8 ounces) sliced water chestnuts, drained and chopped**
- ⅔ **cup chopped pecans**
- 2 **celery ribs, sliced**
- 2 **green onions, sliced**
- 1 **cup mayonnaise**
- 2 **teaspoons prepared mustard**
- ½ **teaspoon garlic pepper blend**
- ¼ **teaspoon salt**
- 8 **lettuce leaves**
- 8 **croissants, split**

1. In a large bowl, combine the turkey, water chestnuts, pecans, celery and onions. Combine the mayonnaise, mustard, garlic pepper and salt; pour over turkey mixture and toss to coat. Cover and refrigerate until serving. Spoon onto lettuce-lined croissants.

Curried Apple Soup

Harvest-fresh soup is a perfect salute to the riches of Indian summer. Sweet apples, spicy curry and tangy lemon strike a delicious balance.

—XAVIER PENNELL MAULDIN, SOUTH CAROLINA

PREP: 20 MINUTES **COOK:** 20 MINUTES
MAKES: 4 SERVINGS

- 1 **medium onion, chopped**
- 2 **tablespoons butter**
- 1 **teaspoon curry powder**
- ¼ **teaspoon ground cinnamon**
- ⅛ **teaspoon salt**
  Dash cayenne pepper
  Dash ground cloves
- 3 **medium McIntosh apples, peeled and sliced**
- 3 **cups chicken broth**
- 1½ **teaspoons lemon juice**
  Crackers and additional ground cinnamon, optional

1. In a small saucepan, saute onion in butter until tender. Add the curry, cinnamon, salt, cayenne and cloves; cook and stir for 1 minute. Add apples and broth; bring to a boil. Reduce heat; cover and simmer for 5-7 minutes or until apples are tender. Cool slightly.
2. In a blender, puree the soup until smooth. Return to the pan. Stir in lemon juice and heat through. Garnish with crackers and additional cinnamon if desired.

Home Style COOKING NOTES

Smoked Salmon Bagel Sandwiches

A memorable pesto salmon I tried in Hawaii inspired these ultra-convenient sandwiches.

—SHERRYL VERA HURLBURT FIELD, FLORIDA

PREP/TOTAL TIME: 10 MINUTES
MAKES: 2 SERVINGS

- 2 tablespoons prepared pesto
- 2 whole wheat bagels, split and toasted
- ⅛ teaspoon coarsely ground pepper
- 4 to 5 ounces smoked salmon or lox
- 2 slices tomato
- 2 Bibb or Boston lettuce leaves

1. Spread pesto over bagel bottoms; sprinkle with pepper. Layer with salmon, tomato and lettuce leaves. Replace tops.

Avocado Tomato Wraps

I eat these super-fast wrap sandwiches all summer long. The creamy avocado and sweet tomato are satisfying and fresh. It doesn't get more simple and delicious than this!

—MEGAN WISENER MILWAUKEE, WISCONSIN

PREP/TOTAL TIME: 10 MINUTES
MAKES: 2 SERVINGS

- 1 medium ripe avocado, peeled and thinly sliced
- 2 flavored tortillas of your choice (10 inches), room temperature
- 2 lettuce leaves
- 1 medium tomato, thinly sliced
- 2 tablespoons shredded Parmesan cheese
- ¼ teaspoon garlic powder
- ⅛ teaspoon salt
- ⅛ teaspoon pepper

1. In a small bowl, mash a fourth of the avocado with a fork; spread over tortillas. Layer with lettuce, tomato and remaining avocado. Sprinkle with cheese, garlic powder, salt and pepper; roll up. Serve immediately.

Chili Verde

This is one of my family's favorite recipes. It can be fixed any time of the year, but it's especially good with fresh peppers from the garden.

—SHERRIE SCETTRINI SALINAS, CALIFORNIA

PREP: 15 MINUTES **COOK:** 1½ HOURS **MAKES:** 6-8 SERVINGS

- 4 tablespoons canola oil, divided
- 4 pounds boneless pork, cut into ¾-inch cubes
- ¼ cup all-purpose flour
- 1 can (4 ounces) chopped green chilies
- ½ teaspoon ground cumin
- ¼ teaspoon salt
- ¼ teaspoon pepper
- 3 garlic cloves, minced
- ½ cup minced fresh cilantro
- ½ to 1 cup salsa
- 1 can (14½ ounces) chicken broth
  Flour tortillas, warmed

1. In a Dutch oven, heat 1 tablespoon oil over medium-high heat. Add 1 pound of pork; cook and stir until lightly browned. Remove and set aside. Repeat with remaining meat, adding more oil as needed. Return all of the meat to Dutch oven.
2. Sprinkle flour over meat; mix well. Add the chilies, cumin, salt, pepper, garlic, cilantro, salsa and broth. Cover and simmer until pork is tender and chili reaches desired consistency, about 1½ hours. Serve with warmed tortillas.

Broccoli Chowder

I serve this comforting soup on chilly, stay-at-home evenings. Nutmeg seasons the light, creamy broth that's chock-full of tender broccoli florets and diced potatoes.
—**SUE CALL** BEECH GROVE, INDIANA

PREP/TOTAL TIME: 30 MINUTES **MAKES:** 6 SERVINGS

- 3 **cups fresh broccoli florets**
- 2 **cups diced peeled potatoes**
- 2 **cups water**
- ⅓ **cup sliced green onions**
- 1 **teaspoon salt**
- ½ **teaspoon pepper**
- 3 **tablespoons butter**
- 3 **tablespoons all-purpose flour**
- ⅛ **teaspoon ground nutmeg**
- 2 **cups milk**
- ½ **cup shredded cheddar cheese**

1. In a large saucepan, combine the first six ingredients. Bring to a boil. Reduce heat; cover and simmer for 12-14 minutes or until vegetables are tender.
2. Meanwhile, in another saucepan, melt butter. Stir in flour and nutmeg until smooth. Gradually add milk. Bring to a boil; cook and stir for 2 minutes or until thickened. Stir into vegetable mixture; heat through. Sprinkle with cheese.

Roasted Red Pepper Soup

If you like cream of tomato soup, try making it with purchased roasted red peppers. Using jarred roasted red peppers makes it extra easy, and pureeing the soup in a blender gives it a nice, smooth texture.
—**TASTE OF HOME TEST KITCHEN**

PREP: 10 MINUTES **COOK:** 25 MINUTES
MAKES: 6 SERVINGS

- 1 **large sweet onion, chopped**
- 2 **teaspoons butter**
- 2 **garlic cloves, minced**
- 2 **jars (15½ ounces each) roasted sweet red peppers, drained**
- 2 **cups vegetable broth**
- ½ **teaspoon dried basil**
- ¼ **teaspoon salt**
- 1 **cup half-and-half cream**

1. In a large saucepan, saute onion in butter for 2-3 minutes or until tender. Add garlic; cook 1 minute longer. Stir in the red peppers, broth, basil and salt. Bring to a boil. Reduce heat; cover and simmer for 20 minutes. Cool slightly.
2. In a blender, cover and process the soup in batches until smooth. Remove 1 cup to a small bowl; stir in the cream. Return remaining puree to the pan. Stir in the cream mixture; heat through (do not boil).

Home Style COOKING NOTES

Hearty Cheese Soup

Thick and creamy, this soup is chock-full of rich cheese flavor. I came home with this recipe after an exchange at my church several years ago, and I have shared it with many. I hope you enjoy it as much as we do.

—SUZANNA SNADER
FREDERICKSBURG, PENNSYLVANIA

PREP: 20 MINUTES **COOK:** 20 MINUTES
MAKES: 2 SERVINGS

- 1½ cups cubed peeled potatoes
- ½ cup water
- ¼ cup sliced celery
- ¼ cup sliced fresh carrots
- 2 tablespoons chopped onion
- ½ teaspoon chicken bouillon granules
- ½ teaspoon dried parsley flakes
- ¼ teaspoon salt
  Dash pepper
- 1½ teaspoons all-purpose flour
- ¾ cup milk
- ¼ pound process cheese (Velveeta), cubed

1. In a small saucepan, combine the first nine ingredients. Bring to a boil. Reduce heat; cover and simmer for 10-12 minutes or until potatoes are tender.

2. In a small bowl, combine flour and milk until smooth. Stir into vegetable mixture. Bring to a boil; cook and stir for 2 minutes or until thickened. Reduce heat to low; stir in the cheese until melted.

Pumpernickel Turkey Hero

Thousand Island dressing adds oomph to each bite of this hearty turkey and Swiss sandwich. A friend brought this loaf to a sandwich luncheon. I asked for the recipe so I could serve it to my family. They liked it, too.

—MILDRED SHERRER FORT WORTH, TEXAS

PREP/TOTAL TIME: 10 MINUTES **MAKES:** 6 SERVINGS

- 1 loaf (1 pound) unsliced pumpernickel bread
- ⅓ cup Thousand Island salad dressing
- 6 lettuce leaves
- 2 medium tomatoes, sliced
- 3 slices red onion, separated into rings
- 6 slices Swiss cheese
- 1 package (12 ounces) thinly sliced deli turkey

1. Cut the bread in half horizontally; spread salad dressing over cut sides. On the bottom half, layer the lettuce, tomatoes, onion, half of the cheese and half of the turkey. Top with remaining cheese and turkey. Replace bread top. Slice before serving.

Split Pea and Ham Soup

Not a winter goes by that I don't fix at least one batch of this traditional pea soup. It's a robust take on a homey meal that really warms up my family.

—LUCILLE SCHREIBER GLEASON, WISCONSIN

PREP: 15 MINUTES **COOK:** 2 HOURS 35 MINUTES **MAKES:** 10 SERVINGS (2¾ QUARTS)

- 1 **pound dried green split peas (2 cups)**
- 7 **cups water**
- 1 **teaspoon canola oil**
- 2 **cups cubed fully cooked ham**
- 2 **cups chopped carrots**
- 1 **cup chopped celery**
- 1 **cup chopped onion**
- 1 **cup diced peeled potato**
- 1 **teaspoon salt, optional**
- ½ **teaspoon garlic powder**
- ½ **teaspoon pepper**
- ¼ **cup minced fresh parsley**

1. In a Dutch oven or stockpot, bring the peas, water and oil to a boil. Reduce heat; cover and simmer for 2 hours, stirring occasionally. Add the next eight ingredients; cover and simmer for 30 minutes or until vegetables are tender. Stir in parsley.

Summer Veggie Sandwiches

A few ingredients make a standout sandwich perfect for lunch or supper. Add bacon, turkey or both for added protein.

—MARY LOU TIMPSON COLORADO CITY, ARIZONA

PREP/TOTAL TIME: 15 MINUTES **MAKES:** 4 SERVINGS

- 4 **ounces cream cheese, softened**
- 8 **slices whole wheat bread**
- 1 **small cucumber, sliced**
- ½ **cup alfalfa sprouts**
- 2 **teaspoons olive oil**
- 2 **teaspoons red wine vinegar**
- 1 **large tomato, sliced**
- 4 **lettuce leaves**
- ¾ **cup sliced pepperoncini**
- 1 **medium ripe avocado, peeled and mashed**

1. Spread cream cheese over four slices of bread; layer with cucumber and sprouts. Combine oil and vinegar; drizzle over sprouts. Layer with tomato, lettuce and pepperoncini. Spread avocado over remaining bread; place over top.

1 celery rib, halved
1 bay leaf
¼ cup minced fresh parsley
¼ teaspoon dried rosemary, crushed
¼ teaspoon dried thyme
¼ teaspoon whole peppercorns

SOUP

⅓ cup medium pearl barley
1½ cups julienned peeled turnips (1-inch pieces)
1 cup coarsely chopped carrots
1 medium leek (white portion only), thinly sliced
¼ teaspoon salt
¼ teaspoon pepper

1. In a Dutch oven, brown lamb shank in oil on all sides; drain. Stir in water and broth. Insert cloves into onion. Add the onion, carrot, celery and seasonings to the pan. Bring to a boil. Reduce heat; cover and simmer for 2 hours or until meat is very tender.

2. Remove shank from broth; cool slightly. Remove meat from bone; cut into small pieces. Discard bone. Strain broth, discarding vegetables and seasonings.

3. Skim fat from broth. In a large saucepan, bring broth to a boil. Stir in barley. Reduce heat; cover and simmer for 40 minutes.

4. Add the turnips, carrots, leek, salt and pepper. Return to a boil. Reduce heat; cover and simmer for 15 minutes or until vegetables are tender. Add lamb; heat through.

Scotch Broth

Add a side of bread to this luscious concoction of lamb, vegetables and barley, and you'll have all a hungry body needs. I skim the fat to fit our lighter way of eating.

—KELSEY HAMILTON HIGHLAND PARK, NEW JERSEY

PREP: 2¼ HOURS **COOK:** 1¼ HOURS **MAKES:** 4 SERVINGS

1 lamb shank (about 1 pound)
2 teaspoons canola oil
4 cups water
2 cans (14½ ounces each) reduced-sodium beef broth
2 whole cloves
1 medium onion, halved
1 medium carrot, halved

Home Style COOKING NOTES

Potato Soup with Spinach Dumplings

I remember my mother often making this soup for Saturday night supper. During the war years, she would cook a lot of stews and soups—she'd start with a big kettle of chicken stock, and it was amazing what she could make! Even though I didn't like spinach much, I liked this soup. I loved to help Mom in the kitchen, and was cooking by myself when I was 10.

—ROSEMARY FLEXMAN
WAUKESHA, WISCONSIN

PREP: 20 MINUTES + STANDING
COOK: 20 MINUTES **MAKES:** 4 SERVINGS

- 2 **cups cubed peeled potatoes**
- ½ **cup chopped onion**
- ½ **cup chopped sweet red pepper**
- 2 **tablespoons butter**
- 3 **cans (14½ ounces each) chicken broth**
- 1 **package (10 ounces) frozen chopped spinach, thawed**
- 1 **cup seasoned dry bread crumbs**
- 1 **egg white, lightly beaten**
  Chopped fresh parsley

1. In a large saucepan, combine potatoes, onion, red pepper, butter and chicken broth; bring to a boil. Reduce heat; cover and simmer about 10 minutes or until the potatoes are tender. Remove from the heat.
2. In a small bowl, combine the spinach, bread crumbs and egg white; let stand for 15 minutes. Shape into 1-in. balls; add to soup. Return to a boil; reduce heat and simmer 10-15 minutes or until dumplings are firm. Sprinkle with parsley.

Shredded Beef au Jus

My mom found this recipe in a farm journal soon after she and my dad got married. The tender beef has been a family favorite for years, and my dad often requests it.
—DANIELLE BRANDT RUTHTON, MINNESOTA

PREP: 10 MINUTES **COOK:** 6 HOURS **MAKES:** 8 SERVINGS

- 1 **boneless beef chuck roast (3 pounds)**
- 2 **cups water**
- 2 **teaspoons beef bouillon granules**
- 1½ **teaspoons dried oregano**
- 1 **teaspoon garlic salt**
- 1 **teaspoon seasoned salt**
- ¼ **teaspoon dried rosemary, crushed**
- 8 **hamburger buns, split**

1. Cut roast in half and place in a 4- or 5-qt. slow cooker. Combine the water, bouillon granules and seasonings; pour over the beef.
2. Cover and cook on low for 6-8 hours or until meat is tender. Remove beef; cool slightly. Meanwhile, skim fat from the cooking liquid.
3. Shred meat with two forks; return to the cooking liquid and heat through. Using a slotted spoon, place ½ cup on each bun. Serve with additional cooking liquid on the side.

Classic Tortellini Soup

My husband's grandmother used to make this soup with her own homemade sausage and homemade tortellini. Since it has been passed down, we don't "hand make" those ingredients but it's almost as good as hers. It's a great way to make spinach extra delicious!

—JOYCE LULEWICZ BRUNSWICK, OHIO

PREP: 10 MINUTES **COOK:** 30 MINUTES **MAKES:** 2 SERVINGS

½ **pound bulk Italian sausage**
1 **small onion, thinly sliced**
1 **garlic clove, minced**
1 **can (14½ ounces) reduced-sodium chicken broth**
½ **cup water**
1½ **cups torn fresh spinach**
¾ **cup refrigerated cheese tortellini**
2 **tablespoons shredded Parmesan cheese**

1. In a small saucepan, cook sausage over medium heat until no longer pink; drain. Add onion; cook and stir until tender. Add garlic; cook 1 minute longer. Stir in broth and water; bring to a boil. Reduce heat; simmer, uncovered, for 10 minutes.

2. Return to a boil. Reduce heat, add spinach and tortellini; cook for 7-9 minutes or until tortellini is tender. Sprinkle with cheese.

our Cheese
stands alone

BY CLARA HEDRICH

Near Chilton, Wisconsin, a busy dairy farm gives a glimpse of what it's like keeping up with the goats.

My husband, Larry, and I first became interested in raising dairy goats when we bought a 22-acre farm in 1978. A pair of milk goats came with the farm, and when he and I got married that year, we spent our honeymoon visiting goat farms!

As our five children became active in 4-H, we started taking our goats to county fairs and livestock shows. Each child had a different preference, so we ended up with six breeds of dairy goats: Alpines, Toggenburgs, Saanens, Nubians, LaManchas and Oberhaslis.

As our hobby herd grew, we decided the goats needed to earn their keep. So we found a market for their milk and built a 20-stall parlor. The truck picked up our first load of milk 16 years ago. Currently, we're milking 350 does twice a day, 365 days a year.

I grew up on a dairy farm and have noticed a few differences between caring for cows versus goats. Some

are positive. For example, goats are smaller, so they're ideal for a woman to handle. They're easy to lead by their neck chains, and they eat less than cattle. Some of the differences aren't so positive. In terms of production, a goat averages 8 pounds of milk a day compared to a cow's 80.

That makes raising goats labor intensive. We need to milk 10 goats to get the output of one cow, which means we trim 40 hooves instead of four. And since twins, triplets and quadruplets aren't uncommon for goats, our kidding seasons are hectic.

You might ask: Why goat's milk? Well, goat's milk is a good alternative for people who are sensitive to cow's milk. It's easy to digest, lower in cholesterol and higher in calcium, phosphorus and vitamins A and B.

Goat's milk is distributed in a similar matter to cow's milk. My husband, Larry, manages a local dairy goat producers' cooperative

that sends our milk out in different directions. Some goes to cheese plants and a fluid milk bottler. Some is used to make butter and even gourmet ice cream.

Four years ago, we started holding back part of our milk to make our own custom artisan cheese. Our daughter Katie recently earned her cheesemaker's license. She went through several batches, trying to make that "just perfect" recipe. Katie named the cheese LaClare Farm Evalon cheese, for Larry's grandmother. We were all thrilled when it won the best-in-show award at the U.S. Championship Cheese Contest last spring, surpassing over 1,604 entries from 30 states.

Evalon is a hard cheese that's carefully aged in curing cellars. It grates and shreds well, which makes it a wonderful cooking cheese.

We're pretty proud of Katie. At 25, she's the youngest cheesemaker to have ever won this contest, and just the second woman. And this is only the second time a goat's milk cheese has been named champion.

Besides our Evalon cheese, Katie started to make goat's milk soap about eight years ago as an FFA project. Once Katie went off to college, her sister Jessica and I began helping make what we call Nitty Gritty Soap.

We mix various oils with the milk, which is a natural moisturizer, and came up with 25 different scents, like lavender, jasmine, mint and strawberry. The soap is long-lasting— it's the only one we use—and it's a good seller at craft shows, farmers markets and specialty stores.

Some people think goats are ornery. But modern dairy goats are about the most sociable and intelligent animals you could hope to raise. As a high school ag teacher for 35 years, I regularly bring kid goats in to teach my students about animal science.

Yes, they're curious. I've learned the hard way that they can turn on water hydrants, lock doors, flip switches—even open electrical boxes and turn off the power!

But Larry and I are fans, obviously. We are also licensed dairy goat judges and hosts at the dairy goat product booth at the Wisconsin State Fair.

In the future, we'd love to diversify the farm enough to make a place for our children, if they show an interest. We plan to open an on-farm retail store, creamery and milking facility. In addition to our regular product line, we'll custom-make and sell items for other dairy farmers as a kind of milk business incubator.

Our daughter Anna and her husband have already purchased 200 dairy goats to provide an additional milk supply. Our son, Greg, is our business manager. Jessica handles package and display design, and Heather, who's in college, takes care of social networking, such as setting us up on Facebook.

Our dairy is a real family affair— with Larry, me, our children and, of course, a couple hundred four-legged kids.

Clara's daughter Katie beams as she holds her best-of-show Evalon goat cheese at the U.S. Championship Cheese Contest.

from Clara's kitchen

Cheese & Ham Filled Sandwiches

Here's a blue-ribbon version of a classic sandwich. When guests try the crusty buns filled with ham and rich melted goat cheese, they quickly reach for seconds.
—**CLARA HEDRICH** CHILTON, WISCONSIN

PREP: 20 MINUTES **BAKE:** 10-14 MINUTES **MAKES:** 4 SERVINGS

- 4 hoagie buns
- 1 small red onion, chopped
- 1 teaspoon olive oil
- 1 cup (4 ounces) shredded fontina cheese
- 1 cup (4 ounces) shredded goat cheese
- 1 cup cubed fully cooked ham
- ⅓ cup roasted sweet red peppers, drained and cut into strips
- 2 teaspoons minced fresh parsley
- ½ teaspoon minced fresh thyme or ¼ teaspoon dried thyme
- ⅛ teaspoon salt
- ⅛ teaspoon pepper

1. Cut a thin slice off the top of each bun. Hollow out bottoms of buns, leaving a ¼-in. shell (discard removed bread or save for another use).
2. In a small skillet, saute onion in oil until tender. Remove from the heat; stir in the cheeses, ham, red peppers, parsley, thyme, salt and pepper.
3. Spoon into shells; replace tops. Wrap each sandwich in foil, leaving top open. Place on a baking sheet. Bake at 375° for 10-14 minutes or until cheese is melted.

Side Dishes & Salads

The items that grace the table with an entree really make the meal. Crunchy salads, steaming mashed potatoes and fresh vegetables cooked to perfection await you on the following pages. Whether dinner is a burger or a roasted chicken, you'll find just the right sides for it.

Sunflower Noodle Coleslaw

(recipe on page 127)

"**D**ressed with sunflower oil and kernels, this slaw is always requested for family get-togethers. Make it once, and it might become your signature dish."

—EILEEN HERMAN
BRINSMADE, NORTH DAKOTA

Cottage Cheese Confetti Salad

When I was growing up, this light but satisfying salad often appeared on the dinner table during the summer months. My mother served it with a platter of smoked fish and good country-style rye bread with unsalted butter.

—LILY JULOW GAINESVILLE, FLORIDA

PREP/TOTAL TIME: 25 MINUTES
MAKES: 7 SERVINGS

- 2 cups (16 ounces) cream-style cottage cheese
- 1 cup (8 ounces) sour cream
- 2 small tomatoes, seeded and finely chopped
- 4 green onions, sliced
- 1 small green pepper, finely chopped
- 4 radishes, finely chopped
- ½ cup chopped seeded peeled cucumber
  Salt and pepper to taste
  Lettuce leaves

1. In a large bowl, combine the cottage cheese, sour cream, tomatoes, onions, green pepper, radishes and cucumber.
2. Season to taste with salt and pepper. Serve in a lettuce-lined bowl.

Home Style COOKING NOTES

Squash au Gratin

My fabulous-tasting squash casserole has an awesome aroma while it's baking. Tart apples add a fruity flavor.

—DEB WILLIAMS PEORIA, ARIZONA

PREP: 20 MINUTES **BAKE:** 1 HOUR **MAKES:** 9 SERVINGS

- 5½ cups thinly sliced peeled butternut squash
- ½ teaspoon salt
- ¼ teaspoon pepper
- ⅛ teaspoon ground nutmeg
- 2 tablespoons olive oil, divided
- 1 cup heavy whipping cream
- 2 medium tart apples, peeled and thinly sliced
- 1 cup (4 ounces) crumbled Gorgonzola cheese

1. In a bowl, combine the squash, salt, pepper, nutmeg and 1 tablespoon oil; toss to coat. Transfer to a greased 11-in. x 7-in. baking dish; pour cream over top.
2. Cover and bake at 325° for 30 minutes.
3. In a small bowl, toss apples in remaining oil. Spoon over squash. Bake, uncovered, for 25-30 minutes or until squash is tender. Sprinkle with cheese; bake 3-5 minutes longer or until cheese is melted.

Winter Endive Salad

Here's a salad with panache! The tangy citrus balances the hint of bitterness in the endive, and the sweet-tart pomegranate seeds add stunning ruby color.

—ALYSHA BRAUN ST. CATHARINES, ONTARIO

PREP/TOTAL TIME: 25 MINUTES **MAKES:** 8 SERVINGS

- 5 **cups torn curly endive**
- 2 **cups watercress**
- 1 **shallot, thinly sliced**
- ⅓ **cup pecan halves, toasted**
- ¼ **cup pomegranate seeds**
- ¼ **cup olive oil**
- 1½ **tablespoons lemon juice**
- 1 **teaspoon grated lemon peel**
- ⅛ **teaspoon salt**
- ⅛ **teaspoon pepper**

1. In a large bowl, combine the endive, watercress and shallot. Sprinkle with pecans and pomegranate seeds.
2. In a small bowl, whisk the oil, lemon juice, lemon peel, salt and pepper. Drizzle over salad; serve immediately.

Shrimp Salad Lemon Baskets

Sunny lemon baskets brimming with shrimp salad are a feast for the eyes and the taste buds.

—RENATA STANKO LEBANON, OREGON

PREP: 55 MINUTES + CHILLING
MAKES: 1 DOZEN

- 2 **envelopes unflavored gelatin**
- 1½ **cups cold water**
- 1 **cup mayonnaise**
- 6 **medium lemons**
- 1 **package (5 ounces) frozen cooked salad shrimp, thawed, divided**
- ½ **cup chopped seeded peeled cucumber**
- ¼ **cup chopped pimiento-stuffed olives**
- 2 **teaspoons sugar**
- 2 **teaspoons prepared horseradish**
- ¼ **teaspoon salt**
- ¼ **teaspoon paprika**
- ½ **cup heavy whipping cream, whipped**
- 12 **sprigs fresh parsley**

1. In a small saucepan, sprinkle gelatin over cold water; let stand for 1 minute. Cook and stir over low heat until the gelatin is completely dissolved. Remove from the heat; whisk in the mayonnaise. Refrigerate for 30 minutes or until partially set.
2. Cut lemons in half; juice lemons, reserving 3 tablespoons juice (save remaining juice for another use). Scoop out and discard pulp. With a sharp knife, cut a thin slice off the bottom of each lemon basket so it sits flat; set aside.
3. Set aside 2 dozen shrimp for garnish; chop remaining shrimp. In a small bowl, combine the cucumber, olives, sugar, horseradish, salt, paprika and reserved lemon juice; fold into gelatin mixture. Fold in chopped shrimp and whipped cream.
4. Spoon into lemon baskets. Garnish with parsley and reserved shrimp. Chill until set.

Blender Yeast Rolls

If you're looking for an easy homemade yeast roll, you'll want to try this recipe. Using a blender speeds things up, and you don't need to knead the dough!

—REGENA NEWTON OKTAHA, OKLAHOMA

PREP: 20 MINUTES + RISING
BAKE: 20 MINUTES
MAKES: ABOUT 1 DOZEN

    1   cup warm 2% milk (110° to 115°)
    1   package (¼ ounce) active dry yeast
    ¼   cup sugar
    2   eggs
    ¼   cup canola oil
  3¼   cups all-purpose flour
    1   teaspoon salt

1. In a blender, combine the warm milk, yeast, sugar, eggs and oil; cover and process on low speed for 30 seconds or until blended.
2. In a large bowl, combine the flour and salt. Add yeast mixture; stir with a spoon until combined (do not knead). Cover and let rise in a warm place until doubled, about 30 minutes.
3. Stir down dough. Fill greased muffin cups half full. Cover and let rise until doubled, about 30 minutes.
4. Bake at 350° for 18-20 minutes or until golden brown. Remove from pans to wire racks. Serve warm.

Potato Bacon Casserole

Bacon and potatoes are terrific together. My hearty and super-easy side works well with most main dishes. Everyone enjoys it so much that it's a regular at our table.

—JOANNE PANZETTA BUSHNELL, FLORIDA

PREP: 20 MINUTES **BAKE:** 35 MINUTES **MAKES:** 8 SERVINGS

    4   cups frozen shredded hash brown potatoes, thawed
    ½   cup finely chopped onion
    8   bacon strips, cooked and crumbled
    1   cup (4 ounces) shredded cheddar cheese
    1   egg
    1   can (12 ounces) evaporated milk
    ½   teaspoon seasoned salt

1. In a greased 8-in. square baking dish, layer half of the potatoes, onion, bacon and cheese. Repeat layers.
2. In a small bowl, whisk the egg, milk and seasoned salt; pour over potato mixture. Cover and bake at 350° for 30 minutes. Uncover; bake 5-10 minutes longer or until a knife inserted near the center comes out clean.

Spinach Salad with Red Currant Dressing

This pretty salad can be put together in less than 20 minutes. It adds lots of color to the table, and the sweet-tart dressing is a wonderful complement to the spinach and fruit.

—KAAREN YAKU SEATTLE, WASHINGTON

PREP: 15 MINUTES + COOLING **MAKES:** 12 SERVINGS

¼ **cup red currant jelly**
3 **tablespoons red wine vinegar**
8 **cups torn fresh spinach**
1 **can (11 ounces) mandarin oranges, drained**
1 **cup sliced fresh strawberries**
2 **green onions, thinly sliced**

1. For dressing, in a small saucepan, cook and stir the jelly and vinegar over medium heat for 1-2 minutes or until melted and smooth. Cool completely.

2. Just before serving, in a large salad bowl, combine the spinach, oranges, strawberries and onions. Drizzle with dressing; toss to coat.

Maple-Glazed Acorn Squash

With a maple syrup and brown sugar glaze, this squash becomes pleasantly sweet. This is comfort food at its easiest. Try pairing it with a pork entree.

—NANCY MUELLER MENOMONEE FALLS, WISCONSIN

PREP: 10 MINUTES **BAKE:** 55 MINUTES **MAKES:** 2 SERVINGS

- 1 medium acorn squash, halved
- 1½ cups water
- ¼ cup maple syrup
- 2 tablespoons brown sugar
- ½ teaspoon ground cinnamon
- ¼ teaspoon ground ginger
- ¼ teaspoon salt

1. Scoop out and discard seeds from squash. Place cut side down in a 13-in. x 9-in. baking dish; add water. Bake, uncovered, at 350° for 45 minutes.

2. Drain water from pan; turn squash cut side up. Combine the syrup, brown sugar, cinnamon, ginger and salt; pour into squash halves. Bake, uncovered, for 10 minutes or until glaze is heated through.

Bacon and Garlic Green Beans

Adding white wine, lemon juice and garlic gives green beans a little kick. It was enough to turn our traditional holiday side into a year-round favorite.

—SHANNON REYNOSO BAKERSFIELD, CALIFORNIA

PREP/TOTAL TIME: 30 MINUTES **MAKES:** 8 SERVINGS

- 6 thick-sliced bacon strips, chopped
- 1 small onion, thinly sliced
- 6 tablespoons butter
- 1 tablespoon olive oil
- 3 garlic cloves, minced
- ¼ cup white wine or chicken broth
- 9 cups frozen French-style green beans, thawed
- ½ teaspoon salt
- ½ teaspoon garlic powder
- ¼ teaspoon pepper
- 2 to 3 tablespoons lemon juice

1. In a large skillet, cook bacon over medium heat until crisp. Remove to paper towels with a slotted spoon; drain. In the same skillet, saute onion in butter and oil until tender. Add garlic; cook 1 minute longer. Stir in wine; bring to a boil. Simmer, uncovered, for 5-8 minutes or until liquid is reduced by half.

2. Add the green beans, salt, garlic powder and pepper; heat through. Stir in lemon juice and bacon.

Southwest Salad

Friends served us this wonderful salad when we were vacationing in Arizona. My husband particularly liked the fresh taste of the citrusy dressing and asked me to be sure to get the recipe before we returned home. It's since become one of our family's favorites.

—SHARON EVANS CLEAR LAKE, IOWA

PREP/TOTAL TIME: 15 MINUTES
MAKES: 6 SERVINGS

SALAD DRESSING
- ½ teaspoon grated orange peel
- ¼ cup orange juice
- ½ cup canola oil
- 2 tablespoons sugar
- 3 tablespoons red wine vinegar
- 1 tablespoon lemon juice
- ¼ teaspoon salt

SALAD
- 3 heads Boston lettuce, torn
- 1 small cucumber, thinly sliced
- 1 medium ripe avocado, peeled and sliced
- 1 small red onion, sliced and separated into rings
- 1 can (11 ounces) mandarin oranges, drained or fresh orange sections

1. In a small bowl, whisk salad dressing ingredients; set aside. Arrange the lettuce, cucumber, avocado, onion and oranges on individual plates. Drizzle with dressing just before serving.

Home Style COOKING NOTES

Broccoli & Horseradish Sauce

This flavorful vegetable dish is popular with my family. We usually serve it alongside prime rib for holidays and special occasions.

—SUE CRAWLEY LANSING, MICHIGAN

PREP/TOTAL TIME: 30 MINUTES
MAKES: 4 SERVINGS (½ CUP SAUCE)

- 1 **bunch broccoli, cut into florets**
- ¼ **cup sour cream**
- ¼ **cup mayonnaise**
- 2 **teaspoons prepared horseradish**
- ¼ **teaspoon Worcestershire sauce**

1. Place broccoli in a steamer basket; place in a saucepan over 1 in. of water. Bring to a boil; cover and steam for 3-4 minutes or until tender.
2. Meanwhile, in a small saucepan, combine the remaining ingredients. Heat over low heat until heated through. Serve with broccoli.

Home Style COOKING NOTES

Minted Fruit Salad

Filled with the season's best and freshest fruit, this salad shouts "summer." The mint adds a refreshing note to the colorful compote.

—EDIE DESPAIN LOGAN, UTAH

PREP: 20 MINUTES + COOLING **MAKES:** 6 SERVINGS

- 1 **cup unsweetened apple juice**
- 2 **tablespoons honey**
- 4 **teaspoons finely chopped crystallized ginger**
- 4 **teaspoons lemon juice**
- 4 **cups cantaloupe balls**
- 1 **cup sliced fresh strawberries**
- 1 **cup fresh blueberries**
- 2 **teaspoons chopped fresh mint leaves**

1. In a small saucepan, combine the apple juice, honey, ginger and lemon juice. Bring to a boil over medium-high heat. Cook and stir for 2 minutes or until mixture is reduced to ¾ cup. Remove from the heat. Cool.
2. In a serving bowl, combine the cantaloupe, strawberries, blueberries and mint. Drizzle with cooled apple juice mixture; gently toss to coat.

Home Style tip

To clean mushrooms, gently wipe with a mushroom brush or a paper towel. Or rinse quickly under cold water, drain, and pat dry with paper towels.

Hot Bacon Macaroni Salad

Start your picnic right with this delicious macaroni salad. It's loaded with diced veggies and bacon, and coated with a zesty dressing similar to one you'd use for German potato salad.

—KAY BELL PALESTINE, TEXAS

PREP/TOTAL TIME: 25 MINUTES **MAKES:** 6 SERVINGS

- 1 **package (7 ounces) elbow macaroni**
- ¼ **pound sliced bacon, diced**
- ½ **pound sliced fresh mushrooms**
- ⅓ **to ½ cup sugar**
- 2 **tablespoons all-purpose flour**
- ½ **teaspoon salt**
- ⅛ **teaspoon pepper**
- ⅔ **cup cider vinegar**
- ½ **cup chopped onion**
- ½ **cup chopped celery**
- ½ **cup sliced radishes**
- 2 **tablespoons minced fresh parsley**

1. Cook macaroni according to the package directions.
2. Meanwhile, in a large skillet, cook bacon over medium heat until crisp. Remove to paper towels with a slotted spoon. In the same skillet, saute mushrooms in drippings until tender; remove with a slotted spoon. Add the sugar, flour, salt and pepper to the skillet; gradually stir in vinegar until smooth. Bring to a boil. Cook and stir for 1-2 minutes or until thickened.
3. Drain macaroni. In a large bowl, combine the macaroni, onion and celery. Drizzle with vinegar mixture. Add mushrooms and bacon; toss to coat. Garnish with radishes and parsley.

Dilly Coleslaw

When I took this coleslaw to a church function, I came home with an empty bowl! You can easily double the recipe for a larger group. With chopped dill pickles and a sweet-tart dressing, it's not your typical slaw.

—CARRIE ROBERTS
PORTERVILLE, CALIFORNIA

PREP: 25 MINUTES + CHILLING
MAKES: 8 SERVINGS

- 8 **cups shredded cabbage**
- ½ **cup chopped dill pickles**
- ¼ **cup finely chopped onion**
- ½ **cup sugar**
- ½ **cup mayonnaise**
- ¼ **cup milk**
- ¼ **cup dill pickle juice**
- 1 **teaspoon salt**
- ¼ **teaspoon garlic powder**
- ¼ **teaspoon pepper**

1. In a large bowl, combine the cabbage, pickles and onion. In a small bowl, whisk remaining ingredients until smooth.
2. Pour over cabbage mixture and toss to coat. Cover and refrigerate for at least 2 hours. Serve with a slotted spoon.

Shoepeg Corn Side Dish

I took this dish to a potluck and everyone asked for the recipe. If shoepeg corn isn't available in your region, regular canned corn works well, too.

—GLORIA SCHUTZ TRENTON, ILLINOIS

PREP: 20 MINUTES **COOK:** 3 HOURS **MAKES:** 8 SERVINGS

- 1 can (14½ ounces) French-style green beans, drained
- 2 cans (7 ounces each) white or shoepeg corn
- 1 can (10¾ ounces) condensed cream of mushroom soup, undiluted
- 1 jar (4½ ounces) sliced mushrooms, drained
- ½ cup slivered almonds
- ½ cup shredded cheddar cheese
- ½ cup sour cream
- ¾ cup French-fried onions

1. In a 3-qt. slow cooker, combine the first seven ingredients. Cover and cook on low for 3-4 hours or until vegetables are tender, stirring occasionally. Sprinkle with French-fried onions during the last 15 minutes of cooking.

Roasted Potato Salad with Feta

Dress up roasted potatoes with savory fixings. This is an easy recipe that delivers big flavor. And you can effortlessly double or triple it for a crowd.

—JENNIFER GALFANO WEST CHESTER, PENNSYLVANIA

PREP: 15 MINUTES **BAKE:** 20 MINUTES **MAKES:** 4 SERVINGS

- 1 **pound small red potatoes, quartered**
- 3 **tablespoons olive oil, divided**
- ½ **teaspoon salt**
- ½ **teaspoon pepper**
- 2 **tablespoons sherry vinegar, divided**
- 1 **teaspoon Dijon mustard**
- ⅔ **cup julienned roasted sweet red peppers**
- 4 **green onions, sliced**
- ⅓ **cup crumbled feta cheese**

1. In a large bowl, toss the potatoes with 1 tablespoon oil, salt and pepper. Transfer to a greased 15-in. x 10-in. x 1-in. baking pan. Bake at 400° for 20-25 minutes or until tender.

2. Immediately drizzle potato mixture with 1 tablespoon vinegar; let stand for 5 minutes. Meanwhile, in a small bowl, combine the mustard and remaining oil and vinegar.

3. In a large bowl, combine the potato mixture, red peppers, onions and cheese. Add dressing and toss to coat.

Parmesan Rice Pilaf

My mom found this recipe in a local newspaper years ago, and it was one of her standby side dishes for a long time. The original recipe was a little bland, so I have doctored it up a little. Sometimes I make more than I need for one meal just so I can have leftovers.

—KELLIE MULLEAVY LAMBERTVILLE, MICHIGAN

PREP/TOTAL TIME: 10 MINUTES
MAKES: 2 SERVINGS

- 1 **small onion, chopped**
- 2 **tablespoons plus 1½ teaspoons butter**
- 1 **cup uncooked instant rice**
- 1 **cup water**
- 1 **teaspoon beef bouillon granules**
- ¼ **teaspoon garlic powder**
- ¼ **teaspoon pepper**
- 2 **tablespoons grated Parmesan cheese**
    Fresh marjoram sprig and shaved Parmesan cheese, optional

1. In a small saucepan, saute onion in butter until tender. Stir in the rice, water, bouillon, garlic powder and pepper; bring to a boil.

2. Remove from the heat; cover and let stand for 5 minutes. Stir in grated Parmesan cheese. Garnish with a sprig of marjoram and shaved Parmesan cheese if desired.

Home Style COOKING NOTES

Green Beans with Herbs

My husband, Jesse, and I love to cook, and we collaborated to create this easy side dish. After a taste, you're sure to agree that our recipe takes plain green beans to a higher level.

—**ANNE FOUST** BLUEFIELD, WEST VIRGINIA

PREP/TOTAL TIME: 20 MINUTES
MAKES: 8-10 SERVINGS

- 1 cup water
- 1½ pounds fresh green beans, trimmed and cut into 1-inch pieces
- 1 medium onion, cut into thin wedges
- 1 celery rib, chopped
- ½ teaspoon dried basil
- ¼ teaspoon dried rosemary, crushed
  Salt and pepper to taste

1. In a large saucepan, bring water to a boil. Add the beans, onion and celery. Reduce heat; cover and cook for 8-10 minutes or until crisp-tender. Drain. Sprinkle with the basil, rosemary, salt and pepper.

Colorful Bean Salad

I had experimented with all kinds of bean salads before I hit on this one. My husband loves all the different bean varieties, and corn adds texture and bright color.

—**DALE BENOIT** MONSON, MASSACHUSETTS

PREP: 30 MINUTES + CHILLING
MAKES: 13 SERVINGS (¾ CUP EACH)

- 2 cups fresh or frozen corn, thawed
- 1 can (16 ounces) kidney beans, rinsed and drained
- 1 can (16 ounces) red beans, rinsed and drained
- 1 can (15½ ounces) white kidney or cannellini beans, rinsed and drained
- 1 can (15¼ ounces) lima beans, rinsed and drained
- 1 can (15 ounces) black beans, rinsed and drained
- 1 can (2¼ ounces) sliced ripe olives, drained
- 1 large green pepper, chopped
- 1 small onion, chopped
- ½ cup chili sauce

- ¼ cup olive oil
- ¼ cup red wine vinegar
- 2 garlic cloves, minced
- 2 teaspoons dried oregano
- ½ teaspoon pepper

1. In a large bowl, combine the first nine ingredients. In a small bowl, whisk the chili sauce, oil, vinegar, garlic, oregano and pepper. Pour over bean mixture; toss to coat.

2. Refrigerate for at least 1 hour before serving.

Honey-Lime Melon Salad

I usually have the ingredients for this melon salad on hand. It's a refreshing side dish for any meal, and it's a good and fast contribution to a potluck. Sliced bananas, strawberries and apples taste great in it, too.
—**FLORI CHRISTENSEN**
BLOOMINGTON, INDIANA

PREP/TOTAL TIME: 10 MINUTES
MAKES: 6-8 SERVINGS

  3 cups cubed honeydew
  2 cups cubed watermelon
  2 cups cubed cantaloupe
  ½ cup seedless red grapes
DRESSING
  2 tablespoons canola oil
  2 tablespoons lime juice
  1 tablespoon honey
  ¼ teaspoon grated lime peel

1. In a large serving bowl, combine the fruits. Whisk together dressing ingredients. Drizzle over fruit; toss to coat. Serve immediately.

Baked Creamed Onions

I often fix this comforting dish for my grown children when they visit. They love it when I double the recipe so they can take leftovers home! You can prepare the recipe a day ahead and refrigerate it before baking.
—**MARGARET BLOMQUIST** NEWFIELD, NEW YORK

PREP: 30 MINUTES **BAKE:** 30 MINUTES **MAKES:** 5 SERVINGS

  5 medium onions, sliced and separated into rings
  3 tablespoons butter
  ¾ cup water
  ⅛ teaspoon ground allspice
  2 tablespoons all-purpose flour
  1 can (5 ounces) evaporated milk
  1 teaspoon sugar
  ½ teaspoon salt
  2 tablespoons grated Parmesan cheese
  2 tablespoons dry bread crumbs

1. In a large skillet, saute onions in butter for 5 minutes. Add water and allspice; bring to a boil. Reduce heat; cover and simmer for 15-20 minutes or until tender.
2. Combine flour and evaporated milk until smooth; gradually stir into the onion mixture. Bring to a boil; cook and stir for 2 minutes or until thickened. Stir in sugar and salt.
3. Transfer to a greased 1-qt. baking dish; sprinkle with cheese and bread crumbs. Bake, uncovered, at 350° for 30-35 minutes or until bubbly.

HOME STYLE tip

"I have trouble keeping foil on my casserole dishes when taking them to potlucks. Instead, I put the baking dish inside a plastic oven bag. The bag traps any spills and doesn't melt."
—**CARLENE H.**
CROSSVILLE, TENNESSEE

Green Beans with Almond Butter

Many beans are grown here in Georgia, so we find lots of ways to serve them. This is one of my favorite side dishes for holiday meals. To make it even more special, substitute hazelnuts for the almonds.

—NANCY STONE CANTON, GEORGIA

PREP/TOTAL TIME: 30 MINUTES
MAKES: 6 SERVINGS

- 1½ pounds fresh green beans, trimmed
- 3 tablespoons butter, softened
- 2 teaspoons lemon juice
- ½ teaspoon grated lemon peel
- ¼ teaspoon salt
- ⅛ teaspoon garlic powder
  Dash pepper
- ¼ cup slivered almonds, toasted and finely chopped

1. Place the beans in a large saucepan and cover with water. Bring to a boil; cook, uncovered, for 8-10 minutes or until crisp-tender.

2. Meanwhile, in a small bowl, combine the butter, lemon juice and peel, salt, garlic powder and pepper. Stir in the almonds. Drain the beans and return to the pan. Add almond butter and toss to coat.

Home Style COOKING NOTES

Summertime Melon Salad

Fun and refreshing, this simple salad is the essence of summer served up in a melon half and dressed with a tangy citrus sauce. Lovely!

—SALLY MALONEY DALLAS, GEORGIA

PREP/TOTAL TIME: 25 MINUTES **MAKES:** 8 SERVINGS

- 1½ cups cantaloupe balls
- 1½ cups honeydew balls
- 1 can (20 ounces) pineapple chunks, drained
- 1 can (11 ounces) mandarin oranges, drained
- 1 cup halved fresh strawberries
- ¾ cup thawed lemonade concentrate
- ½ cup orange marmalade
- 4 medium cantaloupe melons, halved and seeded
  Fresh mint leaves

1. In a large bowl, combine the first five ingredients. In a small bowl, combine the lemonade concentrate and orange marmalade; pour over fruit and toss to coat. Spoon into cantaloupe halves. Garnish with mint.

Butternut Coconut Curry

I love my slow cooker because it's so easy to make dinner with one! The flavorful curry is something I created for a potluck. Since then, I've had lots of requests for the recipe.

—JESS APFE BERKELEY, CALIFORNIA

PREP: 35 MINUTES **COOK:** 4 HOURS **MAKES:** 9 SERVINGS

- **1 cup chopped carrots**
- **1 small onion, chopped**
- **1 tablespoon olive oil**
- **1½ teaspoons brown sugar**
- **1½ teaspoons curry powder**
- **1 garlic clove, minced**
- **½ teaspoon ground cinnamon**
- **¼ teaspoon ground ginger**
- **⅛ teaspoon salt**
- **1 medium butternut squash (about 2½ pounds), cut into 1-inch cubes**

- **2½ cups vegetable broth**
- **¾ cup coconut milk**
- **½ cup uncooked basmati or jasmine rice**

1. In a large skillet, saute carrots and onion in oil until onion is tender. Add the brown sugar, curry, garlic, cinnamon, ginger and salt. Cook and stir 2 minutes longer.

2. In a 3- or 4-qt. slow cooker, combine the butternut squash, broth, coconut milk, rice and carrot mixture. Cover and cook on low for 4-5 hours or until the rice is tender.

Chicken Fiesta Salad

This is a dish I can prepare in 15 minutes! My husband gave me the secret of using the broiler to cook the chicken faster, and I developed the spice blend as I tried to find ways to use his quick-cooking technique. It became a very tasty success.

—KATIE RANKIN COLUMBUS, OHIO

PREP/TOTAL TIME: 30 MINUTES **MAKES:** 2 SERVINGS

1½ teaspoons lemon-pepper seasoning
1½ teaspoons chili powder
1½ teaspoons dried basil
¾ pound boneless skinless chicken breasts, cut into 1-inch pieces
4 cups torn mixed salad greens
⅔ cup canned black beans, rinsed and drained
¼ cup thinly sliced red onion
1 small tomato, sliced
½ cup shredded cheddar cheese
    Tortilla chips, salsa and ranch salad dressing

1. In a large resealable plastic bag, combine the seasonings. Add chicken, a few pieces at a time, and shake to coat.

2. Place chicken on a greased broiler pan. Broil 3-4 in. from the heat for 3-4 minutes on each side or until no longer pink.

3. On two plates, arrange the salad greens, black beans, onion and tomato. Top with chicken and cheese. Serve with tortilla chips, salsa and ranch dressing.

Fall Harvest Salad

For a change, you can swap roasted butternut squash or pumpkin for sweet potatoes in this tasty salad. Any combination of dried fruit and nuts will work as ingredients, so pick your favorites.

—MARY MARLOWE LEVERETTE
COLUMBIA, SOUTH CAROLINA

PREP: 30 MINUTES **BAKE:** 25 MINUTES
MAKES: 6 SERVINGS

 2 **large sweet potatoes, peeled and cubed**
 2 **tablespoons olive oil**
 ¼ **teaspoon salt**
 ¼ **teaspoon pepper**
 2 **cups cubed cooked turkey breast**
 2 **medium apples, cubed**
 1 **cup chopped walnuts, toasted**
 4 **green onions, thinly sliced**
 ½ **cup raisins**
 ½ **cup minced fresh parsley**

DRESSING

 ¼ **cup olive oil**
 2 **tablespoons rice vinegar**
 2 **tablespoons orange juice**
 2 **tablespoons maple syrup**
 1 **tablespoon lemon juice**
 2 **teaspoons minced fresh gingerroot**
 ¼ **teaspoon salt**
 ¼ **teaspoon ground cinnamon**
 ⅛ **teaspoon ground nutmeg**
 ⅛ **teaspoon pepper**

1. Place sweet potatoes in an ungreased 15-in. x 10-in. x 1-in. baking pan; drizzle with oil and sprinkle with salt and pepper. Toss to coat.
2. Bake at 400° for 25-30 minutes or until the sweet potatoes are tender, stirring occasionally. Cool to room temperature.
3. In a large bowl, combine turkey, apples, nuts, onions, raisins, parsley and sweet potatoes.
4. In a small bowl, whisk dressing ingredients. Pour over the turkey mixture; toss to coat. Serve immediately.

Layered Broccoli Salad

Everyone enjoys this simple salad with dinner. The layers look so festive, and the crisp broccoli, sunflower seeds and bacon are a nice, crunchy contrast to the chewy dried cranberries.

—DARLENE BRENDEN SALEM, OREGON

PREP/TOTAL TIME: 20 MINUTES **MAKES:** 8 SERVINGS

 6 **cups chopped fresh broccoli florets**
 1 **small red onion, thinly sliced**
 ⅔ **cup dried cranberries**
 ½ **cup plain yogurt**
 2 **tablespoons mayonnaise**
 2 **tablespoons honey**
 2 **tablespoons cider vinegar**
 1½ **cups (6 ounces) shredded cheddar cheese**
 ¼ **cup sunflower kernels**
 2 **bacon strips, cooked and crumbled**

1. In a large glass bowl, layer the broccoli, onion and cranberries. Combine the yogurt, mayonnaise, honey and vinegar; drizzle over salad. Sprinkle with cheese, sunflower kernels and bacon.

Dilly Stuffed Potatoes

Dill weed and cream cheese give these twice-baked potatoes a tangy taste that makes them a little different. To get a head start, stuff the potato shells beforehand and put them in the fridge. Then finish baking close to dinnertime.

—KOREEN OGG
STE ROSE DU LAC, MANITOBA

PREP: 1 HOUR **BAKE:** 30 MINUTES
MAKES: 4 SERVINGS

- 4 large baking potatoes
- ¼ cup finely chopped onion
- ¼ cup butter, cubed
- 1 cup (4 ounces) shredded cheddar cheese
- 4 ounces cream cheese, cubed
- 1 teaspoon dill weed
- 4 bacon strips, cooked and crumbled

1. Scrub and pierce potatoes. Bake at 400° for 1 hour or until tender. Meanwhile, in a small skillet, saute onion in butter until tender; set aside.

2. When potatoes are cool enough to handle, cut a thin slice off the top of each and discard. Scoop out pulp, leaving a thin shell. In a bowl, mash the pulp with cheddar cheese, cream cheese and dill. Stir in the bacon and reserved onion mixture. Spoon into potato shells.

3. Place potato shells on a baking sheet. Bake at 400° for 30-35 minutes or until heated through.

Home Style COOKING NOTES

Avocado Tomato Salad

My simple salad is terrific with any kind of Mexican food and makes a super appetizer when spooned on a toasted baguette. The recipe combines fresh tomatoes with avocados, a source of healthy fat.

—GINGER BUROW FREDERICKSBURG, TEXAS

PREP/TOTAL TIME: 15 MINUTES **MAKES:** 6-8 SERVINGS

- 4 cups chopped tomatoes
- ½ cup chopped green pepper
- ¼ cup chopped onion
- ½ teaspoon salt
- ⅛ teaspoon pepper
- 2 medium ripe avocados, peeled and cubed
- 1 tablespoon lime juice

1. In a large bowl, combine the tomatoes, green pepper, onion, salt and pepper. Place the avocados in another bowl; sprinkle with lime juice and toss gently to coat. Fold into tomato mixture. Serve immediately.

Baked Sweet Potatoes and Apples

For a pretty and tasty side dish, try a combination of sweet potatoes and apples sprinkled with gingersnap crumbs. It's one of my favorites to serve with turkey at Thanksgiving and Christmas.

—ETTA JOHNSON SOUTH HADLEY, MASSACHUSETTS

PREP: 45 MINUTES **BAKE:** 45 MINUTES **MAKES:** 8-10 SERVINGS

- 6 **medium sweet potatoes**
- 2 **medium tart apples, peeled, cored and cut into rings**
- ½ **cup packed brown sugar**
- ¼ **cup butter**
- 2 **tablespoons unsweetened apple juice**
- ⅔ **cup finely crushed gingersnap cookies (about 10 cookies)**

1. Place the sweet potatoes in a Dutch oven; cover with water. Cover and bring to a boil; cook for 30 minutes or just until tender. Drain; cool slightly. Peel the potatoes and cut into ½-in. slices. Arrange half of the slices in a greased 13-in. x 9-in. baking dish. Top with the apples and remaining sweet potato slices.

2. In a small saucepan, bring the brown sugar, butter and apple juice to a boil, stirring constantly. Pour over potatoes and apples. Bake, uncovered, at 325° for 30 minutes or until apples are tender. Sprinkle with gingersnap crumbs. Bake 15 minutes longer.

Honey-Mustard Turkey Salad

Bring home holiday flavors any time of the year by tossing together this entree salad. Homemade dressing, healthy greens, apples and cheese complement pecan-coated turkey breast slices.

—TASTE OF HOME TEST KITCHEN

PREP: 25 MINUTES **COOK:** 10 MINUTES
MAKES: 7 SERVINGS

- ½ cup olive oil
- ¼ cup honey
- 3 tablespoons white wine vinegar
- 2 teaspoons plus 2 tablespoons Dijon mustard, divided
- ½ teaspoon minced garlic
- ¾ teaspoon salt, divided
- 3 tablespoons plus ¼ cup all-purpose flour, divided
- 3 egg whites
- 2 tablespoons water
- 1⅓ cups ground pecans
- 1 package (17.6 ounces) turkey breast cutlets
- ¼ cup butter, cubed
- 1 package (16 ounces) ready-to-serve salad greens
- 3 medium tart apples, sliced
- 1 medium red onion, sliced
- 2 cups salad croutons
- 1 cup (4 ounces) crumbled blue cheese

HOME STYLE tip

“My wife and I enjoy homemade croutons. I start by cubing the bread, then place it on a baking sheet and spray with a flavored cooking spray. Then I sprinkle on seasonings—Cajun, Italian or onion—and bake until the croutons reach the desired crispiness.”
—BOB K.
GERMANTOWN, TENNESSEE

1. For dressing, in a jar with a tight-fitting lid, combine the oil, honey, vinegar, 2 teaspoons mustard, garlic and ¼ teaspoon salt; shake well. Set aside.

2. Place 3 tablespoons flour in a shallow bowl. In a second bowl, combine the egg whites, water and remaining mustard. In a third bowl, combine the pecans and remaining salt and flour. Coat turkey with flour; dip into mustard mixture, then coat with pecan mixture.

3. In a large skillet over medium heat, cook the turkey in butter in batches for 2-3 minutes on each side or until no longer pink. Keep warm.

4. In a large bowl, combine the greens, apples, onion and croutons. Shake the dressing and pour over salad; toss to coat. Divide among salad bowls. Cut turkey into thin slices; arrange over salads. Sprinkle with blue cheese.

Green Salad with Baked Goat Cheese

I combined my favorite parts of a variety of salads to create this masterpiece. The warm baked cheese and crunchy croutons are wonderful paired with the crisp salad greens.

—DEB MORRIS WEVERTOWN, NEW YORK

PREP/TOTAL TIME: 20 MINUTES **MAKES:** 8 SERVINGS

- 1 log (4 ounces) fresh goat cheese
- 1 tablespoon olive oil
- ¼ cup seasoned bread crumbs
- 1 package (5 ounces) spring mix salad greens
- ½ cup dried cranberries
- ½ cup chopped walnuts, toasted
- 4 bacon strips, cooked and crumbled
- ½ cup Caesar salad croutons
  Salad dressing of your choice

1. Cut goat cheese into eight slices; brush both sides with olive oil and coat with bread crumbs. Place on an ungreased baking sheet. Bake at 350° for 5-6 minutes or until cheese is bubbly.

2. In a large bowl, combine the salad greens, cranberries, walnuts and bacon; transfer to a platter. Top with the cheese and croutons. Serve with dressing of your choice.

To Make Ahead: *This salad is quick to throw together but to save even more time, coat the cheese ahead of time and bake just before serving.*

Sour Cream Potato Salad

Italian dressing and horseradish make this creamy potato salad different from most, and those ingredients really add some zip! It's perfect for picnics or potlucks.

—VEDA LUTTRELL SUTTER, CALIFORNIA

PREP: 20 MINUTES
COOK: 25 MINUTES + CHILLING
MAKES: 8 SERVINGS

- 2 pounds medium red potatoes
- ½ cup Italian salad dressing
- 4 hard-cooked eggs
- ¾ cup sliced celery
- ⅓ cup thinly sliced green onions
- 1 cup mayonnaise
- ½ cup sour cream
- 1½ teaspoons prepared horseradish
- 1½ teaspoons prepared mustard
- 1½ teaspoons celery seed
- ¾ teaspoon salt

1. Place potatoes in a large saucepan and cover with water. Bring to a boil. Reduce heat; cover and cook for 15-20 minutes or until tender. Drain.

2. When cool enough to handle, peel and slice potatoes. Place in a large bowl; add salad dressing and toss gently. Cover and refrigerate for 2 hours.

3. Slice eggs in half; remove yolks and set aside. Chop egg whites; add to potatoes along with celery and onions.

4. In a small bowl, combine the mayonnaise, sour cream, horseradish, mustard, celery seed and salt. Crumble egg yolks; add to mayonnaise mixture and whisk until blended. Spoon over potatoes; toss gently to coat. Cover and chill for at least 2 hours before serving.

Apple Camembert Salad

I like to serve this refreshing main-dish salad with thinly sliced pork roast or diced chicken breast.

—**TRISHA KRUSE** EAGLE, IDAHO

PREP/TOTAL TIME: 15 MINUTES
MAKES: 4 SERVINGS

- 3 **cups torn Boston lettuce**
- ½ **cup chopped apple**
- 2 **ounces Camembert cheese, cubed**
- 2 **tablespoons dried cherries**
- 2 **tablespoons glazed pecans**

DRESSING
- 2 **tablespoons mayonnaise**
- 1 **tablespoon white wine vinegar**
- 1 **tablespoon canola oil**
- 1 **tablespoon maple syrup**
  Dash each sugar, salt and pepper

1. In a large bowl, combine the first five ingredients. In a small bowl, whisk the dressing ingredients. Pour over salad and toss to coat.

Turnip Puff

My family likes turnips with turkey, so my mother used to serve this side dish with our turkey dinner at Christmas. Then I made sure it had a place on the table, and now my daughter, who has taken over preparing Christmas dinner, is carrying on the tradition.

—**HELEN HACKWOOD** MEAFORD, ONTARIO

PREP: 30 MINUTES **BAKE:** 25 MINUTES **MAKES:** 8 SERVINGS

- 3 **medium turnips, peeled and cubed**
- 4 **tablespoons butter, divided**
- 2 **eggs**
- 3 **tablespoons all-purpose flour**
- 1 **tablespoon brown sugar**
- 3 **teaspoons baking powder**
- ¾ **teaspoon salt**
- ¼ **teaspoon pepper**
  Dash ground nutmeg
- ½ **cup dry bread crumbs**

1. Place turnips in a small saucepan and cover with water. Bring to a boil. Reduce heat; cover and simmer for 10-12 minutes or until tender. Drain.
2. In a small bowl, combine the turnips, 2 tablespoons butter and eggs. Combine the flour, brown sugar, baking powder, salt, pepper and nutmeg; add to turnip mixture and mix well. Transfer to a greased 8-in. square baking dish.
3. Melt remaining butter; toss with bread crumbs. Sprinkle over the top. Bake, uncovered, at 375° for 25-30 minutes or until a knife inserted near the center comes out clean. Serve immediately.

Editor's Note: *Carrots, parsnips or rutabagas may be substituted for the turnips.*

Home Style COOKING NOTES

Garlic and Artichoke Roasted Potatoes

I like to put this side into the oven to roast with the main dish. The artichokes make it seem like a gourmet dish!

—**MARIE RIZZIO** INTERLOCHEN, MICHIGAN

PREP: 15 MINUTES **BAKE:** 35 MINUTES **MAKES:** 10 SERVINGS

2½ **pounds medium red potatoes, cut into 1½-inch cubes**
2 **packages (8 ounces each) frozen artichoke hearts**
8 **garlic cloves, halved**
3 **tablespoons olive oil**
¾ **teaspoon salt**
¼ **teaspoon pepper**
¼ **cup lemon juice**
2 **tablespoons minced fresh parsley**
1 **teaspoon grated lemon peel**

1. Place the potatoes, artichokes and garlic in a 15-in. x 10-in. x 1-in. baking pan coated with cooking spray. Combine the oil, salt and pepper; drizzle over vegetables and toss to coat.
2. Bake, uncovered, at 425° for 35-40 minutes or until tender, stirring occasionally. Transfer to a large bowl. Add lemon juice, parsley and lemon peel; toss to coat. Serve warm.

Spinach Salad with Goat Cheese and Beets

Here's an easy, unusual salad that looks and tastes festive and is wonderful for the Christmas season. Vinaigrette dressing coats the greens nicely.

—NANCY LATULIPPE SIMCOE, ONTARIO

PREP: 45 MINUTES + COOLING **MAKES:** 10 SERVINGS

1¼ **pounds fresh beets**
1 **tablespoon balsamic vinegar**
1½ **teaspoons honey**
1½ **teaspoons Dijon mustard**
¼ **teaspoon salt**
¼ **teaspoon pepper**
¼ **cup olive oil**
5 **cups fresh baby spinach**
2 **ounces fresh goat cheese, crumbled**
½ **cup chopped walnuts, toasted**
   Additional pepper, optional

1. Scrub beets and trim tops to 1 in. Place in a Dutch oven and cover with water. Bring to a boil. Reduce heat; cover and simmer for 30-60 minutes or until tender. Remove from the water; cool. Peel beets and cut into 1-in. pieces.

2. In a small bowl, whisk the vinegar, honey, mustard, salt and pepper. Slowly whisk in oil until blended.

3. Place spinach in salad bowl. Drizzle with dressing; toss to coat. Top with beets, goat cheese and walnuts. Sprinkle with additional pepper if desired.

Sweet Potato Waldorf Salad

I came up with my special salad when I promised to bring a potato salad to a picnic but had no regular potatoes on hand. The sweet potatoes were there, so I revised my regular potato salad recipe and a new dish was born! Adding the apples was an extra touch and everybody loved it.

—LOIS JEFFERY CHESTERLAND, OHIO

PREP: 35 MINUTES + CHILLING **MAKES:** 2 SERVINGS

- 1 **small sweet potato**
- 1 **medium apple, cubed**
- ¼ **cup chopped celery**
- 2 **tablespoons chopped walnuts**
- 2 **tablespoons golden raisins**
- 2 **tablespoons miniature marshmallows**
- 2 **tablespoons mayonnaise**
- 2 **tablespoons sour cream**
- ½ **teaspoon lemon juice**
  Leaf lettuce, optional

1. Place the sweet potato in a small saucepan and cover with water. Bring to a boil. Reduce heat; cover and cook for 20 minutes or just until tender. Drain and cool completely.

2. Peel the potato and cut into cubes; place in a small bowl. Add the apple, celery, walnuts, raisins and marshmallows.

3. In another bowl, combine the mayonnaise, sour cream and lemon juice; pour over salad and toss gently. Cover and refrigerate for at least 1 hour.

4. Serve on lettuce-lined plates if desired.

Fried Onion Patties

These crispy patties are a different side dish from the usual potatoes and vegetables. They are wonderful served with a roast or any broiled or grilled meat.

—MARY LEE BOWMAN LAUREL, INDIANA

PREP: 20 MINUTES **COOK:** 15 MINUTES
MAKES: ABOUT 2½ DOZEN

- 1½ **cups all-purpose flour**
- 1 **tablespoon sugar**
- 1 **tablespoon cornmeal**
- 2 **teaspoons salt**
- 2 **teaspoons rubbed sage**
- 2 **teaspoons dried parsley flakes**
- 1 **teaspoon baking powder**
- 1 **egg**
- ¾ **cup milk**
- ¼ **teaspoon hot pepper sauce**
- 2½ **cups finely chopped onions**
  Oil for frying

1. In a large bowl, combine the first seven ingredients. In a small bowl, combine the egg, milk and hot pepper sauce; stir into the dry ingredients just until moistened. Stir in the onions.

2. In a large skillet, heat ½ in. of oil over medium heat. Drop batter by tablespoonfuls into oil; press lightly to flatten. Fry patties for 2-3 minutes on each side or until golden brown; drain on paper towels.

Pear Spinach Salad

When I take a dish to a potluck gathering and everyone asks for the recipe, I know I have a winner. My refreshing salad works well with any entree and has an interesting combination of flavors. It's pretty, too!

—**LOIS TELLONI** LORAIN, OHIO

PREP/TOTAL TIME: 15 MINUTES
MAKES: 5 SERVINGS

- 1 can (15¼ ounces) sliced pears
- 4 cups fresh baby spinach
- 2 green onions, thinly sliced
- 1 medium grapefruit, peeled and sectioned
- 3 bacon strips, cooked and crumbled
- 2 tablespoons white wine vinegar
- 2 tablespoons canola oil
- 1½ teaspoons lime juice
- 1 tablespoon minced fresh parsley
- 1 teaspoon sugar
- ¼ teaspoon salt
- ⅛ teaspoon grated lime peel
  Dash cayenne pepper

1. Drain pears, reserving 2 tablespoons juice. In a salad bowl, combine the spinach and onions. Top with the pears, grapefruit and bacon.

2. In a small bowl, whisk the vinegar, oil, lime juice, parsley, sugar, salt, lime peel, cayenne and reserved pear juice. Pour over salad; gently toss to coat.

Home Style COOKING NOTES

Scalloped Potatoes au Gratin

I found I could cut down the time it takes to prepare scalloped potatoes by first simmering them on top of the stove in an ovenproof skillet. Then I slip the skillet into the oven to finish the potatoes with a nice brown crust.

—**LILY JULOW** GAINESVILLE, FLORIDA

PREP: 35 MINUTES **BAKE:** 15 MINUTES + CHILLING **MAKES:** 2 SERVINGS

- 2 cups thinly sliced peeled potatoes (about 2 large)
- 2 teaspoons all-purpose flour
  Dash each salt, pepper and ground nutmeg
- 2 teaspoons butter
- ⅔ to 1 cup half-and-half cream
- ⅓ cup shredded Gouda cheese

1. Place half the potatoes in a small greased ovenproof skillet; sprinkle with 1 teaspoon flour. Repeat layers. Sprinkle with salt, pepper and nutmeg. Dot with the butter.

2. Add enough cream to fill skillet about three-fourths full. Bring to a boil over medium-high heat. Reduce heat; simmer, uncovered, for 15-20 minutes or until most of the liquid is absorbed.

3. Carefully place skillet in oven. Bake, uncovered, at 350° for 10-15 minutes or until bubbly and potatoes are tender. Sprinkle with cheese; bake 5 minutes longer or until cheese is melted.

Shoepeg Corn Supreme

Dress up canned corn with green pepper, cream of celery soup and cheddar cheese for a deluxe side dish. With a buttery cracker topping, this comfort food is sure to disappear in a hurry.

—LINDA ROBERSON COLLIERVILLE, TENNESSEE

PREP: 10 MINUTES **BAKE:** 25 MINUTES **MAKES:** 8 SERVINGS

1 **small green pepper, chopped**
1 **small onion, chopped**
1 **celery rib, chopped**
2 **tablespoons olive oil**
3 **cans (7 ounces each) white or shoepeg corn, drained**
1 **can (10¾ ounces) condensed cream of celery soup, undiluted**
1 **cup (8 ounces) sour cream**
½ **cup shredded sharp cheddar cheese**
¼ **teaspoon pepper**

1½ **cups crushed butter-flavored crackers**
3 **tablespoons butter, melted**

1. In a large skillet, sauté the green pepper, onion and celery in oil until tender. Remove from the heat; stir in the corn, soup, sour cream, cheese and pepper. Transfer to a greased 11-in. x 7-in. baking dish.

2. Combine cracker crumbs and butter; sprinkle over the top. Bake, uncovered, at 350° for 25-30 minutes or until bubbly.

Brussels Sprouts with Leeks

Since my husband and I both love Brussels sprouts, I often experiment with different combinations to enhance the flavor. We've found leeks give the sprouts a special flavor.

—PATRICIA MICKELSON SAN JOSE, CALIFORNIA

PREP/TOTAL TIME: 15 MINUTES **MAKES:** 2 SERVINGS

10 **Brussels sprouts, trimmed and halved**
 1 **medium leek (white portion only), thinly sliced**
 1 **tablespoon butter**
   Dash salt

1. In a large saucepan, bring 1 in. of water and Brussels sprouts to a boil. Reduce heat; cover and simmer for 8 minutes.

2. Add leek; cover and simmer 2-4 minutes longer or until vegetables are tender. Drain; stir in butter and salt.

Corn and Spinach Salad

As a child, I loved the combination of fresh spinach, crunchy nuts, a good tangy cheese and red onions. I would search different restaurants to discover how chefs prepared such a special salad. Here is my own creation.

—**ROBIN HAAS** CRANSTON, RHODE ISLAND

PREP/TOTAL TIME: 30 MINUTES **MAKES:** 8 SERVINGS (½ CUP DRESSING)

- ½ cup chopped walnuts
- 1 tablespoon sugar
- 1½ teaspoons cider vinegar
- 1 package (6 ounces) fresh baby spinach
- 1 medium sweet red pepper, diced
- 1 medium red onion, diced
- 1 cup fresh or frozen corn, thawed
- 1 cup crumbled goat cheese
- ¼ cup dried cranberries

DRESSING

- 3 tablespoons cider vinegar
- 2 tablespoons orange marmalade
- 2 tablespoons mayonnaise
- ½ teaspoon salt
- ½ teaspoon pepper
- ¼ teaspoon Worcestershire sauce

1. In a small heavy skillet, cook walnuts over medium heat until toasted, about 3 minutes. Sprinkle with sugar and vinegar. Cook and stir for 2-4 minutes or until sugar is melted. Spread on foil to cool.

2. In a large bowl, combine the spinach, red pepper, onion, corn, cheese and cranberries; sprinkle with walnuts. In a small bowl, whisk the dressing ingredients. Serve with salad.

Rosemary Mashed Potatoes

These special-occasion mashed potatoes call for whipping cream instead of milk. I must admit that I was a little shocked when a good friend suggested this substitution, but I couldn't argue after tasting the results! It makes ordinary mashed potatoes taste exceptional.

—**SUE GRONHOLZ** BEAVER DAM, WISCONSIN

PREP/TOTAL TIME: 30 MINUTES
MAKES: 12 SERVINGS

- 8 large potatoes (about 4 pounds), peeled and quartered
- 1½ teaspoons salt, divided
- ¾ cup heavy whipping cream
- ¼ cup butter, cubed
- ½ teaspoon minced fresh rosemary
- ¼ teaspoon ground nutmeg
- ¼ teaspoon pepper

1. Place the potatoes in a Dutch oven; add 1 teaspoon salt. Cover with water. Bring to a boil. Reduce heat; cover and simmer for 15-20 minutes or until tender. Drain.

2. Place potatoes in a large bowl. Add the cream, butter, rosemary, nutmeg, pepper and remaining salt; beat until smooth.

Chicken 'n' Fruit Salad

This salad has been on my menu for more than 20 years. We love to make it when we're traveling in our motor home during the summer, as it's so easy to fix and we carry most of the ingredients with us. It's also a good dish for potlucks. Serve it with assorted crackers and cheeses if you like.

—BETTY HUNTER SALINA, KANSAS

PREP: 15 MINUTES + CHILLING
MAKES: 2 SERVINGS

- 1 cup cubed cooked chicken or 1 can (5 ounces) chunk white chicken, drained
- 1 cup green grapes, halved
- ½ cup sliced fresh strawberries
- ¼ cup mayonnaise
- 2 teaspoons lime juice
- ¼ teaspoon honey
- ½ cup sliced ripe banana
- 2 lettuce leaves

1. In a small bowl, combine the chicken, grapes and strawberries. In another bowl, combine the mayonnaise, lime juice and honey. Pour over the chicken mixture; toss to coat. Cover and refrigerate for at least 30 minutes.

2. Just before serving, stir in banana. Spoon onto lettuce-lined plates.

Twice-Baked Mashed Potatoes

My simple recipe delivers big flavor by dressing up a favorite comfort food with savory additions. And it's hardly any work at all to double or triple it for a crowd.

—ANNA MAYER FORT BRANCH, INDIANA

PREP: 30 MINUTES **BAKE:** 30 MINUTES
MAKES: 6 SERVINGS

- 2½ pounds medium potatoes, peeled
- 1 cup (8 ounces) sour cream
- ¼ cup milk
- 2 tablespoons butter, melted
- 1½ cups (6 ounces) shredded cheddar cheese, divided
- ½ cup chopped onion
- 5 bacon strips, cooked and crumbled

- ½ teaspoon salt
- ⅛ teaspoon pepper

1. Place potatoes in a large saucepan and cover with water. Bring to a boil. Reduce heat; cover and cook for 15-20 minutes or until tender. Drain.

2. In a large bowl, mash potatoes. Add the sour cream, milk, butter and 1 cup cheese. Stir in the onion, bacon, salt and pepper. Spoon into a greased 2-qt. baking dish. Sprinkle with remaining cheese.

3. Bake, uncovered, at 350° for 30-35 minutes or until heated though.

Turkey Waldorf Salad

A perfect combination of refreshing and filling, my salad is ideal for days when you don't want to heat up the kitchen. Serve it stuffed in pita bread for a yummy lunch.

—TRISHA KRUSE EAGLE, IDAHO

PREP: 20 MINUTES + CHILLING **MAKES:** 4 SERVINGS

- ¼ cup sour cream
- ¼ cup mayonnaise
- 1 tablespoon rice vinegar
- 2 teaspoons brown sugar
- 1 teaspoon reduced-sodium soy sauce
- ¼ teaspoon salt
- ¼ teaspoon lemon-pepper seasoning
- 2 cups cubed cooked turkey breast
- 2 celery ribs, thinly sliced
- ¼ cup dried cranberries
- 1 large apple, diced
- ⅔ cup chopped walnuts, toasted
- 4 Bibb lettuce leaves

1. In a small bowl, whisk together the first seven ingredients.
2. In a large bowl, combine the turkey, celery and cranberries. Pour dressing over mixture; toss to coat. Cover and refrigerate for at least 1 hour.
3. Just before serving, stir in apple and walnuts. Serve on lettuce leaves.

Orzo Vegetable Salad

Heading to a cookout and need something to share? Tangy lemon dressing over cool orzo and vegetables combine to provide everything you want in a summer dish.

—TERRI CRANDALL GARDNERVILLE, NEVADA

PREP/TOTAL TIME: 30 MINUTES
MAKES: 6 SERVINGS

- ½ cup uncooked orzo pasta
- 3 plum tomatoes, chopped
- 1 cup marinated quartered artichoke hearts, chopped
- 1 cup coarsely chopped fresh spinach
- 2 green onions, chopped
- ½ cup crumbled feta cheese
- 1 tablespoon capers, drained

DRESSING
- ⅓ cup olive oil
- 4 teaspoons lemon juice
- 1 tablespoon minced fresh tarragon or 1 teaspoon dried tarragon
- 2 teaspoons grated lemon peel
- 2 teaspoons rice vinegar
- ½ teaspoon salt
- ¼ teaspoon pepper

1. Cook the orzo according to the package directions.
2. Meanwhile, in a large bowl, combine the tomatoes, artichokes, spinach, onions, cheese and capers. In a small bowl, whisk the dressing ingredients.
3. Drain orzo and rinse in cold water. Add to vegetable mixture. Pour dressing over the salad; toss to coat. Refrigerate, covered, until serving.

Home Style COOKING NOTES

Sunflower Power
Summer's always sunny at our place.
BY EILEEN HERMAN

> Luminous blooms get dawn-to-dusk attention from my husband, Reg, and me. We harvest sunflower seeds for oil and snacks.

During the summer months, sunflowers rise and shine as far as the eye can see on our family's North Dakota acres.

Passers-by may pay little attention to the lush stretches of soy, barley, wheat and other crops we grow. But when they spot 800 acres of solid sunflower gold, their cars slow and they circle back to take pictures.

Sunflowers are raised from the northern Plains to the Texas Panhandle. However, North Dakota farmers are responsible for growing about half the nation's crop, which is used for oil and confection seeds.

We grow both types on our farm near Brinsmade, which has been in Reg's family for five generations.

Confection sunflowers produce larger black-and-white striped seeds. Those can be roasted and salted in the shell for snacks, or hulled and used as kernels in food products like baked goods and salads.

The smaller black oil seeds are pressed for cooking oil. Both varieties of seed can be turned into birdseed.

We plant in May, and the sunflowers grow quickly from tiny green shoots into towering 6-foot stalks with heads the size of dinner plates and manes of yellow petals. Our crop blooms from early July into the beginning of August, when the seeds form. Each head can contain as many as 2,000 seeds.

We wait to harvest the sunflowers until after a hard freeze in October, when the seeds' moisture is low. Then we go in with our combine, which cuts several rows of stalks at a time. The combine separates the seeds, then chops up and spits out the stalks.

It looks like a monster gobbling through the field! A movable auger arm carries the seeds into grain carts. Later, the seed is loaded into trucks and hauled to the farm for drying.

Dryer fans force heat over the seeds and blow off fine dust. When dried to 10 percent moisture so they won't spoil, the seeds go into bins and on to a processing plant. Confection seeds are graded primarily according to size—the larger, the better. The other seeds are graded by oil content.

Most every season, sunflower growers face their nemesis: blackbirds. We try several options to chase them away, like boomers—machines placed in the fields that make loud, explosive sounds. Other scare tactics include everything from natural bird repellent sprays to noisy helicopter flyovers.

I have to hurry to beat the birds to the prettiest flowers, because I like to cut them for table arrangements. My parents grew sunflowers, too, so I've always loved them. They're the kind of plant that makes you happy to have them around.

With five children, the family goes through plenty of sunflower seeds and oil in the kitchen, too.

I use confection seeds in many recipes for the crunchy, nutty taste. The oil is great for cooking. It's high in vitamin E, lower in saturated fat and has a light, clean flavor.

Every year, we host a sunflower harvest party on our farm. Friends, family and members of our church come out for hayrides, outdoor games and a potluck supper. My Sunflower Noodle Coleslaw (at right) is always on the menu, no matter what else I make!

Sunflowers are considered a specialty crop, and I think they really are special. Whether you're looking at one or eating its seeds, you just have to smile.

from Eileen's kitchen

Sunflower Noodle Coleslaw

Dressed with sunflower oil and kernels, this slaw is always requested for family get-togethers. Make it once, and it might become your signature dish.

—EILEEN HERMAN BRINSMADE, NORTH DAKOTA

PREP/TOTAL TIME: 15 MINUTES **MAKES:** 10 SERVINGS

- 1 **package (3 ounces) chicken ramen noodles**
- 1 **package (14 ounces) coleslaw mix**
- ½ **cup unsalted sunflower kernels**
- ¼ **cup chopped green pepper**
- ⅓ **cup sunflower oil**
- ¼ **cup white vinegar**
- 3 **tablespoons sugar**
- 1 **tablespoon poppy seeds**
- ¾ **teaspoon pepper**

1. Break noodles into small pieces. In a large bowl, combine the noodles, coleslaw mix, sunflower kernels and green pepper.
2. In a small bowl, whisk the oil, vinegar, sugar, poppy seeds, pepper and contents of seasoning packet. Pour over the salad and toss to coat. Refrigerate, covered, until serving.

Turning HEADS

In Greek mythology, the nymph Clytie loved the sun god Apollo so deeply, she was transformed into a beautiful sunflower that turned its head to follow the light.

This was the ancient Greeks' explanation for the phenomenon known as heliotropism. A sunflower plant in the growing bud stage tracks the sun's movement in a 180-degree arc, horizon to horizon. Overnight, it resets to face east, and then follows the sun west again.

Once the flower opens, movement stops, with the mature plant facing east.

Everyday Cooking

Lure your family to the dinner table with the easy-to-make dishes that follow. While they won't task the cook, they'll please the palate and look as good as they taste. You'll be rewarded with thanks as your gang cleans their plates.

Broiled Fish with Tarragon Sauce

(recipe on page 163)

"The delicate flavor of this fish pairs perfectly with the tangy sauce. A yummy hint of honey comes through. Serve it with crusty bread, mixed vegetables or rice to help soak up the sauce."

—ROBIN PRATT ATHENS, GEORGIA

Creamed Chicken Over Corn Bread

This comforting dish was a favorite with our kids, and now our grandkids request it. The recipe is easily doubled or tripled for our Sunday family dinners.

—NANCY LANGE HINDSBORO, ILLINOIS

PREP: 15 MINUTES **BAKE:** 20 MINUTES
MAKES: 6 SERVINGS

- 1 **package (8½ ounces) corn bread/muffin mix**
- 1 **tablespoon chopped onion**
- ⅛ **teaspoon minced garlic**
- ¼ **cup butter, cubed**
- 2 **cups cubed rotisserie chicken**
- 1 **package (16 ounces) frozen chopped broccoli, thawed**
- 2 **tablespoons all-purpose flour**
- 1½ **teaspoons salt**
- 2 **egg yolks, lightly beaten**
- 1 **cup (8 ounces) sour cream**
- ¾ **cup milk**
  Shredded cheddar cheese

Home Style COOKING NOTES

1. Prepare corn bread batter and bake according to package directions, using a 9-in. round baking pan.
2. Meanwhile, in a large skillet, saute the onion and garlic in butter for 2-3 minutes; stir in the chicken and broccoli. Cook and stir for 5-7 minutes or until heated through.
3. In a small bowl, combine flour and salt; stir in the egg yolks, sour cream and milk until smooth. Add to the chicken mixture; cook and stir for 3-5 minutes or until thickened.
4. Cut warm corn bread into wedges; top with the chicken mixture. Sprinkle with the cheese.

Super Short Ribs

My mom passed her short rib recipe down to me. As any good cook would do, I added a few ingredients to her original to suit my taste.

—COLEEN CARTER MALONE, NEW YORK

PREP: 20 MINUTES **COOK:** 8 HOURS **MAKES:** 6 SERVINGS

- 3 **medium onions, cut into wedges**
- 3 **to 3½ pounds bone-in beef short ribs**
- 1 **bay leaf**
- 1 **bottle (12 ounces) light beer or nonalcoholic beer**
- 2 **tablespoons brown sugar**
- 2 **tablespoons Dijon mustard**
- 2 **tablespoons tomato paste**
- 2 **teaspoons dried thyme**
- 2 **teaspoons beef bouillon granules**
- 1 **teaspoon salt**
- ¼ **teaspoon pepper**
- 3 **tablespoons all-purpose flour**
- ½ **cup cold water**
  Hot cooked noodles

1. Place onions in a 5-qt. slow cooker; add ribs and bay leaf. Combine the beer, brown sugar, mustard, tomato paste, thyme, bouillon, salt and pepper. Pour over meat. Cover and cook on low for 8-10 hours or until meat is tender.

2. Remove meat and vegetables to a serving platter; keep warm. Discard bay leaf. Skim fat from cooking juices; transfer juices to a small saucepan. Bring liquid to a boil.

3. Combine flour and water until smooth. Gradually stir into the pan. Bring to a boil; cook and stir for 2 minutes or until thickened. Serve with meat and noodles.

Turkey Piccata

With an appealing lemon flavor, this classic skillet supper never goes out of style. It can also be prepared with boneless chicken breasts or pork cutlets.

—PERLENE HOEKEMA
LYNDEN, WASHINGTON

PREP: 15 MINUTES **COOK:** 20 MINUTES
MAKES: 8 SERVINGS

- 2 **eggs**
- 2 **tablespoons milk**
- 3½ **cups fresh bread crumbs (about 8 slices)**
- 2 **packages (14 to 16 ounces each) uncooked turkey cutlets or half of a 5-pound to 6-pound frozen turkey breast, thawed and cut into ¼-inch-thick slices**
  About ¾ cup butter
- 2 **large lemons, divided**
- 1½ **cups water**
- 2 **teaspoons chicken bouillon granules**
- ½ **teaspoon salt**
  Parsley sprigs

1. Beat the eggs with milk in shallow dish until well blended. Place the bread crumbs on waxed paper. Dip cutlets in egg mixture then in crumbs, coating both sides.

2. Melt the butter, as needed, in a 12-in. skillet over a medium high heat. Brown cutlets, four to six at a time, on both sides. Remove to a plate; keep warm.

3. Reduce heat to low. Squeeze juice of 1 lemon (about ¼ cup) into pan drippings in skillet; stir in the water, bouillon and salt until well mixed. Scrape brown bits from the bottom. Return the turkey to skillet; cover and simmer 15 minutes.

4. Thinly slice remaining lemon. To serve, arrange cutlets on large warm platter and garnish with lemon slices. Pour remaining sauce over cutlets; sprinkle with parsley.

Tater Crust Tuna Pie

I make the tuna pie a lot because it's quick and easy. My husband and I like the combination of potato flakes and french-fried onions in the pastry crust.

—CYNTHIA KOLBERG SYRACUSE, INDIANA

PREP: 15 MINUTES **BAKE:** 30 MINUTES **MAKES:** 6-8 SERVINGS

CRUST
- **1 cup all-purpose flour**
- **½ cup mashed potato flakes**
- **½ cup cold butter**
- **3 to 4 tablespoons ice water**
- **1 can (2.8 ounces) french-fried onions, divided**

FILLING
- **1 egg**
- **1 can (10¾ ounces) reduced-fat reduced-sodium condensed cream of mushroom soup, undiluted**
- **1 cup (4 ounces) shredded cheddar cheese, divided**
- **¾ cup mashed potato flakes**
- **1 can (6½ ounces) light water-packed tuna, drained and flaked**
- **2 tablespoons chopped pimiento-stuffed green olives**

1. In a small bowl, combine flour and potato flakes; cut in butter until crumbly. Add water, 1 tablespoon at a time, until dough is moist enough to hold together. Press pastry over bottom and up sides of an ungreased 9-in. pie plate. Flute edge. Set aside ½ cup onions for topping. Sprinkle remaining onions into pastry crust.

2. In a large bowl, combine the egg, soup, ½ cup cheese, potato flakes, tuna and olives. Spoon into pastry crust.

3. Bake at 350° for 25 minutes or until crust is golden. Sprinkle with remaining cheese and reserved onions; bake 5-10 minutes longer or until cheese is melted. Let stand for 5 minutes before serving.

Chicken Crescent Almondine

Easy and elegant-looking , the casserole is nice enough for special occasions...but you'll make it for family too! For a fun flavor substitute, use turkey or tuna instead of the chicken. You'll win raves all around the table.

—NANCY REICHERT THOMASVILLE, GEORGIA

PREP: 15 MINUTES **BAKE:** 20 MINUTES **MAKES:** 8 SERVINGS

- 1 can (10¾ ounces) condensed cream of chicken soup, undiluted
- ⅔ cup Miracle Whip
- ½ cup sour cream
- 2 tablespoons dried minced onion
- 3 cups cubed cooked chicken
- 1 can (8 ounces) sliced water chestnuts, drained
- 1 can (4 ounces) mushroom stems and pieces, drained
- ½ cup chopped celery
- 1 tube (8 ounces) refrigerated crescent rolls

TOPPING
- ⅔ cup shredded Swiss or American cheese
- ½ cup slivered almonds
- 2 tablespoons butter, melted

1. In large saucepan, combine the soup, Miracle Whip, sour cream and onion. Stir in the chicken, water chestnuts, mushrooms and celery; cook over medium heat until mixture is hot and bubbly.

2. Pour into ungreased 13-in. x 9-in. baking dish. Unroll crescent dough and separate into two rectangles, trimming to fit dish. Place dough rectangles over hot chicken mixture. Combine cheese and almonds; sprinkle over the dough. Drizzle with butter.

3. Bake, uncovered, at 375° for 20-25 minutes or until crust is a deep golden brown. Serve immediately.

Spaghetti with Roasted Red Pepper Sauce

Sparked by jarred red peppers, my pasta entree is an excellent company dish. Guests won't believe how easy it is until they try making it.

—DIANE LOMBARDO NEW CASTLE, PENNSYLVANIA

PREP/TOTAL TIME: 30 MINUTES
MAKES: 5 SERVINGS

- 12 ounces uncooked spaghetti
- 1 jar (12 ounces) roasted sweet red peppers, drained
- 2 large tomatoes, seeded and chopped
- 1 tablespoon red wine vinegar
- 1 garlic clove, peeled and halved
- ½ teaspoon salt
- ¼ teaspoon pepper
- ½ cup olive oil
- 5 tablespoons grated Parmesan cheese

1. Cook spaghetti according to the package directions. Meanwhile, in a food processor, combine the peppers, tomatoes, vinegar, garlic, salt and pepper. Cover and process until blended. While processing, gradually add oil in a steady stream.

2. Transfer to a small saucepan; bring to a boil. Reduce heat; simmer, uncovered, for 10 minutes. Drain spaghetti; serve with sauce. Sprinkle with cheese.

Home Style COOKING NOTES

> **66** I use leftover chicken or brisket for quesadillas. Butter one side of a tortilla and place butter side down in skillet and layer with refried beans, meat and cheese. Cover with another buttered tortilla and cook until lightly browned. **99**
>
> —**KATE B.,** DUNCANVILLE, TEXAS

HOME STYLE tip

Savory Orange Salmon

Citrus sauce adds zip to the succulent salmon. I serve it with anything from steamed broccoli to stunning yellow saffron rice.

—**ROSEANNE TURNER** DENVER, INDIANA

PREP/TOTAL TIME: 25 MINUTES
MAKES: 4 SERVINGS

- 2 garlic cloves, minced
- 1 teaspoon fennel seed
- 1 teaspoon olive oil
- 4 salmon fillets (1 inch thick and 4 ounces each)
- ½ teaspoon salt
- 1 cup orange juice

1. In a large nonstick skillet coated with cooking spray, cook the garlic and fennel seed in oil for 2 minutes. Sprinkle salmon with salt; add to skillet. Top with orange juice. Bring to a boil. Reduce heat; cover and simmer for 8-12 minutes or until fish flakes easily with a fork.

2. Remove salmon and keep warm. Simmer sauce, uncovered, for 6-9 minutes or until slightly thickened. Spoon over fillets.

Black Bean Quesadillas

Need a quick snack or appetizer? These bean and cheese quesadillas are the answer. I got the recipe at a Mexican festival held at our children's school. It's been served at our house regularly ever since.

—**DIXIE TERRY** GOREVILLE, ILLINOIS

PREP/TOTAL TIME: 25 MINUTES **MAKES:** 4 SERVINGS

- 1 cup canned black beans, rinsed and drained
- 1 green onion, chopped
- 2 tablespoons chopped red onion
- 2 tablespoons finely chopped roasted sweet red pepper
- 1 tablespoon minced fresh cilantro
- 1 tablespoon lime juice
- 1 garlic clove, minced
- 4 flour tortillas (10 inches)
- 1 cup (4 ounces) shredded Muenster or Monterey Jack cheese

1. In a small bowl, mash beans with a fork; stir in the green onion, red onion, pepper, cilantro, lime juice and garlic. Spread ¼ cup bean mixture over half of each tortilla; top with ¼ cup cheese. Fold over.

2. Cook on a griddle coated with cooking spray over low heat for 1-2 minutes on each side or until cheese is melted. Cut into wedges.

Creamy Chicken Angel Hair

Our pasta-loving family often requests this recipe featuring chicken and vegetables. Lemon adds a light touch to the sauce, which is delightfully seasoned with garlic and herbs.

—VANESSA SORENSON ISANTI, MINNESOTA

PREP: 15 MINUTES **COOK:** 20 MINUTES **MAKES:** 6 SERVINGS

1	**package (16 ounces) angel hair pasta**
1¼	**pounds boneless skinless chicken breasts, cut into 1-inch cubes**
½	**teaspoon salt**
¼	**teaspoon pepper**
3	**tablespoons olive oil, divided**
1	**large carrot, diced**
2	**tablespoons butter**
1	**medium onion, chopped**
1	**celery rib, diced**
3	**large garlic cloves, minced**
2	**cups heavy whipping cream**
5	**bacon strips, cooked and crumbled**
3	**tablespoons lemon juice**
1	**teaspoon Italian seasoning**
1	**cup shredded Parmesan cheese**

1. Cook pasta according to the package directions. Meanwhile, in a large skillet, saute the chicken, salt and pepper in 2 tablespoons oil until no longer pink. Remove and keep warm.

2. In the same skillet, saute carrot in butter and remaining oil for 1 minute. Add onion and celery; saute 3-4 minutes longer or until tender. Add garlic; cook for 1 minute.

3. Stir in the cream, bacon, lemon juice and Italian seasoning. Bring to a boil. Reduce heat; simmer, uncovered, for 2-3 minutes or until slightly thickened, stirring constantly. Return chicken to the pan.

4. Drain pasta; toss with chicken mixture. Garnish with cheese.

Hearty Beef Enchilada

Deliciously spicy, meaty and cheesy, this slow-cooker favorite will please everyone in your family. Serve it with sour cream, avocado and additional enchilada sauce. It's perfect for potlucks and other fun get-togethers!

—MARINA CASTLE CANYON COUNTY, CALIFORNIA

PREP: 10 MINUTES **COOK:** 6 HOURS **MAKES:** 10 SERVINGS

- 1½ **pounds lean ground beef (90% lean)**
- 1 **small onion, chopped**
- 1 **garlic clove, minced**
- 1 **envelope taco seasoning**
- ½ **teaspoon salt**
- ½ **teaspoon pepper**
- 9 **corn tortillas (6 inches)**
- ½ **cup chicken broth**
- ½ **cup tomato sauce**
- 1 **can (10 ounces) enchilada sauce**
- 1½ **cups (6 ounces) shredded cheddar cheese**
- 2 **cans (15 ounces each) pinto beans, rinsed and drained**
- 1 **can (11 ounces) Mexicorn, drained**

- 1 **can (4 ounces) chopped green chilies, drained**
- 1 **can (2¼ ounces) chopped ripe olives, drained**
  Optional ingredients: Sour cream and avocado slices

1. In a large skillet, cook the beef, onion and garlic over medium heat until meat is no longer pink; drain. Stir in the taco seasoning, salt and pepper.

2. In a greased 5-qt. slow cooker, layer 3 tortillas, beef mixture, broth, tomato sauce and enchilada sauce; sprinkle with ½ cup cheese. Add 3 tortillas, beans, Mexicorn, green chilies, half of the olives and a ½ cup cheese. Top with remaining tortillas, cheese and olives.

3. Cover and cook on low for 6-7 hours. Serve with sour cream and avocado if desired.

Meat-and-Potato Casserole

For variety, you can use another kind of cream soup (cream of mushroom, for instance). But try it this way first!

—MARNA HEITZ FARLEY, IOWA

PREP: 10 MINUTES **BAKE:** 50 MINUTES **MAKES:** 6 SERVINGS

- 4 **cups thinly sliced peeled potatoes**
- 2 **tablespoons butter, melted**
- ½ **teaspoon salt**
- 1 **pound ground beef**
- 1 **package (10 ounces) frozen corn**
- 1 **can (10¾ ounces) condensed cream of celery soup, undiluted**
- ⅓ **cup milk**
- ¼ **teaspoon garlic powder**
- ⅛ **teaspoon pepper**
- 1 **tablespoon chopped onion**
- 1 **cup (4 ounces) shredded cheddar cheese, divided**
   Minced fresh parsley, optional

1. Toss potatoes with butter and salt; arrange on the bottom and up the sides of a greased 13-in. x 9-in. baking dish. Bake, uncovered, at 400° for 25-30 minutes or until potatoes are almost tender.

2. Meanwhile, in a large skillet, cook beef over medium heat until no longer pink; drain. Sprinkle beef and corn over potatoes. Combine the soup, milk, garlic powder, pepper, onion and ½ cup cheese; pour over beef mixture.

3. Bake, uncovered, at 400° for 20 minutes or until vegetables are tender. Sprinkle with remaining cheese. Bake 2-3 minutes longer or until cheese is melted. Sprinkle with parsley if desired.

Italian Beef Sandwiches

After a hectic day, our family loves coming home to the inviting smell of Italian beef wafting from our slow cooker. Use the broth from my recipe as an au jus sauce—it's perfect for dipping.

—KEITH SADLER ORAN, MISSOURI

PREP: 20 MINUTES **COOK:** 6 HOURS
MAKES: 8 SERVINGS

- 1 **beef sirloin tip roast (2 pounds), cut into ¼-inch strips**
- 2 **jars (11½ ounces each) pepperoncini, undrained**
- 1 **small onion, sliced and separated into rings**
- 3 **teaspoons dried oregano**
- 1½ **teaspoons garlic salt**
- 1 **can (12 ounces) beer or nonalcoholic beer**
   Mayonnaise, optional
- 8 **hoagie buns, split**
- 8 **slices provolone cheese**

1. In a 5-qt. slow cooker, layer the beef, pepperoncini and onion; sprinkle with the oregano and garlic salt. Pour beer over the top. Cover and cook on low for 6 hours or until meat is tender.

2. Spread mayonnaise on cut sides of rolls if desired. Place cheese on roll bottoms. With a slotted spoon, place meat mixture over cheese.

Home Style COOKING NOTES

"If you don't have any leftover chicken for Barbecued Chicken Pizza, you can poach, bake or microwave some chicken breasts. You'll need about 6 to 8 ounces of boneless, skinless chicken breasts to make 1 cup of cubes. Another super easy way to have cubed chicken is to buy two fried bone-in chicken breasts at your supermarket. The cooking is done and all you need to do is remove the bones and skin and cube the meat."

—TASTE OF HOME TEST KITCHEN

Carribbean Jerk Chicken

Get ready to rock the grill with this spicy and wonderfully fragrant chicken. The zippy marinade includes hints of cinnamon, cayenne and thyme. We like to think of this dish as "chicken with attitude."

—JUDY KAMALIEH NEBRASKA CITY, NEBRASKA

PREP: 15 MINUTES + MARINATING **GRILL:** 35 MINUTES **MAKES:** 4 SERVINGS

- 4 **chicken leg quarters, skin removed**
- ¼ **cup olive oil**
- 2 **tablespoons brown sugar**
- 2 **tablespoons reduced-sodium soy sauce**
- 1 **envelope Italian salad dressing mix**
- 1 **teaspoon dried thyme**
- 1 **teaspoon ground cinnamon**
- ½ **teaspoon cayenne pepper**

1. With a sharp knife, cut leg quarters at the joints if desired. In a large resealable plastic bag, combine the remaining ingredients; add chicken. Seal bag and turn to coat; refrigerate for 2-4 hours.
2. Drain and discard marinade. Using long-handled tongs, moisten a paper towel with cooking oil and lightly coat the grill rack. Grill chicken, covered, over medium heat for 35-45 minutes or until a thermometer reads 180°, turning occasionally.

Barbecued Chicken Pizza

I often cut this easy pizza into little squares and serve it as an appetizer at parties.

—PATRICIA RICHARDSON VERONA, ONTARIO

PREP/TOTAL TIME: 20 MINUTES
MAKES: 4 SERVINGS

- 1 **prebaked 12-inch pizza crust**
- ⅔ **cup honey garlic barbecue sauce**
- 1 **small red onion, chopped**
- 1 **cup cubed cooked chicken**
- 2 **cups (8 ounces) shredded part-skim mozzarella cheese**

1. Place the crust on a 14-in. pizza pan. Spread barbecue sauce to within ½ in. of edges. Sprinkle with onion, chicken and cheese. Bake at 350° for 10 minutes or until cheese is melted.

Spiced Salmon

Salmon fillets are very quick and easy to prepare. The fish gets a little sweetness from brown sugar but overall the seasonings are mild and give this dish broad appeal. It's a great way to enjoy healthy salmon.

—**DONNA REYNOLDS** INNISFAIL, ALBERTA

PREP/TOTAL TIME: 20 MINUTES **MAKES:** 6-8 SERVINGS

     3 **tablespoons brown sugar**
    ½ **teaspoon garlic powder**
    ½ **teaspoon ground mustard**
    ½ **teaspoon paprika**
    ½ **teaspoon pepper**
    ¼ **teaspoon dill weed**
        Dash salt
        Dash dried tarragon
        Dash cayenne pepper
     2 **tablespoons butter, melted**
     2 **tablespoons olive oil**
     2 **tablespoons soy sauce**
     1 **salmon fillet (2 pounds)**

1. In a small bowl, combine the first nine ingredients. Add the butter, oil and soy sauce; spoon over salmon.

2. Using long-handled tongs, moisten a paper towel with cooking oil and lightly coat the grill rack. Place salmon skin side down on rack. Grill, covered, over medium heat or broil 4 in. from the heat for 10-15 minutes or until fish flakes easily with a fork.

Dilly Turkey Burgers

I changed this recipe from ground lamb to ground turkey since my family prefers turkey. Dill is a great herb to enhance the flavor of turkey.

—**ANDREA ROS**
    MOON TOWNSHIP, PENNSYLVANIA

PREP/TOTAL TIME: 20 MINUTES
MAKES: 4 SERVINGS

    1 **egg, lightly beaten**
    2 **tablespoons lemon juice**
    1 **to 2 tablespoons snipped fresh dill**
        or 1 to 2 teaspoons dill weed
    1 **garlic clove, minced**
    ½ **teaspoon salt**
    ½ **teaspoon dried oregano**
    ¼ **teaspoon pepper**
    ½ **cup soft bread crumbs**
    1 **pound ground turkey**
    4 **hamburger buns, split**
        Lettuce leaves
    8 **slices tomato, optional**
    2 **tablespoons mayonnaise, optional**

1. In a large bowl, combine the first eight ingredients. Crumble turkey over mixture and mix well. Shape mixture into four patties.

2. Grill patties, covered, over medium heat or broil 4 in. from the heat for 8-10 minutes or until a thermometer reads 165°, turning once. Serve on the buns with lettuce, tomato and mayonnaise if desired.

Home Style COOKING NOTES

Stroganoff-Style Spaghetti 'n' Meatballs

When the nights turn chilly, I turn to this rich, creamy entree. Convenience products save time, but it still tastes like it simmered for hours.

—SHARON YLKANEN MARENISCO, MICHIGAN

PREP/TOTAL TIME: 30 MINUTES
MAKES: 4 SERVINGS

- ½ pound uncooked spaghetti
- 1 package (12 ounces) frozen fully cooked Italian meatballs, thawed
- 2 tablespoons finely chopped onion
- 1 garlic clove, minced
- 1 tablespoon olive oil
- 1 can (10¾ ounces) condensed cream of mushroom soup, undiluted
- ¼ cup 2% milk
- 1 tablespoon concentrated au jus sauce
- ⅛ teaspoon Cajun seasoning
- 1 cup (8 ounces) sour cream

1. Cook spaghetti according to the package directions. Meanwhile, in a large skillet, saute the meatballs, onion and garlic in oil for 4-5 minutes or until meatballs are browned. Stir in the soup, milk, au jus sauce and seasoning. Bring to a boil. Reduce the heat; simmer, uncovered, for 10-12 minutes or until mixture is heated through.

2. Gradually stir in sour cream; heat through (do not boil). Drain spaghetti; stir into skillet. Serve immediately.

HOME STYLE tip

"When basting with marinade, reserve some for basting before adding the meat to the remaining marinade. For food safety concerns never use the liquid from marinating meat for basting.**"**

—TASTE OF HOME TEST KITCHEN

Grilled Chops with Rosemary Lemon Marinade

I'm not "chicken" about experimenting in the kitchen—I discovered this mouthwatering marinade in a poultry cookbook and decided to try it with pork chops. My family's glad because it has become a favorite! Don't be bashful about basting a pork roast or ribs with the marinade, either. I did, and I discovered two more family-favorite taste treats.

—PEGGY GWILLIM STRASBOURG, SASKATCHEWAN

PREP: 10 MINUTES + MARINATING **GRILL:** 15 MINUTES **MAKES:** 4 SERVINGS

- 2 garlic cloves, minced
- ½ cup lemon juice
- 2 teaspoons grated lemon peel
- 2 tablespoons olive oil
- 1 tablespoon minced fresh rosemary or 1 teaspoon dried rosemary, crushed
- ⅛ teaspoon dried basil
- ⅛ teaspoon lemon-pepper seasoning
- 4 bone-in pork loin chops (1 inch thick)

1. In a small bowl, whisk garlic, lemon juice, peel, oil, rosemary, basil and pepper. Pour ⅓ cup marinade into a large resealable plastic bag; add the pork. Seal bag and turn to coat; refrigerate for at least 2 hours or overnight, turning occasionally. Cover and refrigerate remaining marinade.

2. Drain marinade from pork; brush the remaining marinade on the chops while cooking. Grill chops over medium heat about 4-5 minutes per side or until a thermometer reads 145°. Let meat stand for 5 minutes before serving.

Crunchy Chicken Casserole

My 96-year-old mother wanted me to spread the word about her favorite recipe. It's both creamy and crunchy. I hope you enjoy it as much as our family does.

—BLANCHE HOLLINGWORTH RICHMOND, INDIANA

PREP: 15 MINUTES **BAKE:** 30 MINUTES **MAKES:** 6-8 SERVINGS

- 1 cup chopped celery
- 1 tablespoon butter
- 2 cups cubed cooked chicken
- 1½ cups cooked rice
- 1 can (10¾ ounces) condensed cream of chicken soup, undiluted
- ¾ cup mayonnaise
- 1 can (8 ounces) sliced water chestnuts; drained
- ½ cup sliced almonds
- 2 tablespoons chopped onion
  Salt and pepper to taste

TOPPING
- 1 tablespoon butter, melted
- ½ cup crushed cornflakes
  Sliced almonds, optional

1. In a skillet, saute celery in butter until tender. Remove from the heat; add the next nine ingredients. Spoon into an ungreased 2½-qt. baking dish.

2. Combine melted butter and cornflakes; sprinkle on top of casserole. Sprinkle with almonds if desired. Bake, uncovered, at 350° for 30 minutes.

Spicy Pork Tenderloin Skewers

My healthy prep-ahead skewers are easy to grill at the last minute. Red pepper flakes add a nice bite. Serve with steamed rice or broccoli.

—DAWN E. BRYANT THEDFORD, NEBRASKA

PREP: 15 MINUTES + MARINATING
GRILL: 10 MINUTES **MAKES:** 6 SERVINGS

- 1 large onion, chopped
- ⅓ cup reduced-sodium soy sauce
- ¼ cup water
- 2 tablespoons brown sugar
- 1 tablespoon ground coriander
- 1 tablespoon ground cumin
- 1 tablespoon minced fresh gingerroot
- 1 tablespoon lemon juice
- 1 tablespoon canola oil
- 2 teaspoons crushed red pepper flakes
- ½ teaspoon pepper
- 2 pork tenderloins (¾ pound each), cut into 1-inch cubes

1. In a blender, combine the first 11 ingredients; cover and process until smooth. Pour into a large resealable plastic bag; add pork. Seal bag and turn to coat; refrigerate for 6 hours or overnight.

2. Drain and discard marinade. Thread pork cubes onto six metal or soaked wooden skewers. Grill, covered, over medium heat for 8-10 minutes or until juices run clear, turning occasionally.

Home Style COOKING NOTES

Beef and Noodle Casserole

When I was working on the local election board in the '50s, one of my co-workers gave me this recipe, and it has been a family favorite ever since. It's quick to make for unexpected company or easily doubled for a potluck.

—MARY HINMAN ESCONDIDO, CALIFORNIA

PREP: 20 MINUTES **BAKE:** 45 MINUTES
MAKES: 8 SERVINGS

- 1½ **pounds ground beef**
- 1 **tablespoon butter**
- 1 **large onion, chopped**
- 1 **cup chopped green pepper**
- 1 **tablespoon Worcestershire sauce**
- 6¼ **cups uncooked wide egg noodles, cooked and drained**
- 2 **cans (10¾ ounces each) condensed tomato soup, undiluted**
- 1 **can (10¾ ounces) condensed cream of mushroom soup, undiluted**
- 1 **cup (4 ounces) shredded cheddar cheese**

1. In a large skillet, cook the beef over medium heat until no longer pink; drain. In the same skillet, melt the butter over medium-high heat. Saute onion and pepper until tender. Stir in the beef, Worcestershire sauce, noodles and soups.

2. Transfer to a greased 3-qt. baking dish; top with cheese. Bake, uncovered, at 350° for 45-50 minutes or until heated through.

Tarragon Chicken with Grapes and Linguine

Grapes are definitely a different addition to an entree, but their sweet, subtle flavor pairs well with savory tarragon sauce.

—GAIL LONG O'FALLON, ILLINOIS

PREP/TOTAL TIME: 30 MINUTES **MAKES:** 4 SERVINGS

- 8 **ounces uncooked linguine**
- 4 **boneless skinless chicken breast halves (6 ounces each)**
- ¼ **teaspoon salt**
- ¼ **teaspoon pepper**
- 2 **tablespoons olive oil**
- 2 **tablespoons butter**
- ½ **cup white wine or chicken broth**
- ½ **cup heavy whipping cream**
- 1 **cup green grapes, halved**
- 2 **tablespoons minced fresh tarragon**

1. Cook linguine according to package directions. Meanwhile, sprinkle chicken with salt and pepper.

2. In a large skillet over medium heat, cook chicken in oil and butter for 5-8 minutes on each side or until juices run clear. Remove and keep warm.

3. Add wine to skillet; stir to loosen brown bits. Bring to a boil; cook until liquid is reduced by half. Stir in cream; cook and stir until thickened. Add the grapes, tarragon and chicken; heat through. Drain linguine. Serve with chicken mixture.

Maple Pork Chops

Tender pork chops simmer in a maple glaze that makes every bite absolutely succulent. We brought together common household ingredients for this hearty, dazzling entree that delivers a lot of flavor with just a little fuss.

—TASTE OF HOME TEST KITCHEN

PREP/TOTAL TIME: 30 MINUTES **MAKES:** 4 SERVINGS

4 **boneless pork loin chops (1 inch thick and 6 ounces each)**

1 **teaspoon minced fresh thyme or ¼ teaspoon dried thyme**

½ **teaspoon salt**

½ **teaspoon pepper**

1 **tablespoon olive oil**

½ **cup brewed coffee**

¼ **cup maple syrup**

1 **tablespoon Dijon mustard**

2 **teaspoons Worcestershire sauce**

1. Sprinkle the pork chops with thyme, salt and pepper. In a large skillet, brown chops in oil. Remove and keep warm.

2. Add remaining ingredients to skillet. Bring to a boil; cook until liquid is reduced by half.

3. Return pork chops to skillet. Reduce heat; cover and simmer for 10-12 minutes or until meat is tender, turning once. Serve with sauce.

Place boneless chicken breasts between two pieces of waxed paper or plastic wrap or in a resealable plastic bag. Starting in the center and working out to edges, pound lightly with the flat side of a meat mallet until the chicken is even in thickness.

Chicken Stuffed with Walnuts, Apples & Brie

When I want a simple-to-do weeknight dinner, I often turn to chicken. In this recipe, the stuffing combines sweet and savory flavors, and the sauce makes the dish memorable.

—NICOLE PAVELICH LEXINGTON, KENTUCKY

PREP: 20 MINUTES **COOK:** 25 MINUTES
MAKES: 2 SERVINGS

- ¼ cup chopped onion
- 3 tablespoons butter, divided
- ½ cup chopped peeled apple
- 2 tablespoons chopped walnuts, toasted
- ⅛ teaspoon dried rosemary, crushed
  Dash plus ¼ teaspoon salt, divided
  Dash plus ¼ teaspoon pepper, divided
- 2 boneless skinless chicken breast halves (6 ounces each)
- ⅛ teaspoon garlic powder
- 2 ounces Brie cheese, cubed
- ¼ cup cider vinegar
- ¾ cup unsweetened apple juice, divided
- 1½ teaspoons cornstarch

1. In a large skillet, saute onion in 1 tablespoon butter for 1 minute. Add the apple; cook 2-3 minutes longer or until apple is golden brown. Remove from the heat; add walnuts, rosemary, and a dash of salt and pepper.
2. Flatten chicken to ¼-in. thickness; sprinkle with garlic powder and remaining salt and pepper. Place apple mixture and Brie on half of each chicken breast; fold chicken over. Secure with toothpicks if necessary.
3. In the same skillet, brown chicken in remaining butter. Stir in vinegar and ¼ cup apple juice. Bring to a boil. Reduce heat; cover and cook for 15-20 minutes or until a thermometer reads 170°.
4. Remove the chicken to a serving platter; discard toothpicks. Combine the cornstarch and remaining apple juice; add to the pan. Bring to a boil; cook and stir for 2 minutes or until thickened. Serve with chicken.

Sausage-Corn Bake

This is true comfort food: creamy and loaded with noodles and pork sausage. The aroma is fantastic while the casserole bakes.

—BERNICE MORRIS MARSHFIELD, MISSOURI

PREP: 20 MINUTES **BAKE:** 30 MINUTES **MAKES:** 6-8 SERVINGS

- 1½ pounds bulk pork sausage
- 1 medium green pepper, chopped
- 1 medium onion, chopped
- 4 tablespoons butter, divided
- 3 tablespoons all-purpose flour
- ½ teaspoon salt
- ½ teaspoon white pepper
- 1½ cups milk
- 1 can (14¾ ounces) cream-style corn
- 3½ cups (10 ounces) egg noodles, cooked and drained
- ¼ cup shredded cheddar cheese
- ½ cup dry bread crumbs

1. In a large skillet, cook the sausage, green pepper and onion over medium heat until sausage is no longer pink; drain and set aside.

2. In a large saucepan, melt 3 tablespoons butter over medium heat. Stir in the flour, salt and pepper. Gradually add milk. Bring to a boil; cook and stir for 2 minutes or until thickened. Stir in corn. Add noodles and corn mixture to the sausage mixture. Fold in the cheese.

3. Transfer to a greased 13-in. x 9-in. baking dish. Melt remaining butter; stir in bread crumbs. Sprinkle over casserole. Bake, uncovered, at 325° for 30-40 minutes or until heated through.

Mustard-Lover's Grilled Chicken

I'm a big fan of all types of mustard. So I knew I had to try this recipe. My family loves the unique, robust sauce.

—LESLIE BERNARD KINGWOOD, TEXAS

PREP: 5 MINUTES **GRILL:** 30 MINUTES **MAKES:** 6-8 SERVINGS

- ¼ cup butter, cubed
- 1⅓ cups prepared mustard
- ¼ cup white vinegar
- ½ teaspoon salt
- ½ teaspoon pepper
- 2 garlic cloves, minced
- 3 drops hot pepper sauce
- 3½ pounds chicken legs or thighs

1. In a small saucepan, melt butter over low heat. Stir in mustard, vinegar, salt, pepper, garlic and hot pepper sauce. Cook and stir until heated through; remove from the heat.

2. Grill the chicken, covered, over medium heat, turning occasionally, for 20 minutes. Brush with sauce. Continue basting and turning chicken several times for an additional 10 minutes or until a thermometer reads 180°.

Home Style COOKING NOTES

Gnocchi with Meat Sauce

This dish from my mother-in-law is the Italian version of a meat-and-potatoes meal. I recently served it to friends who immediately wanted the recipe.

—**KARIN NOLTON** ORTONVILLE, MICHIGAN

PREP: 30 MINUTES **COOK:** 15 MINUTES
MAKES: 6 SERVINGS

- ½ pound lean ground beef (90% lean)
- 1 large onion, finely chopped
- 4 garlic cloves, minced
- 2 cans (15 ounces each) tomato sauce
- 1 can (14½ ounces) diced tomatoes
- 1 teaspoon dried oregano
- 1 teaspoon dried basil
- ½ teaspoon dried rosemary, crushed
- 1 to 2 teaspoons sugar
- ½ teaspoon salt
- ⅛ teaspoon pepper

GNOCCHI

- 2 cups mashed potato flakes
- 1½ cups boiling water
- 2 eggs, beaten
- 1½ cups all-purpose flour
- ¼ teaspoon salt
  Grated Parmesan cheese, optional

1. In a large saucepan, cook the beef, onion and garlic over medium heat until meat is no longer pink; drain. Stir in the tomato sauce, diced tomatoes and seasonings. Bring to a boil. Reduce heat; cover and simmer for 15-20 minutes or until heated through.

2. Place potato flakes in a large bowl; stir in boiling water until blended. Stir in eggs. Add flour and salt all at once; stir just until combined. Divide into fourths; turn each onto a floured surface. Roll into ¾-in.-thick ropes; cut ropes into ¾-in. pieces.

3. In a large saucepan, bring water to a boil. Cook gnocchi, in batches, for 30-60 seconds or until gnocchi float. Remove with a slotted spoon. Place in a large bowl; top with sauce. Gently stir to coat. Sprinkle with cheese.

Tater Brat Bake

My husband suggested a brats-and-kraut lunch for friends back for their high school reunion. Rather than cut his visiting time, I made this. It was so easy!

—**PAULINE LENTZ** MESA, ARIZONA

PREP: 25 MINUTES **BAKE:** 25 MINUTES **MAKES:** 6 SERVINGS

- 1 package (1¼ pounds) uncooked bratwurst links
- 2 bottles (12 ounces each) beer or nonalcoholic beer
- 2 tablespoons butter
- 1 can (16 ounces) sauerkraut, rinsed, drained and chopped
- 1 can (10¾ ounces) condensed cheddar cheese soup, undiluted
- ½ cup milk
- 1 package (32 ounces) frozen Tater Tots
- 1 cup (4 ounces) shredded cheddar cheese

1. In a large saucepan, combine bratwurst and beer. Bring to a boil. Reduce heat. Cover and simmer for 10-15 minutes or until a thermometer reads 160°. Drain and cut into ¼-in. slices. In a large skillet, brown brats in butter over medium-high heat; drain on paper towels.

2. Spoon sauerkraut into a greased 13-in. x 9-in. baking dish. Top with brats. Combine soup and milk; drizzle over brats. Top with Tater Tots. Bake at 450° for 20-25 minutes or until potatoes are lightly browned.

3. Sprinkle with cheese; bake 5 minutes longer or until cheese is melted.

Saucy Chicken Strips

For a quick and easy meal, try this chicken recipe. The sauce is so tasty, your family will request it often.

—BARIANNE WILSON FALFURRIAS, TEXAS

PREP/TOTAL TIME: 25 MINUTES **MAKES:** 4 SERVINGS

- **1 pound boneless skinless chicken breast halves**
- **2 tablespoons butter**
- **½ cup chopped onion**
- **½ cup chopped green pepper**
- **1 can (4 ounces) mushroom stems and pieces, drained**
- **1 envelope onion soup mix**
- **1¼ cups water**
- **1 tablespoon Worcestershire sauce**
- **1 tablespoon cornstarch**
- **3 tablespoons cold water**

1. Cut chicken breast in 2-in. x ½-in. strips. Melt butter in a large skillet; add chicken and brown on all sides. Remove the chicken from skillet, reserving the drippings.

2. Add the onion, green pepper and mushrooms to the pan; saute until crisp-tender. Return chicken to skillet. In a small bowl, combine the soup mix, water and Worcestershire sauce; pour over chicken. Reduce heat; cover and simmer for 10 minutes.

3. Remove the chicken to a warm platter. Combine cornstarch and water until smooth; add to sauce. Bring to a boil. Cook and stir for 2 minutes or until thickened and bubbly. Pour over chicken.

Chicken Artichoke Casserole

With a flavor that's similar to artichoke dip, my rich and comforting chicken entree will warm you up on chilly nights.

—AMY NUTONI LA CRESCENT, MINNESOTA

PREP: 20 MINUTES **BAKE:** 25 MINUTES **MAKES:** 6 SERVINGS

- 2 **cups uncooked bow tie pasta**
- 2 **cups cubed cooked chicken**
- 1 **can (14 ounces) water-packed artichoke hearts, rinsed, drained and chopped**
- 1 **can (10¾ ounces) condensed cream of chicken soup, undiluted**
- 1 **cup shredded Parmesan cheese**
- 1 **cup mayonnaise**
- ⅓ **cup 2% milk**
- 1 **garlic clove, minced**
- ½ **teaspoon onion powder**
- ½ **teaspoon pepper**
- 1 **cup onion and garlic salad croutons, coarsely crushed**

1. Cook pasta according to the package directions. Meanwhile, in a large bowl, combine the chicken, artichokes, soup, cheese, mayonnaise, milk, garlic, onion powder and pepper. Drain pasta; add to the chicken mixture.

2. Transfer to a greased 2-qt. baking dish. Sprinkle with croutons. Bake, uncovered, at 350° for 25-30 minutes or until heated through.

Eggplant Zucchini Bolognese

I roast the veggies while the pasta cooks, making for a quick dish. This meal in one blends rustic comfort with fresh flavors.

—TRISHA KRUSE EAGLE, IDAHO

PREP: 30 MINUTES **COOK:** 20 MINUTES **MAKES:** 8 SERVINGS

- 1 **package (16 ounces) penne pasta**
- 1 **small eggplant, peeled and cut into 1-inch pieces**
- 1 **medium zucchini, cut into ¼-inch slices**
- 1 **medium yellow summer squash, cut into ¼-inch slices**
- 1 **cup chopped onion**
- 2 **tablespoons olive oil**
- 2 **teaspoons minced garlic**
- 1 **teaspoon salt**
- ½ **teaspoon pepper**
- 1 **pound lean ground beef (90% lean)**
- 1 **can (28 ounces) tomato puree**
- 1 **tablespoon Italian seasoning**
- 1 **tablespoon brown sugar**
- 8 **teaspoons grated Parmesan cheese**

1. Cook pasta according to the package directions.

2. In a large bowl, combine the eggplant, zucchini, squash, onion, oil, garlic, salt and pepper. Transfer to two 15-in. x 10-in. x 1-in. baking pans coated with cooking spray. Bake at 425° for 20-25 minutes or until tender.

3. Meanwhile, in a large skillet, cook beef over medium heat until no longer pink; drain. Stir in the tomato puree, Italian seasoning and brown sugar.

4. Drain pasta; stir in the tomato mixture and roasted vegetables. Sprinkle with cheese.

Grilled Lemon Pork Chops

These melt-in-your-mouth pork chops are always a hit with my family and with company, too. Lemonade concentrate is what gives them their tangy lemon flavor. They're so easy to make that we have them often.

—ANGELA OELSCHLAEGER TONGANOXIE, KANSAS

PREP: 15 MINUTES + MARINATING
GRILL: 10 MINUTES **MAKES:** 6 SERVINGS

- 1 **can (12 ounces) frozen lemonade concentrate, thawed**
- ⅔ **cup soy sauce**
- 2 **teaspoons seasoned salt**
- 1 **teaspoon celery salt**
- ¼ **teaspoon garlic powder**
- 6 **boneless butterflied pork chops (½ inch thick and 6 ounces each)**

1. In a small bowl, combine the lemonade concentrate, soy sauce, seasoned salt, celery salt and garlic powder. Pour 1½ cups into a large resealable plastic bag; add pork chops. Seal bag and turn to coat; refrigerate for at least 4 hours. Cover and refrigerate remaining marinade for basting.

2. Drain and discard marinade. Using long-handled tongs, moisten a paper towel with cooking oil and lightly coat the grill rack. Grill pork chops, covered, over medium heat or broil 4-5 in. from the heat for 3-4 minutes on each side or until a thermometer reads 145°, basting occasionally with reserved marinade. Let meat stand for 5 minutes before serving.

Home Style COOKING NOTES

Baked Spaghetti

My satisfying pasta bake pleases young and old, family and friends! Add a tossed green salad and breadsticks to round out a memorable menu.

—**BETTY RABE** MAHTOMEDI, MINNESOTA

PREP: 20 MINUTES
BAKE: 30 MINUTES + STANDING
MAKES: 6 SERVINGS

- 8 ounces uncooked spaghetti, broken into thirds
- 1 egg
- ½ cup fat-free milk
- ½ pound lean ground beef (90% lean)
- ½ pound Italian turkey sausage links, casings removed
- 1 small onion, chopped
- ¼ cup chopped green pepper
- 1 jar (14 ounces) meatless spaghetti sauce
- 1 can (8 ounces) no-salt-added tomato sauce
- ½ cup shredded part-skim mozzarella cheese

1. Cook spaghetti according to package directions; drain. In a large bowl, beat egg and milk. Add spaghetti; toss to coat. Transfer to a 13-in. x 9-in. baking dish coated with cooking spray.
2. In a large skillet, cook the beef, sausage, onion and green pepper over medium heat until meat is no longer pink; drain. Stir in the spaghetti sauce and tomato sauce. Spoon over the spaghetti mixture.
3. Bake casserole, uncovered, at 350° for 20 minutes. Sprinkle with cheese. Bake 10 minutes longer or until cheese is melted. Let stand for 10 minutes before cutting.

Ham and Asparagus Casserole

With hard-cooked eggs and asparagus, this family-favorite casserole is perfect for all occasions. But it's especially nice for springtime brunches.

—**DONETTA BRUNNER** SAVANNA, ILLINOIS

PREP: 15 MINUTES **BAKE:** 25 MINUTES **MAKES:** 4 SERVINGS

- 1 package (10 ounces) frozen cut asparagus or 1 pound fresh asparagus, ½-inch cuts
- 4 hard-cooked eggs, peeled and chopped
- 1 cup cubed fully cooked ham
- 2 tablespoons quick-cooking tapioca
- ¼ cup shredded process cheese (Velveeta)
- 2 tablespoons chopped green pepper
- 2 tablespoons chopped onion
- 1 tablespoon minced fresh parsley
- 1 tablespoon lemon juice
- ½ cup half-and-half cream or evaporated milk
- 1 cup condensed cream of mushroom soup, undiluted

TOPPING
- 1 cup soft bread crumbs
- 2 tablespoons butter, melted

1. In a large saucepan, bring ½ in. of water to a boil. Add asparagus; cover and boil for 3 minutes. Drain and immediately place asparagus in ice water. Drain and pat dry.
2. In a 2½-qt. baking dish, combine the asparagus, eggs and ham; sprinkle tapioca evenly over all. Stir in the cheese, green pepper, onion and parsley.
3. In a small bowl, combine the lemon juice, cream and soup; add to casserole and mix thoroughly. Combine topping ingredients; sprinkle over top.
4. Bake, uncovered, at 375° for 25-30 minutes or until heated through. Let stand a few minutes before serving.

Sage-Dusted Chicken

I use this "express" recipe for family meals and last-minute dinner parties. It's always met with rave reviews. The golden-brown chicken looks scrumptious served over spinach.

—**VERONICA CALLAGHAN** GLASTONBURY, CONNECTICUT

PREP/TOTAL TIME: 25 MINUTES **MAKES:** 4 SERVINGS

- 4 **boneless skinless chicken breast halves (6 ounces each)**
- 3 **teaspoons rubbed sage**
- 1 **teaspoon salt**
- ½ **teaspoon pepper**
- 2 **tablespoons butter**
- 2 **teaspoons olive oil**
- ¼ **cup heavy whipping cream**

1. Flatten chicken to ½-in. thickness; sprinkle with sage, salt and pepper.

2. In a large skillet over medium heat, cook chicken in butter and oil for 5-6 minutes on each side or until juices run clear. Remove and keep warm.

3. Add cream to the skillet, stirring to loosen browned bits. Cook and stir until sauce is thickened, about 4 minutes. Serve with chicken.

Cheddar Turkey Casserole

This recipe comes with lots of mass appeal, thanks to its cheesy sauce. Pasta, veggies and leftover turkey combine to create a filling meal.

—STEVE FOY KIRKWOOD, MISSOURI

PREP: 20 MINUTES **BAKE:** 35 MINUTES **MAKES:** 6 SERVINGS

- 4 **cups uncooked spiral pasta**
- 1 **garlic clove, minced**
- 3 **tablespoons butter**
- 3 **tablespoons all-purpose flour**
- 1 **teaspoon salt**
- ¼ **teaspoon prepared mustard**
- ¼ **teaspoon dried thyme**
- ¼ **teaspoon pepper**
- 2 **cups 2% milk**
- 1½ **cups (6 ounces) shredded cheddar cheese**
- 2 **cups cubed cooked turkey**
- 2 **cups frozen mixed vegetables, thawed**
- ½ **cup slivered almonds**

1. Cook pasta according to the package directions. Meanwhile, in a large saucepan, saute garlic in butter until tender. Stir in flour, salt, mustard, thyme and pepper. Gradually stir in milk. Bring to a boil; cook and stir for 2 minutes or until thickened. Remove from heat; stir in cheese until melted. Drain pasta; place in a bowl. Toss with turkey, vegetables and cheese sauce.

2. Transfer to a greased 13-in. x 9-in. baking dish. Sprinkle with almonds. Bake, uncovered, at 350° for 35-40 minutes or until heated through.

3. Serve immediately, or before baking, cover and freeze casserole for up to 3 months.

To use frozen casserole: *Thaw in the refrigerator overnight. Remove from the refrigerator 30 minutes before baking. Bake according to directions.*

Slow-Cooked Moroccan Chicken

I would recommend this chicken go into everyone's pot, whether served as a comforting supper or a meal for special company. Its simplicity—I put it together in the morning, walk away, and come back to a fabulous and colorful main dish—makes it a family favorite.

—KATHY MORGAN RIDGEFIELD, WASHINGTON

PREP: 20 MINUTES **COOK:** 6 HOURS **MAKES:** 4 SERVINGS

- 4 **medium carrots, sliced**
- 2 **large onions, halved and sliced**

- 1 **broiler/fryer chicken (3 to 4 pounds), cut up, skin removed**
- ½ **teaspoon salt**
- ½ **cup chopped dried apricots**
- ½ **cup raisins**
- 2 **tablespoons all-purpose flour**
- 1 **can (14½ ounces) reduced-sodium chicken broth**
- ¼ **cup tomato paste**
- 2 **tablespoons lemon juice**
- 2 **garlic cloves, minced**
- 1½ **teaspoons ground ginger**
- 1½ **teaspoons ground cumin**
- 1 **teaspoon ground cinnamon**
- ¾ **teaspoon pepper**
  Hot cooked couscous

1. Place carrots and onions in a greased 5-qt. slow cooker. Sprinkle chicken with salt; add to slow cooker. Top with apricots and raisins.

2. In a small bowl, combine flour and broth until smooth; whisk in the tomato paste, lemon juice, garlic, ginger, cumin, cinnamon and pepper. Pour over chicken.

3. Cover and cook on low for 6 to 7 hours or until chicken is tender. Serve with couscous.

Home Style COOKING NOTES

Beef Stew with Cheddar Dumplings

This stew is perfect for company. It's easy, and everyone comments on the cheese in the dumplings.

—**JACKIE RILEY** GARRETTSVILLE, OHIO

PREP: 25 MINUTES **COOK:** 1½ HOURS
MAKES: 6-8 SERVINGS

- ½ cup all-purpose flour
- ½ teaspoon salt
- ½ teaspoon pepper
- 2 to 3 pounds beef stew meat, cut into 1-inch pieces
- 2 tablespoons canola oil
- ½ teaspoon onion salt
- ½ teaspoon garlic salt
- 1 tablespoon browning sauce, optional
- 5 cups water
- 5 teaspoons beef bouillon granules
- 4 medium carrots, sliced
- 1 medium onion, cut into wedges
- 1 can (14½ ounces) cut green beans, drained

DUMPLINGS

- 2 cups biscuit/baking mix
- 1 cup (4 ounces) shredded cheddar cheese
- ⅔ cup milk

1. Combine flour, salt and pepper. Coat the meat with flour mixture. In a Dutch oven, heat oil over medium-high. Brown meat on all sides.

2. Add onion salt and garlic salt, browning sauce, water and bouillon. Bring to a boil; reduce heat and simmer, covered, for 1 hour.

3. Add carrots and onion. Cover and simmer until vegetables for 15 minutes or until tender. Stir in green beans.

4. For dumplings, combine biscuit mix and cheese. Stir in enough milk to form a soft dough. Drop by tablespoonful into bubbling stew. Cover and simmer 12 minutes (do not lift cover) or until a toothpick inserted in dumplings comes out clean.

Presto Paprika Chicken

On busy evenings, I wing it for dinner. The mild, paprika-spiced sauce nicely coats the rotisserie chicken and noodles.

—**GLORIA WARCZAK** CEDARBURG, WISCONSIN

PREP/TOTAL TIME: 30 MINUTES **MAKES:** 6 SERVINGS

- 1 medium onion, chopped
- 3 tablespoons butter
- 4 teaspoons all-purpose flour
- 2 cups chicken broth
- 2 tablespoons plus 1½ teaspoons paprika
- 1 bay leaf
- 1½ cups (12 ounces) sour cream
- 1 rotisserie chicken, cut into serving-size pieces
  Hot cooked noodles

1. In a large skillet, saute onion in butter. Stir in flour until blended; gradually add the broth, paprika and bay leaf. Bring to a boil; cook and stir for 2 minutes or until thickened.

2. Reduce heat to low. Stir in sour cream. Add chicken; heat through. Discard bay leaf. Serve with noodles.

Mom's Meat Loaf

My mother made her tender, moist meat loaf at least every other week, and always served it with scalloped potatoes. It was one of my favorite meals growing up. You'll be amazed by all the flavor from just a handful of pantry ingredients!

—HELEN LIPKO MARTINSBURG, PENNSYLVANIA

PREP: 10 MINUTES **BAKE:** 35 MINUTES **MAKES:** 8 SERVINGS

1 egg, lightly beaten
1 can (5½ ounces) V8 juice
½ cup seasoned bread crumbs
1 envelope onion soup mix
¼ cup grated Parmesan cheese
¼ teaspoon garlic powder
1½ pounds ground beef
⅓ cup ketchup

1. In a large bowl, combine the egg, V8 juice, bread crumbs, soup mix, cheese and garlic powder. Crumble beef over mixture and mix well. Pat into an ungreased 9-in. x 5-in. loaf pan.

2. Bake, uncovered, at 350° for 30 minutes. Spread ketchup over top; bake 5-10 minutes longer or until no pink remains and a thermometer reads 160°.

3. Serve immediately or before baking, cover and freeze meat loaf for up to 3 months.

To use frozen meat loaf: *Thaw in the refrigerator overnight. Bake as directed.*

Perfect Pork Chop Bake

This recipe is especially useful on busy days when we're short on time. It's packed with pork, potatoes and carrots for a filling meal.

—JAN LUTZ STEVENS POINT, WISCONSIN

PREP: 15 MINUTES **BAKE:** 45 MINUTES **MAKES:** 6 SERVINGS

6   pork chops (5 ounces each)
½   teaspoon salt, divided, optional
1   medium onion, thinly sliced and separated into rings
3   medium potatoes, peeled and thinly sliced
6   medium carrots, thinly sliced
1   teaspoon dried marjoram
3   tablespoons all-purpose flour
¾   cup milk
1   can (10¾ ounces) condensed cream of mushroom soup, undiluted

1. Coat a large skillet with cooking spray; cook chops over medium heat for 2-3 minutes on each side or until lightly browned. Place in an ungreased 13-in. x 9-in. baking dish; sprinkle with ¼ teaspoon salt if desired. Layer with the onion, potatoes and carrots. Sprinkle with marjoram and remaining salt if desired.

2. In a small bowl, whisk flour and milk until smooth; add soup. Pour over vegetables. Cover and bake at 350° for 30-35 minutes. Uncover; bake 10-15 minutes longer or until meat is tender.

1 teaspoon dried oregano
1 garlic clove, minced
¼ teaspoon salt
¼ teaspoon pepper

FAJITAS

½ medium onion, sliced
1 medium sweet red pepper, sliced into thin strips
2 tablespoons canola oil, divided
8 flour tortilla shells, warmed
2 avocados, peeled and sliced
  Salsa
  Sour cream

1. Cut the steak cut across the grain into ¼-in. strips; set aside.

2. In a large resealable bag, combine marinade ingredients; add beef. Seal and refrigerate for 3-6 hours or overnight, turning several times.

3. Discard marinade. In a skillet, saute the onion and pepper in 1 tablespoon oil until crisp-tender; remove from pan. Add remaining oil and saute the meat until no longer pink, about 4 minutes. Add the vegetables to pan and heat through.

4. To serve, place a spoonful of meat-vegetable mixture on a warmed tortilla and top with avocado, salsa and sour cream. Roll tortilla around filling.

Home Style COOKING NOTES

Fantastic Beef Fajitas

The first time I made these fajitas, my family couldn't get enough. The next time I had to make a double batch. This is a favorite evening meal for me, too, because it fixes up so quick. It would turn any get-together into a fiesta!

—**MARLA BRENNEMAN** GOSHEN, INDIANA

PREP: 15 MINUTES + MARINATING **COOK:** 10 MINUTES **MAKES:** 4-6 SERVINGS

1 **pound beef top sirloin steak or flank steak, trimmed**

MARINADE

3 **tablespoons canola oil**
2 **tablespoons lemon juice**

Chicken and Rice Casserole

Everyone loves this casserole because it's a tasty combination of hearty and crunchy ingredients mixed in a creamy sauce.

—MYRTLE MATTHEWS MARIETTA, GEORGIA

PREP: 15 MINUTES **BAKE:** 1 HOUR
MAKES: 12 SERVINGS

- 4 cups cooked white rice or a combination of wild and white rice
- 4 cups diced cooked chicken
- ½ cup slivered almonds
- 1 small onion, chopped
- 1 can (8 ounces) sliced water chestnuts, drained
- 1 package (10 ounces) frozen peas, thawed
- ¾ cup chopped celery
- 1 can (10¾ ounces) condensed cream of celery soup, undiluted
- 1 can (10¾ ounces) condensed cream of chicken soup, undiluted
- 1 cup mayonnaise
- 2 teaspoons lemon juice
- 1 teaspoon salt
- 2 cups crushed potato chips
  Paprika

1. In a greased 13-in. x 9-in. baking dish, combine first seven ingredients. In a large bowl, combine the soups, mayonnaise, lemon juice and salt. Pour over chicken mixture and toss to coat.
2. Sprinkle with the potato chips and paprika. Bake at 350° for 1 hour or until heated through.

Home Style COOKING NOTES

Cheese-Topped Sloppy Joes

My Aunt Nellie gave me her recipe for the quick-to-fix sandwiches. As busy farm wife, she used to serve them to the harvest crew. Microwaved leftovers taste just as delicious the next day.

—MARY DEMPSEY OVERLAND PARK, KANSAS

PREP/TOTAL TIME: 25 MINUTES **MAKES:** 6 SERVINGS

- 1 pound ground beef
- 2 celery ribs, chopped
- 1 tablespoon chopped onion
- 1 tablespoon all-purpose flour
- 1 tablespoon brown sugar
- ½ teaspoon ground mustard
- ¾ cup ketchup
- 6 hamburger buns, split
- 6 slices Swiss cheese

1. In a large skillet, cook the beef, celery and onion over medium heat until meat is no longer pink; drain. Stir in the flour, brown sugar, mustard and ketchup.
2. Bring to a boil. Reduce heat; simmer, uncovered, for 10 minutes, stirring occasionally. Serve on buns with cheese.

Spanish Turkey Tenderloins

If you're hungry for warm-weather fare, try this grilled turkey. The bright, sunny colors of the relish look like summer.
—**ROXANNE CHAN** ALBANY, CALIFORNIA

PREP: 20 MINUTES **GRILL:** 15 MINUTES **MAKES:** 6 SERVINGS

- 1   **package (20 ounces) turkey breast tenderloins**
- 1   **tablespoon olive oil**
- ½   **teaspoon salt**
- ½   **teaspoon pepper**
- ¼   **teaspoon paprika**

RELISH
- 1   **plum tomato, chopped**
- 1   **large navel orange, peeled, sectioned and chopped**
- ¼   **cup sliced pimiento-stuffed olives**
- 1   **green onion, finely chopped**
- 2   **tablespoons minced fresh oregano or 2 teaspoons dried oregano**
- 2   **tablespoons sliced almonds**
- 2   **tablespoons minced fresh parsley**

- 1   **large garlic clove, minced**
- 1   **tablespoon capers, drained**
- 1   **teaspoon lemon juice**
- ½   **teaspoon grated lemon peel**
- ¼   **teaspoon salt**

1. Rub turkey with oil; sprinkle with salt, pepper and paprika.

2. Grill, covered, over medium heat or broil 4 in. from the heat for 15-20 minutes or until a thermometer reads 170°, turning occasionally. Let stand for 5 minutes before slicing.

3. Meanwhile, in a small bowl, combine the relish ingredients. Serve with turkey.

Pork Chops with Scalloped Potatoes

My sister's recipe was originally a casserole baked in the oven, but I've also fixed it in the slow cooker and on the stovetop. Everyone who has tasted it loves it.

—**ELIZABETH JOHNSTON** GLENDALE, ARIZONA

PREP: 30 MINUTES **COOK:** 8 HOURS
MAKES: 6 SERVINGS

- 4 medium potatoes, peeled and thinly sliced
- 6 bone-in pork loin chops (7 ounces each)
- 1 tablespoon canola oil
- 2 large onions, sliced and separated into rings
- 2 teaspoons butter
- 3 tablespoons all-purpose flour
- ¼ teaspoon salt
- ¼ teaspoon pepper
- 1 can (14½ ounces) reduced-sodium chicken broth
- 1 cup fat-free milk

1. Place potatoes in a 5- or 6-qt. slow cooker coated with cooking spray. In a large nonstick skillet, brown pork chops in oil in batches.
2. Place chops over potatoes. Saute onions in drippings until tender; place over chops. Melt butter in skillet. Combine the flour, salt, pepper and broth until smooth. Stir into pan. Add milk. Bring to a boil; cook and stir for 2 minutes or until thickened.
3. Pour sauce over onions. Cover and cook on low for 8-10 hours or until pork is tender. Skim fat and thicken cooking juices if desired.

Beef & Veggie Stew

This healthy, hearty stew is one of my husband's favorite meals. I always use fresh mushrooms, and I toss low-sodium bouillon cubes right into the roaster.

—**PATRICIA KILE** ELIZABETHTOWN, PENNSYLVANIA

PREP: 25 MINUTES **COOK:** 4 HOURS
MAKES: 8 SERVINGS

- ¼ cup all-purpose flour
- 2 pounds boneless beef chuck roast, trimmed and cut into 1-inch cubes

- 2 tablespoons canola oil
- 1 can (10¾ ounces) condensed tomato soup, undiluted
- 1 cup water or red wine
- 2 reduced-sodium beef bouillon cubes
- 3 teaspoons Italian seasoning
- 1 bay leaf
- ½ teaspoon coarsely ground pepper
- 6 white onions or yellow onions, quartered
- 4 medium potatoes, cut into 1½-inch slices
- 3 medium carrots, cut into 1-inch slices
- 12 large fresh mushrooms
- ½ cup sliced celery

1. Place flour in a large resealable plastic bag. Add beef, a few pieces at a time, and shake to coat.
2. In a large skillet, brown meat in oil in batches; drain. Transfer to a 5-qt. slow cooker. Combine the tomato soup, water or wine, bouillon and seasonings; pour over beef. Add the onions, potatoes, carrots, mushrooms and celery.
3. Cover and cook on low for 4-5 hours or until meat is tender. Discard bay leaf. Serve with noodles or French bread.

Cranberry Chicken

I love to collect cookbooks and try new recipes. This dish is so good, I reach for it more often than others. It's delicious, easy and lovely when served with rice and a side vegetable.

—EDITH HOLLIDAY FLUSHING, MICHIGAN

PREP: 10 MINUTES **COOK:** 5 HOURS **MAKES:** 6 SERVINGS

- 1 **broiler/fryer chicken (3 to 4 pounds), cut up**
- 1 **can (14 ounces) whole-berry cranberry sauce**
- 1 **cup barbecue sauce**
- 1 **small onion, finely chopped**
- 1 **celery rib, finely chopped**
- ½ **teaspoon salt**
- ¼ **teaspoon pepper**
  Hot cooked rice

1. Place chicken in a 3-qt. slow cooker. In a small bowl, combine the cranberry sauce, barbecue sauce, onion, celery, salt and pepper; pour over chicken. Cover and cook on low for 5-6 hours or until chicken is tender. Serve with rice.

Sweet on Honey

It's easy to get stuck on backyard beekeeping.

BY ROBIN PRATT

Bee-liever. Robin Pratt finds many benefits in beekeeping.

I seemed to have generated quite a buzz around my peaceful neighborhood in Athens, Georgia. Because I moved in lock, stock and beehive.

The first time I checked my honeybees after moving here, I looked up to see half a dozen neighbors watching from the edge of my lawn. Now they come up right to the hive to chat. I've found beekeeping is a great way to meet people.

Seven years ago, I left a successful job as a website designer in downtown Atlanta to work for the College of Agriculture at the University of Georgia-Athens.

I signed up for a beekeeping course offered by our ag extension. In the first 10 minutes of class, I caught the bee bug. I began with a starter kit, including a hive and keepers' accessories. Then I got 4,000 bees for $50 from a farm that raises them for sale. I introduced the queen to her new kingdom—my backyard beehive.

The compact white hive consists of three stacked boxes, each containing 10 frames. The bees build wax combs inside the frames. The two bottom boxes, called "deeps," are where the queen lays her eggs and where the bee brood develops into grown bees. The top box, called the "super," contains combs of hexagonal cells that the bees fill with honey.

I'm in awe of the queen bee. She's the heart and soul of the colony. After mating, she returns to the hive and can lay around 2,000 eggs per day during the spring season.

The unfertilized eggs become male drones, while the fertilized ones turn into female worker bees that collect food to feed the colony.

In Georgia, the bees' pollen and nectar sources are a mix of everything that blooms from early spring through summer, including locust, kudzu, tulip, poplar, wild cherry, clover, privet, wildflowers and more. I love to pull out the frames and see them filled with pollen in a rainbow of colors— red, pink, neon green and school-bus yellow. They remind me of stained glass windows.

I typically harvest the honey in late August, donning canvas gloves, a hat with a screen veil, a chambray shirt and corduroy pants.

My daughter, Sadie, who's 6, is absolutely fearless around bees, so she's a big help at harvesttime. I use an old-fashioned method, scraping the honeycomb off the frame and into a strainer. It sits over a big pot for several hours until most of the honey has drained out. Then Sadie helps me pour the honey into sterilized mason jars. We freeze the wax to make candles at a later date.

I'll harvest three of the 10 frames, and leave the rest to nourish the bees in winter. I net about six pints from the three frames. I keep two pints and pour the rest into smaller jelly jars for gifts or trading with neighbors.

A great thing about Athens is our underground economy based on bartering. I've traded a couple of jars of honey for homemade bread, homegrown veggies, a winter's worth of firewood, and lessons in everything from canning to rain-barrel making.

I'm so thankful to my bees for demonstrating what a working, functional society is. We humans can be individualistic and isolated at times. The bees prove that we have to work together to make something as golden as honey. There's a place and a role for everyone.

Benefits of beekeeping

Dan Harris, a professional beekeeper who teaches beginners, says the hobby requires only moderate upkeep and offers many benefits:

- Bees help pollinate nearby gardens and farm crops.
- Backyard hives help keep aggressive, defensive types of bees from settling nearby.
- Local raw honey maintains pollens, enzymes and nutrients that may be lost in pasteurization. Plus, it's often tastier.
- Wax from honeycombs can be used to make natural candles, moisturizer, lip balm and furniture polish.

Want to learn more? Check with your local extension office or local beekeeping groups.

Robin checks a super for honey and then puts it back on the hive. A full honey super weighs 80 to 100 pounds.

from Robin's kitchen

Broiled Fish with Tarragon Sauce

The delicate flavor of this fish pairs perfectly with the tangy sauce. A yummy hint of honey comes through. Serve it with crusty bread, mixed vegetables or rice to help soak up the sauce.

—ROBIN PRATT ATHENS, GEORGIA

PREP/TOTAL TIME: 25 MINUTES **MAKES:** 8 SERVINGS

2 pounds cod or red snapper fillets
1 tablespoons cornstarch
½ cup cold water
½ cup honey
¼ cup white wine or chicken broth
¼ cup lemon juice
1 teaspoon garlic salt
½ teaspoon grated lemon peel
1 tablespoon minced fresh tarragon

1. Place fish on a lightly greased 15-in. x 10-in. x 1-in. baking pan. Broil 4 in. from the heat for 8-10 minutes or until fish flakes easily with a fork.

2. Meanwhile, in a small saucepan, whisk cornstarch and water until smooth. Stir in the honey, wine, lemon juice, garlic salt and lemon peel. Bring to a boil. Cook and stir for 3-5 minutes or until thickened. Remove from the heat; stir in tarragon. Serve with fish.

Sunday Dinners

Gather family and friends for one of the most enduring traditions of all: Sunday dinner. Whether you're planning a cookout with the neighbors, preparing a succulent roast for your in-laws, or just carving out some slow-down time for your family, the following foods will create lasting memories.

Steak with Chipotle-Lime Chimichurri

(recipe on page 192)

"**S**teak gets a flavor kick from chimichurri. This piquant all-purpose herb sauce is so versatile, it complements most any grilled meat, poultry or fish."

—LAUREEN PITTMAN
RIVERSIDE, CALIFORNIA

Turkey Meat Loaf

For a holiday meal any time of year, this tender turkey meat loaf is perfect. Jazzed up with a cranberry glaze, it's a mouthwatering dish.

—MOLLIE BROWN LOS ANGELES, CALIFORNIA

PREP: 30 MINUTES + STANDING
BAKE: 45 MINUTES **MAKES:** 6 SERVINGS

- 1 **cup seasoned stuffing cubes**
- ½ **cup milk**
- 1 **egg, beaten**
- 1 **celery rib, finely chopped**
- 1 **small onion, grated**
- 1 **small carrot, grated**
- ¼ **cup dried cranberries**
- ½ **teaspoon salt**
- ¼ **teaspoon pepper**
- 3 **to 4½ teaspoons minced fresh sage, divided**
- 3 **teaspoons minced fresh rosemary, divided**
- 1½ **pounds lean ground turkey**
- ½ **cup whole-berry cranberry sauce**
- ½ **cup ketchup**
- ⅛ **teaspoon hot pepper sauce**

> **HOME STYLE tip**
>
> **66**To ensure a tender meat loaf, avoid overmixing. Follow the recipe to combine the other loaf ingredients, then crumble meat over the top and mix just until combined. Gently pat the mixture into a loaf shape. Try different meat loaf toppings. Salsa, marinara, barbecue sauce and even jarred tapenade could yield tasty results. **99**
>
> **—TASTE OF HOME TEST KITCHEN**

1. In a large bowl, combine stuffing cubes and milk. Let stand for 10 minutes; break up stuffing cubes with a fork. Stir in the egg, celery, onion, carrot, cranberries, salt and pepper. Combine sage and rosemary; add half to the mixture. Crumble turkey over mixture and mix well. Pat into an ungreased 9-in. x 5-in. loaf pan.

2. Bake, uncovered, at 375° for 25 minutes; drain if necessary. Combine the cranberry sauce, ketchup, pepper sauce and remaining herbs; spread over meat loaf. Bake 20-25 minutes longer or until no pink remains and a thermometer reads 165°.

Autumn Pot Roast

This is one of my all-time-favorite slow cooker recipes. When the weather turns chilly, it's always comforting to come home to a warm home-cooked meal like this one.

—**MARY HANKINS** KANSAS CITY, MISSOURI

PREP: 30 MINUTES **COOK:** 6 HOURS **MAKES:** 6 SERVINGS

- 1 **boneless beef chuck roast (3 pounds)**
- 1 **teaspoon salt, divided**
- ½ **teaspoon pepper, divided**
- 1 **tablespoon olive oil**
- 1½ **pounds sweet potatoes, cut into 1-inch pieces**
- 2 **medium parsnips, cut into ½ inch pieces**
- 1 **large sweet onion, cut into chunks**
- ⅓ **cup sun-dried tomatoes (not packed in oil)**
- 3 **garlic cloves, minced**
- 1 **teaspoon dried thyme**
- 2 **bay leaves**
- 1 **can (14½ ounces) reduced-sodium beef broth**
- ¾ **cup dry red wine or additional reduced-sodium beef broth**

1. Cut roast in half; sprinkle with ½ teaspoon salt and ¼ teaspoon pepper. In a large skillet, brown meat in oil on all sides; drain.

2. Transfer to a 5-qt. slow cooker. Top with sweet potatoes, parsnips, onion, sun-dried tomatoes, garlic, thyme, bay leaves and remaining salt and pepper. Combine broth and wine; pour over vegetables.

3. Cover and cook on low for 6-8 hours or until meat and vegetables are tender. Skim fat. Discard bay leaves. If desired, thicken cooking juices.

Grilled Marinated Pork Tenderloin

My sister, who has always had a knack for tossing spices and ingredients together, introduced this dish to our family at a barbecue she hosted. She worked at the ingredients until she came up with a recipe she could proudly share with all of us.

—**LISA PETERS** DEWITT, NEW YORK

PREP: 15 MINUTES + MARINATING
GRILL: 25 MINUTES
MAKES: 6 SERVINGS (⅔ CUP SAUCE)

- ¾ **cup canola oil**
- ½ **cup soy sauce**
- ¼ **cup white vinegar**
- 2 **tablespoons lemon juice**
- 2 **tablespoons Worcestershire sauce**
- 1 **tablespoon minced fresh parsley**
- 1 **garlic clove, minced**
- ¼ **teaspoon salt**
- ¼ **teaspoon pepper**
- 2 **pork tenderloins (1 pound each)**

MUSTARD SAUCE
- ½ **cup mayonnaise**
- 2 **tablespoons Dijon mustard**
- 2 **teaspoons prepared horseradish**
- 1 **teaspoon Worcestershire sauce**
- ⅛ **teaspoon crushed red pepper flakes, optional**

1. In a large resealable plastic bag, combine the first nine ingredients; add pork. Seal bag and turn to coat; refrigerate overnight.

2. Prepare grill for indirect heat. Drain and discard marinade. Moisten a paper towel with cooking oil; using long-handled tongs, lightly coat the grill rack.

3. Grill pork, covered, over indirect medium-hot heat for 25-40 minutes or until a thermometer reads 160°. Let stand for 5 minutes before slicing.

4. In a small bowl, combine the sauce ingredients; serve with pork.

Donna Lasagna

My traditional lasagna is a real crowd-pleaser. With ground beef, Italian sausage, a from-scratch tomato sauce and rich cheeses, it's hearty and delicious. I get lots of compliments when I put together and share this wonderful dish.

—DONNA PATTERSON DAVENPORT, IOWA

PREP: 40 MINUTES **BAKE:** 1 HOUR + STANDING **MAKES:** 12 SERVINGS

1 pound lean ground beef (90% lean)
8 ounces mild or hot Italian sausage
1 can (15 ounces) tomato puree
2 cans (6 ounces each) tomato paste
3 tablespoons dried parsley flakes, divided
2 tablespoons sugar
1 tablespoon dried basil
1½ teaspoons salt, divided
1 garlic clove, minced
2 eggs, lightly beaten
3 cups (24 ounces) cream-style cottage cheese
½ cup grated Parmesan cheese
½ teaspoon pepper
9 lasagna noodles, cooked and drained
4 cups (16 ounces) shredded part-skim mozzarella cheese

1. In a Dutch oven, cook beef and sausage over medium heat until no longer pink; drain. Add the tomato puree, tomato paste, 1 tablespoon parsley, sugar, basil, 1 teaspoon salt and garlic. Bring to a boil. Reduce heat; simmer, uncovered, for 30 minutes.

2. In a large bowl, combine the eggs, cottage cheese, Parmesan cheese, pepper, and the remaining parsley and salt.

3. Spread ½ cup meat mixture in a greased 13-in. x 9-in. baking dish. Layer with three noodles, a third of the cheese mixture, 1⅓ cups mozzarella cheese and a third of remaining meat sauce. Repeat layers twice.

4. Bake at 350° for 1 hour or until a thermometer reads 160°. Let stand for 15 minutes before cutting.

½ teaspoon pepper
2 tablespoons olive oil
1 large sweet onion, quartered
1 can (10½ ounces) condensed beef consomme, undiluted
2 tablespoons Worcestershire sauce
1 tablespoon stone-ground mustard
1 bay leaf
3 to 4 drops browning sauce, optional
½ pound sliced fresh mushrooms
1 bottle (12 ounces) light beer or nonalcoholic beer
1 teaspoon dried thyme
3 tablespoons cornstarch
3 tablespoons cold water

1. With a sharp knife, cut six 1-in.-long slits in meat; insert a garlic clove half into each slit. Combine the brown sugar, salt and pepper; rub over roast.

2. In an ovenproof Dutch oven, brown roast in oil on all sides. Add the onion, beef consomme, Worcestershire sauce, mustard, bay leaf and browning sauce if desired.

3. Cover and bake at 350° for 1¾ to 2¼ hours or until meat is tender. Remove roast to a serving platter; keep warm.

4. Discard bay leaf. Add the mushrooms, beer and thyme to the pan. Bring to a boil. Cook until liquid is reduced by half. Combine cornstarch and water until smooth; gradually stir into pan. Bring to a boil; cook and stir for 2 minutes or until thickened. Serve with roast.

Home Style COOKING NOTES

Country Chuck Roast with Mushroom Gravy

My tender, savory beef roast practically melts in your mouth. The recipe looks a little complex, but the hands-free oven time makes it my go-to company recipe on chilly winter days.

—**MARY KAY LABRIE** CLERMONT, FLORIDA

PREP: 30 MINUTES **COOK:** 1¾ HOURS **MAKES:** 8 SERVINGS

1 boneless beef chuck roast (2½ to 3 pounds)
3 garlic cloves, halved
1 tablespoon brown sugar
1½ teaspoons kosher salt

Applesauce Meatballs

These savory homemade meatballs are always well-received. Folks really like the tangy sauce that showcases hot pepper sauce to give the meatballs a little kick.

—**BETSY SMITH** SAN DIEGO, CALIFORNIA

PREP: 30 MINUTES **BAKE:** 45 MINUTES
MAKES: 4 SERVINGS

- 1   egg, lightly beaten
- ½   cup unsweetened applesauce
- 1   cup soft bread crumbs
- 1   teaspoon salt
- ¼   teaspoon pepper
- 1   pound ground beef

SAUCE

- 1   can (10¾ ounces) condensed tomato soup, undiluted
- ¼   cup water
- ½   teaspoon sugar
- ½   teaspoon prepared horseradish
- 3   to 5 drops Worcestershire sauce
- 3   to 5 drops hot pepper sauce

1. In a large bowl, combine the first five ingredients. Crumble beef over mixture and mix well. Shape into 1½-in. balls. In a large skillet, gently brown meatballs over medium heat; drain. Transfer to an ungreased 2-qt. baking dish.

2. Combine sauce ingredients; pour over meatballs. Cover and bake at 325° for 45-50 minutes or until meat is no longer pink.

Chicken Spaghetti Casserole

Here's a creamy, cheesy casserole that makes second helpings a must!

—**LYNNE GERMAN** CUMMING, GEORGIA

PREP: 25 MINUTES **BAKE:** 25 MINUTES
MAKES: 6 SERVINGS

- 8   ounces uncooked spaghetti, broken into 3-inch pieces
- 3   cups cubed cooked chicken
- 1   can (10¾ ounces) condensed cream of chicken soup, undiluted
- 1   medium onion, chopped
- 1   cup 2% milk
- 1   cup (4 ounces) shredded sharp cheddar cheese, divided
- 1   cup (4 ounces) shredded Swiss cheese, divided
- 1   can (4 ounces) mushroom stems and pieces, drained
- ½   cup chopped roasted sweet red peppers
- 3   tablespoons mayonnaise
- 1½   teaspoons steak seasoning
- ½   teaspoon dried basil

1. Cook spaghetti according to package directions. Meanwhile, in a large bowl, combine the chicken, soup, onion, milk, ½ cup cheddar cheese, ½ cup Swiss cheese, mushrooms, peppers, mayonnaise, steak seasoning and basil.

2. Drain spaghetti. Add to chicken mixture; toss to coat. Transfer to a greased 13-in. x 9-in. baking dish. Cover and bake at 350° for 20 minutes. Uncover; sprinkle with remaining cheeses. Bake 5-10 minutes longer or until heated through and cheese is melted.

Editor's Note: *This recipe was tested with McCormick's Montreal Steak Seasoning. Look for it in the spice aisle.*

Mashed Potato Sausage Bake

Smoked sausage and zesty seasonings like onion and garlic taste great in this casserole. It's especially satisfying during the colder months.

—JENNIFER SEEVERS NORTH BEND, OREGON

PREP: 35 MINUTES **BAKE:** 10 MINUTES **MAKES:** 5 SERVINGS

- 5 **medium potatoes, peeled and quartered**
- ½ **cup reduced-fat sour cream**
- ¼ **cup reduced-sodium chicken broth**
- 1 **package (14 ounces) smoked turkey kielbasa, sliced**
- ½ **pound sliced fresh mushrooms**
- 1 **cup chopped onion**
- 1 **garlic clove, minced**
- ¼ **cup shredded reduced-fat cheddar cheese**
- 1 **teaspoon dried parsley flakes**
- 1 **teaspoon dried oregano**

1. Place potatoes in a large saucepan; cover with water. Bring to a boil. Reduce heat; cover and simmer for 20-25 minutes or until very tender; drain.

2. Transfer to a large bowl. Add sour cream and broth; beat on low speed until smooth; set aside. In a large skillet, cook the sausage, mushrooms and onion until vegetables are tender. Add garlic; cook 1 minute longer.

3. Spread half of the potato mixture into a 9-in. x 5-in. loaf pan coated with cooking spray. Top with sausage mixture and remaining potatoes. Sprinkle with the cheese, parsley and oregano.

4. Bake, uncovered, at 350° for 10-15 minutes or until cheese is melted.

Pear 'n' Prosciutto Pork Loin

Slightly sweet roast pork is magnificent served on a bed of mesclun with fresh goat cheese and roasted veggies. If prosciutto is unavailable, use thin deli ham in the stuffing.

—ANTHONY GUAETTA PEABODY, MASSACHUSETTS

PREP: 50 MINUTES **BAKE:** 1½ HOURS + STANDING **MAKES:** 12 SERVINGS

- 1 **bottle (750 milliliters) sweet white wine**
- 2 **cups water**
- 2 **cups sugar**
- 2 **tablespoons ground ginger**
- 2 **cinnamon sticks (3 inches)**
- 3 **whole cloves**
- 4 **medium Bosc pears, peeled and quartered**
- 1 **boneless pork loin roast (3 to 4 pounds)**
- ¾ **teaspoon salt, divided**
- ½ **teaspoon pepper, divided**
- 8 **thin slices prosciutto (about 4 ounces)**
- ¼ **cup butter, cubed**

1. In a saucepan, combine the wine, water, sugar, ginger, cinnamon sticks and cloves; bring to a boil. Reduce heat; simmer, uncovered, for 10 minutes. Add pears; cover and simmer for 15-20 minutes or until tender.

2. Using a slotted spoon, carefully remove pears and cool to room temperature. Continue to simmer poaching liquid, uncovered, for 15-25 minutes or until reduced to 2 cups. Remove and discard cinnamon sticks and cloves. Set liquid aside.

3. Cut a lengthwise slit down center of roast to within ½ in. of bottom. Open roast so it lies flat; cover with plastic wrap. Flatten to ¾-in. thickness. Remove plastic; sprinkle the meat with ½ teaspoon salt and ¼ teaspoon pepper. Top with prosciutto and pears. Roll up jelly-roll style, starting with a long side; tie roast with kitchen string.

4. Place in a shallow roasting pan lined with heavy-duty foil. Bake, uncovered, at 350° for 1½ to 2 hours or until a thermometer reads 160°. Cover and let stand 10-15 minutes before slicing.

5. Add remaining salt and pepper to poaching liquid and bring to a boil. Reduce heat; simmer, uncovered, for 5 minutes. Stir in butter until melted. Serve with meat.

Herbed Beef Stew with Puff Pastry

Guests will be so surprised by the beautiful presentation of homemade beef stew. Puff pastry makes a fancy (yet easy) crust.

—SARA MARTIN BROOKFIELD, WISCONSIN

PREP: 1¼ HOURS **BAKE:** 30 MINUTES **MAKES:** 6 SERVINGS

- 1 **pound beef stew meat, cut into 1-inch cubes**
- 1 **tablespoon canola oil**
- 3 **medium carrots, cut into 1-inch pieces**
- 1 **to 2 medium red potatoes, cut into 1-inch pieces**
- 1 **cup sliced celery (½-inch pieces)**
- ½ **cup chopped onion**
- 1 **garlic clove, minced**
- 2 **cans (10½ ounces each) condensed beef broth, undiluted**
- 1 **can (14½ ounces) diced tomatoes, undrained**
- 1 **teaspoon each dried parsley flakes, thyme and marjoram**
- ¼ **teaspoon pepper**
- 2 **bay leaves**
- 1 **cup cubed peeled butternut squash**
- 3 **tablespoons quick-cooking tapioca**
- 1 **to 2 packages (17.3 ounces each) frozen puff pastry, thawed**
- 1 **egg yolk**
- ¼ **cup heavy whipping cream**

1. In a Dutch oven, brown the beef in oil; drain. Stir in the carrots, potatoes, celery, onion, garlic, broth, tomatoes and seasonings.

2. Bring to a boil. Reduce heat; cover and simmer for 1 hour or until meat is almost tender. Discard bay leaves. Stir in squash and tapioca; return to a boil. Cook for 5 minutes. Remove from the heat; let cool for 10 minutes.

3. Meanwhile, on a lightly floured surface, roll out puff pastry to ¼-in. thickness. Using a 10-oz. ramekin for a pattern, cut out six pastry circles 1 in. larger than the diameter of the ramekin.

4. Fill six greased 10-oz. ramekins with beef mixture; top each with a pastry circle. Seal pastry to edges of ramekins; cut slits in each pastry. If desired, use the pastry scraps to cut out 30 strips. Twist strips; place five strips on each ramekin. Pinch edges to seal. Combine egg yolk and cream; brush over tops.

5. Place on a baking sheet. Bake at 400° for 30-35 minutes or until golden brown. Let stand for 5 minutes before serving.

Home Style COOKING NOTES

Turkey Wild Rice Casserole

Here's a sensational meal in one. The wild rice mixture bakes in the same dish as the turkey tenderloins, which makes serving and clean-up a breeze.

—LOIS KINNEBERG PHOENIX, ARIZONA

PREP: 1 HOUR **BAKE:** 1 HOUR
MAKES: 6 SERVINGS

- 3 cups water
- 1 cup uncooked wild rice
- ½ cup chopped onion
- ½ cup chopped carrot
- ½ cup chopped celery
- 1 tablespoon butter
- 1 tablespoon canola oil
- 3 tablespoons all-purpose flour
- ½ teaspoon rubbed sage
- ½ teaspoon salt, divided
- ⅛ teaspoon pepper
- ¾ cup reduced-sodium chicken broth
- ½ cup fat-free milk
- 2 turkey breast tenderloins (¾ pound each)
- 1 teaspoon dried parsley
- ⅛ teaspoon paprika

1. In a saucepan, bring the water, wild rice and onion to a boil. Reduce heat; cover and simmer for 55-60 minutes or until rice is tender. Meanwhile, in another saucepan, saute carrot and celery in butter and oil until tender.
2. Combine the flour, sage, ¼ teaspoon salt and pepper; stir into carrot mixture until blended. Gradually add broth and milk. Bring to a boil; cook and stir for 1 minute or until thickened. Remove from the heat. Stir in rice. Transfer to a 2-qt. baking dish coated with cooking spray.
3. Place turkey over rice mixture. Combine the parsley, paprika and remaining salt; sprinkle over turkey.
4. Cover casserole and bake at 350° for 60-70 minutes or until a thermometer inserted in turkey reads 170°. Slice turkey; serve with rice.

Family-Favorite Spaghetti Sauce

My friend Mary shared the wonderful recipe for spaghetti sauce that's become an annual tradition at our campers' potluck.

—HELEN ROWE SPRING LAKE, MICHIGAN

PREP: 30 MINUTES **COOK:** 6 HOURS **MAKES:** 9 SERVINGS (2¼ QUARTS)

- 1 pound bulk Italian sausage
- ½ pound ground beef
- 1 large onion, chopped
- 1 celery rib, chopped
- 3 garlic cloves, minced
- 1 tablespoon olive oil
- 1 can (28 ounces) diced tomatoes
- 1 can (10¾ ounces) condensed tomato soup, undiluted
- 1 can (8 ounces) mushroom stems and pieces, drained
- 1 can (8 ounces) tomato sauce
- 1 can (6 ounces) tomato paste
- 1 tablespoon sugar
- ½ teaspoon pepper
- ½ teaspoon dried basil
- ¼ teaspoon dried oregano
  Hot cooked spaghetti

1. In a large skillet, cook the sausage, beef, onion, celery and garlic in oil over medium heat until meat is no longer pink; drain. In a 4-qt. slow cooker, combine the diced tomatoes, tomato soup, mushrooms, tomato sauce, tomato paste, sugar and seasonings. Stir in sausage mixture.
2. Cover and cook on low for 6-8 hours or until flavors are blended. Serve sauce with spaghetti.

Savory Rubbed Roast Chicken

A blend of paprika, onion powder, garlic and cayenne go on the skin and inside the cavity to create a delicious, slightly spicy roast chicken. The aroma of this dish while it's cooking drives my family nuts.

—MARGARET COLE IMPERIAL, MISSOURI

PREP: 20 MINUTES **BAKE:** 2 HOURS + STANDING **MAKES:** 8 SERVINGS

- 2 **teaspoons paprika**
- 1 **teaspoon salt**
- 1 **teaspoon onion powder**
- 1 **teaspoon dried thyme**
- 1 **teaspoon white pepper**
- 1 **teaspoon cayenne pepper**
- ¾ **teaspoon garlic powder**
- ½ **teaspoon pepper**
- 1 **roasting chicken (6 to 7 pounds)**
- 1 **large onion, peeled and quartered**

1. In a small bowl, combine the seasonings; set aside. Place chicken breast side up on a rack in a shallow roasting pan; pat dry. Tuck wings under chicken; tie drumsticks together. Rub seasoning mixture over the outside and inside of chicken. Place onion inside cavity.

2. Bake, uncovered, at 350° for 2 to 2½ hours or until a thermometer inserted in the thigh reads 180°, basting occasionally with pan drippings. (Cover loosely with foil if chicken browns too quickly.) Cover and let stand for 15 minutes before carving.

Ham and Creamy Potato Scallops

Everyone loves rich and cheesy scalloped potatoes. This dish is my own creation—it's a combination of three different recipes! Besides tasting good, it's foolproof to make. The ingredients won't separate during baking.

—MABEL COURTNEY WAUSEON, OHIO

PREP: 25 MINUTES **BAKE:** 50 MINUTES **MAKES:** 12 SERVINGS

5 **pounds medium potatoes**
3 **tablespoons butter**
¼ **cup all-purpose flour**
1 **can (14½ ounces) chicken broth**
1 **pound diced fully cooked ham**
1 **cup process cheese sauce**
½ **cup sliced celery**
¼ **cup chopped onion**
¼ **cup mayonnaise**
Salt and pepper to taste

1. Place potatoes in a Dutch oven and cover with water. Bring to a boil. Reduce heat; cover and cook for 20-25 minutes or until partially cooked. Drain and cool potatoes. Peel and cut into ¼-in. slices. Spread in greased 3-qt. baking dish.

2. In large saucepan, melt butter. Stir in flour until smooth; add the broth. Bring to a boil. Cook and stir for 1-2 minutes or until thickened and bubbly. Remove from the heat. Stir in the remaining ingredients. Pour over potatoes and toss gently to coat.

3. Bake, uncovered, at 350° for 50-60 minutes or until potatoes are tender.

Caramelized Onion Chuck Roast

Wonderfully fork-tender, this tasty roast with sweet onions makes the perfect comfort food at the end of a long day.

—**JEANNIE KLUGH** LANCASTER, PENNSYLVANIA

PREP: 25 MINUTES **COOK:** 8 HOURS **MAKES:** 8 SERVINGS

- 1 **cup water**
- 1 **cup beer or beef broth**
- ½ **cup beef broth**
- ¼ **cup packed brown sugar**
- 3 **tablespoons Dijon mustard**
- 2 **tablespoons cider vinegar**
- 1 **boneless beef chuck roast (4 pounds), trimmed**
- 1 **teaspoon onion salt**
- 1 **teaspoon coarsely ground pepper**
- 1 **tablespoon olive oil**
- 3 **large sweet onions, halved and sliced**
- 2 **tablespoons cornstarch**
- 2 **tablespoons cold water**

1. In a large bowl, combine the first six ingredients; set aside. Sprinkle roast with onion salt and pepper. In a large skillet, brown meat in oil on all sides. Place onions and roast in a 5-qt. slow cooker; pour beer mixture over top. Cover and cook on low for 8-10 hours or until meat is tender.

2. Remove roast and onions and keep warm. Skim fat from cooking juices; transfer 2 cups to a small saucepan. Bring liquid to a boil. Combine cornstarch and water until smooth; gradually stir into the pan. Bring to a boil; cook and stir for 2 minutes or until thickened.

Chicken Potpie

Chicken potpie was a favorite childhood food, but my mother never wrote the recipe down. After some trial and error, I came up with a version that tastes just like hers!

—**BRENDA SAWATZKY** NIVERVILLE, MANITOBA

PREP: 20 MINUTES **BAKE:** 45 MINUTES
MAKES: 6 SERVINGS

- 1 **cup chopped celery**
- ¼ **cup chopped onion**
- 2 **tablespoons butter**
- 2¼ **cups water, divided**
- 1½ **cups diced cooked chicken**
- 1 **cup frozen mixed vegetables**
- ¾ **cup uncooked thin egg noodles**
- 1 **tablespoon chicken bouillon granules**
- ¼ **teaspoon pepper**
- 2 **tablespoons cornstarch**
  Pastry for single-crust pie (10 inches)

1. In a medium saucepan, saute celery and onion in butter until tender. Add 2 cups water, chicken, vegetables, noodles, bouillon and pepper. Cook, uncovered, over medium heat for 5 minutes or just until noodles are tender, stirring occasionally.

2. Combine cornstarch and remaining water; add to saucepan. Bring to a boil. Reduce heat; cook and stir for 2 minutes or until thickened and bubbly.

3. Pour into an ungreased 10 in. pie plate. Roll out pastry to fit plate; place over filling. Cut several 1-in. slits in the top.

4. Bake at 350° for 45-55 minutes or until browned. Let stand 5 minutes before serving.

Home Style COOKING NOTES

Company's Coming Turkey

My turkey recipe accomplishes every cook's wish—a bird that brings the flavor of seasonings and herbs in every bite. It's the perfect centerpiece for your celebration, and it's very easy to prepare.

—CAROLINE WAMELINK
CLEVELAND HEIGHTS, OHIO

PREP: 20 MINUTES **BAKE:** 3½ HOURS + STANDING
MAKES: 14 SERVINGS

- 8 **tablespoons butter, softened, divided**
- 3 **garlic cloves, minced**
- 1 **tablespoon poultry seasoning**
- 1 **tablespoon minced fresh rosemary**
- 1 **tablespoon minced fresh thyme**
- 1 **turkey (14 to 16 pounds)**
- ¾ **teaspoon salt**
- ¾ **teaspoon pepper**
- 3 **large onions, quartered, divided**
- 3 **garlic cloves**
- 2 **fresh rosemary sprigs**
- 2 **fresh thyme sprigs**
- 2 **cans (14½ ounces each) chicken broth**
- 3 **cups white wine or additional chicken broth**
- 3 **celery ribs, cut into 2-inch pieces**
- 3 **medium carrots, cut into 2-inch pieces**

1. In a small bowl, combine 5 tablespoons butter, minced garlic, poultry seasoning and minced rosemary and thyme. With fingers, carefully loosen skin from the turkey breast; rub butter mixture under the skin. Rub remaining butter over skin of turkey. Sprinkle salt and pepper over turkey and inside cavity.
2. Place two onions, garlic cloves and rosemary and thyme sprigs inside the cavity. Place turkey on a rack in a large shallow roasting pan. Pour broth and wine into pan. Add celery, carrots and remaining onion.
3. Bake, uncovered, at 325° for 3½ to 4 hours or until a thermometer reads 180°, basting occasionally. Cover loosely with foil if turkey browns too quickly. Cover and let stand for 20 minutes before slicing. If desired, thicken pan drippings for gravy.

Big Daddy's BBQ Ribs

There's nothing left on the platter when I make these for the guys at work. The spices and brown sugar make an excellent rub.

—ERIC BRZOSTEK EAST ISLIP, NEW YORK

PREP: 30 MINUTES + CHILLING **BAKE:** 1½ HOURS **MAKES:** 8 SERVINGS

- ¾ **cup packed brown sugar**
- 2 **tablespoons mesquite seasoning**
- 4½ **teaspoons garlic powder**
- 4½ **teaspoons paprika**
- 1 **tablespoon dried minced onion**
- 1 **tablespoon seasoned salt**
- 1 **tablespoon ground cinnamon**
- 1 **tablespoon ground cumin**
- 1 **tablespoon pepper**
- 1 **teaspoon salt**
- 8 **pounds pork spareribs, cut into serving size pieces**
- 3½ **cups barbecue sauce**

1. In a small bowl, combine the first 10 ingredients. Rub over ribs; cover and refrigerate overnight.
2. Place ribs bone side down on a rack in a shallow roasting pan. Cover and bake at 350° for 1 hour; drain. Brush some of the barbecue sauce over ribs. Bake, uncovered, for 30-45 minutes or until tender, basting occasionally with barbecue sauce.

Crusted Baked Chicken

Moist and tender on the inside and crispy on the outside, my recipe is like fried chicken without the work or mess.

—BILL EGAN BURLINGTON, MASSACHUSETTS

PREP: 20 MINUTES + STANDING **BAKE:** 55 MINUTES **MAKES:** 6 SERVINGS

- 1 **cup dry bread crumbs**
- 1 **tablespoon seafood seasoning**
- ½ **teaspoon garlic salt**
- ½ **teaspoon Creole seasoning**
- ½ **teaspoon dried basil**
- ½ **teaspoon dried oregano**
- ½ **teaspoon dried thyme**
- ⅛ **teaspoon pepper**
- ¾ **cup buttermilk**
- ½ **cup all-purpose flour**
- 1 **broiler/fryer chicken (4 to 5 pounds), cut up**
- 1 **tablespoon butter, melted**

1. In a shallow bowl, combine the first eight ingredients. Place buttermilk and flour in separate shallow bowls. Coat chicken with flour, then dip in buttermilk and coat with crumb mixture. Place in a greased 15-in. x 10-in. x 1-in. baking pan. Let stand for 10 minutes.

2. Bake, uncovered, at 350° for 45 minutes. Drizzle with butter. Bake 10-15 minutes longer or until juices run clear.

Editor's Note: *The following spices may be substituted for 1 teaspoon Creole seasoning: ¼ teaspoon each salt, garlic powder and paprika; and a pinch each of dried thyme, ground cumin and cayenne pepper.*

When creating the pockets in the pork chops, use a paring knife to make a slit in the chop's fatty side. Cut almost to the other side but not through to the bone. Spoon stuffing mixture into the pocket and secure the opening with toothpicks.

Stuffing-Stuffed Pork Chops

You'll want to make stuffing more often once you try these elegant pork chops. Just a few ingredients give them such fabulous flavor!

—TASTE OF HOME TEST KITCHEN

PREP: 30 MINUTES **BAKE:** 25 MINUTES
MAKES: 4 SERVINGS

  4 **bone-in pork loin chops (8 ounces each)**
  2 **cups cooked stuffing**
  ¼ **teaspoon pepper**
  1 **tablespoon canola oil**
  2 **garlic cloves, minced**
  ¼ **teaspoon dried thyme**
  ½ **cup white wine or chicken broth**
  2 **tablespoons all-purpose flour**
  ¾ **cup chicken broth**

1. Cut a pocket in each chop by slicing almost to the bone. Fill each chop with ½ cup stuffing; secure with toothpicks if necessary. Sprinkle with pepper.

2. In a large ovenproof skillet, brown chops in oil. Bake, uncovered, at 350° for 25-30 minutes or until a thermometer reads 160°. Remove pork chops and set aside. Keep warm.

3. In the same skillet, cook garlic and thyme in pan drippings over medium heat for 1 minute. Add wine, stirring to loosen browned bits from pan. In a small bowl, combine flour and broth until smooth. Gradually add to pan. Bring to a boil; cook and stir for 2 minutes or until thickened.

4. Remove toothpicks from pork chops; serve chops with gravy.

Meatball Stew

My stew recipe is chock-full of tender meatballs and veggies. It's sure to warm you up when there's an autumn chill in the air.
—JOAN CHASSE BERLIN, CONNECTICUT

PREP: 1 HOUR **COOK:** 30 MINUTES **MAKES:** 10 SERVINGS (2½ QUARTS)

   3 **eggs, lightly beaten**
   ⅔ **cup seasoned bread crumbs**
   ⅓ **cup grated Parmesan cheese**
       Dash pepper
   ½ **pound each ground beef, pork and veal**
   4 **medium potatoes, peeled and cubed**
   3 **medium carrots, sliced**
   1½ **cups chopped celery**
   1 **medium onion, cut into wedges**
   1 **garlic clove, minced**
   1 **envelope onion soup mix**
   2¼ **cups water**
   1 **cup frozen peas**
   4½ **teaspoons minced fresh parsley**

1. In a large bowl, combine the eggs, bread crumbs, cheese and pepper. Crumble beef, pork and veal over mixture and mix well. Shape into 1½-in. balls.
2. Place meatballs on a greased rack in a shallow baking pan. Bake at 350° for 20-25 minutes or until no longer pink.
3. Place the meatballs, potatoes, carrots, celery, onion and garlic in a Dutch oven. In a small bowl, combine soup mix and water; pour over meatball mixture. Bring to a boil. Reduce heat; cover and simmer for 25-30 minutes or until vegetables are tender. Stir in peas and parsley; heat through.

Braised Short Ribs

Very hearty and very delicious is how I describe these ribs. I sometimes finish them in a slow cooker for 8-10 hours on low, instead of baking.

—SUSAN KINSELLA
EAST FALMOUTH, MASSACHUSETTS

PREP: 30 MINUTES **BAKE:** 1½ HOURS
MAKES: 8 SERVINGS

   4 **pounds bone-in beef short ribs**
   1 **teaspoon pepper, divided**
   ½ **teaspoon salt**
   3 **tablespoons canola oil**
   3 **celery ribs, chopped**
   2 **large carrots, chopped**
   1 **large yellow onion, chopped**
   1 **medium sweet red pepper, chopped**
   1 **garlic clove, minced**
   1 **cup dry red wine or reduced-sodium beef broth**
   4 **cups reduced-sodium beef broth**
   1 **fresh rosemary sprig**
   1 **fresh oregano sprig**
   1 **bay leaf**

1. Sprinkle ribs with ½ teaspoon pepper and salt. In an ovenproof Dutch oven, brown ribs in oil in batches. Remove and set aside.
2. In the drippings, saute the celery, carrots, onion, red pepper and garlic until tender. Add wine, stirring to loosen browned bits from the pan. Bring to a boil; cook until liquid is reduced by half.
3. Return ribs to the pan. Add broth and remaining pepper; bring to a boil. Place rosemary, oregano and bay leaf on a double thickness of cheesecloth; bring up corners of cloth and tie with kitchen string to form a bag. Add to Dutch oven.
4. Cover and bake at 325° for 1½ to 2 hours or until meat is tender.
5. Remove ribs and keep warm. Discard herb bag. Skim fat from pan juices; thicken if desired.

Crunch Top Ham and Potato Casserole

Hash browns, ham and cheese make a dish that's sure to satisfy the whole family. You'll love that it preps in just 10 minutes!

—**NANCY SCHMIDT** DELHI, CALIFORNIA

PREP: 10 MINUTES **BAKE:** 1 HOUR
MAKES: 10 SERVINGS

- 1 package (32 ounces) frozen cubed hash brown potatoes, thawed
- 2 cups cubed cooked ham
- 2 cups (16 ounces) sour cream
- 1½ cups (6 ounces) shredded cheddar cheese
- 1 can (10¾ ounces) condensed cream of chicken soup, undiluted
- ½ cup butter, melted
- ⅓ cup chopped green onions
- ½ teaspoon pepper

TOPPING
- 2 cups crushed cornflakes
- ¼ cup butter, melted

1. In a large bowl, combine the first eight ingredients. Transfer to a greased 13-in. x 9-in. baking dish. Combine the topping ingredients; sprinkle over top.
2. Bake, uncovered, at 350° for 1 hour or until heated through.

Home Style COOKING NOTES

Satisfying Beef Stew

This stew is so hearty and tastes even better the next day—if there are any leftovers! It goes great with fresh hot bread.

—**ABBEY MUELLER** ENID, OKLAHOMA

PREP: 30 MINUTES **COOK:** 6 HOURS **MAKES:** 8 SERVINGS

- 2 pounds beef stew meat, cut into 1-inch cubes
- 1 medium onion, chopped
- 2 tablespoons canola oil
- 2 cups water
- ¼ cup all-purpose flour
- 3 medium carrots, sliced
- 3 medium potatoes, peeled and cubed
- 2 cups frozen corn
- 1½ cups frozen cut green beans
- 1 can (15 ounces) Italian tomato sauce
- 2 teaspoons Worcestershire sauce
- 1 teaspoon salt
- 1 teaspoon paprika
- 1 teaspoon pepper
  Dash ground cloves
- 2 bay leaves

1. In a large skillet, brown the beef and onion in oil; drain. Transfer to a 5-qt. slow cooker. Combine water and flour; pour over beef. Stir in the remaining ingredients.
2. Cover and cook on low for 6-8 hours or until meat and vegetables are tender. Discard bay leaves.

Hearty Shepherd's Pie

Fresh rosemary adds great flavor to the convenience products used in a comforting shepherd's pie. Great on cold days, it makes a filling meal served with slices of corn bread.

—MELISSA HASS GILBERT, SOUTH CAROLINA

PREP: 35 MINUTES **BAKE:** 20 MINUTES **MAKES:** 6 SERVINGS

- 1 **pound lean ground beef (90% lean)**
- 1 **medium onion, chopped**
- 1 **can (10¾ ounces) condensed cream of celery soup, undiluted**
- 1 **can (8½ ounces) peas and carrots, drained**
- 1 **jar (4½ ounces) sliced mushrooms, drained**
- ¼ **cup water**
- 1 **tablespoon minced fresh rosemary or 1 teaspoon dried rosemary, crushed**
- 1 **teaspoon garlic powder, divided**
- ½ **teaspoon salt**
- ¼ **teaspoon pepper**
- 2 **cups prepared instant mashed potatoes**
- 1 **package (3 ounces) cream cheese, softened and cubed**
- ¼ **cup sour cream**
- ¼ **cup grated Parmesan cheese**

1. In a large skillet, cook beef and onion over medium heat until meat is no longer pink; drain. Stir in the soup, peas and carrots, mushrooms, water, rosemary, ½ teaspoon garlic powder, salt and pepper; heat through. Transfer to a greased 9-in. deep-dish pie plate.

2. In a large bowl, beat the mashed potatoes, cream cheese, sour cream and remaining garlic powder until blended. Spread over top of pie. Sprinkle with Parmesan cheese.

3. Bake, uncovered, at 350° for 20-25 minutes or until heated through and potatoes are lightly browned.

Jambalaya

My family has enjoyed this delicious Cajun specialty for many years.

—LIZZIE H. WHITTEN OAK GROVE, LOUISIANA

PREP: 25 MINUTES **BAKE:** 1 HOUR **MAKES:** 8 SERVINGS

12 small pork sausage links, cut into 1-inch pieces
1 cup finely chopped onion
1 cup finely chopped green pepper
4 garlic cloves, minced
2 tablespoons canola oil
1½ cups cubed cooked chicken
1½ cups cubed fully cooked ham
1 can (28 ounces) diced tomatoes, undrained
1 cup uncooked long-grain rice
1 can (14½ ounces) chicken broth
3 tablespoons minced fresh parsley
1 teaspoon salt
½ to 1 teaspoon pepper
½ to ¾ teaspoon dried thyme

1. In a large heavy skillet, saute the sausage, onion, green pepper and garlic in oil until vegetables are tender. Add chicken and ham; cook for 5 minutes. Stir in the remaining ingredients.

2. Transfer to a 2-qt. baking dish. Cover and bake at 350° for 1 hour or until rice is tender and liquid is absorbed.

Crumb-Crusted Pork Roast with Root Vegetables

Perfect for fall, this hearty meal combines sweet roasted veggies and pork with a savory crumb coating.

—TASTE OF HOME TEST KITCHEN

PREP: 25 MINUTES **BAKE:** 1½ HOURS + STANDING **MAKES:** 8 SERVINGS

- 1 boneless pork loin roast (2 to 3 pounds)
- 4½ teaspoons honey
- 1 tablespoon molasses
- 1½ teaspoons spicy brown mustard
- 2 teaspoons rubbed sage
- 1 teaspoon dried thyme
- 1 teaspoon dried rosemary, crushed
- ½ cup soft whole wheat bread crumbs
- 2 tablespoons grated Parmesan cheese
- 1 large celery root, peeled and cut into ½-inch cubes
- 1 large rutabaga, peeled and cut into ½-inch cubes
- 1 large sweet potato, peeled and cut into ½-inch cubes
- 1 large onion, cut into wedges
- 2 tablespoons canola oil
- ½ teaspoon salt
- ¼ teaspoon pepper

1. Place roast on a rack in a shallow roasting pan coated with cooking spray. In a small bowl, combine the honey, molasses and mustard; brush over roast. In another small bowl, combine the sage, thyme and rosemary; set aside. Combine the bread crumbs, Parmesan cheese and 2 teaspoons of the herb mixture; press onto roast.

2. In a resealable plastic bag, combine the celery root, rutabaga, sweet potato, onion, oil, salt, pepper and remaining herb mixture; toss to coat. Arrange vegetables around roast.

3. Bake, uncovered, at 350° for 1½ to 1¾ hours or until a thermometer reads 160°. Transfer to a warm serving platter. Let stand for 10-15 minutes before slicing.

Horseradish-Encrusted Beef Tenderloin

Wow friends and family with tender beef encased in a golden horseradish crust. Roasted garlic boosts the mouthwatering flavor even more.

—LAURA BAGOZZI DUBLIN, OHIO

PREP: 30 MINUTES + COOLING
BAKE: 45 MINUTES + STANDING
MAKES: 8 SERVINGS

- 1 whole garlic bulb
- 1 teaspoon olive oil
- ⅓ cup prepared horseradish
- ¼ teaspoon salt
- ¼ teaspoon dried basil
- ¼ teaspoon dried thyme
- ¼ teaspoon pepper
- ⅓ cup soft bread crumbs
- 1 beef tenderloin roast (3 pounds)

1. Remove papery outer skin from garlic (do not peel or separate cloves). Cut top off garlic bulb; brush with oil. Wrap in heavy-duty foil. Bake at 425° for 30-35 minutes or until softened. Cool for 10-15 minutes.

2. Squeeze softened garlic into a small bowl; stir in the horseradish, salt, basil, thyme and pepper. Add bread crumbs; toss to coat. Spread over top of tenderloin. Place on a rack in a large shallow roasting pan.

3. Bake at 400° for 45-55 minutes or until meat reaches desired doneness (for medium-rare, a thermometer should read 145°; medium, 160°; well-done, 170°). Let stand for 10 minutes before slicing.

Double Layered Souffle

This simple souffle bursts with flavor. The crispy topping of cheese hides a creamy layer of turkey underneath. If I don't have turkey on hand, I use chicken instead.

—**SHARON AMIDON** GUTHRIE, OKLAHOMA

PREP: 40 MINUTES **BAKE:** 1¼ HOURS
MAKES: 8 SERVINGS

6 eggs
¼ cup butter, cubed
1 cup chopped fresh mushrooms
¼ cup all-purpose flour
½ teaspoon salt
2 cups 2% milk
3 cups cubed cooked turkey breast

SOUFFLE LAYER
⅓ cup butter, cubed
1 shallot, finely chopped
⅓ cup all-purpose flour
½ teaspoon salt
1½ cups 2% milk
1 package (10 ounces) frozen chopped spinach, thawed and squeezed dry
1½ cups (6 ounces) shredded Swiss cheese

> **66** Room-temperature egg whites beat up fluffier than cold ones, producing a light and airy souffle. Beat egg whites just until they hold stiff peaks when the beaters are lifted. Stir a small portion into the souffle batter, then quickly and gently fold in the rest. Have your baking dish ready and the oven preheated so you can start baking right away. **99**
>
> **HOME STYLE tip**
>
> —**TASTE OF HOME TEST KITCHEN**

1. Separate eggs; let stand at room temperature for 30 minutes. Grease a 2½-qt. souffle dish and lightly sprinkle with flour; set aside.

2. In a large skillet over medium-high heat, melt butter. Add mushrooms; saute until tender. Stir in flour and salt until blended; gradually whisk in milk. Bring to a boil, stirring constantly; cook and stir for 2-3 minutes or until thickened. Add turkey; heat through. Transfer to prepared dish.

3. For souffle layer, in a small saucepan over medium-high heat, melt butter. Add shallot; saute until tender. Stir in flour and salt until blended; gradually whisk in milk. Bring to a boil, stirring constantly; cook and stir for 2-3 minutes or until thickened. Transfer to a large bowl; stir in spinach and cheese.

4. Stir a small amount of hot spinach mixture into egg yolks; return all to the bowl, stirring constantly. Allow to cool slightly.

5. In a large bowl with clean beaters, beat the egg whites until stiff peaks form. With a spatula, stir a fourth of the egg whites into spinach mixture until no white streaks remain. Fold in remaining egg whites until combined. Pour over turkey layer.

6. Bake at 325° for 1¼ to 1½ hours or until the top is puffed and center appears set. Serve immediately.

Cranberry-Gorgonzola Stuffed Chicken

Chicken breasts go from ordinary to extraordinary when filled with tart cranberries and creamy Gorgonzola. Serve it with couscous and a freshly tossed green salad.

—KARA FIRSTENBERGER CARDIFF, CALIFORNIA

PREP: 30 MINUTES **BAKE:** 35 MINUTES **MAKES:** 6 SERVINGS

- 6 **boneless skinless chicken breast halves (6 ounces each)**
- 1 **cup (4 ounces) crumbled Gorgonzola cheese**
- ½ **cup dried cranberries**
- ⅔ **cup chopped walnuts**
- ⅓ **cup packed fresh parsley sprigs**
- ⅔ **cup dry bread crumbs**
- ½ **teaspoon salt**
- ½ **teaspoon pepper**
- 2 **eggs**
- 1 **tablespoon Dijon mustard**
- ½ **cup all-purpose flour**

1. Flatten chicken to ¼-in. thickness. In a small bowl, combine cheese and cranberries. Spoon ¼ cup cheese mixture down the center of each chicken breast. Roll up and secure with toothpicks.

2. Place walnuts and parsley in a food processor, cover and process until ground. Transfer to a shallow bowl; stir in the bread crumbs, salt and pepper. In another shallow bowl, combine eggs and mustard. Place flour in a third shallow bowl. Coat chicken with flour, then dip in egg mixture and coat with walnut mixture.

3. Place seam side down in a greased 15-in. x 10-in. x 1-in. baking pan. Bake at 350° for 35-40 minutes or until a thermometer reads 170°. Discard toothpicks.

Glazed Corned Beef

Tender corned beef brisket is a wonderful treat for St. Patrick's Day. The tangy sauce is a perfect complement.

—PAT SCHMELING
GERMANTOWN, WISCONSIN

PREP: 2¾ HOURS
BAKE: 25 MINUTES + STANDING
MAKES: 12 SERVINGS

- 1 **corned beef brisket with spice packet (3 pounds), trimmed**
- 1 **medium onion, sliced**
- 1 **celery rib, sliced**
- ¼ **cup butter**
- 1 **cup packed brown sugar**
- ⅔ **cup ketchup**
- ⅓ **cup white vinegar**
- 2 **tablespoons prepared mustard**
- 2 **teaspoons prepared horseradish**

1. Place corned beef and contents of seasoning packet in a Dutch oven; cover with water. Add onion and celery. Bring to a boil. Reduce heat; cover and simmer for 2½ hours or until meat is tender.

2. Drain and discard liquid and vegetables. Place beef on a rack in a shallow roasting pan; set aside.

3. In a saucepan, melt butter over medium heat. Stir in the remaining ingredients. Cook and stir until sugar is dissolved. Brush over beef. Bake, uncovered, at 350° for 25 minutes. Let stand for 10 minutes before slicing.

Home Style COOKING NOTES

Flank Steak with Wine Sauce

For the best results, I like to serve this lean and tasty flank steak rare. Deglaze the pan with wine, making sure to scrape up all the savory browned bits with a wooden spoon.

—WARNER BEATTY NIAGARA FALLS, ONTARIO

PREP: 40 MINUTES + COOLING
COOK: 30 MINUTES
MAKES: 6 SERVINGS (¾ CUP SAUCE)

- 1 whole garlic bulb
- 1½ teaspoons olive oil, divided
- 1 beef flank steak (1½ pounds)
- 1 teaspoon coarsely ground pepper
- ¾ teaspoon salt
- 2 tablespoons butter, divided
- ½ cup reduced-sodium beef broth
- 1 cup dry red wine or ¼ cup grape juice and ¾ cup additional reduced-sodium beef broth
- ¼ cup thinly sliced green onions

1. Remove papery outer skin from garlic bulb (do not peel or separate cloves). Cut top off of garlic bulb; brush with ½ teaspoon oil. Wrap bulb in heavy-duty foil. Bake at 425° for 30-35 minutes or until softened. Cool for 10-15 minutes. Squeeze softened garlic into a small bowl; mash and set aside.

2. Sprinkle steak with pepper and salt. In a large nonstick skillet coated with cooking spray, cook steak over medium-high heat in remaining oil for 3-4 minutes on each side or until browned.

3. Reduce heat to medium; add 1 tablespoon butter. Cook steak 4-8 minutes longer on each side or until meat reaches desired doneness (for medium-rare, a thermometer should read 145°; medium, 160°; well-done, 170°). Remove and keep warm.

4. Gradually add broth and wine to the pan, stirring to loosen browned bits. Bring to a boil. Stir in mashed garlic. Reduce heat; simmer, uncovered, until liquid is reduced by half.

5. Strain sauce and return to pan; stir in remaining butter until melted. Thinly slice steak across the grain. Sprinkle with onions; serve with sauce.

Shrimp and Fontina Casserole

Looking for a seafood casserole that tastes gourmet? Try my recipe. The Cajun flavor comes through the cheese topping, and the confetti of green onions and red peppers makes it a pretty dish to serve guests.

—EMORY DOTY JASPER, GEORGIA

PREP: 35 MINUTES **BAKE:** 15 MINUTES + STANDING **MAKES:** 8 SERVINGS

- ½ cup all-purpose flour
- 1 tablespoon Cajun seasoning
- ½ teaspoon pepper
- 2 pounds uncooked large shrimp, peeled and deveined
- 2 tablespoons olive oil
- 4 thin slices prosciutto or deli ham, cut into thin strips
- ½ pound medium fresh mushrooms, quartered
- 2 tablespoons butter
- 4 green onions, chopped
- 2 garlic cloves, minced
- 1 cup heavy whipping cream
- 8 ounces fontina cheese, cubed
- 1 jar (7 ounces) roasted sweet red peppers, drained and chopped
- ¼ cup grated Parmigiano-Reggiano cheese
- ¼ cup grated Romano cheese

1. In a large resealable plastic bag, combine the flour, Cajun seasoning and pepper. Add shrimp, a few at a time, and shake to coat.

2. In a large skillet over medium heat, cook shrimp in oil in batches until golden brown. Drain on paper towels. Transfer to an ungreased 13-in. x 9-in. baking dish; top with prosciutto. Set aside.

3. In the same skillet, saute mushrooms in butter until tender. Add onions and garlic; cook 1 minute longer. Add cream and fontina cheese; cook and stir until cheese is melted. Remove from the heat; stir in peppers. Pour over prosciutto. Sprinkle with remaining cheeses.

4. Bake, uncovered, at 350° for 15-20 minutes or until bubbly and cheese is melted. Let stand for 10 minutes before serving.

Prime Rib with Horseradish Cream

Here's the perfect dish for a memorable family dinner. Mouths will water over this juicy prime rib.

—MARGARET DADY GRAND ISLAND, NEBRASKA

PREP: 30 MINUTES **BAKE:** 3 HOURS + STANDING **MAKES:** 12 SERVINGS (1½ CUPS CREAM)

1	**bone-in beef rib roast (6 to 8 pounds)**
3	**garlic cloves, sliced**
1	**teaspoon pepper**

HORSERADISH CREAM

1	**cup heavy whipping cream**
2	**tablespoons prepared horseradish**
2	**teaspoons red wine vinegar**
1	**teaspoon ground mustard**
¼	**teaspoon sugar**
⅛	**teaspoon salt**
	Dash pepper

1. Place roast fat side up in a shallow roasting pan. Cut slits into roast; insert garlic slices. Sprinkle with pepper. Bake, uncovered, at 450° for 15 minutes. Reduce heat to 325°; bake 2¾ to 3¼ hours longer or until meat reaches desired doneness (for medium-rare, a thermometer should read 145°; medium, 160°; well-done, 170°).

2. Meanwhile, in a small bowl, beat cream until soft peaks form. Fold in the horseradish, vinegar, mustard, sugar, salt and pepper. Cover and refrigerate for 1 hour.

3. Remove roast to a serving platter and keep warm; let stand for 15 minutes. Serve with cream.

Sneaky Lasagna

Lasagna's always been a family favorite. Because my children and husband aren't very fond of veggies, I started sneaking them into my lasagna and they hardly notice! The recipe feeds a crowd and is great for family reunions.

—CATHERINE YODER NEW PARIS, INDIANA

PREP: 25 MINUTES **BAKE:** 55 MINUTES + STANDING **MAKES:** 10-12 SERVINGS

- 2 **pounds ground beef**
- 1 **package (16 ounces) frozen California-blend vegetables**
- 2 **eggs, beaten**
- 3 **cups (24 ounces) 2% cottage cheese**
- 2 **jars (26 ounces each) spaghetti sauce**
- 12 **no-cook lasagna noodles**
- 2 **cups (8 ounces) shredded part-skim mozzarella cheese**

1. In a Dutch oven, cook beef over medium heat until no longer pink. Meanwhile, cook vegetables according to package directions; drain. Finely chop the vegetables; place in a bowl. Stir in eggs and cottage cheese; set aside.

2. Drain beef; stir in spaghetti sauce. Spread 2 cups meat mixture into a greased 13-in. x 9-in. baking dish. Top with four noodles. Spread half of the vegetable mixture to edges of noodles. Layer with 2 cups meat mixture and 1 cup mozzarella cheese. Top with four noodles, remaining vegetable mixture and 2 cups meat mixture. Layer with remaining noodles, meat mixture and mozzarella cheese.

3. Cover and bake at 375° for 50 minutes or until a thermometer reads 160°. Uncover; bake 5-10 minutes longer or until bubbly and cheese is melted. Let stand for 15 minutes before cutting.

1 can (10 ounces) hot enchilada sauce
1 can (10 ounces) green enchilada sauce
1 cup (8 ounces) sour cream
1 cup mayonnaise
2 cans (4 ounces each) chopped green chilies
2 cans (10 ounces each) mild enchilada sauce
4 cups (16 ounces) shredded Colby-Monterey Jack cheese
24 flour tortillas (6 inches), warmed
1 bunch green onions, thinly sliced
2 tablespoons chopped ripe olives

1. Place fillets on a greased baking sheet. Sprinkle with salt, pepper and cayenne. Bake, uncovered, at 350° for 15-20 minutes or until fish flakes easily with a fork.

2. Meanwhile, in a large skillet, saute onion and green pepper in oil until tender. Add garlic; cook 1 minute longer.

3. Flake fish with two forks; set aside. In a large bowl, combine the hot enchilada sauce, green enchilada sauce, sour cream, mayonnaise, chilies, onion mixture and fish. Spread ½ cup mild enchilada sauce into each of two greased 13-in. x 9-in. baking dishes. Sprinkle each with 1 cup cheese.

4. Place a heaping ⅓ cup halibut mixture down the center of each tortilla. Roll up each and place seam side down over cheese. Pour remaining sauce over top.

5. Cover and bake at 350° for 30 minutes. Sprinkle with the green onions, olives and remaining cheese. Bake enchiladas, uncovered, 10-15 minutes longer or until cheese is melted.

Halibut Enchiladas

To create a tasty dinner where north meets south of the border, I roll local Alaskan halibut fillets into flour tortillas. It's one of my most-requested recipes and a mainstay for potlucks.

—CAROLE DERIFIELD VALDEZ, ALASKA

PREP: 45 MINUTES **BAKE:** 40 MINUTES **MAKES:** 12 SERVINGS

3 pounds halibut fillets
½ teaspoon salt
⅛ teaspoon pepper
⅛ teaspoon cayenne pepper
1 medium onion, finely chopped
1 medium green pepper, finely chopped
1 tablespoon canola oil
2 garlic cloves, minced

Home Style COOKING NOTES

Steak with Chipotle-Lime Chimichurri

Steak gets a flavor kick from chimichurri. This piquant all-purpose herb sauce is so versatile, it complements most any grilled meat, poultry or fish.

—LAUREEN PITTMAN RIVERSIDE, CALIFORNIA

PREP/TOTAL TIME: 30 MINUTES
MAKES: 8 SERVINGS

- 2   cups chopped fresh parsley
- 1½ cups chopped fresh cilantro
- 1   small red onion, quartered
- 5   garlic cloves, quartered
- 2   chipotle peppers in adobo sauce
- ½   cup plus 1 tablespoon olive oil, divided
- ¼   cup white wine vinegar
- ¼   cup lime juice
- 1   tablespoon dried oregano
- 1   teaspoon grated lime peel
- 1¼ teaspoons salt, divided
- ¾   teaspoon pepper, divided
- 2   beef flat iron steaks or top sirloin steaks (1 pound each)

Home Style COOKING NOTES

1. For chimichurri, place the parsley, cilantro, onion, garlic and chipotle peppers in a food processor; cover and pulse until minced. Add ½ cup oil, vinegar, lime juice, oregano, lime peel, ½ teaspoon salt and ¼ teaspoon pepper; cover and process until blended. Cover and refrigerate until serving.

2. Drizzle steaks with remaining oil; sprinkle with remaining salt and pepper. Grill, covered, over medium heat for 8-10 minutes on each side or until meat reaches desired doneness (for medium-rare, a thermometer should read 145°; medium, 160°; well-done, 170°). Thinly slice across the grain; serve with chimichurri.

Maple Chicken 'n' Ribs

With its generous portions, my sweet and spicy recipe is great for feeding a crowd. I love this entree because the chicken thighs and country-style ribs are affordable.

—PHYLLIS SCHMALZ KANSAS CITY, KANSAS

PREP: 15 MINUTES + MARINATING **BAKE:** 1½ HOURS **MAKES:** 8 SERVINGS

> 1½ cups apple cider or juice
> ½ cup maple syrup
> 9 garlic cloves, peeled and crushed
> 3 tablespoons canola oil
> 3 tablespoons soy sauce
> 2 cinnamon sticks (3 inches)
> 3 whole star anise
> ¾ teaspoon crushed red pepper flakes
> 8 pork spareribs (about 5½ pounds)
> 8 bone-in chicken thighs (about 3 pounds)

1. In a large bowl, combine the first eight ingredients. Divide 1½ cups marinade between two large resealable plastic bags; add spareribs and chicken to separate bags. Seal bags and turn to coat; refrigerate for at least 8 hours or overnight. Cover and refrigerate remaining marinade.

2. Drain and discard marinade. Place ribs and chicken, skin side up, in separate greased shallow roasting pans.

3. Bake at 350° for 1½ to 2 hours or until tender, basting occasionally with reserved marinade.

Caraway Beef Roast

It's wonderful to have a beef roast that's both extra special and extra easy. This one delivers on both counts.

—BEVERLY SWANSON RED OAK, IOWA

PREP: 20 MINUTES **BAKE:** 3 HOURS
MAKES: 12 SERVINGS

> 1 boneless beef rump roast or chuck roast (3 pounds)
> 3 tablespoons canola oil
> 1 cup hot water
> 1½ teaspoons beef bouillon granules
> ¼ cup ketchup
> 1 tablespoon dried minced onion
> 1 tablespoon Worcestershire sauce
> 2 teaspoons caraway seeds
> 1 teaspoon salt
> ½ teaspoon pepper
> 2 bay leaves
> 2 tablespoons all-purpose flour
> ¼ cup cold water
> Cooked potatoes and carrots, optional

1. In an ovenproof Dutch oven over medium heat, brown roast in oil on all sides; drain.

2. In a small bowl, combine the hot water and bouillon; add the ketchup, onion, Worcestershire sauce, caraway, salt and pepper. Pour over roast. Add bay leaves.

3. Cover and bake at 325° for 3 hours or until tender. Remove roast to serving platter; keep warm.

4. In a small bowl, combine flour and cold water until smooth. Stir into pan juices; bring to a boil. Cook and stir for 1-2 minutes or until thickened, adding additional water if necessary. Discard bay leaves. Serve with cooked potatoes and carrots if desired.

Easy Beef-Stuffed Shells

Here's a rich and comforting dish that's terrific right away or made ahead and baked the next day. Pesto makes a surprising filling for the cheesy and satisfying shells.

—**BLAIR LONERGAN** ROCHELLE, VIRGINIA

PREP: 45 MINUTES + CHILLING
BAKE: 45 MINUTES **MAKES:** 10 SERVINGS

- 20 uncooked jumbo pasta shells
- 1 pound ground beef
- 1 large onion, chopped
- 1 carton (15 ounces) ricotta cheese
- 2 cups (8 ounces) shredded Italian cheese blend, divided
- ½ cup grated Parmesan cheese
- ¼ cup prepared pesto
- 1 egg, beaten
- 1 jar (26 ounces) spaghetti sauce, divided

1. Cook pasta shells according to package directions to al dente; drain and rinse in cold water. In a large skillet, cook beef and onion over medium heat until meat is no longer pink; drain. In a large bowl, combine the ricotta cheese, 1½ cups Italian cheese blend, Parmesan cheese, pesto, egg and half of the beef mixture.

2. Spread ¾ cup spaghetti sauce into a greased 13-in x 9-in. baking dish. Spoon cheese mixture into pasta shells; place in baking dish. Combine remaining beef mixture and spaghetti sauce; pour over shells. Sprinkle with remaining cheese. Cover and refrigerate overnight.

3. Remove casserole from refrigerator 30 minutes before baking. Cover and bake at 350° for 40 minutes. Uncover; bake 5-10 minutes longer or until cheese is melted.

Meatballs Stroganoff

This is one of my oldest, best-loved recipes from my mother. I like to serve it over hot, buttery egg noodles.

—**NANCY CARNES** CLEARWATER, MINNESOTA

PREP: 40 MINUTES **COOK:** 25 MINUTES **MAKES:** 4 SERVINGS

- 1 egg, lightly beaten
- ½ cup soft bread crumbs
- 2 tablespoons chopped onion
- ½ teaspoon celery salt
- ¼ teaspoon dried marjoram
- ⅛ teaspoon garlic salt
- ⅛ teaspoon pepper
- 1 pound ground beef
- 2 tablespoons all-purpose flour
- 1 tablespoon canola oil
- 1 can (10¾ ounces) condensed cream of mushroom soup, undiluted
- ¾ cup water
- ⅓ cup sour cream
    Hot cooked egg noodles

1. In a large bowl, combine the first seven ingredients. Crumble beef over mixture and mix well. Shape into 1½-in. balls.

2. Place flour in a large shallow bowl; gently roll meatballs in flour. In a large skillet, brown meatballs in oil. Drain; return to the pan. Combine soup and water; pour over meatballs. Bring to a boil. Reduce heat; cover and simmer for 20-25 minutes or until meat is no longer pink, stirring occasionally.

3. Stir in sour cream; heat through (do not boil). Serve with noodles.

Roasted Pork Loin with Fig Sauce

Roast pork with fruit is a classic preparation, but this recipe gives it a superb twist when pork loin is paired with tender figs. Family and friends will be thrilled with the wonderful combination.

—RIAN MACDONALD POWDER SPRINGS, GEORGIA

PREP: 1 HOUR **BAKE:** 1½ HOURS **MAKES:** 16 SERVINGS (6¼ CUPS SAUCE)

- **1 pound dried figs, quartered**
- **1 cup sherry or reduced-sodium chicken broth**
- **1 medium lemon, sliced**
- **1 cinnamon stick (3 inches)**
- **2 whole cloves**
- **1 boneless rolled pork loin roast (4 to 5 pounds)**
- **1 teaspoon salt**
- **¼ teaspoon ground cinnamon**
- **¼ teaspoon pepper**
- **½ cup orange juice**
- **¼ cup honey**
- **2 tablespoons cornstarch**
- **2 cups reduced-sodium chicken broth**

1. In a large saucepan, combine the first five ingredients. Bring to a boil. Reduce heat; simmer, uncovered, for 10 minutes. Remove from the heat. Cover and steep for 1 hour. Strain figs, discarding the lemon, cinnamon stick and cloves. Reserve liquid and set aside.

2. Sprinkle roast with salt, ground cinnamon and pepper. Place on a rack in a shallow roasting pan. Bake, uncovered, at 350° for 1 hour. In a small bowl, combine the orange juice, honey and reserved liquid; brush over pork. Bake 30-60 minutes longer or until a thermometer reads 160°, basting occasionally.

3. Remove meat to a serving platter; keep warm. Skim fat from cooking juices; transfer to a large saucepan. Add figs. Combine cornstarch and broth until smooth. Gradually stir into the pan. Bring to a boil; cook and stir for 2 minutes or until thickened. Serve with pork.

Spinach Lasagna Roll-Ups

With five kinds of cheese and a rich cream sauce, these pasta roll-ups are so flavorful. Keep them in mind when you want an impressive main course for special Sunday guests.

—MARY JANE JONES WILLIAMSTOWN, WEST VIRGINIA

PREP: 35 MINUTES **BAKE:** 30 MINUTES + STANDING **MAKES:** 10 SERVINGS

- 10 **uncooked lasagna noodles**
- 1 **package (8 ounces) cream cheese, softened**
- 2 **packages (10 ounces each) frozen chopped spinach, thawed and squeezed dry**
- 1 **carton (15 ounces) ricotta cheese**
- 2 **cups (8 ounces) shredded part-skim mozzarella cheese**
- 1 **cup grated Parmesan cheese**
- 1½ **teaspoons Italian seasoning**
- ¼ **teaspoon salt**

SAUCE
- 3 **tablespoons butter**
- 4 **tablespoons all-purpose flour**
- ½ **teaspoon pepper**
- ¼ **teaspoon salt**
- 2 **cups chicken broth**
- 1 **cup heavy whipping cream**

TOPPING
- ½ **cup shredded Gruyere cheese**
- ½ **cup grated Parmesan cheese**

1. Cook lasagna noodles according to package directions; drain. In a large bowl, beat cream cheese until smooth. Stir in the spinach, ricotta, mozzarella, Parmesan, Italian seasoning and salt. Spread ½ cup cheese mixture over each noodle; carefully roll up.

2. For sauce, in a large saucepan, melt butter over medium heat. Whisk in the flour, pepper and salt until smooth. Gradually whisk in broth. Bring to a boil; cook and stir for 2 minutes or until thickened. Remove from the heat; stir in cream.

3. Pour 1 cup sauce into a greased 13-in. x 9-in. baking dish. Cut lasagna roll-ups in half widthwise; place cut side down in dish. Top with remaining sauce; sprinkle with Gruyere and Parmesan.

4. Cover and bake at 350° for 20-25 minutes. Uncover; bake 10 minutes longer or until bubbly. Let stand for 15 minutes before serving.

TOPPING

1½ cups all-purpose flour
2 teaspoons sugar
1½ teaspoons baking powder
1 teaspoon dried thyme
¼ teaspoon baking soda
¼ teaspoon salt
2 tablespoons cold butter
1 cup buttermilk
1 tablespoon canola oil

1. In a Dutch oven, saute mushrooms and onion in oil until tender. Stir in the turkey, peas and carrots, salt and pepper. Combine cornstarch and broth until smooth; gradually stir into the pan. Bring to a boil. Reduce heat; cook and stir for 2 minutes or until thickened. Stir in sour cream. Transfer to eight greased 8-oz. ramekins.

2. In a large bowl, combine the flour, sugar, baking powder, thyme, baking soda and salt. Cut in butter until mixture resembles coarse crumbs. In a small bowl, combine buttermilk and oil; stir into dry ingredients just until moistened. Drop by heaping teaspoonfuls over filling.

3. Bake, uncovered, at 400° for 20-25 minutes or until topping is golden brown and filling is bubbly. Let stand 5 minutes before serving.

Turkey Potpies

I always use the leftovers from our big holiday turkey to make these little potpies. I think my family enjoys them more than the original feast!

—LILY JULOW GAINESVILLE, FLORIDA

PREP: 40 MINUTES **BAKE:** 20 MINUTES **MAKES:** 8 SERVINGS

4⅓ cups sliced baby portobello mushrooms
1 large onion, chopped
1 tablespoon olive oil
2½ cups cubed cooked turkey
1 package (16 ounces) frozen peas and carrots
¼ teaspoon salt
¼ teaspoon pepper
¼ cup cornstarch
2½ cups chicken broth
¼ cup sour cream

Home Style COOKING NOTES

Honey-Glazed Pork Tenderloins

Honey, smoky chipotle pepper and soy sauce help to flavor this no-fuss pork tenderloin. Serve it with veggies or rice for a satisfying meal.

—DIANE COTTON FRANKLIN, NORTH CAROLINA

PREP: 15 MINUTES **BAKE:** 20 MINUTES **MAKES:** 6 SERVINGS

- ½ **teaspoon garlic powder**
- ½ **teaspoon ground chipotle pepper**
- ½ **teaspoon pepper**
- 2 **pork tenderloins (1 pound each)**
- 1 **tablespoon canola oil**
- ½ **cup honey**
- 2 **tablespoons reduced-sodium soy sauce**
- 1 **tablespoon balsamic vinegar**
- 1 **teaspoon sesame oil**

1. Combine the first three ingredients; rub over pork. In a large ovenproof skillet, brown pork in canola oil on all sides.

2. In a small bowl, combine the honey, soy sauce, vinegar and sesame oil; spoon over pork. Bake, uncovered, at 350° for 20-25 minutes or until a thermometer reads 145°, basting occasionally with pan juices. Let stand for 5 minutes before slicing.

Tourtiere

When temperatures drop, people in our region start craving the ultimate French-Canadian comfort food—savory meat pie, or tourtiere.

—VIVIANNE REMILLARD ST. JOSEPH, MANITOBA

PREP: 25 MINUTES **BAKE:** 50 MIN.
MAKES: 6 SERVINGS

- **Pastry for double-crust pie (9 inches)**
- 1¼ **pounds lean ground beef (90% lean)**
- 1¼ **pounds ground pork**
- 1 **medium onion, chopped**
- ⅓ **cup water**
- ¾ **teaspoon salt**
- ¾ **teaspoon ground cinnamon**
- ¼ **teaspoon dried sage leaves**
- ¼ **teaspoon ground cloves**
- ¼ **teaspoon pepper**
- ½ **cup soft bread crumbs**

1. Line a 9-in. pie plate with bottom pastry; trim pastry even with edge of plate. Set aside.

2. In a large skillet, cook the beef, pork and onion over medium heat until meat is no longer pink; drain. Stir in water and seasonings, then bread crumbs.

3. Spoon into prepared pastry. Roll out remaining pastry to fit top of pie; place over filling. Trim, seal and flute edges. Cut slits in top of pie.

4. Bake at 375° for 50-60 minutes or until crust is golden brown.

Home Style COOKING NOTES

Company's Coming

Small-town suppers are a big part of our fall social calendar in rural Canada.

BY VIVIANNE REMILLARD

When my neighbors and I have people over for supper, we go all out—inviting a thousand of our closest friends, relatives and complete strangers with a taste for good home cooking.

Our St. Joseph Fall Supper is one of countless community meals that have become a tradition in Manitoba and across the Canadian prairie. The menus vary; what stays the same is that the workers are local volunteers, the food is made from family recipes, and the diners come back for seconds and walk away happy and full!

Most of these meals are held in the fall as fundraisers. Ours began 19 years ago as a way to finance a community hall. Now it's an annual event here, held the third Sunday in October in the new hall we've built with the proceeds. As the supper's volunteer organizer, I've watched attendance grow to our present record: 1,125 hungry guests.

Since this is a French area, we spotlight ethnic dishes such as tourtiere (meat pie), pork hock ragout (stew) and tarte au sucre (sugar pie). We always get high marks from those who rate community fall suppers on their food, friendliness and service. One couple drove all night from the next province to eat with us again. That's quite a testimonial!

My main duty is making sure there are enough helpers for our workstations. Luckily, St. Joseph is known for its community spirit. More than half our population of 150 will take part as cooks, servers, dishwashers and greeters. To get a head start, we meet a few weekends in advance to prepare the meat pies, peel potatoes and dice veggies for several kinds of salads. Local women help bake 90 dozen white, brown, multigrain and raisin buns.

Big-batch cooking is familiar, since many of us have families and farmhands to feed. Harvest is usually over by the time fall supper rolls around. But sometimes we end up rushing from the fields to the hall kitchen, swapping our work boots for aprons.

Early on supper day, we begin barbecuing 450 pounds of beef on a rotisserie 4 feet deep and 6 feet long. My husband, Rheal, and his brothers built the titanic barbecue to accommodate 33 roasts at once! At suppertime, Rheal and our sons, Rejean and Marcel, are among the volunteers who man the meat-carving station. Daughter Julie clears tables, while Josee, our youngest, serves as one of the kitchen minions filling punch-bowl-size serving dishes with hominy, coleslaw, green and yellow beans and mashed potatoes.

Josee loves working beside experienced cooks. Last fall, she learned about meatballs from a woman who prepared them as rations for World War II. A lady who helps make our pie shells taught her how to roll out a crust with a glass bottle.

Diners begin arriving shortly before 4 p.m., and we try to keep the buffet moving. That was quite a trick the day three charter buses from Winnipeg came in a convoy! Usually people don't mind the wait, because they enjoy visiting before filling their plates. For many, socializing is every bit as important as the food.

Our kitchen crew always takes time to check the food line for familiar faces. The next day, a few of us come back to the hall to make a Monday lunch from leftovers. We often serve another hundred who couldn't make it to the supper or who want to chat about the night before.

It's rewarding to see generations of neighbors working as a team, just as our ancestors built the town we live in today. And our fall supper-goers truly appreciate the big helpings of food and togetherness. There's always room for more friends—and some pie!

Gatherings

From breathtaking holiday roasts and heartwarming breads to festive drinks and whimsical treats, you'll discover new recipes to cherish in this chapter. Whether you're celebrating Easter, Independence Day or the most joyous season of all, new family traditions are just waiting to be created.

Over-the-Top Chocolate Cake

(recipe on page 220)

"Traditionally served for the holidays, this dessert has already become a family heirloom recipe."
—**VANESSA JOHNSON**
HEYBURN, IDAHO

Winter Plum Punch

The plum jam and spices in this punch create a delightful holiday flavor and aroma. For a festive look, we filled the ice ring with cinnamon sticks, mint leaves and fruit.

—TASTE OF HOME TEST KITCHEN

PREP: 20 MINUTES + FREEZING
MAKES: 13 SERVINGS (¾ CUP EACH)

- 5 **cups water, divided**
  Assorted fresh fruit (cranberries and lemon and orange slices)
  Fresh mint leaves
  Cinnamon sticks (3 inches), crushed
- 1 **cup plum jam**
- 1 **teaspoon ground cinnamon**
- ½ **teaspoon ground nutmeg**
- 4 **cups cranberry juice, chilled**
- 1 **cup orange juice, chilled**
- ¼ **cup lemon juice**
- 4 **cups club soda, chilled**

1. Lightly coat a decorative tube cake pan or gelatin mold with cooking spray; add ½ cup of water. Arrange the fruit, mint and cinnamon pieces in pan as desired. Freeze until solid. Add remaining water; arrange more fruit, mint and cinnamon pieces as desired. Freeze until ready to use.

2. In a microwave, melt jam; stir until smooth. Add ground cinnamon and nutmeg. Cool. Just before serving, in a punch bowl, combine the juices and jam mixture. Stir in soda.
3. Unmold ice ring by wrapping the bottom of the mold in a hot, damp dishcloth. Invert onto a baking sheet; place fruit side up in punch bowl.

Home Style COOKING NOTES

Pumpkin Cranberry Muffins

Spicy pumpkin perks up these muffins, and cranberries lend a sweet-and-sour tang. Made with nutritious whole wheat, they're great to bring to a brunch.

—LYNNE PARRISH PHOENIX, ARIZONA

PREP: 20 MINUTES **BAKE:** 15 MINUTES **MAKES:** 1 DOZEN

- 1¼ **cups whole wheat flour**
- ¾ **cup sugar**
- ¼ **cup oat bran**
- 1½ **teaspoons ground cinnamon**
- 1 **teaspoon baking powder**
- 1 **teaspoon baking soda**
- ½ **teaspoon salt**
- 2 **eggs, beaten**
- 1 **cup canned pumpkin**
- ⅔ **cup plain yogurt**
- ¼ **cup canola oil**
- ¾ **cup dried cranberries**

1. In a large bowl, combine the first seven ingredients. In another bowl, combine the eggs, pumpkin, yogurt and oil. Stir into dry ingredients just until moistened. Fold in cranberries. Coat muffin cups with cooking spray or use paper liners; fill three-fourths full with batter.

2. Bake at 400° for 15-20 minutes or until a toothpick comes out clean. Cool for 5 minutes before removing from pan to a wire rack.

American Flag Berry Pie

We host Fourth of July at my home every year and this is the delicious pie I serve. My family always enjoys it because it's so patriotic and festive.

—SHERRY CLUBINE
INDEPENDENCE, KANSAS

PREP: 40 MINUTES + STANDING
BAKE: 50 MINUTES + COOLING
MAKES: 8 SERVINGS

- **Pastry for a double-crust pie (9 inches)**
- 2½ **cups pitted dark sweet cherries**
- 2½ **cups fresh blueberries**
- ¾ **cup sugar**
- ¼ **cup all-purpose flour**
- ½ **teaspoon ground cinnamon**
- 1 **tablespoon butter**
- **Additional sugar**

1. Line a 9-in. pie plate with bottom crust; trim pastry even with edge. Set crust aside.

2. In a large bowl, gently combine cherries and blueberries. Combine the sugar, flour and cinnamon; stir into fruit. Let stand for 10 minutes. Pour into crust; dot with butter.

3. Roll out remaining pastry into a 10-in. circle. Cut pastry in half. Cut one half into two wedges. Using a 1-in. star cookie cutter, cut out stars from one wedge. Place cutout pastry wedge over filling. Discard cutout stars.

4. Cut remaining pastry pieces into ½-in.-wide strips; position over filling to resemble a flag. Seal and flute edges. Sprinkle pastry with additional sugar. Cover edges with foil.

5. Bake at 425° for 15 minutes. Reduce heat to 350°; bake 35-40 minutes longer or until pastry is golden brown and filling is bubbly. Cool on a wire rack.

Roasted Leg of Lamb

Lamb is succulent with a flavorful rub of rosemary, garlic, onion and olive oil.

—SUZY HORVATH GLADSTONE, OREGON

PREP: 10 MINUTES
BAKE: 2 HOURS + STANDING
MAKES: 10-12 SERVINGS

- ⅓ cup olive oil
- ¼ cup minced fresh rosemary
- ¼ cup finely chopped onion
- 4 garlic cloves, minced
- ½ teaspoon salt
- ¼ teaspoon pepper
- 1 bone-in leg of lamb (5 to 6 pounds), trimmed

1. Combine the first six ingredients; rub over lamb. Place fat side up on a rack in a shallow roasting pan.

2. Bake, uncovered, at 325° for 2 to 2½ hours or until meat reaches desired doneness (for medium-rare, a thermometer should read 145°; medium, 160°; well-done, 170°), basting occasionally with pan juices. Let stand for 15 minutes before slicing.

Christmas Brunch Casserole

No one leaves the table hungry when I serve my savory brunch casserole. In fact, folks rave about it! I like how easy it is to serve a crowd.

—MARY ECKLER LOUISVILLE, KENTUCKY

PREP: 20 MINUTES **BAKE:** 55 MINUTES **MAKES:** 12 SERVINGS

- 2 pounds bulk pork sausage
- 1 large onion, chopped
- 2 cups cooked rice
- 3 cups crisp rice cereal
- 3 cups (12 ounces) shredded cheddar cheese
- 6 eggs
- 2 cans (10¾ ounces each) condensed cream of celery soup, undiluted
- ½ cup milk

1. In a skillet, cook sausage and onion over medium heat until meat is no longer pink; drain. Place in a lightly greased 13-in. x 9-in. baking dish. Layer with the rice, cereal and cheddar cheese. In a bowl, beat the eggs, soup and milk. Spread over top.

2. Bake, casserole, uncovered, at 350° for 55-60 minutes or until a knife inserted near the center comes out clean. Let stand for 5 minutes before cutting. Refrigerate leftovers.

Ham & Gruyere Mini Quiches

By making these in muffin cups, I get to serve everyone their own individual quiches. I have also doubled the recipe, used jumbo muffin cups and baked the little treats about 10 minutes longer to great success.

—**GENA STOUT** RAVENDEN, ARKANSAS

PREP: 30 MINUTES **BAKE:** 20 MINUTES **MAKES:** 10 MINI QUICHES

4	**eggs, lightly beaten**
1	**cup 2% cottage cheese**
¼	**cup 2% milk**
2	**tablespoons all-purpose flour**
½	**teaspoon baking powder**
¼	**teaspoon ground nutmeg**
¼	**teaspoon pepper**
1½	**cups (6 ounces) shredded Gruyere or Swiss cheese**
¾	**cup finely chopped fully cooked ham**
3	**tablespoons thinly sliced green onions**

1. In a large bowl, combine the first seven ingredients; fold in the Gruyere cheese, ham and onions. Fill greased muffin cups three-fourths full.

2. Bake at 375° for 18-22 minutes until a knife inserted near the center comes out clean. Cool for 5 minutes before removing from pans to wire racks.

3. Transfer quiches to a large resealable plastic freezer bag. May be frozen for up to 3 months.

To use frozen mini quiches: *Thaw in the refrigerator overnight. Transfer to a greased baking sheet; bake at 350° for 10-14 minutes or until heated through.*

Fruit-Stuffed Crown Roast

Absolutely sensational is the only way to describe this crown roast! Moist and full of fruit-flavored stuffing, it's a natural choice for any dinner that calls for a special presentation.

—SHAARON HETLAND CHILLIWACK, BRITISH COLUMBIA

PREP: 15 MINUTES **BAKE:** 3 HOURS + STANDING **MAKES:** 16 SERVINGS

1½ cups red currant jelly
½ cup orange liqueur or juice
1 pork crown rib roast (16 ribs and about 8 pounds)
¼ cup butter, cubed
1 large onion, chopped
1 celery rib, chopped
6 cups unseasoned stuffing cubes
1 can (15¼ ounces) apricot halves, drained and quartered
1 can (8 ounces) sliced water chestnuts, drained
1 large tart apple, peeled and chopped
1 egg, beaten
1 teaspoon salt
½ teaspoon rubbed sage
½ teaspoon dried thyme

1. In a small saucepan, heat jelly and orange liqueur over low heat until jelly is melted; brush over roast. Place roast on a rack in a large shallow roasting pan. Cover rib ends with foil. Bake, uncovered, at 350° for 2 hours.

2. In a large skillet, melt butter over medium heat. Add onion and celery; cook and stir until tender. Transfer to a large bowl; add remaining ingredients and mix well.

3. Carefully spoon stuffing into center of roast. Bake 1 hour longer or until a thermometer reads 160° in meat and stuffing.

4. Transfer to a serving platter; let stand for 10-15 minutes. Discard foil. Cut between ribs to serve.

Editor's Note: *Extra stuffing may be baked, covered, in a greased baking dish for 45-60 minutes or until a thermometer reads 160°.*

Lemon Sorbet Torte

Oohs and aahs are sure to follow when you serve my elegant dessert. The unique almond- and cinnamon-flavored crust is topped with a layer of strawberry jam, then filled with prepared lemon sorbet. I serve the torte with a fruit sauce and additional fresh berries.

—SARAH BRADLEY ATHENS, TEXAS

PREP: 30 MINUTES + FREEZING **MAKES:** 12 SERVINGS

- 3 **cups slivered almonds, toasted**
- ½ **cup sugar**
- ¼ **teaspoon ground cinnamon**
- 5 **tablespoons butter, melted**
- ⅓ **cup seedless strawberry jam**
- 3 **pints lemon sorbet, softened**

STRAWBERRY-RHUBARB SAUCE

- ½ **cup sugar**
- ¼ **cup water**
- 2½ **cups sliced fresh or frozen rhubarb**
- 2½ **cups frozen unsweetened strawberries, partially thawed and sliced**
- ¾ **teaspoon vanilla extract**
- 1 **pint fresh strawberries, sliced**

1. Place the almonds, sugar and cinnamon in a food processor; cover and process until finely chopped. Stir in the butter. Press onto the bottom and 2 in. up the sides of an ungreased 9-in. springform pan.

2. Place pan on a baking sheet. Bake at 350° for 15-20 minutes or until lightly browned. Cool completely on a wire rack.

3. In a small saucepan over low heat, melt jam; spread over bottom of crust. Top with sorbet. Freeze until firm.

4. Meanwhile, for sauce, combine sugar and water in a large saucepan. Bring to a boil. Add rhubarb; return to a boil. Reduce heat; cover and simmer for 5-8 minutes or until rhubarb is tender. Add thawed strawberries; bring to a boil. Remove from the heat; cool to room temperature. Stir in vanilla. Cool sauce; refrigerate until chilled.

5. Just before serving, remove sides of springform pan. Spoon ½ cup sauce onto center of torte; top with fresh strawberries. Serve with remaining sauce.

Holiday Brussels Sprouts

Peas and sprouts mixed with crunchy celery and flavorful bacon make an appealing winter side dish. I often add it to my holiday menus.

—JODIE BECKMAN COUNCIL BLUFFS, IOWA

PREP/TOTAL TIME: 25 MINUTES
MAKES: 6 SERVINGS

- 1 **package (16 ounces) frozen Brussels sprouts**
- 1 **package (10 ounces) frozen peas**
- 2 **medium celery ribs, chopped**
- 2 **tablespoons butter**
- 2 **bacon strips, cooked and crumbled**
- 2 **tablespoons minced chives**

1. Cook Brussels sprouts and peas according to package directions.

2. Meanwhile, in a small skillet, saute celery in butter until crisp-tender. Transfer to a large bowl; add bacon and chives. Drain Brussels sprouts and peas; add to celery mixture and stir until blended.

Home Style COOKING NOTES

Keep your hands and the countertop clean by shaping a cheese ball on plastic wrap. Working from the underside of the wrap, pat the mixture into a ball. Finish as directed.

Pumpkin Cheese Ball

Everyone will get a kick out of this pumpkin-shaped cheese ball. You can make it a day ahead.

—**SUZANNE MCKINLEY** LYONS, GEORGIA

PREP: 20 MINUTES + CHILLING **MAKES:** 2½ CUPS

- 1 package (8 ounces) cream cheese, softened
- 1 carton (8 ounces) spreadable chive and onion cream cheese
- 2 cups (8 ounces) shredded sharp cheddar cheese
- 2 teaspoons paprika
- ½ teaspoon cayenne pepper
- 1 celery rib or broccoli stalk
  Sliced apples and assorted crackers

1. In a small bowl, beat cream cheeses until smooth. Stir in the cheddar cheese, paprika and cayenne. Shape into a ball; wrap in plastic wrap. Refrigerate for 4 hours or until firm.

2. With a knife, add vertical lines to the cheese ball to resemble a pumpkin; insert a celery rib or broccoli stalk for the stem. Serve with apples and crackers.

Harvest Stuffing

Chock-full of veggies and studded with colorful dried fruits, my unique stuffing boasts the very best of autumn's harvest. It's also delicious served with pork.

—**RUTH HASTINGS** LOUISVILLE, ILLINOIS

PREP: 25 MINUTES **BAKE:** 40 MINUTES **MAKES:** 6 SERVINGS

- 1½ cups water, divided
- 1 cup each chopped carrots, celery and onion
- 10 dried plums, halved
- 10 dried apricots, halved
- 1 teaspoon salt-free herb seasoning blend
- ½ teaspoon salt
- 8 slices cinnamon-raisin bread, cubed
- ¼ cup unsweetened apple juice

1. In a large saucepan, combine 1 cup water, carrots, celery, onion, plums, apricots, seasoning blend and salt. Bring to a boil. Reduce heat; cover and simmer for 15-20 minutes or until fruit and vegetables are tender.

2. Meanwhile, place the bread cubes in a single layer on baking sheets. Bake at 350° for 8-10 minutes or until lightly toasted. Transfer vegetable mixture to a large bowl. Stir in the bread cubes, apple juice and remaining water; toss gently to combine.

3. Transfer to a greased 1½-qt. baking dish. Cover and bake at 350° for 30 minutes. Uncover; bake 10-15 minutes longer or until heated through.

Jeweled Buffet Ham

Cranberry sauce and mandarin oranges make a beautiful, aromatic glaze for cooked ham. This recipe will be a crowd-pleaser!

—AGNES WARD STRATFORD, ONTARIO

PREP: 10 MINUTES **BAKE:** 2½ HOURS **MAKES:** 15 SERVINGS

- 1 bone-in fully cooked spiral-sliced ham (7 pounds)
- 1 can (14 ounces) whole-berry cranberry sauce
- 1 can (11 ounces) mandarin oranges, drained
- 1 can (8 ounces) jellied cranberry sauce
- ½ cup orange juice
- ½ teaspoon garlic powder
- ⅛ teaspoon hot pepper sauce

1. Place ham on a rack in a shallow roasting pan. Bake ham, uncovered, at 325° for 2 hours.

2. In a large saucepan, combine the remaining ingredients. Cook and stir over medium heat until heated through. Brush ham with some of the glaze; bake 30-60 minutes longer or until a thermometer reads 140°, brushing occasionally with remaining glaze.

Garlic, Bacon & Stilton Mashed Potatoes

Creamy and savory, these mashed potatoes are a perfect partner for just about any entree. They're a snap to put together in advance.

—JAMIE BROWN-MILLER NAPA, CALIFORNIA

PREP: 30 MINUTES **COOK:** 20 MINUTES **MAKES:** 8 SERVINGS

- 6 garlic cloves, peeled
- 1 teaspoon olive oil
- 2½ pounds small red potatoes, scrubbed
- 4 ounces cream cheese, softened
- ½ cup butter, cubed
- ½ cup 2% milk
- ½ teaspoon salt
- ½ teaspoon pepper
- ⅓ pound Stilton cheese, crumbled
- 6 bacon strips, cooked and crumbled
- 3 tablespoons minced fresh parsley, divided

1. Place garlic on a double thickness of heavy-duty foil. Drizzle with oil. Wrap foil around garlic. Bake at 425° for 15-20 minutes or until softened. Cool garlic for 10-15 minutes.

2. Meanwhile, place potatoes in a large saucepan and cover with water. Bring to a boil. Reduce heat; cover and cook for 15-20 minutes or until tender. Drain; transfer to a large bowl.

3. Squeeze softened garlic into potatoes. Add the cream cheese, butter, milk, salt and pepper. Mash potatoes until combined. Stir in the Stilton cheese, bacon and 2 tablespoons parsley. Sprinkle with remaining parsley before serving.

Roasted Garlic Twice-Baked Potato

A creamy potato filling flavored with roasted garlic makes this side dish a winner. It's easy to prepare and a perfect choice to accompany a hearty meat entree like steak.

—NANCY MUELLER
MENOMONEE FALLS, WISCONSIN

PREP: 1 HOUR **BAKE:** 25 MINUTES
MAKES: 2 SERVINGS

- 1 **large baking potato**
- 1 **teaspoon canola oil, divided**
- 6 **garlic cloves, unpeeled**
- 2 **tablespoons butter, softened**
- 2 **tablespoons 2% milk**
- 2 **tablespoons sour cream**
- ¼ **teaspoon minced fresh rosemary or dash dried rosemary, crushed**
- ⅛ **teaspoon salt**
- ⅛ **teaspoon pepper**

1. Scrub and pierce potato; rub with ½ teaspoon oil. Place garlic on a double thickness of heavy-duty foil. Drizzle with remaining oil. Wrap foil around garlic. Place potato and garlic on a baking sheet. Bake at 400° for 15 minutes. Remove garlic; bake potato 45 minutes longer or until tender.

2. When cool enough to handle, cut potato in half lengthwise. Scoop out the pulp, leaving thin shells.

3. Squeeze softened garlic into a small bowl; add potato pulp and mash. Stir in remaining ingredients. Spoon into potato shells. Place on an ungreased baking sheet. Bake at 350° for 25-30 minutes or until heated through.

Lemon Easter Bread

This yeast bread is an Easter tradition at my house, but I also bake it other times of the year. While the bread is in the oven, the aroma is irresistible!

—ELIZABETH IMBLUM WARREN, OHIO

PREP: 20 MINUTES + RISING **BAKE:** 25 MINUTES **MAKES:** 2 LOAVES (12 SLICES EACH)

- 1 **package (¼ ounce) active dry yeast**
- ½ **cup warm water (110° to 115°)**
- 1 **cup warm milk (110° to 115°)**
- ¼ **cup butter, softened**
- 1 **package (3.4 ounces) instant lemon pudding mix**
- 3 **eggs, lightly beaten**
- 5 **to 5½ cups all-purpose flour**

1. In a large bowl, dissolve yeast in warm water. Add the milk, butter, pudding mix, eggs and 3 cups flour; beat until smooth. Stir in enough remaining flour to form a soft dough.

2. Turn onto a floured surface; knead until smooth and elastic, about 6-8 minutes. Place in a greased bowl, turning once to grease top. Cover and rise in a warm place until doubled, about 1 hour.

3. Punch dough down. Turn onto a lightly floured surface; divide in half. Shape into loaves. Place in two greased 8-in. x 4-in. loaf pans. Cover and let rise until doubled, about 30 minutes.

4. Bake at 350° for 25-30 minutes or until golden brown. Remove from pans to wire racks to cool.

Eggnog Sweet Potato Pie

Pies are therapy to me. This is one I make for special events and holiday celebrations. The eggnog and sweet potato make a soft filling that goes nicely with the coconut topping's lovely crunch.

—**SARAH SPAUGH** WINSTON-SALEM, NORTH CAROLINA

PREP: 25 MINUTES **BAKE:** 55 MINUTES + COOLING **MAKES:** 8 SERVINGS

¼ **cup caramel ice cream topping**
1 **unbaked pastry shell (9 inches)**
2 **cups mashed sweet potatoes**
¾ **cup eggnog**
1 **egg, lightly beaten**
2 **tablespoons butter, melted**
½ **teaspoon vanilla extract**
½ **cup sugar**
½ **cup packed brown sugar**
¾ **teaspoon ground cinnamon**

TOPPING
½ **cup flaked coconut**
⅓ **cup all-purpose flour**
¼ **cup packed brown sugar**
⅓ **cup cold butter, cubed**
¼ **cup chopped pecans**

1. Carefully spread caramel topping over bottom of pastry shell; set aside. In a small bowl, combine the sweet potatoes, eggnog, egg, butter and vanilla. Stir in the sugars and cinnamon. Carefully spoon over caramel layer.

2. Bake at 400° for 15 minutes. Reduce heat to 350°; bake 30 minutes longer.

3. Meanwhile, in a small bowl, combine the coconut, flour and brown sugar. Cut in butter until crumbly; stir in pecans. Sprinkle over pie.

4. Bake for 10-15 minutes or until a knife inserted near the center comes out clean and topping is golden brown (cover edges with foil if necessary to prevent overbrowning). Cool completely on a wire rack. Store in the refrigerator.

Editor's Note: *This recipe was tested with commercially prepared eggnog.*

Pumpkin Torte

A local newspaper featured this potluck-friendly torte years ago. A creamy and playful-looking alternative to pumpkin pie, it quickly became one of my favorites.

—PEGGY SHEA LOWELL, INDIANA

PREP: 30 MINUTES **BAKE:** 25 MINUTES + CHILLING **MAKES:** 15 SERVINGS

1⅔ cups graham cracker crumbs
⅓ cup sugar
½ cup butter, melted

CREAM CHEESE FILLING

2 packages (8 ounces each) cream cheese, softened
¾ cup sugar
2 eggs, lightly beaten

PUMPKIN FILLING

2 envelopes unflavored gelatin
½ cup cold water
1 can (30 ounces) pumpkin pie filling
1 can (5½ ounces) evaporated milk
2 eggs, lightly beaten

TOPPING

1 carton (12 ounces) frozen whipped topping, thawed

1. In a small bowl, combine the crumbs, sugar and butter. Press onto the bottom of an ungreased 13-in. x 9-in. baking dish; set aside. In a large bowl, beat cream cheese and sugar until smooth. Add eggs; beat on low speed just until combined. Pour over crust. Bake at 350° for 25-30 minutes or until center is almost set.

2. Meanwhile, in a small bowl, sprinkle gelatin over cold water; let stand for 1 minute. In a large saucepan, combine pie filling and evaporated milk. Bring to a boil. Add gelatin; stir until dissolved. Whisk a small amount of hot mixture into the eggs. Return all to the pan, whisking constantly.

3. Cook and stir over low heat until mixture is thickened and coats the back of a spoon. Cool for 10 minutes. Spread over cream cheese layer. Spread whipped topping over top. Cover and chill overnight.

1. In a double boiler or metal bowl over simmering water, heat chocolate and butter until melted, stirring frequently. Whisk a small amount of mixture into egg yolks. Return all to the heat, whisking constantly. Cook and stir until mixture reaches at least 160° and coats the back of a spoon.
2. Remove from the heat; stir in the cranberries, orange juice concentrate and extract. Cool to room temperature, stirring occasionally. Refrigerate for 1 hour or until easy to handle. Shape into 1-in. balls.
3. In a microwave, melt candy coating. Dip truffles in coating; allow excess to drip off. Place on waxed paper-lined baking sheets; immediately sprinkle with almonds. Drizzle with bittersweet chocolate and garnish with dried cranberries. Refrigerate for 2 hours or until firm. Store in an airtight container in the refrigerator.

Crispy Star Pops

These patriotic pops are a hit at our annual Fourth of July get-together. Serve them as an after-picnic dessert. Or slip them into cellophane bags, tie on ribbons and give them as favors.
—**COLLEEN STURMA** MILWAUKEE, WISCONSIN

PREP: 30 MINUTES
COOK: 15 MINUTES + COOLING **MAKES:** 15 POPS

    8 cups miniature marshmallows
    6 tablespoons butter, cubed
   12 cups Rice Krispies
   12 Popsicle sticks
    1 cup white baking chips
   ½ teaspoon shortening
       Red, white and blue sprinkles

1. In a Dutch oven, heat marshmallows and butter until melted. Remove from the heat; stir in cereal and mix well. Press into a greased 15-in. x 10-in. x 1-in. baking pan. Cut out with a 3-in. star-shaped cookie cutter. Insert a Popsicle stick into the side of each star; place on waxed paper.
2. In a microwave, melt white chips and shortening; stir until smooth. Spread over stars. Decorate with sprinkles.

Cranberry Orange Truffles

Homemade truffles are a delicacy my family looks forward to every holiday. We love the combination of tart cranberries and rich chocolate—and the orange and almond nuances put this recipe over the top.
—**TERRYANN MOORE** VINELAND, NEW JERSEY

PREP: 1 HOUR + CHILLING **MAKES:** ABOUT 3 DOZEN

   12 ounces bittersweet chocolate, chopped
   ½ cup unsalted butter, cubed
    4 egg yolks, beaten
    1 cup dried cranberries, chopped
    3 tablespoons thawed orange juice concentrate
    1 teaspoon almond extract
   COATING
   12 ounces white candy coating, chopped
   ⅓ cup finely chopped almonds
    1 ounce bittersweet chocolate, melted
   ¼ cup dried cranberries

Sweet Potato Eggnog Casserole

For an extra-special Christmas side, try this heavenly casserole that gives sweet potatoes a twist. They're dressed up with eggnog, spices and a crunchy pecan topping.

—KATIE WOLLGAST FLORISSANT, MISSOURI

PREP: 20 MINUTES **BAKE:** 30 MINUTES
MAKES: 8 SERVINGS

 6 cups mashed sweet potatoes (about 3 pounds)
 ⅔ cup eggnog
 ½ cup golden raisins
 2 tablespoons sugar
 1 teaspoon salt

TOPPING

 ¼ cup all-purpose flour
 ¼ cup quick-cooking oats
 ¼ cup packed brown sugar
 ¼ cup chopped pecans
 3 tablespoons butter, melted
 ¾ teaspoon ground cinnamon
 ¼ teaspoon ground nutmeg

1. In a large bowl, combine the potatoes, eggnog, raisins, sugar and salt. Transfer to a greased 2-qt. baking dish. Combine topping ingredients; sprinkle over top.

2. Bake, uncovered, at 350° for 30-35 minutes or until heated through.

Editor's Note: *This recipe was tested with commercially prepared eggnog.*

Layered Christmas Gelatin

Christmastime always means that instructions for this fruity dish come out of my recipe box. The traditional holiday colors make my table so pretty.

—DIANE SCHEFELKER IRETON, IOWA

PREP: 30 MINUTES + CHILLING
MAKES: 10 SERVINGS

 1 package (3 ounces) lime gelatin
 1 cup boiling water
 ⅓ cup unsweetened pineapple juice
 1 cup crushed pineapple, drained

CREAM CHEESE LAYER

 1 teaspoon unflavored gelatin

 2 tablespoons cold water
 1 package (8 ounces) cream cheese, softened
 ⅓ cup milk

BERRY LAYER

 2 packages (3 ounces each) strawberry gelatin
 2 cups boiling water
 1 can (14 ounces) whole-berry cranberry sauce
   Whipped topping, optional

1. Dissolve lime gelatin in boiling water; stir in pineapple juice. Stir in pineapple. Pour into an 11-in. x 7-in. dish; refrigerate until set.

2. In a small saucepan, sprinkle unflavored gelatin over cold water; let stand for 1 minute. Heat over low heat, stirring until gelatin is completely dissolved. Transfer to a small bowl. Beat in cream cheese and milk until smooth. Spread over lime layer; refrigerate until set.

3. Dissolve strawberry gelatin in boiling water; stir in cranberry sauce. Cool for 10 minutes. Carefully spoon over cream cheese layer. Refrigerate until set.

4. Cut into squares. Garnish with whipped topping if desired.

Gorgonzola Baked Apples with Balsamic Syrup

Gorgonzola cheese and a balsamic vinegar reduction are pleasing partners to sweet apples. Serve them alongside any entree

—**CRYSTAL HOLSINGER** SURPRISE, ARIZONA

PREP: 20 MINUTES **BAKE:** 40 MINUTES **MAKES:** 6 SERVINGS

⅓ cup chopped hazelnuts
¼ cup butter, chopped
3 tablespoons crumbled Gorgonzola cheese
1 tablespoon brown sugar
¼ teaspoon ground cinnamon
⅛ teaspoon salt
⅛ teaspoon onion powder
6 medium tart apples, cored
1 cup balsamic vinegar

1. In a small bowl, combine the first seven ingredients. Stuff apples with mixture and place in a greased 11-in. x 7-in. baking dish. Bake, uncovered, at 325° for 40-45 minutes or until apples are tender.
2. Meanwhile, in a small saucepan, bring vinegar to a boil; cook until liquid is reduced to ⅓ cup. Drizzle over apples.

Triple Cranberry Sauce

Cranberry fans will ask for this sauce again and again. It's loaded with their favorite fruit—in fresh, dried and juice form. Orange and allspice make it awesome.

—**ARLENE SMULSKI** LYONS, ILLINOIS

PREP: 10 MINUTES
COOK: 15 MINUTES + CHILLING
MAKES: 3 CUPS

1 package (12 ounces) fresh or frozen cranberries
1 cup thawed cranberry juice concentrate
½ cup dried cranberries
⅓ cup sugar
3 tablespoons orange juice
3 tablespoons orange marmalade
2 teaspoons grated orange peel
¼ teaspoon ground allspice

1. In a small saucepan, combine the fresh or frozen cranberries, cranberry juice concentrate, dried cranberries and sugar.
2. Cook over medium heat until the berries pop, about 15 minutes.
3. Remove from the heat; stir in the orange juice, marmalade, orange peel and allspice. Transfer to a small bowl; refrigerate until chilled

HOME STYLE tip

❝I use leftover cranberry sauce to fill apples before baking them. The blend of flavors is delicious.❞

—**LORRAINE V.**
BEAVER DAM, WISCONSIN

Red-White-and-Blue Berry Delight

Loaded with fresh strawberries and blueberries, this luscious treat is perfect for any Fourth of July celebration!

—CONSTANCE FENNELL
GRAND JUNCTION, MICHIGAN

PREP: 25 MINUTES + CHILLING
MAKES: 8 SERVINGS

- ½ cup sugar
- 2 envelopes unflavored gelatin
- 4 cups white cranberry-peach juice drink, divided
- 1 tablespoon lemon juice
- 2 cups fresh strawberries, halved
- 2 cups fresh blueberries

CREAM
- ½ cup heavy whipping cream
- 1 tablespoon sugar
- ¼ teaspoon vanilla extract

1. In a large saucepan, combine sugar and gelatin. Add 1 cup cranberry-peach juice; cook and stir over low heat until gelatin is completely dissolved, about 5 minutes. Remove from the heat; stir in lemon juice and remaining cranberry-peach juice.

2. Place strawberries in an 8-cup ring mold coated with cooking spray; add 2 cups gelatin mixture. Refrigerate until set but not firm, about 30 minutes. Set aside remaining gelatin mixture.

3. Stir blueberries into remaining gelatin mixture; spoon over strawberry layer. Refrigerate overnight. Unmold onto a serving platter.

4. In a small bowl, beat cream until it begins to thicken. Add sugar and vanilla; beat until stiff peaks form. Serve with gelatin.

Christmas Vegetable Salad

My sister gave me this recipe at a family gathering one year, and I've been making her colorful, crisp salad for holiday get-togethers, dinner parties and potlucks ever since. The festive salad travels well and holds up beautifully on the buffet table, so it's ideal for making ahead. Serve it in a clear bowl so everyone can see the pretty combination of colors.

—MARY DEAN EAU CLAIRE, WISCONSIN

PREP: 15 MINUTES + MARINATING **MAKES:** 6 SERVINGS

- ¼ cup canola oil
- 1 tablespoon plus 1½ teaspoons lemon juice
- 1 tablespoon plus 1½ teaspoons white wine vinegar
- 1 teaspoon salt
- ½ teaspoon sugar
  Coarsely ground pepper
- 2 cups thinly sliced cauliflower
- ½ cup sliced pimiento-stuffed olives
- ⅓ cup chopped green pepper
- ⅓ cup chopped red pepper

1. In a jar with a tight-fitting lid, combine the first six ingredients; shake well. In a salad bowl, combine the cauliflower, olives and peppers; drizzle with dressing and toss to coat. Cover and refrigerate for several hours or overnight.

Cranberry Bread Pudding

This down-home dessert takes on a touch of elegance when I serve it warm and drizzled with a thin orange custard sauce. It's so pretty that I often make it for dinner guests.

—**MARGERY RICHMOND** FORT COLLINS, COLORADO

PREP: 35 MINUTES + STANDING **BAKE:** 65 MINUTES **MAKES:** 12 SERVINGS

16 slices bread, crusts removed and cubed
1½ cups fresh or frozen cranberries, thawed
1 tablespoon grated orange peel
¼ cup butter, melted
6 eggs
4 cups milk
¾ cup plus 1 tablespoon sugar, divided
1 teaspoon vanilla extract

ORANGE CUSTARD SAUCE

3 egg yolks
¼ cup sugar
1 cup heavy whipping cream
1 orange peel strip (¼ inch)
½ teaspoon orange extract

1. In a greased 13-in. x 9-in. baking dish, layer half of the bread cubes, cranberries and orange peel. Repeat layers. Drizzle with butter.

2. In a large bowl, beat the eggs, milk, ¾ cup sugar and vanilla until blended; pour over bread mixture. Let stand for 15-30 minutes. Sprinkle with remaining sugar.

3. Bake, uncovered, at 375° for 65-75 minutes or until a knife inserted near the center comes out clean.

4. For sauce, in a heavy saucepan, beat egg yolks and sugar. Stir in cream and orange peel. Cook and stir over low heat for 20-25 minutes or until mixture is thickened and coats the back of a spoon. Remove from the heat; discard orange peel. Stir in extract. Refrigerate until chilled. Serve with bread pudding.

Peppermint Stick Cookies

With cool mint flavor and a festive look, these whimsical creations will make you feel like you're at the North Pole. The chilled dough is easy to shape, too.

—NANCY KNAPKE FORT RECOVERY, OHIO

PREP: 1 HOUR + CHILLING **BAKE:** 10 MINUTES/BATCH + COOLING **MAKES:** 4 DOZEN

- 1 **cup unsalted butter, softened**
- 1 **cup sugar**
- 1 **egg**
- 2 **teaspoons mint extract**
- ½ **teaspoon vanilla extract**
- 2¾ **cups all-purpose flour**
- ½ **teaspoon salt**
- 12 **drops green food coloring**
- 12 **drops red food coloring**
- 1½ **cups white baking chips**
  Crushed mint candies

1. In a bowl, cream butter and sugar until light and fluffy. Beat in egg and extracts. Combine flour and salt; gradually add to the creamed mixture and mix well.

2. Set aside half of the dough. Divide remaining dough in half; add green food coloring to one portion and red food coloring to the other. Wrap dough separately in plastic wrap. Refrigerate for 1-2 hours or until easy to handle.

3. Divide green and red dough into 24 portions each. Divide plain dough into 48 portions. Roll each into a 4-in. rope. Place each green rope next to a white rope; press together gently and twist. Repeat with red ropes and remaining white ropes. Place 2 in. apart on ungreased baking sheets.

4. Bake at 350° for 10-12 minutes or until set. Cool for 2 minutes before carefully removing from pans to wire racks to cool completely.

5. In a microwave, melt white chips; stir until smooth. Dip cookie ends into melted chips; allow excess to drip off. Sprinkle with crushed candies and place on waxed paper. Let stand until set. Store in an airtight container.

Holiday English Trifles

This recipe has everything I want in a holiday dessert. It's decadent, easy to prepare and beautiful.
—**BONNIE L. CAMERON** COLBERT, WASHINGTON

PREP: 35 MINUTES **BAKE:** 35 MINUTES + CHILLING **MAKES:** 15 SERVINGS

- 1 **package (18¼ ounces) yellow cake mix**
- ⅓ **cup orange juice or orange liqueur**
- ⅓ **cup sherry or additional orange juice**
- 1 **jar (18 ounces) seedless raspberry jam**
- 1½ **cups cold 2% milk**
- 1 **package (3.4 ounces) instant vanilla pudding mix**
- 1 **cup (8 ounces) reduced-fat sour cream**
- 2 **cups heavy whipping cream**
- 3 **tablespoons confectioners' sugar**
- 1½ **cups fresh raspberries**

1. Prepare and bake the cake according to package directions, using a greased 13-in. x 9-in baking pan. Cool; cut into 1-in. cubes.
2. In a small bowl, combine orange juice and sherry. In another bowl, whisk jam. In a large bowl, whisk milk and pudding mix for 2 minutes. Whisk in sour cream. Let stand for 2 minutes or until soft-set.
3. Divide half of the cake cubes among 15 parfait glasses or dessert dishes; drizzle with half of the orange juice mixture. Layer each with jam and pudding mixture. Top with remaining cake cubes; drizzle with remaining orange juice mixture. Cover and refrigerate for at least 4 hours.
4. Just before serving, in a large bowl, beat cream until it begins to thicken. Add confectioners' sugar; beat until stiff peaks form. Dollop over trifles and garnish with raspberries.

Tender Sugar Cookies

Want to simplify your sugar cookies? Roll the buttery dough into balls, then dip them into colored sugar before baking.
—**TASTE OF HOME TEST KITCHEN**

PREP: 30 MINUTES + CHILLING
BAKE: 10 MINUTES/BATCH **MAKES:** 5½ DOZEN

- ¾ **cup butter-flavored shortening**
- 1½ **cups sugar**
- 2 **eggs**
- ½ **teaspoon almond extract**
- ½ **teaspoon vanilla extract**
- 3 **cups all-purpose flour**
- 1 **teaspoon baking powder**
- 1 **teaspoon baking soda**
- ½ **teaspoon salt**
- ⅓ **cup buttermilk**
  Colored sugar and/or coarse sugar

1. In a large bowl, cream shortening and sugar until light and fluffy. Add eggs, one at a time, beating well after each addition. Beat in extracts. Combine the flour, baking powder, baking soda and salt; add to the creamed mixture alternately with buttermilk, beating well after each addition. Cover and refrigerate for at least 2 hours.
2. Roll into 1-in. balls; dip tops in sugar. Place 2 in. apart on parchment paper-lined baking sheets. Bake at 375° for 9-11 minutes or until lightly browned and tops are cracked. Remove to wire racks to cool.

Home Style COOKING NOTES

Over-the-Top Chocolate Cake

Coming up with this decadent cake was a real family affair. The cake recipe is from my sister-in-law, I created the frosting, and my husband, Alan, thought of studding the cake with made-from-scratch English toffee. Traditionally served for the holidays, this dessert has already become a family heirloom recipe.

—VANESSA JOHNSON HEYBURN, IDAHO

PREP: 1½ HOURS **BAKE:** 20 MINUTES + COOLING
MAKES: 16 SERVINGS

- 1 teaspoon plus ¾ cup butter, divided
- 1 cup sugar
- 2 tablespoons water
  Dash salt
- ½ cup coarsely chopped pecans
- 1 teaspoon vanilla extract

CAKE

- 2 cups sugar
- 1 cup water
- 1 cup 2% milk
- ½ cup canola oil
- 2 eggs
- 2 teaspoons vanilla extract
- 1¾ cups all-purpose flour
- ¾ cup baking cocoa
- 1½ teaspoons baking powder
- 1½ teaspoons baking soda
- 1 teaspoon salt

FROSTING

- 2 cups heavy whipping cream
- 1 package (8 ounces) cream cheese, softened
- ½ cup mascarpone cheese
- 9 ounces white baking chocolate, melted
- 1 cup confectioners' sugar
- 1 teaspoon vanilla extract
- 1 cup dulce de leche, divided

1. Line a 13-in. x 9-in. baking pan with foil and grease the foil with 1 teaspoon butter; set aside.

2. In a large heavy saucepan, combine the sugar, water, salt and remaining butter. Cook and stir over medium heat until a candy thermometer reads 300° (hard-crack stage). Remove from heat; stir in pecans and vanilla. Immediately pour into prepared pan. Let stand until set, about 1 hour. Break into small pieces.

3. In a large bowl, beat the sugar, water, milk, oil, eggs and vanilla until well blended.

Combine the flour, cocoa, baking powder, baking soda and salt; gradually beat into sugar mixture until blended. Transfer batter to three greased and floured 9-in. round baking pans.

4. Bake at 350° for 18-22 minutes or until a toothpick comes out clean. Cool for 10 minutes before removing from pans to wire racks to cool completely.

5. In a large bowl, beat whipping cream until stiff peaks form. In a another bowl, beat cheeses until smooth; add the chocolate, confectioners' sugar and vanilla. Fold in whipped cream and ½ cup dulce de leche.

6. Place bottom cake layer on a serving plate; spread with 2 cups frosting and sprinkle with ¼ cup toffee. Repeat layers once. Top with remaining cake layer. Spread remaining frosting over top and sides of cake.

7. Drop remaining dulce de leche by teaspoonfuls over top of cake; cut through frosting with a knife to swirl. Press remaining toffee into top and sides of cake. Refrigerate leftovers.

Editor's Note: *We recommend that you test your candy thermometer before each use by bringing water to a boil; the thermometer should read 212°. Adjust your recipe temperature up or down based on your test. This recipe was tested with Nestle dulce de leche. Look for it in the international foods section.*

Squash Dressing

I got this recipe from my husband's cousin. She always made the luscious dressing for her mother at Thanksgiving.

—ANNA MAYER FORT BRANCH, INDIANA

PREP: 30 MINUTES + COOLING **BAKE:** 40 MINUTES **MAKES:** 8 SERVINGS

- 1 package (8½ ounces) corn bread/muffin mix
- ½ cup water
- 4 cups chopped yellow summer squash
- ½ cup butter
- ½ cup each chopped onion, celery and green pepper
- 1 can (10¾ ounces) condensed cream of chicken soup, undiluted
- 1 cup milk
- 1 teaspoon salt
- ½ teaspoon pepper

1. Prepare corn bread according to package directions. Cool and crumble into a large bowl; set aside.

2. In a large saucepan, bring ½ in. of water to a boil. Add squash; cook, covered, for 3-5 minutes or until crisp-tender. Drain. Meanwhile, in a large skillet, melt butter. Add the onion, celery and green pepper; saute until tender.

3. Add vegetable mixture and squash to the corn bread. In a small bowl, combine the soup, milk, salt and pepper; add to corn bread and stir until blended. Transfer to a greased 11-in. x 7-in. baking dish.

4. Bake, uncovered, at 350° for 40-45 minutes or until golden brown.

New Year's Eve Tenderloin Steaks

I found the instructions for these delicious beef filets in a cookbook I bought on a cruise. My friend and I tried them and they're one of our favorites—easy, quick to prepare and so elegant on the table.

—AGNES WARD STRATFORD, ONTARIO

PREP: 30 MINUTES **BROIL:** 5 MINUTES
MAKES: 2 SERVINGS

- 2 beef tenderloin steaks (1 inch thick and 5 ounces each)
- ¼ teaspoon pepper
- 1 tablespoon canola oil
- 3 shallots, finely chopped
- 2 tablespoons Cognac
- ¼ teaspoon whole peppercorns, crushed
- ½ cup dry red wine or beef broth
- ¼ cup beef broth
- 2 ounces fresh goat cheese, crumbled

1. Sprinkle steaks with pepper. In a large skillet, cook steaks in oil over medium heat for 4-6 minutes on each side or until meat reaches desired doneness (for medium-rare, a thermometer should read 145°; medium, 160°; well-done, 170°). Remove to a baking sheet and keep warm.

2. Reduce heat to low; add the shallots, Cognac and peppercorns, stirring to loosen browned bits from pan. Stir in wine and broth. Bring to a boil over medium heat; cook until liquid is reduced to ½ cup.

3. Top steaks with cheese. Broil 6 in. from the heat for 2-3 minutes or until cheese is softened. Serve sauce mixture with steaks.

Pumpkin Eggnog Rolls

I needed to use up some eggnog, so I swapped it for milk in my sweet-roll recipe. Even those who might pass up eggnog otherwise go back for seconds of these yummy frosted treats.

—REBECCA SOSKE DOUGLAS, WYOMING

PREP: 40 MINUTES + RISING **BAKE:** 20 MINUTES
MAKES: 1 DOZEN

- 4½ **cups all-purpose flour**
- ½ **cup sugar**
- 1 **package (¼ ounce) active dry yeast**
- ½ **teaspoon salt**
- ¾ **cup eggnog**
- ½ **cup butter, cubed**
- ¼ **cup canned pumpkin**
- 2 **eggs**

FILLING
- ¼ **cup butter, melted**
- ½ **cup sugar**
- 1 **teaspoon ground cardamom**
- 1 **teaspoon ground allspice**

FROSTING
- 2 **ounces cream cheese, softened**
- 2 **tablespoons eggnog**
- 1 **tablespoon canned pumpkin**
- ¼ **teaspoon ground cardamom**
- 2 **cups confectioners' sugar**

Home Style COOKING NOTES

1. In a large bowl, combine 2 cups flour, sugar, yeast and salt. In a small saucepan, heat the eggnog, butter and pumpkin to 120°-130°. Add to dry ingredients; beat on medium speed for 2 minutes. Add eggs and ½ cup flour; beat 3 minutes longer. Stir in enough remaining flour to form a firm dough.

2. Turn onto a floured surface; knead until smooth and elastic, about 6-8 minutes. Place in a greased bowl, turning once to grease the top. Cover and let rise in a warm place until doubled, about 1 hour. Punch dough down.

3. Roll into an 18-in. x 12-in. rectangle. Brush with melted butter. Combine the sugar, cardamom and allspice. Sprinkle to within ½ in. of edges. Roll up jelly-roll style, starting with a long side; pinch seams to seal. Cut into 1½-in. slices.

4. Place rolls, cut side down, in a greased 13-in. x 9-in. baking pan. Cover and let rise in a warm place until doubled, about 45 minutes. Bake at 350° for 20-25 minutes or until golden brown.

5. In a small bowl, beat the cream cheese, eggnog, pumpkin and cardamom until blended. Add confectioners' sugar; beat until smooth. Spread over warm rolls. Cool on a wire rack.

Editor's Note: *This recipe was tested with commercially prepared eggnog.*

⅓ cup plus 4 teaspoons water
1¼ teaspoons vanilla extract
5 cups confectioners' sugar
1 tablespoon plus ¾ teaspoon meringue powder

DECORATING
Red and blue colored sugar
Coarse sugar
Red and blue paste food coloring
1 tablespoon light corn syrup

1. Prepare and bake cake according to package directions, using two greased 9-in. round baking pans. Cool for 10 minutes before removing from pans to wire racks to cool completely.

2. In a large bowl, combine cookie dough and flour. On a lightly floured surface, roll out dough to ¼-in. thickness. Cut out 12 cookies with a floured 2-in. star cookie cutter; insert lollipop sticks into dough. Cut out eight cookies with a floured 1-in. star cookie cutter.

3. Place 1 in. apart on ungreased baking sheets. Bake at 350° for 7-9 minutes or until edges are light golden brown. Cool on wire racks.

4. For buttercream, using a heavy-duty stand mixer, combine the shortening, water and vanilla. Combine confectioners' sugar and meringue powder; beat into shortening mixture.

5. Spread 2 cups buttercream between layers and over top and sides of cake. Sprinkle the top with colored sugar. Frost cookie pops; sprinkle with red, blue and clear sugars.

6. Tint ⅓ cup frosting red and ⅓ cup blue; leave remaining frosting white. Using a #18 star tip and white frosting, pipe a border around bottom of cake. Using a #4 round tip with blue frosting and an additional #18 star tip with red frosting, pipe four flags on sides of cake.

7. In a microwave, heat corn syrup for 10 seconds or just until bubbly. Brush over one side of small star cookies; sprinkle with red and blue sugars. Press onto sides of cake. Press cookie pops into top of cake.

Editor's Note: *Meringue powder is available from Wilton Industries. Call 800-794-5866 or visit* wilton.com.

Buttercream Blast Layer Cake

The decorations on this patriotic dessert remind me of a fireworks display. Since the recipe includes both cookies and cake, people can take their pick—or have both!
—**JENNIFER LINDSTROM** BROOKFIELD, WISCONSIN

PREP: 1 HOUR 20 MINUTES **BAKE:** 25 MINUTES + COOLING **MAKES:** 12 SERVINGS

1 package (18¼ ounces) white cake mix
1 tube (16½ ounces) refrigerated sugar cookie dough, softened
⅔ cup all-purpose flour
12 lollipop sticks
BUTTERCREAM
1¼ cups shortening

Rhubarb Cheese Pie

This tangy rhubarb pie is topped with a luscious cream cheese layer. It's a match made in heaven!

—STACEY MEYER PLYMOUTH, WISCONSIN

PREP: 35 MINUTES **BAKE:** 25 MINUTES + CHILLING **MAKES:** 8 SERVINGS

Pastry for single-crust pie (9 inches)
4½ teaspoons all-purpose flour
1 tablespoon cornstarch
1 cup sugar, divided
½ cup water
3 cups sliced fresh or frozen rhubarb
1 teaspoon vanilla extract, divided
12 ounces cream cheese, softened
2 eggs, lightly beaten
1 egg yolk

1. Line a 9-in. pie plate with pastry; flute edges. Line unpricked pastry shell with a double thickness of heavy-duty foil. Bake at 450° for 8 minutes. Remove foil; bake 5 minutes longer. Cool on a wire rack.

2. In a small saucepan, combine the flour, cornstarch and ½ cup sugar. Add water and rhubarb; stir until blended. Bring to a boil; cook and stir for 2 minutes or until thickened. Remove from the heat; stir in ½ teaspoon vanilla. Transfer to prepared pastry.

3. In a bowl, beat cream cheese with remaining sugar and vanilla until smooth. Add eggs and egg yolk; beat on low speed just until combined. Spread over top of pie.

4. Cover edges with foil. Bake at 325° for 25-30 minutes or until set. Cool on a wire rack for 1 hour. Refrigerate for at least 4 hours before serving.

Editor's Note: *If using frozen rhubarb, measure rhubarb while still frozen, then thaw completely. Drain in a colander, but do not press liquid out.*

3 **fresh rosemary sprigs**
3 **sprigs fresh sage**
3 **cups chicken broth, divided**
¼ **cup all-purpose flour**
   Additional citrus fruits and herb sprigs,
   optional

1. Pat turkey dry. Combine butter and Italian seasoning. With fingers, carefully loosen skin from the turkey breast; rub half of the butter under skin. Rub remaining mixture over the skin. Rub cavity with salt and pepper and fill with onion, lemon, orange, rosemary and sage. Tuck wings under turkey; tie drumsticks together. Place breast side up on a rack in a roasting pan. Pour 2 cups broth into pan.

2. Bake at 325° for 2¾ to 3¼ hours or until a thermometer reads 180°, basting occasionally with pan drippings. Cover loosely with foil if turkey browns too quickly. Cover and let stand for 20 minutes before carving.

3. Pour drippings into a small saucepan; skim fat. Combine flour and remaining broth until smooth; whisk into the pan. Bring to a boil; cook and stir for 2 minutes or until thickened.

4. Discard onion, lemon, orange and herbs from the turkey; transfer turkey to a serving platter. Garnish the platter with additional citrus fruits and herb sprigs if desired. Serve turkey with gravy.

Roasted Citrus & Herb Turkey

Thanksgiving has never been the same since I tried this recipe. I have made it for the past 3 years, and it has never failed to impress both in presentation and flavor. This turkey is a true showstopper!

—NANCY NIEMERG DIETERICH, ILLINOIS

PREP: 30 MINUTES **BAKE:** 2¾ HOURS **MAKES:** 14-16 SERVINGS (2 CUPS GRAVY)

1 **turkey (14 to 16 pounds)**
¼ **cup butter, softened**
2 **tablespoons Italian seasoning**
2 **teaspoons salt**
2 **teaspoons pepper**
1 **large onion, quartered**
1 **medium lemon, quartered**
1 **medium orange, quartered**

Home Style COOKING NOTES

Lemon Carrot Bread

Lemon and carrot flavors combine for a unique flavor sensation in moist and tender quick bread. I know it's a winner because I bring a loaf to our church festival every year, and I always get requests to bake it again.

—HAZEL SCHULTZ PAINESVILLE, OHIO

PREP: 20 MINUTES
BAKE: 40 MINUTES + COOLING
MAKES: 2 LOAVES (12 SLICES EACH)

- ¾ cup butter, softened
- 1½ cups sugar
- 3 eggs
- 1 tablespoon lemon juice
- 2¼ cups all-purpose flour
- 2 teaspoons baking powder
- ½ teaspoon baking soda
- ¼ teaspoon salt
- ½ cup milk
- 1 cup shredded carrots
- ¾ cup chopped pecans
- 2 tablespoons grated lemon peel

1. In a large bowl, cream butter and sugar until light and fluffy. Add eggs, one at a time, beating well after each addition. Stir in lemon juice. Combine the flour, baking powder, baking soda and salt; add to the creamed mixture alternately with milk. Stir in the carrots, pecans and lemon peel.

2. Transfer to two greased 8-in. x 4-in. loaf pans. Bake at 350° for 40-45 minutes or until a toothpick inserted near the center comes out clean. Cool for 10 minutes before removing from pans to wire racks.

Grandma's Christmas Cake

One bite of this old-fashioned spice cake will bring back memories. Chock-full of raisins and nuts, it tastes extra special drizzled with a rich, buttery sauce.

—LINDA STEMEN MONROEVILLE, INDIANA

PREP: 25 MINUTES **BAKE:** 45 MINUTES + COOLING **MAKES:** 12 SERVINGS

- 2 cups sugar
- 2 cups raisins
- 2 cups water
- 1 cup butter, cubed
- 3½ cups all-purpose flour
- 1 teaspoon baking soda
- 1 teaspoon ground cinnamon
- ½ teaspoon each ground nutmeg and cloves
- 1 cup chopped pecans

BRANDY BUTTER SAUCE

- 1 cup heavy whipping cream
- 1 cup butter, cubed
- 1 cup sugar
- 4 egg yolks, lightly beaten
- ¼ cup brandy

1. In a large saucepan, combine the sugar, raisins, water and butter. Bring to a boil. Reduce heat to medium; cook, uncovered, for 5 minutes or until sugar is dissolved. Remove from the heat; cool.

2. In a large bowl, combine the flour, baking soda, cinnamon, nutmeg and cloves. Add raisin mixture; beat until blended. Fold in pecans.

3. Pour into a greased and floured 10-in. fluted tube pan. Bake at 350° for 45-55 minutes or until cake springs back when lightly touched. Cool for 10 minutes before removing from pan to a wire rack to cool completely.

4. For sauce, in a large saucepan, bring cream to a boil; stir in butter and sugar until smooth. Reduce heat; stir a small amount of hot liquid into egg yolks. Return all to the pan, stirring constantly. Cook until sauce is slightly thickened and coats the back of a spoon (do not boil). Remove from the heat; stir in brandy. Serve warm with cake.

Pumpkin-Sweet Potato Pie with Sugared Pecans

This is not your typical pumpkin pie! With a smooth, creamy filling and pretty arrangement of nuts on top, it's a sensational dessert.

—LORETTA LAWRENCE MYRTLE BEACH, SOUTH CAROLINA

PREP: 20 MINUTES **BAKE:** 40 MINUTES + COOLING **MAKES:** 8 SERVINGS

1 can (15 ounces) solid-pack pumpkin
1 cup mashed sweet potatoes
¾ cup packed brown sugar
1½ teaspoons ground cinnamon
½ teaspoon salt
½ teaspoon ground ginger
½ teaspoon ground nutmeg
¼ teaspoon ground cloves
3 eggs, beaten
1¼ cups heavy whipping cream
1 can (5 ounces) evaporated milk
1 tablespoon dark rum
    Pastry for single-crust pie (9 inches)

PECANS
2 cups pecan halves
½ cup packed brown sugar
¼ cup heavy whipping cream
    Whipped cream

1. In a large bowl, combine the first eight ingredients. Add the eggs, cream, milk and rum; mix well. Line a 9-in. deep-dish pie plate with pastry; trim and flute edges. Pour pumpkin mixture into pastry.

2. Bake at 400° for 40-45 minutes or until a knife inserted near the center comes out clean. Cool on a wire rack.

3. In a small bowl, combine the pecans, brown sugar and cream. Spread into a greased 15-in. x 10-in. x 1-in. baking pan. Bake at 350° for 15-20 minutes or until toasted, stirring once. Cool completely.

4. Top pie with sugared pecans; serve with whipped cream. Refrigerate leftovers.

Cranberry Corn Bread Casserole

What could be better on a cold day than a warm casserole and creamy sweet corn bread put together? Since it starts with a mix, this side takes no time to make. Just bake, scoop and eat. Yum!

—**VALERY ANDERSON** STERLING HTS, MICHIGAN

PREP: 15 MINUTES **BAKE:** 20 MINUTES **MAKES:** 9 SERVINGS

- ½ cup dried cranberries
- ½ cup boiling water
- 1 package (8½ ounces) corn bread/muffin mix
- 1 teaspoon onion powder
- ¼ teaspoon rubbed sage
- 1 egg
- 1 can (14¾ ounces) cream-style corn
- 2 tablespoons butter, melted
- ¼ cup chopped pecans
- ½ teaspoon grated orange peel

1. Place cranberries in a small bowl; cover with boiling water. Let stand for 5 minutes; drain and set aside.

2. In a small bowl, combine the muffin mix, onion powder and sage. In another bowl, whisk the egg, corn and butter; stir into dry ingredients just until moistened. Fold in the pecans, orange peel and cranberries.

3. Transfer to a greased 8-in. square baking dish. Bake uncovered at 400° for 20-25 minutes or until set.

Hot Apple Pie Drink

A perfect holiday treat for adults, these hot drinks are simple and fun to make. They definitely take the chill off.

—**TASTE OF HOME TEST KITCHEN**

PREP/TOTAL TIME: 20 MINUTES
MAKES: 2 SERVINGS

- 2 cups unsweetened apple juice
- 4 teaspoons brown sugar
- 2 teaspoons lemon juice
- ¼ teaspoon ground cinnamon
  Dash ground cloves
  Dash ground nutmeg
- 1½ ounces orange liqueur
- 1½ ounces brandy
  Sweetened whipped cream and additional ground nutmeg, optional

1. In a small saucepan, heat the first six ingredients until sugar is dissolved. Remove mixture from the heat; stir in the orange liqueur and brandy.

2. Pour into mugs; garnish with whipped cream and additional nutmeg if desired.

Easter Fruit Salad

Both young and old alike are sure to enjoy this colorful Easter fruit salad that uses pastel marshmallows. I recommend making it the day before it's served.

—DEANNA RICHTER ELMORE, MINNESOTA

PREP: 25 MINUTES + CHILLING
MAKES: 12 SERVINGS

- 1 can (20 ounces) unsweetened pineapple chunks
- ¾ cup sugar
- 2 tablespoons all-purpose flour
- 2 eggs, lightly beaten
- 1 tablespoon lemon juice
- 1 cup heavy whipping cream, whipped
- 1 can (11 ounces) mandarin oranges, drained
- 1 package (10½ ounces) pastel miniature marshmallows
- 1 jar (10 ounces) maraschino cherries, drained and chopped

1. Drain pineapple, reserving the juice; set pineapple aside. In a heavy saucepan, combine the sugar, flour, eggs, lemon juice and reserved pineapple juice until smooth. Cook and stir over medium-low heat until mixture is thickened and reaches 160°. Cool to room temperature.

2. Fold in whipped cream. In a large bowl, combine the oranges, marshmallows, cherries and reserved pineapple; fold in cooked dressing. Refrigerate until chilled.

Pumpkin Patch Biscuits

I often bake a double batch of these moist, fluffy biscuits to meet the enthusiastic demand. My dad loves their pumpkiny goodness and requests them for holidays, Father's Day and his birthday.

—LIZA TAYLOR SEATTLE, WASHINGTON

PREP: 20 MINUTES **BAKE:** 20 MINUTES **MAKES:** 6 BISCUITS

- 1¾ cups all-purpose flour
- ¼ cup packed brown sugar
- 2½ teaspoons baking powder
- ½ teaspoon salt
- ¼ teaspoon baking soda
- ½ cup plus 1½ teaspoons cold butter, divided
- ¾ cup canned pumpkin
- ⅓ cup buttermilk

1. Combine the flour, brown sugar, baking powder, salt and baking soda. Cut in ½ cup of the butter until mixture resembles coarse crumbs. Combine the pumpkin and buttermilk; stir into crumb mixture just until moistened.

2. Turn onto a lightly floured surface; knead 8-10 times. Pat or roll out to 1-in. thickness; cut with a floured 2½-in. biscuit cutter. Place 1 in. apart on a greased baking sheet.

3. Bake at 425° for 18-22 minutes or until golden brown. Melt remaining butter; brush over biscuits. Serve warm.

Home Style COOKING NOTES

Marshmallow Easter Eggs

I've been making this wonderful Easter candy for years. The eggs are a big hit with everyone who loves marshmallows.
—**BETTY CLAYCOMB** ALVERTON, PENNSYLVANIA

PREP: 45 MINUTES + STANDING **COOK:** 15 MINUTES **MAKES:** 3 DOZEN

- 25 **cups all-purpose flour (about 8 pounds)**
- 1 **large egg**
- 2 **tablespoons unflavored gelatin**
- ½ **cup cold water**
- 2 **cups sugar**
- 1 **cup light corn syrup, divided**
- ¾ **cup hot water**
- 2 **teaspoons vanilla extract**
- 1 **pound dark chocolate candy coating, melted**
- 2 **ounces white candy coating, melted**

1. Spread 7 cups flour in each of three 13-in. x 9-in. pans and 4 cups flour in a 9-in. square pan. Carefully wash the egg in a mild bleach solution (1 teaspoon chlorine bleach to 1 qt. warm water); dry. Press washed egg halfway into the flour to form an impression. Repeat 35 times; set aside.

2. In a small bowl, sprinkle the gelatin over cold water; set aside. In a large saucepan, combine the sugar, ½ cup corn syrup and hot water. Bring to a boil over medium heat, stirring constantly, until a candy thermometer reads 238° (soft-ball stage). Remove from the heat; stir in remaining corn syrup.

3. Pour into a large bowl. Add reserved gelatin, 1 tablespoon at a time, beating on high speed until candy is thick and has cooled to lukewarm, about 10 minutes. Beat in vanilla.

4. Spoon lukewarm gelatin mixture into egg depressions; dust with flour. Let stand for 3-4 hours or until set.

5. Brush excess flour off marshmallow eggs. Dip each in chocolate candy coating. Place flat side down on waxed paper. Let stand until set. Pour white candy coating into a heavy-duty resealable plastic bag; cut a hole in one corner. Drizzle over eggs.

Editor's Note: *For safety reasons, we recommend that you discard the egg and all of the flour. We recommend that you test your candy thermometer before each use by bringing water to a boil; the thermometer should read 212°. Adjust your recipe temperature up or down based on your test.*

Cranberry-White Chocolate Cinnamon Rolls

A basket of warm cinnamon rolls is a sure way to impress family and friends. Add cranberries and chocolate to the ingredient mix, and these treats are irresistible.

—**MEG MARRIOTT** TACOMA, WASHINGTON

PREP: 45 MINUTES + CHILLING **BAKE:** 30 MINUTES + COOLING **MAKES:** 16 SERVINGS

- 2 **packages (¼ ounce each) active dry yeast**
- 2 **cups warm water (110° to 115°)**
- 1 **cup butter, melted**
- ½ **cup sugar**
- 2 **teaspoons salt**
- 5 **to 6 cups all-purpose flour**

FILLING
- 1 **cup butter, softened**
- ½ **cup packed brown sugar**
- 2 **teaspoons ground cinnamon**
- 1 **package (10 to 12 ounces) white baking chips**
- 1 **cup dried cranberries**
- ½ **cup chopped pecans**

GLAZE
- 2 **cups confectioners' sugar**
- 2 **teaspoons vanilla extract**
- 5 **to 6 tablespoons heavy whipping cream**

1. In a large bowl, dissolve yeast in warm water. Add the butter, sugar, salt and 4 cups flour; beat until smooth. Stir in enough remaining flour to form a soft dough.

2. Turn onto a floured surface; knead until smooth and elastic, about 6-8 minutes. Place in a greased bowl, turning once to grease the top. Cover and refrigerate overnight.

3. Punch dough down. On a lightly floured surface, roll into a 24-in. x 12-in. rectangle. For filling, combine the butter, brown sugar and cinnamon; spread over dough to within ½ in. of edges. Sprinkle with chips, cranberries and pecans. Roll up jelly-roll style, starting with a long side; pinch seam to seal.

4. Cut into 16 slices. Place cut side down in two greased 13-in. x 9-in. baking pans. Cover and let rise in a warm place until doubled, about 45 minutes.

5. Bake at 350° for 30-35 minutes or until golden brown. Meanwhile, in a small bowl, combine the confectioners' sugar, vanilla and enough cream to achieve desired consistency; drizzle over warm rolls. Cool on wire racks.

Home Style COOKING NOTES

Pineapple Coconut Potatoes

This recipe gives potatoes a bit of tropical flair with pineapple, coconut, soy sauce and ginger. The potatoes are a hit whenever I've served them— at barbecues, holidays and more— and I've often had requests for the recipe.

—PAULA PELIS
LENHARTSVILLE, PENNSYLVANIA

PREP: 20 MINUTES **BAKE:** 1¼ HOURS
MAKES: 4-6 SERVINGS

- 1 can (20 ounces) unsweetened pineapple chunks
- 2 cups diced peeled potatoes
- 1 cup flaked coconut, divided
- 1 medium onion, sliced
- ¼ cup packed brown sugar
- 2 tablespoons all-purpose flour
- ½ teaspoon salt
- ½ teaspoon ground ginger
- ¼ cup cider vinegar
- 1 tablespoon soy sauce

1. Drain pineapple, reserving juice. In a large bowl, combine the pineapple, potatoes, ¾ cup coconut and onion. Transfer to a greased 1-qt. baking dish; set aside.

2. In a small saucepan, whisk the brown sugar, flour, salt, ginger, vinegar, soy sauce and reserved pineapple juice until smooth. Bring to a boil; cook and stir for 2 minutes or until thickened. Pour over potato mixture and toss to coat.

3. Cover and bake at 350° for 65-70 minutes or until potatoes are tender. Sprinkle with remaining coconut. Bake, uncovered, for 10 minutes or until lightly browned.

Jack-o'-Lantern Cupcakes

Carve out a little time to decorate these Halloween pumpkins with jack-o'-lantern faces. They're a cute and fun treat to make and share!

—TASTE OF HOME TEST KITCHEN

PREP: 1 HOUR **MAKES:** 1 DOZEN

- 1 can vanilla frosting (16 ounces)
  Orange food coloring
- 12 cupcakes of your choice
  Assorted candies: spice drops, fruit leather, green licorice and licorice whips, candy corn, miniature and peanut M&Ms, jelly beans

1. Tint frosting orange; frost cupcakes. Roll spice drops to ¼-in. thickness; cut spice drops and fruit leather into triangles for eyes and noses.

2. Cut licorice into 1-in. lengths for stems. Cut licorice whips into 2- to 3-in. lengths and twist as desired to form pumpkin vines. Make jack-o'-lantern faces with candies.

Cranberry Sweet Potato Bake

Here's a perfect side dish for Thanksgiving, with a tasty combination of sweet potatoes, cranberries and apples. I find it convenient to cook the sweet potatoes in the morning and assemble the dish, then bake it later.

—**ISABELL BURROWS** LIVERMORE, CALIFORNIA

PREP: 40 MINUTES **BAKE:** 30 MINUTES **MAKES:** 8 SERVINGS

- 2 **large sweet potatoes**
- 3 **tablespoons butter**
- ½ **cup packed brown sugar**
- 2 **medium apples, peeled and cubed**
- ½ **cup dried cranberries**
- ½ **teaspoon ground cinnamon**
- ½ **teaspoon ground nutmeg**

1. Place sweet potatoes in a large saucepan and cover with water. Bring to a boil. Reduce heat; cover and cook for 30-45 minutes or just until tender. Drain; cool slightly. Peel potatoes and cut into ½-in. slices; set aside.

2. In a large skillet, melt butter and brown sugar over medium heat. Add apples; cook and stir until crisp-tender. Stir in the cranberries, cinnamon and nutmeg.

3. In a greased 1½-qt. baking dish, layer half of the sweet potatoes and half of the apple mixture; repeat layers. Cover and bake at 375° for 30-35 minutes or until bubbly.

Pumpkin Chili

This unique chili freezes well, but it still doesn't last around our farmhouse very long, especially when my five children and 13 grandchildren are around! They often are—we're a very close-knit family.

—**BETTY BUTLER** GREENCASTLE, INDIANA

PREP: 10 MINUTES **COOK:** 70 MINUTES
MAKES: 11 SERVINGS

- 3 **pounds ground beef**
- 1 **medium onion, chopped**
- 2 **cans (16 ounces each) hot chili beans, undrained**
- 2 **bottles (12 ounces each) chili sauce**
- 2 **cans (10¾ ounces each) condensed tomato soup, undiluted**
- 1 **cup canned pumpkin**
- 2 **teaspoons pumpkin pie spice**
- 1 **teaspoon salt**
- 1 **teaspoon sugar**
- 1 **teaspoon pepper**
- 1 **teaspoon chili powder**

1. In a Dutch oven, cook the beef and onion over medium heat until no longer pink; drain. Stir in the remaining ingredients. Add water to thin if desired. Bring to a boil. Reduce heat; cover and simmer for 1 hour.

Home Style COOKING NOTES

Parmesan Potatoes au Gratin

This recipe represents my philosophy of cooking at its best—cooking with love. A good test to see if you have enough cream in the recipe is to gently press on the top of the layers (once it's assembled). If there is enough cream, you should see it coming out on the sides, but not overflowing. Letting the au gratin rest is very important, even though it's so delicious that you will want to jump right in. If you like onions, slice thinly and add between the layers.

—THERESA DANOS HYDE PARK, NEW YORK

PREP: 20 MINUTES **BAKE:** 1½ HOURS + STANDING **MAKES:** 9 SERVINGS

- 2 cups grated Parmesan cheese
- 1 tablespoon minced fresh thyme or 1 teaspoon dried thyme
- 1 tablespoon grated lemon peel
- ½ teaspoon salt
- ½ teaspoon pepper
- 2 pounds red potatoes, very thinly sliced
- 2½ cups heavy whipping cream

1. Combine the first five ingredients. Layer a third of the potatoes and ⅔ cup cheese mixture in a greased 8-in. square baking dish; repeat layers. Top with remaining potatoes; pour cream over top. Sprinkle with remaining cheese mixture.
2. Cover and bake at 325° for 65 minutes. Increase temperature to 375°. Uncover; bake 25-30 minutes longer or until potatoes are tender and top is golden brown. Let stand for 10 minutes before serving.

Grandma's Pumpkin Bread

The aroma of pumpkin bread baking never fails to whet the appetite. This classic recipe is tender, moist and perfectly spiced and creates a sugary crust around the edges.

—KATHLEENE S. BAKER PLANO, TEXAS

PREP: 25 MIN. **BAKE:** 55 MIN. + COOLING
MAKES: 2 LOAVES (16 SLICES EACH)

- ⅔ cup shortening
- 2⅔ cups sugar
- 4 eggs
- 1 can (15 oz.) solid-pack pumpkin
- ⅔ cup water
- 3⅓ cups all-purpose flour
- 1 teaspoon baking soda
- 1 teaspoon ground cinnamon
- ½ teaspoon baking powder
- ½ teaspoon salt
- ⅛ teaspoon ground nutmeg
- ⅔ cup chopped pecans or walnuts

1. In a large bowl, cream shortening and sugar until light and fluffy. Beat in the eggs, pumpkin and water (mixture will appear curdled). Combine flour, baking soda, cinnamon, baking powder, salt and nutmeg; gradually beat into pumpkin mixture until blended. Stir in nuts.
2. Transfer mixture to two greased 9-in. x 5-in. loaf pans. Bake at 350° for 55-65 minutes or until a toothpick inserted near the center comes out clean. Cool for 10 minutes before removing from pans to wire racks.

Home Style COOKING NOTES

Connected

How my recipe collection feeds my soul

BY KATHLEENE S. BAKER

Early November always finds me wandering down memory lane as I fumble through my untidy batch of recipes. I'm not the sort who creates efficient recipe folders on my computer, nor do I alphabetize my collection in a cute recipe box. What I have instead is an embarrassing hodgepodge of cards, scraps of paper and even a few envelopes.

Finding my favorites for the holidays is never difficult, though. Some I recognize by the handwriting of the person who jotted a recipe down for me. Others, scribbled on any notepad that was handy at the time, I search out by the color of the paper I happen to recall it was written on.

One recipe card stands out among the others. The handwriting is faded, the yellowed edges are bent, and it has amassed an array of smudges over the years. Still, it's far from being just another dog-eared recipe card. It's a special keepsake from my mother, now deceased. Recently I recognized how faint her handwriting had become on the aged card, and placed it in a plastic bag for protection.

While I pop my loaf pans into my electric oven, I try to imagine my grandma baking this pumpkin bread recipe for her 11 children, using a woodstove in a drafty farmhouse. I can only wonder about the size of her mixing bowls and the number of loaves she had to make to feed a family that large!

I grew up in rural Kansas. Our house sat at the foot of a hill on the Plains, and Mother's country kitchen was to be envied. The window over her kitchen sink provided a view of pastureland where cattle grazed regularly. From there, Mom could see most everything afoot in her domain—as well as any tomboyish prank I might have in the making. I can't count the number of times the aroma of that pumpkin bread caught me by surprise. It never failed to lure me into the house and away from my latest escapade.

That ragged old recipe card has traveled with me from state to state, kitchen to kitchen, and has been the start of more loaves of pumpkin bread than I would dare to count. Many were devoured at family dinners; countless others became holiday gifts, embellished with colorful ribbons and bows.

And that card started a collection of recipes I gathered from old friends, new friends and relatives, each sharing a special dish. Some, like the pumpkin bread, have become part of my traditional holiday fare.

Put those cards and other bits of paper together and they form a roadmap of my adult life, passing along tranquil country roads and scenic city boulevards. True, I've encountered my share of bumps and detours along the way. But upon reflection, I'm more than thankful for each hill and valley—and more than that, for every person who touched my life and who shared a recipe to sustain me.

> "The handwriting is faded, the yellowed edges are bent, and it has amassed an array of smudges over the years. Still, it's far from being just another dog-eared recipe card. It's a special keepsake from my mother . . ."

Sweet Treats

"Save room for dessert!" You'll be thankful for the dinner-table reminder when you end your meal with one of our scrumptious treats. With the fantastic array of pies, cakes, ice creams and bars that follow, prepare to find the perfect ending for every meal.

Green Tomato Lattice Pie

(recipe on page 263)

"My bounty of garden tomatoes ends up in countless family-favorite recipes...including dessert! Your pie-loving friends will be tempted by the sweet aroma. One slice will have them lining up for seconds."

—ELIZABETH COURTNEY DAYTON, TEXAS

Moist Lemon Angel Cake Roll

Tart and delicious, our pretty cake roll will tickle any lemon lover's fancy. Its feathery angel-food texture enhances its guilt-free goodness.

—TASTE OF HOME TEST KITCHEN

PREP: 30 MINUTES **BAKE:** 15 MINUTES + COOLING
MAKES: 10 SERVINGS

- 9 **egg whites**
- 1½ **teaspoons vanilla extract**
- ¾ **teaspoon cream of tartar**
- 1 **cup plus 2 tablespoons sugar**
- ¾ **cup cake flour**
- 1 **tablespoon confectioners' sugar**

FILLING

- 1 **cup sugar**
- 3 **tablespoons cornstarch**
- 1 **cup water**
- 1 **egg, lightly beaten**
- ¼ **cup lemon juice**
- 1 **tablespoon grated lemon peel**
  Yellow food coloring, optional
  Additional confectioners' sugar

1. Place the egg whites in a large bowl; let stand at room temperature for 30 minutes. Meanwhile, line a 15-in. x 10-in. x 1-in. baking pan with waxed paper; lightly coat paper with cooking spray and set aside.

2. Add vanilla and cream of tartar to the egg whites; beat on medium speed until soft peaks form. Gradually beat in sugar, 2 tablespoons at a time, on high until stiff glossy peaks form and sugar is dissolved. Fold in flour, about ¼ cup at a time.

3. Carefully spread batter into prepared pan. Bake at 350° for 15-20 minutes or until cake springs back when lightly touched. Cool for 5 minutes.

4. Turn cake onto a kitchen towel dusted with 1 tablespoon confectioners' sugar. Gently peel off waxed paper. Roll up cake in the towel jelly-roll style, starting with a short side. Cool completely on a wire rack.

5. In a large saucepan, combine sugar and cornstarch; stir in water until smooth. Cook and stir over medium-high heat until thickened and bubbly. Reduce heat; cook and

stir 2 minutes longer. Remove from the heat. Stir a small amount of hot mixture into egg; return all to the pan, stirring constantly. Bring to a gentle boil; cook and stir 2 minutes longer.

6. Remove from the heat. Gently stir in lemon juice, peel and food coloring if desired. Cool to room temperature without stirring.

7. Unroll cake; spread filling to within ½ in. of edges. Roll up again. Place seam side down on a serving plate; sprinkle with additional confectioners' sugar.

Lime Pudding Cakes

My mother baked this old-time dessert for us and it was always a real treat. Now I share it with my loved ones.

—ETHEL KOZMA WESTPORT, NEW YORK

PREP: 20 MINUTES **BAKE:** 40 MINUTES **MAKES:** 6 SERVINGS

- 2 **tablespoons butter, softened**
- 1½ **cups sugar**
- ⅓ **cup all-purpose flour**
- ¼ **teaspoon salt**
- ½ **cup lime or lemon juice**
- 1 **teaspoon grated lime or lemon peel**
- 3 **eggs, separated**
- 1¼ **cups 2% milk**

1. In a small bowl, beat butter and sugar until crumbly. Add the flour, salt, lime juice and peel; mix well. Beat in egg yolks and milk until smooth. In another bowl, beat egg whites until stiff peaks form; gently fold into batter.

2. Pour into six ungreased 6-oz. custard cups. Place cups in a large baking pan; add 1 in. of boiling water to pan.

3. Bake, uncovered, at 325° for 40-45 minutes or until a knife inserted near the center comes out clean and top is golden. Serve warm or at room temperature.

Peaches and Cream Torte

When I'm craving something cool and fruity, I turn to my recipe for peach torte. Cream cheese adds zing to the fluffy filling.

—ELVA ROBERTS SUMMERSIDE, PRINCE EDWARD ISLAND

PREP: 40 MINUTES + CHILLING
MAKES: 12 SERVINGS

- 2 **cups graham cracker crumbs**
- ⅓ **cup packed brown sugar**
- ½ **cup butter, melted**

FILLING

- 1 **can (29 ounces) sliced peaches**
- 1¼ **cups sugar, divided**
- 2 **tablespoons cornstarch**
- 1 **package (8 ounces) cream cheese, softened**
- 2 **cups heavy whipping cream**

1. In a small bowl, combine the graham cracker crumbs and brown sugar; stir in butter. Set aside ¼ cup for topping. Press remaining crumb mixture onto the bottom and 1 in. up the sides of a greased 9-in. springform pan.

2. Place pan on a baking sheet. Bake at 350° for 10 minutes. Cool on a wire rack.

3. Drain peaches, reserving syrup in a 2-cup measuring cup. Add enough water to measure 1½ cups. In a large saucepan, combine ¼ cup sugar and cornstarch; stir in syrup mixture until smooth. Add peaches. Bring to a boil over medium heat; cook and stir for 2 minutes or until thickened. Cool to room temperature, stirring occasionally.

4. Meanwhile, in a large bowl, beat cream cheese and remaining sugar until smooth. In a small bowl, beat cream until stiff peaks form; fold into cream cheese mixture.

5. Spread half of the cream cheese mixture over crust. Top with half of the peach mixture; repeat layers. Sprinkle with reserved crumb mixture. Cover and refrigerate for 8 hours or overnight. Remove sides of pan before slicing.

Rhubarb Ice Cream

I sampled a scoop of rhubarb-flavored treat at an ice cream shop and knew I had to try making my own. So I raided my garden for rhubarb and added lemon and ginger. It came out yummy!

—**DENISE LINNETT** PICTON, ONTARIO

PREP: 45 MINUTES + CHILLING
PROCESS: 20 MINUTES + FREEZING
MAKES: 1 QUART

- 3 **cups sliced fresh or frozen rhubarb**
- 2 **cups sugar**
- 1 **cup milk**
- 1 **cup heavy whipping cream**
- 2 **teaspoons lemon juice**
- 1 **teaspoon minced fresh gingerroot**

1. Place rhubarb in an ungreased 13-in. x 9-in. baking dish. Sprinkle with sugar; toss to coat. Cover and bake at 375° for 30-40 minutes or until tender, stirring occasionally.
2. Cool slightly. Process rhubarb in batches in a food processor; transfer to a bowl. Cover and refrigerate until mixture is chilled.
3. In a large bowl, combine the milk, cream, lemon juice and ginger; stir in the rhubarb.
4. Fill cylinder of ice cream freezer two-thirds full; freeze according to manufacturer's directions. Transfer to a freezer container; freeze for 2-4 hours before serving.

Scotch Shortbread Cookies

This simple three-ingredient recipe makes wonderfully rich, tender cookies. Serve them with fresh berries of the season for a nice, light dessert. You'll get miles of smiles when you provide these for afternoon tea or at a bridal shower.

—**MARLENE HELLICKSON** BIG BEAR CITY, CALIFORNIA

PREP: 15 MINUTES **BAKE:** 25 MINUTES **MAKES:** 4 DOZEN

- 4 **cups all-purpose flour**
- 1 **cup sugar**
- 1 **pound cold butter, cubed**

1. In a large bowl, combine flour and sugar. Cut in butter until mixture resembles fine crumbs. Knead dough until smooth, about 6-10 times. Pat dough into an ungreased 15-in. x 10-in. x 1-in. baking pan. Pierce with a fork.
2. Bake at 325° for 25-30 minutes or until lightly browned. Cut into squares while warm. Cool on a wire rack.

Editor's Note: *This recipe makes a dense, crisp bar, so it does not call for baking powder or baking soda.*

Caramel Pecan Pie

Of all of the pecan pie recipes I've collected over the years, this is the most decadent. It simply oozes goodness! Even kids eat it slowly so they can enjoy every bite.

—DIANA BARTELINGS ROCK CREEK, BRITISH COLUMBIA

PREP: 45 MINUTES **BAKE:** 35 MINUTES + COOLING **MAKES:** 6-8 SERVINGS

1⅔ cups all-purpose flour
¼ teaspoon salt
½ cup cold butter, cubed
⅓ cup sweetened condensed milk
2 egg yolks

FILLING

1½ cups sugar
½ cup plus 2 tablespoons butter
⅓ cup maple syrup
3 eggs
3 egg whites
½ teaspoon vanilla extract
2 cups ground pecans

1. In a large bowl, combine flour and salt; cut in butter until mixture resembles coarse crumbs. Combine milk and egg yolks; stir into crumb mixture until the dough forms a ball. Press onto the bottom and up the sides of an ungreased 9-in. deep-dish pie plate; flute edges. Cover and refrigerate.

2. In a large saucepan, combine the sugar, butter and syrup; bring to a boil over medium heat, stirring constantly. Remove from the heat.

3. In a large bowl, beat the eggs, egg whites and vanilla. Gradually add hot syrup mixture. Stir in pecans. Pour into pastry shell.

4. Cover edges loosely with foil. Bake at 350° for 35-40 minutes or until pie is set. Cool on a wire rack. Refrigerate leftovers.

Baked Apple Dumplings

These versatile dumplings can be made with peaches or mixed berries in place of apples, and drizzled with hot caramel sauce instead of icing. Add vanilla custard or ice cream, and it's the perfect dessert.

—EVANGELINE BRADFORD ERLANGER, KENTUCKY

PREP: 35 MINUTES **BAKE:** 15 MINUTES **MAKES:** 1½ DOZEN

½ cup sugar
3 tablespoons dry bread crumbs
4½ teaspoons ground cinnamon
   Dash ground nutmeg
1 package (17.3 ounces) frozen puff pastry, thawed
1 egg, beaten
2¼ cups chopped peeled tart apples

STREUSEL

⅓ cup chopped pecans, toasted
⅓ cup packed brown sugar
⅓ cup all-purpose flour
2 tablespoons plus 1½ teaspoons butter, melted

ICING

1 cup confectioners' sugar
2 tablespoons 2% milk
1 teaspoon vanilla extract

1. In a small bowl, combine the sugar, bread crumbs, cinnamon and nutmeg. On a lightly floured surface, roll pastry into two 12-in. squares. Cut each sheet into nine 4-in. squares.

2. Brush squares with the egg. Place 1 teaspoon sugar mixture in the center of a square; top with 2 tablespoons chopped apple and 1 teaspoon sugar mixture. Gently bring up corners of pastry to center; pinch the edges to seal. Repeat with the remaining pastry, crumb mixture and apples. Place on greased baking sheets.

3. In a small bowl, combine the streusel ingredients. Brush remaining egg over dumplings; press streusel over tops.

4. Bake at 400° for 14-18 minutes or until golden brown. Place pans on wire racks. Combine icing ingredients; drizzle over dumplings.

Pumpkin Dessert Bars

For a different dessert other than the traditional pumpkin pie, try this recipe. It captures familiar pumpkin flavor in a new, different form.

—TENA HUCKLEBY GREENEVILLE, TENNESSEE

PREP: 35 MINUTES **BAKE:** 20 MINUTES + CHILLING **MAKES:** 15 SERVINGS

- 1¾ cups graham cracker crumbs
- 1⅓ cups sugar, divided
- ½ cup butter, melted
- 1 package (8 ounces) cream cheese, softened
- 5 eggs
- 1 can (15 ounces) solid-pack pumpkin
- ½ cup packed brown sugar
- ½ cup milk
- ½ teaspoon salt
- ½ teaspoon ground cinnamon
- 1 envelope unflavored gelatin
- ¼ cup cold water
  Whipped topping, optional

1. In a small bowl, combine graham cracker crumbs and ⅓ cup sugar; stir in butter. Press into a greased 13-in. x 9-in. baking dish.

2. In a small bowl, beat cream cheese and ⅔ cup sugar until smooth. Beat in 2 eggs just until blended. Pour over crust. Bake at 350° for 20-25 minutes or until set. Cool on a wire rack.

3. Meanwhile, separate the remaining eggs and set whites aside. In a large saucepan, combine the yolks, pumpkin, brown sugar, milk, salt and cinnamon. Cook and stir over low heat for 10-12 minutes or until mixture is thickened and reaches 160°. Remove from the heat.

4. In a small saucepan, sprinkle gelatin over cold water; let stand for 1 minute. Heat over low heat, stirring until gelatin is completely dissolved. Stir into pumpkin mixture; set aside.

5. In a large heavy saucepan, combine reserved egg whites and remaining sugar. With a portable mixer, beat on low speed for 1 minute. Continue beating over low heat until mixture reaches 160°, about 12 minutes. Remove from the heat; beat until stiff glossy peaks form and sugar is dissolved.

6. Fold into pumpkin mixture; spread over cream cheese layer. Refrigerate 4 hours or until set. Garnish with whipped topping if desired.

Chocolate Strawberry Truffle Brownies

Every summer, I make strawberry jam. One day I decided to add some to brownies. These delectable treats are a hit with my family.

—TERESA JANSEN ADVANCE, MISSOURI

PREP: 30 MINUTES **BAKE:** 30 MINUTES + CHILLING **MAKES:** ABOUT 2 DOZEN

- 1¼ cups semisweet chocolate chips
- ½ cup butter, cubed
- ¾ cup packed brown sugar
- 2 eggs
- 1 teaspoon instant coffee granules
- 2 tablespoons hot water
- ¾ cup all-purpose flour
- ½ teaspoon baking powder

TRUFFLE FILLING
- 1 cup (6 ounces) semisweet chocolate chips
- ¼ teaspoon instant coffee granules
- 1 package (8 ounces) cream cheese, softened
- ¼ cup sifted confectioners' sugar
- ⅓ cup strawberry jam or preserves

GLAZE
- ¼ cup semisweet chocolate chips
- 1 teaspoon shortening

1. In a microwave, melt chocolate chips and butter; stir until smooth. Cool slightly. In a large bowl, beat brown sugar and eggs. Stir in chocolate mixture. Dissolve coffee in water; add to chocolate mixture. Combine flour and baking powder; gradually add to batter.

2. Spread into a greased and floured 9-in. square baking pan. Bake brownies at 350° for 30-35 minutes or until a toothpick inserted near the center comes out clean. Cool.

3. For filling, melt chocolate chips with coffee granules; stir until smooth. Set aside. In a small bowl, beat cream cheese until smooth. Add confectioners' sugar and jam; mix well. Beat in chocolate mixture. Spread over brownies.

4. For glaze, in a microwave, melt chocolate and shortening; stir until smooth. Drizzle over filling. Chill for at least 1 hour.

Grandma's Orange Milk Sherbet

My dear grandma made this sherbet for my birthday party in the 1930s. She squeezed whole oranges to get the juice for it. I often double the recipe. It's so refreshing on a hot summer day.
—**MARILYNN ENGELBRECHT** HARRISONVILLE, MISSOURI

PREP: 20 MINUTES + FREEZING **MAKES:** ABOUT 2 QUARTS

- 1½ cups orange juice
- ¾ cup sugar
- 3 cups milk, scalded and cooled
- 1 can (16 ounces) crushed pineapple in natural juices

1. In a large bowl, combine orange juice and sugar; blend thoroughly. Add milk and mix. Place in chilled ice cube trays without dividers or a shallow pan; freeze until mushy.
2. Place mixture in a bowl and whip. Add pineapple and juices. Return to trays or pan and freeze.

Yogurt Ice Pops

These fun and refreshing peach pops get their creamy goodness from yogurt. Any fruit can be substituted for peaches in the recipe. We've even used all bananas. Yum!
—**DENISE PATTERSON** BAINBRIDGE, OHIO

PREP: 20 MINUTES + FREEZING **MAKES:** 16 POPS

- 1 envelope unflavored gelatin
- 1 cup cold water
- ½ cup sugar
- 1½ cups (12 ounces) peach yogurt
- 2 cups sliced peeled fresh or frozen peaches
- 1 medium ripe banana, quartered
- 16 Popsicle molds or paper cups (3 ounces each) and Popsicle sticks

1. In a small saucepan, sprinkle gelatin over cold water; let stand for 1-2 minutes. Stir in sugar. Cook and stir over low heat until gelatin and sugar are dissolved.
2. Transfer gelatin mixture to a blender; add yogurt, peaches and banana. Cover and process until smooth.
3. Fill each mold or cup with ¼ cup peach mixture; top with holders or insert sticks into cups. Freeze.

Toasted Butter Pecan Cake

If you like butter pecan ice cream, you'll adore this cake. Loads of nuts are folded into the batter, and more are sprinkled over the delectable frosting.

—PHYLLIS EDWARDS FORT VALLEY, GEORGIA

PREP: 25 MINUTES **BAKE:** 25 MINUTES + COOLING **MAKES:** 12-16 SERVINGS

- 1 cup plus 2 tablespoons butter, softened, divided
- 2⅔ cups chopped pecans
- 2 cups sugar
- 4 eggs
- 2 teaspoons vanilla extract
- 3 cups all-purpose flour
- 2 teaspoons baking powder
- ½ teaspoon salt
- 1 cup 2% milk

FROSTING

- 2 packages (one 8 ounces, one 3 ounces) cream cheese, softened
- ⅔ cup butter, softened
- 6½ cups confectioners' sugar
- 1½ teaspoons vanilla extract
- 1 to 2 tablespoons 2% milk

1. In a small heavy skillet, melt 2 tablespoons butter. Add pecans; cook over medium heat until toasted, about 4 minutes. Set aside to cool.

2. In a large bowl, cream sugar and remaining butter until light and fluffy. Add eggs, one at a time, beating well after each addition. Beat in vanilla. Combine the flour, baking powder and salt; add to creamed mixture alternately with milk. Beat just until combined. Fold in 2 cups reserved pecans.

3. Spread evenly into three greased and waxed paper-lined 9-in. round baking pans. Bake at 350° for 25-30 minutes or until a toothpick inserted near the center comes out clean. Cool for 10 minutes before removing from pans to wire racks to cool completely.

4. For frosting, in a large bowl, beat the cream cheese, butter, confectioners' sugar and vanilla until smooth. Beat in enough milk to achieve spreading consistency. Spread frosting between layers and over top and sides of cake. Sprinkle with remaining pecans. Store in the refrigerator.

Strawberry Dessert

I like to garnish this dessert with strawberry slices arranged to look like poinsettias. It's festive and feeds a crowd!

—DELORES ROMYN STRATTON, ONTARIO

PREP: 20 MINUTES + CHILLING
MAKES: 12-15 SERVINGS

- 1 package (3 ounces) ladyfingers, split
- 1 package (4¾ ounces) strawberry Junket Danish Dessert
- 1¾ cups cold water
- 2 pints fresh strawberries, sliced
- 1 carton (8 ounces) frozen whipped topping, thawed
  Additional sliced strawberries, optional

1. Place ladyfingers in a single layer in a 13-in. x 9-in. dish; set aside. In a saucepan, bring dessert mix and water to a boil. Cook and stir for 1 minute. Cool for 4-5 minutes; fold in strawberries. Spoon over ladyfingers; spread gently. Cover and refrigerate for 3-4 hours. Spread with whipped topping. Garnish with additional strawberries if desired.

Editor's Note: *Look for strawberry Junket Danish Dessert in the gelatin section.*

Home Style COOKING NOTES

Lemon Pound Cake

When you're in the mood for a treat
but don't want a large cake or batch of
cookies, turn to my pound cake recipe.
It bakes in a small loaf pan and makes six
delicious slices.

—CORKEY ADDCOX
MT. SHASTA, CALIFORNIA

PREP: 20 MINUTES
BAKE: 30 MINUTES + COOLING
MAKES: 1 LOAF (6 SLICES)

- ⅓ cup sugar
- 1 egg
- 3 tablespoons canola oil
- 3 tablespoons orange juice
- ½ teaspoon lemon extract
- ⅔ cup all-purpose flour
- ¾ teaspoon baking powder
- ⅛ teaspoon salt
- 1 teaspoon poppy seeds, optional
- ⅓ cup confectioners' sugar
- 2 tablespoons lemon juice

1. In a small bowl, combine sugar, egg,
oil, orange juice and extract. Combine
the flour, baking powder and salt; add to
egg mixture and mix well. Stir in poppy
seeds if desired.

2. Pour into a greased and floured
5¾-in. x 3-in. x 2-in. loaf pan. Bake
at 350° for 30-35 minutes or until a
toothpick inserted near the center
comes out clean. Cool for 10 minutes
before removing from pan to a wire rack
to cool completely.

3. For glaze, in a small bowl, whisk
confectioners' sugar and lemon juice
until smooth; drizzle over cake.

Banana Split Ice Cream Cake

Every time they visit, my children and grandkids request my fantastic frozen dessert.
It takes time to assemble, but it's worth the effort when I see all those smiling faces.

—GLADYS MCCOLLUM ABEE MCKEE, KENTUCKY

PREP: 30 MINUTES + FREEZING **MAKES:** 12 SERVINGS

- 12 ice cream sugar cones, finely crushed
- ½ cup finely chopped walnuts
- 6 tablespoons butter, melted

CAKE
- 1¾ quarts low-fat vanilla frozen yogurt, softened, divided
- 2 medium ripe bananas, mashed
- 1 teaspoon banana extract, optional
- 1 jar (16 ounces) hot fudge ice cream topping
- 1 cup chopped walnuts
- 1 cup strawberry ice cream topping
- 1 carton (8 ounces) frozen whipped topping, thawed

1. In a small bowl, combine crushed cones, walnuts and butter; press onto the
bottom of a greased 9-in. springform pan.

2. In another small bowl, combine 3 cups yogurt, bananas and extract if desired.
Spread over crust. In a small bowl, combine fudge topping and walnuts; spread
over yogurt. Cover and freeze for 2 hours or until firm.

3. Top with remaining yogurt; spread with strawberry topping. Cover and
freeze for 8 hours or overnight until firm. Garnish with whipped topping.

Cookie Dough Brownies

When I take these rich brownies to any get-together, I carry the recipe, too, because it always gets requested. Children of all ages love the tempting cookie dough filling. This special treat is typically the first to disappear from the buffet table—even before the entrees!

—WENDY BAILEY ELIDA, OHIO

PREP: 20 MINUTES + CHILLING **BAKE:** 30 MINUTES + COOLING **MAKES:** 3 DOZEN

 4 **eggs**
 1 **cup canola oil**
 2 **cups sugar**
 2 **teaspoons vanilla extract**
 1½ **cups all-purpose flour**
 ½ **cup baking cocoa**
 ½ **teaspoon salt**
 ½ **cup chopped walnuts, optional**

FILLING

 ½ **cup butter, softened**
 ½ **cup packed brown sugar**
 ¼ **cup sugar**
 2 **tablespoons 2% milk**
 1 **teaspoon vanilla extract**
 1 **cup all-purpose flour**

GLAZE

 1 **cup (6 ounces) semisweet chocolate chips**
 1 **tablespoon shortening**
 ¾ **cup chopped walnuts**

1. In a large bowl, beat eggs, oil, sugar and vanilla until well blended. Combine flour, cocoa and salt; gradually beat into egg mixture. Stir in walnuts if desired.

2. Pour into a greased 13-in. x 9-in. baking pan. Bake at 350° for 30 minutes or until brownies test done. Cool completely on a wire rack.

3. For filling, in a large bowl, cream the butter and sugars until light and fluffy. Beat in milk and vanilla. Gradually beat in the flour. Spread over the brownies; chill until firm.

4. For glaze, in a microwave, melt chocolate chips and shortening; stir until smooth. Spread over filling. Immediately sprinkle with the nuts, pressing down slightly. Let stand until set.

Sour Cream-Lemon Pie

I first tasted this pie at a local restaurant and hunted around until I found a similar recipe. Now it's my husband's favorite.

—MARTHA SORENSEN FALLON, NEVADA

PREP: 20 MINUTES + CHILLING **MAKES:** 8 SERVINGS

   Pastry for single-crust pie (9 inches)
1 **cup sugar**
3 **tablespoons plus 1½ teaspoons cornstarch**
1 **cup milk**
½ **cup lemon juice**
3 **egg yolks, lightly beaten**
¼ **cup butter, cubed**
1 **tablespoon grated lemon peel**
1 **cup (8 ounces) sour cream**
1 **cup heavy whipping cream, whipped**

1. Roll out pastry to fit a 9-in. pie plate. Transfer to pie plate; trim to ½ in. beyond edge of plate. Flute edges. Line unpricked pastry with a double thickness of heavy-duty foil. Bake at 450° for 8 minutes. Remove foil; bake 5-7 minutes longer or until golden brown. Cool on a wire rack.

2. In a large heavy saucepan, combine sugar and cornstarch. Whisk in milk and lemon juice until smooth. Cook and stir over medium-high heat until thickened and bubbly. Reduce heat to low; cook and stir 2 minutes longer. Remove from heat.

3. In a small bowl, whisk a small amount of hot mixture into egg yolks; return all to the pan, whisking constantly. Bring to a gentle boil; cook and stir 2 minutes. Remove from heat. Stir in butter and lemon peel. Cool without stirring.

4. Stir in sour cream. Add filling to crust. Top with whipped cream. Store in the refrigerator.

the flour, baking soda, baking powder and salt; add to creamed mixture alternately with buttermilk, beating well after each addition.

2. Fill paper-lined muffin cups two-thirds full. Bake at 375° for 18-22 minutes or until a toothpick inserted near the center comes out clean. Cool for 10 minutes before removing from pan to a wire rack to cool completely.

3. In a small bowl, combine the frosting ingredients; beat until light and fluffy. Frost the cooled cupcakes.

Cherry Banana Cupcakes: *Fold ⅓ cup each chopped maraschino cherries and walnuts into the batter. In the frosting, substitute milk for lemon juice.*

Buttery Almond Pear Cake

Pears and almonds make a tasty duo in this cake. It looks pretty with the fruit on top. How can something this simple taste so wonderful?

—LILY JULOW GAINESVILLE, FLORIDA

PREP: 25 MINUTES **BAKE:** 40 MINUTES
MAKES: 6-8 SERVINGS

- 1¼ **cups blanched almonds**
- ½ **cup plus 4½ teaspoons sugar, divided**
- ⅓ **cup all-purpose flour**
- ¼ **teaspoon salt**
- 5 **tablespoons cold butter, divided**
- 2 **eggs**
- ¼ **cup milk**
- 1 **can (15¼ ounces) pear halves, drained and thinly sliced**

1. In a food processor, combine almonds and ½ cup sugar. Cover and process until blended; transfer to a bowl. Stir in flour and salt. In a microwave-safe bowl, melt 4 tablespoons butter; whisk in eggs and milk. Stir into the almond mixture.

2. Pour into a greased 9-in. fluted tart pan with a removable bottom. Arrange pear slices over batter. Sprinkle with remaining sugar; dot with remaining butter.

3. Place on a baking sheet. Bake at 350° for 40-45 minutes or until the crust is golden brown. Serve warm or at room temperature. Refrigerate leftovers.

Banana Cupcakes

Go bananas with baking—especially when you have a bunch to use up. Ripe bananas are the secret to these down-home cupcakes. They look, smell and taste the best!

—JANE DEARING NORTH LIBERTY, INDIANA

PREP: 25 MINUTES **BAKE:** 20 MINUTES + COOLING **MAKES:** 1½ DOZEN

- ½ **cup shortening**
- 1½ **cups sugar**
- 2 **eggs**
- 1 **cup mashed ripe bananas (about 2 medium)**
- 1 **teaspoon vanilla extract**
- 2 **cups all-purpose flour**
- ¾ **teaspoon baking soda**
- ½ **teaspoon baking powder**
- ½ **teaspoon salt**
- ½ **cup buttermilk**

LEMON BUTTER FROSTING

- 2 **cups confectioners' sugar**
- ⅓ **cup butter, softened**
- 3 **tablespoons mashed ripe banana**
- 1 **tablespoon lemon juice**

1. In a bowl, cream shortening and sugar until light and fluffy. Add eggs, one at a time, beating well after each addition. Beat in bananas and vanilla. Combine

White Chocolate Cheesecake

This is my all-time favorite cheesecake recipe—and I have a lot of them! A friend gave it to me years ago and I've made so many of these delicious cakes over the years. I have even had them requested as birthday cakes. I always hear compliments when I serve one.

—JANET GILL TANEYTOWN, MARYLAND

PREP: 40 MINUTES **BAKE:** 45 MINUTES + CHILLING
MAKES: 12 SERVINGS

- 7 whole cinnamon graham crackers, crushed
- ¼ cup sugar
- ⅓ cup butter, melted

FILLING
- 4 packages (8 ounces each) cream cheese, softened
- ½ cup plus 2 tablespoons sugar
- 1 tablespoon all-purpose flour
- 1 teaspoon vanilla extract
- 4 eggs, lightly beaten
- 2 egg yolks, lightly beaten
- 8 ounces white baking chocolate, melted and cooled

STRAWBERRY SAUCE
- ½ cup sugar
- 2 tablespoons cornstarch
- ½ cup water
- 1½ cups chopped fresh strawberries
  Red food coloring, optional
  Melted white chocolate

Home Style COOKING NOTES

1. In a small bowl, combine cracker crumbs and sugar; stir in butter. Press onto the bottom and 1 in. up the sides of a greased 10-in. springform pan.
2. In a large bowl, beat the cream cheese, sugar, flour and vanilla until well blended. Add eggs and yolks; beat on low speed just until combined. Stir in white chocolate. Pour over crust. Place pan on a baking sheet.
3. Bake at 350° for 45-50 minutes or until center is just set. Cool on a wire rack for 10 minutes. Carefully run a knife around edge of pan to loosen; cool 1 hour longer. Refrigerate overnight.
4. For sauce, in a large saucepan, combine the sugar, cornstarch and water until smooth. Add strawberries. Bring to a boil; cook and stir until thickened. Remove from the heat; stir in a few drops of food coloring if desired. Cool.
5. Spread strawberry sauce over top of cheesecake; drizzle with melted white chocolate. Refrigerate leftovers.

Apple Upside-Down Cake

Topped with walnuts and caramelized tart apple slices, this cake is both easy and dazzling. It never fails to make tasters say, "Wow!"

—LINDA WETSCH MANDAN, NORTH DAKOTA

PREP: 25 MINUTES **BAKE:** 30 MINUTES + COOLING **MAKES:** 8 SERVINGS

- ⅓ cup butter, melted
- 1 cup packed brown sugar
- 3 medium tart apples, peeled and sliced
- ½ cup chopped walnuts

CAKE

- 3 tablespoons butter, softened
- ¾ cup sugar
- 2 eggs
- 1 cup all-purpose flour
- ¾ teaspoon baking powder
- ½ teaspoon baking soda
- ¼ teaspoon salt
- ¼ teaspoon ground cinnamon
- ⅓ cup buttermilk
- 3 tablespoons sour cream
- 1 teaspoon apple brandy or rum, optional

1. Pour butter into an ungreased 9-in. round baking pan; sprinkle with ½ cup brown sugar. Arrange the apples in a single layer over brown sugar; layer with walnuts and remaining brown sugar.

2. In a bowl, cream butter and sugar until light and fluffy. Add eggs, one at a time, beating well after each addition. Combine the flour, baking powder, baking soda, salt and cinnamon; add to the creamed mixture alternately with buttermilk and sour cream, beating well after each addition. Beat in brandy if desired.

3. Spoon batter over brown sugar layer. Bake at 350° for 30-35 minutes or until a toothpick inserted near the center comes out clean. Cool for 10 minutes before inverting onto a serving plate. Serve warm.

Lemon Velvet Dessert

The first time I whipped up this light and lemony mousse, everyone oohed and aahed. But no one believed me when I told them how simple it was to make.

—MARIA BARNET
ELKINS PARK, PENNSYLVANIA

PREP: 15 MINUTES + CHILLING
MAKES: 8 SERVINGS

- 1 package (8 ounces) cream cheese, softened
- ½ cup lemon curd
- 1 envelope unflavored gelatin
- ½ cup water
- 1 cup heavy whipping cream, whipped
- 1 teaspoon grated lemon peel

1. In a small bowl, beat cream cheese and lemon curd until smooth; set aside.
2. In a small saucepan, sprinkle gelatin over water; let stand for 1 minute. Cook and stir over low heat until gelatin is completely dissolved, about 2 minutes.
3. Beat gelatin into cream cheese mixture. Fold in whipped cream and lemon peel. Pour into eight dessert cups. Cover and refrigerate for 1 hour or until firm.

HOME STYLE tip

66 When picking apples for baking and cooking, it's hard to know which apple is good for your needs. For tart apples for the cake at left, choose from Granny Smith, Jonathan, Northern Spy or Pippin. 99

—TASTE OF HOME TEST KITCHEN

Cherry Almond Pie

My dad loves all kinds of fruit pies, especially this one, so I make it for his birthday every year.

—JOHANNA GEROW RAYTOWN, MISSOURI

PREP: 40 MINUTES **BAKE:** 35 MINUTES + COOLING **MAKES:** 6-8 SERVINGS

2 cans (14 ounces each) pitted tart cherries
1 cup sugar
¼ cup cornstarch
⅛ teaspoon salt
2 tablespoons butter
½ teaspoon almond extract
½ teaspoon vanilla extract
¼ teaspoon red food coloring, optional
   Pastry for double-crust pie (9 inches)
1 egg yolk, lightly beaten
   Additional sugar

1. Drain cherries, reserving 1 cup juice. Set cherries aside. In a large saucepan, combine the sugar, cornstarch and salt; gradually stir in reserved cherry juice until smooth. Bring to a boil; cook and stir for 2 minutes or until thickened. Remove from the heat; stir in the butter, extracts and food coloring if desired. Fold in cherries. Cool slightly.

2. Line a 9-in. pie plate with bottom crust; trim the pastry even with edge. Pour filling into crust. Roll out remaining pastry; make a lattice crust. Trim, seal and flute edges. Brush lattice top with egg yolk. Sprinkle with additional sugar.

3. Cover edges loosely with foil. Bake at 425° for 15 minutes. Remove foil. Bake 20-25 minutes longer or until crust is golden brown and filling is bubbly. Cool on a wire rack.

Chocolate Guinness Cake

One bite and everyone will propose a toast to my moist and chocolaty cake. The cream cheese frosting resembles the foamy head on a pint.

—MARJORIE HENNIG SEYMOUR, INDIANA

PREP: 25 **BAKE:** 45 MINUTES + COOLING **MAKES:** 12 SERVINGS

- 1 cup Guinness (dark beer)
- ½ cup butter, cubed
- 2 cups sugar
- ¾ cup baking cocoa
- 2 eggs, beaten
- ⅔ cup sour cream
- 3 teaspoons vanilla extract
- 2 cups all-purpose flour
- 1½ teaspoons baking soda

TOPPING
- 1 package (8 ounces) cream cheese, softened
- 1½ cups confectioners' sugar
- ½ cup heavy whipping cream

1. Grease a 9-in. springform pan and line the bottom with parchment paper; set aside.

2. In a small saucepan, heat beer and butter until butter is melted. Remove from the heat; whisk in sugar and cocoa until blended. Combine the eggs, sour cream and vanilla; whisk into beer mixture. Combine flour and baking soda; whisk into beer mixture until smooth. Pour batter into prepared pan.

3. Bake at 350° for 45-50 minutes or until a toothpick inserted near the center comes out clean. Cool completely in pan on a wire rack. Remove sides of pan.

4. In a large bowl, beat cream cheese until fluffy. Add confectioners' sugar and cream; beat until smooth (do not over-beat). Remove cake from the pan and place on a platter or cake stand. Ice top of cake so that it resembles a frothy pint of beer. Refrigerate leftovers.

Strawberries with Vanilla Mascarpone and Balsamic Drizzle

Fresh strawberries shine in a simple yet sophisticated treat. The balsamic syrup adds an interesting sweet-savory quality to the dessert.

—CATHY MCINNES RANDOLPH, NEW JERSEY

PREP/TOTAL TIME: 20 MINUTES
MAKES: 4 SERVINGS

- ¼ cup sugar
- ¼ cup balsamic vinegar
- 1 cup Mascarpone cheese
- 2 tablespoons confectioners' sugar
- 1 teaspoon vanilla extract
- 1 pound fresh strawberries, sliced

1. In a small saucepan, bring sugar and vinegar to a boil; cook until liquid is reduced to ¼ cup, about 2 minutes.

2. In a small bowl, combine the cheese, confectioners' sugar and vanilla. Divide strawberries among four dessert plates. Top with cheese mixture; drizzle with balsamic mixture.

Pecan Chocolate Puddles

Since my grandchildren like frosted cookies, I came up with this chocolate-topped version that satisfies them and is almost fuss-free for me. I have used the recipe for years and now make them for my great-grandchildren.

—JOYCE KUTZLER CLINTON, MINNESOTA

PREP: 20 MINUTES
BAKE: 15 MINUTES/BATCH
MAKES: 4 DOZEN

- ½ cup butter, softened
- 1 cup packed brown sugar
- 1 egg
- 1 teaspoon vanilla extract
- 1 cup all-purpose flour
- ½ cup quick-cooking oats
- ½ teaspoon salt
- ½ teaspoon baking powder
- 1 cup chopped pecans
- 1 cup (6 ounces) miniature semisweet chocolate chips

FILLING
- 1 cup (6 ounces) semisweet chocolate chips
- ½ cup sweetened condensed milk
- 48 pecan halves

1. In a large bowl, cream butter and brown sugar until light and fluffy. Beat in egg and vanilla. Combine the flour, oats, salt and baking powder; gradually add to creamed mixture and mix well. Stir in chopped pecans and miniature chocolate chips.

2. In a microwave, melt chocolate chips and milk; stir until smooth. Roll dough into 1-in. balls. Place 2 in. apart on ungreased baking sheets.

3. Using the end of a wooden spoon handle, make an indentation in the center of each ball. Fill with a rounded teaspoonful of melted chocolate; top with a pecan half.

4. Bake at 350° for 14-16 minutes or until the edges are lightly browned. Remove to wire racks to cool.

Caramel Heavenlies

My mom made these dressy, sweet cookies for cookie exchanges when I was a little girl, letting me sprinkle on the almonds and coconut. They're so easy to fix that sometimes I can't wait 'til Christmas to make a batch.

—DAWN BURNS LAKE ST. LOUIS, MISSOURI

PREP: 20 MINUTES **BAKE:** 15 MINUTES **MAKES:** ABOUT 6 DOZEN

- 12 whole graham crackers
- 2 cups miniature marshmallows
- ¾ cup butter
- ¾ cup packed brown sugar
- 1 teaspoon ground cinnamon
- 1 teaspoon vanilla extract
- 1 cup sliced almonds
- 1 cup flaked coconut

1. Line a 15-in. x 10-in. x 1-in. baking pan with foil. Place graham crackers in pan; cover with marshmallows. In a saucepan over medium heat, cook and stir butter, brown sugar and cinnamon until the butter is melted and sugar is dissolved. Remove from the heat; stir in vanilla.

2. Spoon over the marshmallows. Sprinkle with almonds and coconut. Bake at 350° for 14-16 minutes or until browned. Cool completely. Cut into 2-in. squares, then cut each square in half to form triangles.

Cherry-Chip Ice Cream Sandwiches

You can make these marvelous ice cream treats days ahead. Just wrap and freeze! My kids created them one afternoon after I made the ice cream.

—SALLY HOOK MONTGOMERY, TEXAS

PREP: 15 MINUTES + CHILLING **PROCESS:** 20 MINUTES + FREEZING **MAKES:** 10 SERVINGS

1½ cups 2% milk
½ cup sugar
   Dash salt
1 cup heavy whipping cream
1 teaspoon vanilla extract
⅔ cup chopped dried cherries
½ cup miniature semisweet chocolate chips
10 whole chocolate graham crackers

1. In a large saucepan over medium heat, cook and stir the milk, sugar and salt until sugar is dissolved. Remove from the heat; stir in cream and vanilla. Transfer to a bowl; refrigerate until chilled.

2. Line a 13-in. x 9-in. pan with waxed paper; set aside. Fill cylinder of ice cream freezer with milk mixture; freeze according to manufacturer's directions. Stir in cherries and chocolate chips. Spread into prepared pan; cover and freeze overnight.

3. Cut or break graham crackers in half. Using waxed paper, lift ice cream out of pan; discard waxed paper. Cut ice cream into squares the same size as the graham cracker halves; place ice cream between cracker halves. Wrap sandwiches in plastic wrap. Freeze until serving.

Ginger Creme Sandwich Cookies

With a lemony filling, these spiced cookies go over big because they have old-fashioned comfort food appeal. Your party guests will snatch them up.

—CAROL WALSTON GRANBURY, TEXAS

PREP: 25 MINUTES + CHILLING **BAKE:** 10 MINUTES/BATCH + COOLING **MAKES:** 2½ DOZEN

- ¾ cup shortening
- 1 cup packed light brown sugar
- 1 egg
- ¼ cup molasses
- 2¼ cups all-purpose flour
- 3 teaspoons ground ginger
- 2 teaspoons baking soda
- 1 teaspoon ground cinnamon
- ½ teaspoon salt
- ¼ cup sugar

FILLING

- 1 package (3 ounces) cream cheese, softened
- ⅓ cup butter, softened
- 2 teaspoons lemon extract
- 2 cups confectioners' sugar
- 1 teaspoon vanilla extract

1. In a large bowl, cream shortening and brown sugar until light and fluffy. Beat in egg and molasses. Combine the flour, ginger, baking soda, cinnamon and salt; gradually add to creamed mixture and mix well. Cover and refrigerate overnight.

2. Shape into 1-in. balls; roll in sugar. Place 2 in. apart on ungreased baking sheets. Flatten with a fork, forming a crisscross pattern. Bake at 375° for 8-10 minutes or until set (do not overbake). Remove to wire racks to cool.

3. In a small bowl, combine filling ingredients until smooth. Spread over the bottoms of half of the cookies; top with remaining cookies. Store in the refrigerator.

Surprise Red Cupcakes

Our family loves these special filled cupcakes. They often disappear on the same day I make them!

—BETTY CLAYCOMB ALVERTON, PENNSYLVANIA

PREP: 1 HOUR **BAKE:** 20 MINUTES + COOLING **MAKES:** 2 DOZEN

- 2 cups sugar, divided
- 3 tablespoons plus 2 cups all-purpose flour, divided
- ½ cup milk
- ½ cup plus ⅓ cup shortening, divided
- 2 eggs
- 1 bottle (1 ounce) red food coloring
- 1 tablespoon white vinegar
- 2 teaspoons vanilla extract, divided
- 3 tablespoons baking cocoa
- 1 teaspoon baking soda
- 1 cup buttermilk
- ½ cup butter, softened
- 3 tablespoons confectioners' sugar

FROSTING

- 1 cup (6 ounces) semisweet chocolate chips
- ⅓ cup plus 1 to 3 teaspoons evaporated milk, divided
- 1½ cups confectioners' sugar

1. In a heavy saucepan, combine ½ cup sugar, 3 tablespoons flour and milk until smooth. Bring to a boil; cook and stir for 1-2 minutes or until thickened. Remove from the heat; cool.

2. In a large bowl, cream ½ cup shortening and remaining sugar until light and fluffy. Add eggs, one at a time, beating well after each addition. Beat in the food coloring, vinegar and 1 teaspoon vanilla. Combine the cocoa, baking soda and remaining flour; gradually add to creamed mixture alternately with buttermilk, beating well after each addition.

3. Fill paper-lined muffin cups two-thirds full. Bake at 350° for 20-25 minutes or until a toothpick insert near the center comes out clean. Cool for 10 minutes before removing from pans to wire racks to cool completely.

4. In a small bowl, beat butter and remaining shortening until smooth. Beat in confectioners' sugar, cooled sugar mixture and remaining vanilla until light and fluffy, about 3 minutes. Insert a large round tip into a pastry or plastic bag; fill with filling. Insert the tip halfway into the center of each cupcake and fill with a small amount of filling.

5. For frosting, in a heavy saucepan, melt chips with ⅓ cup evaporated milk over low heat; stir until smooth. Remove from the heat. Beat in confectioners' sugar. Add enough remaining milk to achieve spreading consistency. Frost the cooled cupcakes.

Cherries on a Cloud

Our Amish friend Naomi Yoder makes this meringue heart topped with cream cheese and pie filling whenever we visit. Her family's farm is a stop on our wagon train vacation.

—**JUDY HERBKERSMAN** COLLINS, OHIO

PREP: 20 MINUTES **BAKE:** 1½ HOURS + COOLING
MAKES: 6 SERVINGS

- 3 **egg whites**
- ¼ **teaspoon cream of tartar**
- ¾ **cup sugar**

FILLING
- 1 **package (3 ounces) cream cheese, softened**
- ¼ **cup confectioners' sugar**
- ½ **teaspoon vanilla extract**
- 1 **cup heavy whipping cream, whipped**
- 1 **can (21 ounces) cherry pie filling**

1. Place egg whites in a small bowl; let stand at room temperature for 30 minutes. Add cream of tartar and beat on medium speed until soft peaks form. Gradually beat in the sugar, 1 tablespoon at a time, on high until stiff glossy peaks form and sugar is dissolved. Spoon onto a parchment paper-lined baking sheet. Using the back of a spoon, form meringue into a 9-in. heart shape, building up edges slightly.

2. Bake at 275° for 1½ hours. Turn oven off and do not open door; leave meringue in the oven for 1 hour. Remove meringue from the oven; cool completely.

3. In a small bowl, beat the cream cheese, confectioners' sugar and vanilla until smooth. Fold in whipped cream until mixture is well blended. To serve, place heart on a serving platter; fill with cream cheese mixture and top with pie filling.

Home Style COOKING NOTES

Cinnamon Peach Kuchen

This favorite dessert—a recipe from my mom—is one I make for many of my dinner guest. It tastes incredible warm or cold.

—**RACHEL GARCIA** ARLINGTON, VIRGINIA

PREP: 25 MINUTES **BAKE:** 45 MINUTES + COOLING **MAKES:** 10 SERVINGS

- 2 **cups all-purpose flour**
- 2 **tablespoons sugar**
- ½ **teaspoon salt**
- ¼ **teaspoon baking powder**
- ½ **cup cold butter, cubed**
- 2 **cans (15¼ ounces each) peach halves, drained and patted dry**
- 1 **cup packed brown sugar**
- 1 **teaspoon ground cinnamon**
- 2 **egg yolks, lightly beaten**
- 1 **cup heavy whipping cream**

1. In a small bowl, combine the flour, sugar, salt and baking powder; cut in butter until crumbly. Press onto the bottom and 1½ in. up the sides of a greased 9-in. springform pan.

2. Place pan on a baking sheet. Arrange peach halves, cut side up, in the crust. Combine brown sugar and cinnamon; sprinkle over peaches.

3. Bake at 350° for 20 minutes. Combine egg yolks and cream; pour over peaches. Bake 25-30 minutes longer or until top is set. Cool on a wire rack. Refrigerate leftovers.

Sweet Corn Creme Brulee

The starch in corn acts as a natural thickener for this dessert and adds an extra sweetness. The caramelized sugar crust and fruit garnish make a lovely presentation.

—MARYANNE JENSEN-GOWAN PELHAM, NEW HAMPSHIRE

PREP: 25 MINUTES **BAKE:** 45 MINUTES + CHILLING **MAKES:** 6 SERVINGS

    1½ cups frozen corn, thawed
    4½ teaspoons butter
     3 cups heavy whipping cream
     1 cup 2% milk
     8 egg yolks
    1¼ cups plus 2 tablespoons sugar, divided
     2 tablespoons vanilla extract
        Fresh raspberries and mint leaves

1. In a large saucepan, saute corn in butter until tender. Reduce heat. Add cream and milk; heat until bubbles form around sides of pan. Cool slightly. Transfer to a blender; cover and process until smooth. Strain and discard corn pulp. Return to pan.

2. In a small bowl, whisk egg yolks and 1¼ cups sugar. Stir a small amount of hot cream into egg mixture. Return all to the pan, stirring constantly. Stir in vanilla.

3. Transfer to six 6-oz. ramekins. Place in a baking pan; add 1 in. of boiling water to pan. Bake, uncovered, at 325° for 40-45 minutes or until centers are just set (mixture will jiggle). Remove ramekins from water bath; cool for 10 minutes. Cover and refrigerate for at least 4 hours.

4. If using a creme brulee torch, sprinkle custards with remaining sugar. Heat sugar with the torch until caramelized. Serve immediately.

5. If broiling the custards, place ramekins on a baking sheet; let stand at room temperature for 15 minutes. Sprinkle with sugar. Broil 8 in. from the heat for 4-7 minutes or until sugar is caramelized. Refrigerate for 1-2 hours or until firm.

6. Garnish servings with raspberries and mint leaves.

Personal Pear Pies

Talk about cutie pies! These tasty pear mini pies, baked in ramekins, are super easy. Frozen puff pastry makes it simple to treat your family to personal-size desserts.

—BARBARA ENGELHART
BLOOMFIELD HILLS, MICHIGAN

PREP: 30 MINUTES **BAKE:** 25 MINUTES
MAKES: 4 SERVINGS

     2 tablespoons sugar
     1 tablespoon cornflake crumbs
     1 tablespoon brown sugar
     ¼ teaspoon ground ginger
     2 cups finely chopped peeled
        Anjou pears
     2 cups finely chopped peeled
        Bartlett pears
     1 tablespoon orange juice
     2 tablespoons butter, divided
     ½ sheet frozen puff pastry, thawed
     1 egg, beaten
        Vanilla ice cream

1. In a small bowl, combine the sugar, cornflake crumbs, brown sugar and ginger. In a large bowl, combine the pears and orange juice; add crumb mixture and toss to coat.

2. With 1 tablespoon butter, grease the bottoms and sides of four 8-oz. ramekins (do not butter rims). Divide pear mixture between ramekins; dot with remaining butter.

3. Without unfolding pastry, cut widthwise into fourteen ¼-in. strips. Carefully unfold strips. Cut into shorter lengths and make a lattice crust over each ramekin. Gently press dough to rims to seal edges. Brush with egg.

4. Place ramekins on a baking sheet. Bake at 400° for 25-30 minutes or until filling is bubbly and top is golden brown. Cool on a wire rack. Serve with vanilla ice cream.

An egg-rich custard is fully cooked when it is thickened and coats the back of a spoon. To determine doneness, dip a spoon in the mixture and run your finger across the back of the spoon. The cooked mixture will hold a firm line and not run down onto the stripe you've made. A mixture that's not fully cooked will be too thin to hold the line.

Frozen Vanilla Custard

I used to make this treat when we went to Grandma's house. Now, whenever I make it, I think of her.

—DUAINE KURTZBEIN
MONTEVIDEO, MINNESOTA

PREP: 20 MINUTES + FREEZING
MAKES: 1 QUART

- 1 **cup half-and-half cream**
- ⅔ **cup sugar**
- 3 **eggs, beaten**
- 1 **cup heavy whipping cream**
- 1 **teaspoon vanilla extract**
- ¼ **teaspoon salt**

1. In a heavy saucepan, combine the first three ingredients. Cook, stirring constantly, until thickened. Cool. Pour into a shallow pan. Freeze to a mush (do not harden). Whip cream with vanilla and salt. Fold into partially frozen mixture. Return to pan and freeze.

Spiced Peach Puffs

We always made cream puffs for special occasions when I was growing up in a family of seven. My favorite filling, then and now, is whipped cream and peaches.

—AGNES WARD STRATFORD, ONTARIO

PREP: 70 MINUTES **BAKE:** 25 MINUTES + COOLING **MAKES:** 3 DOZEN

- 1 **cup water**
- ½ **cup butter, cubed**
- 1 **teaspoon ground nutmeg**
- ⅛ **teaspoon salt**
- 1 **cup all-purpose flour**
- 4 **eggs**
- 2 **cups heavy whipping cream**
- ½ **cup confectioners' sugar**
- 1 **teaspoon vanilla extract**
- 2 **cups chopped peeled fresh or frozen peaches, thawed**
  Additional confectioners' sugar

1. In a large saucepan, bring the water, butter, nutmeg and salt to a boil. Add flour all at once and stir until a smooth ball forms. Remove from the heat; let stand for 5 minutes. Add eggs, one at a time, beating well after each addition. Continue beating until mixture is smooth and shiny.

2. Drop by tablespoonfuls 2 in. apart onto greased baking sheets. Bake at 400° for 25-30 minutes or until golden brown. Remove to a wire rack. Immediately split puffs open; remove tops and set aside. Discard soft dough from inside. Cool puffs.

3. For filling, in a large bowl, beat cream until it begins to thicken. Add confectioners' sugar and vanilla; beat until stiff peaks form.

4. Just before serving, fill puffs with whipped cream and peaches. Dust with confectioners' sugar.

Lemon Snowdrops

My crunchy butter cookies have a perfect lemon filling. I usually save them for special occasions.

—BERNICE MARTINONI PETALUMA, CALIFORNIA

PREP/TOTAL TIME: 30 MINUTES **MAKES:** ABOUT 4 DOZEN

1 **cup butter, softened**
½ **cup confectioners' sugar**
1 **teaspoon lemon extract**
2 **cups all-purpose flour**
¼ **teaspoon salt**
LEMON BUTTER FILLING
1 **egg, lightly beaten**
⅔ **cup sugar**
3 **tablespoons lemon juice**
  Grated peel of 1 lemon
4½ **teaspoons butter, softened**
  Additional confectioners' sugar

1. In a small bowl, cream butter and sugar until light and fluffy. Beat in extract. Combine flour and salt; gradually add to creamed mixture and mix well.

2. Roll teaspoonfuls of dough into balls. Place 1 in. apart on ungreased baking sheets; flatten slightly. Bake at 350° for 10-12 minutes or until lightly browned.

3. Meanwhile, for filling, combine the egg, sugar, lemon juice, peel and butter in a heavy saucepan. Cook and stir until thickened and a thermometer reads 160°, about 20 minutes. Refrigerate for 1 hour or until completely cooled.

4. Spread lemon filling on the bottoms of half of the cookies; top with remaining cookies and dust with confectioners' sugar. Store in the refrigerator.

White Chocolate Cran-Pecan Cookies

There are lots of good, tasty things packed in my yummy cookie...cranberries, white chips and pecans. They make a delicious change from the classic chocolate chip cookie.

—BARB GARRETT JACKSONVILLE, NORTH CAROLINA

PREP: 15 MINUTES **BAKE:** 10 MINUTES/ BATCH **MAKES:** ABOUT 2½ DOZEN

½ cup butter, softened
½ cup sugar
½ cup packed brown sugar
1 egg
1½ teaspoons vanilla extract
1½ cups all-purpose flour
½ teaspoon baking soda
1 cup dried cranberries
¾ cup white baking chips
½ cup chopped pecans

1. In a large bowl, cream butter and sugars until light and fluffy. Beat in egg and vanilla. Combine flour and baking soda; gradually add to creamed mixture and mix well. Fold in cranberries, baking chips and pecans.
2. Drop by tablespoonfuls 2 in. apart onto ungreased baking sheets. Bake at 375° for 8-10 minutes or until lightly browned. Remove to wire racks.

3 tablespoons lemon juice
2 tablespoons grated lemon peel
2 tablespoons butter, melted
¼ teaspoon salt
½ teaspoon ground cinnamon, divided
¼ teaspoon ground nutmeg
   Dash ground cloves
¼ cup cold butter, cubed

1. In a large bowl, combine flour and salt; cut in shortening until crumbly. Gradually add water, tossing with a fork until dough forms a ball. Divide in half; flatten into disks. Wrap each disk in plastic wrap. Refrigerate for 1 hour or until easy to handle.

2. Meanwhile, place tomatoes in a large bowl; cover with boiling water. Cover and let stand for 20 minutes or until slightly cooled. Drain well.

3. In a small bowl, combine 1 cup sugar, flour, lemon juice, lemon peel, melted butter, salt, ¼ teaspoon cinnamon, nutmeg and cloves. Gently stir in tomatoes.

4. Roll out half of the pastry to fit a 9-in. pie plate; transfer pastry to pie plate. Add filling and dot with cold butter. Roll out remaining pastry; make a lattice crust. Trim, seal and flute edges. Combine remaining sugar and cinnamon; sprinkle over top.

5. Bake at 450° for 10 minutes. Reduce heat to 375°; bake 35-40 minutes longer for until crust is lightly browned. Cool completely on a wire rack before cutting. Refrigerate leftovers.

Green Tomato Lattice Pie

My bounty of garden tomatoes ends up in countless family-favorite recipes…including dessert! Your pie-loving friends will be tempted by the sweet aroma. One slice will have them lining up for seconds.

—ELIZABETH COURTNEY DAYTON, TEXAS

PREP: 25 MINUTES + CHILLING **BAKE:** 45 MINUTES **MAKES:** 8 SERVINGS

2 cups all-purpose flour
¾ teaspoon salt
⅔ cup shortening
6 to 7 tablespoons cold water
FILLING
6 cups thinly sliced green tomatoes
1 cup plus 1 tablespoon sugar, divided
3 tablespoons all-purpose flour

Home Style COOKING NOTES

Strawberry Cheesecake Mousse

You'll be happy to indulge your sweet tooth with this refreshing berry dessert. I've been making it for years. It's like a no-bake cheesecake without the crust.

—VIRGINIA ANTHONY
JACKSONVILLE, FLORIDA

PREP: 20 MINUTES + CHILLING
MAKES: 6 SERVINGS

- ½ teaspoon unflavored gelatin
- ¼ cup cold water
- 1 quart fresh strawberries, halved
- 2 tablespoons reduced-sugar strawberry preserves
- 1 package (8 ounces) reduced-fat cream cheese
- ½ cup sugar, divided
- ¼ cup reduced-fat sour cream, divided
- ½ cup heavy whipping cream

1. Sprinkle gelatin over cold water; let stand for 1 minute. Microwave on high for 20 seconds. Stir and let stand for 1 minute or until gelatin is completely dissolved. Meanwhile, combine strawberries and preserves; set aside.

2. In a large bowl, beat the cream cheese, ¼ cup sugar and 2 tablespoons sour cream until blended; set aside.

3. In another bowl, beat whipping cream and remaining sour cream until it begins to thicken. Add the gelatin mixture and remaining sugar; beat until stiff peaks form. Fold into cream cheese mixture.

4. In each of six dessert dishes, layer ½ cup strawberry mixture and ⅓ cup cream cheese mixture. Refrigerate until chilled.

Caramel-Pecan Cheesecake Pie

In fall or any time of year, this nutty, rich and delicious pie is one I'm proud to serve. While it seems very special, it's a snap to make.

—REBECCA RUFF MCGREGOR, IOWA

PREP: 15 MINUTES **BAKE:** 35 MINUTES + CHILLING **MAKES:** 6-8 SERVINGS

- 1 sheet refrigerated pie pastry
- 1 package (8 ounces) cream cheese, softened
- ½ cup sugar
- 4 eggs
- 1 teaspoon vanilla extract
- 1¼ cups chopped pecans
- 1 jar (12¼ ounces) fat-free caramel ice cream topping
  Additional fat-free caramel ice cream topping, optional

1. Line a 9-in. deep-dish pie plate with pastry. Trim and flute edges. In a small bowl, beat the cream cheese, sugar, 1 egg and vanilla until smooth. Spread into pastry shell; sprinkle with pecans.

2. In a small bowl, whisk remaining eggs; gradually whisk in caramel topping until blended. Pour slowly over pecans.

3. Bake at 375° for 35-40 minutes or until lightly browned (loosely cover edges with foil after 20 minutes if pie browns too quickly). Cool on a wire rack for 1 hour. Refrigerate for 4 hours or overnight before slicing. If desired, garnish with additional caramel ice cream topping.

Editor's Note: *This recipe was tested with Smucker's ice cream topping.*

Blueberry Citrus Cake

My husband and I grow blueberries for market-and this cake is my favorite way to use them. Our fresh berries are enhanced by the light, citrusy frosting. I bring this beauty to all potlucks.

—SHIRLEY COOPER SALEMBURG, NORTH CAROLINA

PREP: 40 MINUTES **BAKE:** 20 MINUTES + COOLING **MAKES:** 12 SERVINGS

- 1 **package (18¼ ounces) yellow cake mix**
- 3 **eggs**
- 1 **cup orange juice**
- ⅓ **cup canola oil**
- 1½ **cups fresh blueberries**
- 1 **tablespoon grated lemon peel**
- 1 **tablespoon grated orange peel**

CITRUS FROSTING
- 1 **package (3 ounces) cream cheese, softened**
- ¼ **cup butter, softened**
- 3 **cups confectioners' sugar**
- 2 **tablespoons orange juice**
- 2 **teaspoons grated orange peel**
- 1 **teaspoon grated lemon peel**
- 2 **cups whipped topping**

1. In a large bowl, combine the cake mix, eggs, orange juice and oil; beat on low speed for 30 seconds. Beat on medium for 2 minutes. Fold in the blueberries and peels. Pour into two greased and floured 9-in. round baking pans.

2. Bake at 350° for 20-25 minutes or until a toothpick inserted near the center comes out clean. Cool for 10 minutes before removing from pans to wire racks to cool completely.

3. For frosting, in a small bowl, combine cream cheese and butter until fluffy. Add the confectioners' sugar, orange juice and peels; beat until blended. Fold in the whipped topping.

4. Spread frosting between layers and over the top and sides of cake. Refrigerate until serving.

Ginger Plum Tart

Looking for a quick and easy dessert that's pretty as a picture? Try this mouthwatering tart. For an extra-special effect, crown it with a scoop of low-fat ice cream, yogurt or a dollop of reduced-fat whipped topping.

—TASTE OF HOME TEST KITCHEN

PREP: 15 MINUTES **BAKE:** 20 MINUTES + COOLING **MAKES:** 8 SERVINGS

Pastry for single-crust pie (9 inches)
3½ cups sliced unpeeled fresh plums
 3 tablespoons plus 1 teaspoon coarse sugar, divided
 1 tablespoon cornstarch
 2 teaspoons finely chopped crystallized ginger
 1 egg white
 1 tablespoon water

1. Roll pastry into a 12-in. circle. Transfer to a large baking sheet lined with parchment paper. In a large bowl, combine plums, 3 tablespoons sugar and cornstarch. Arrange plums in a pinwheel pattern over pastry to within 2 in. of edges; sprinkle with ginger. Fold edges of pastry over plums.

2. Beat egg white and water; brush over pastry. Sprinkle with remaining sugar. Bake at 400° for 20-25 minutes or until crust is lightly browned. Cool for 15 minutes before removing from pan to a serving platter.

Peanut Butter Meringue Pie

My four sons clamor for this peanut butter pie. My mom found the recipe from a farm-wife magazine in the 1960s, and now I'm teaching my sons' wives to make it.

—JUDY HERNKE MUNDELEIN, ILLINOIS

PREP: 45 MINUTES + CHILLING **BAKE:** 15 MINUTES + COOLING **MAKES:** 8 SERVINGS

    Pastry for single-crust pie (9 inches)
¾ cup confectioners' sugar
½ cup creamy peanut butter
⅔ cup sugar
3 tablespoons cornstarch
2 tablespoons all-purpose flour
    Dash salt
3 cups 2% milk
3 egg yolks
2 tablespoons butter
1 teaspoon vanilla extract

MERINGUE
3 egg whites
    Dash cream of tartar
¼ cup sugar

1. Roll out pastry to fit a 9-in. pie plate. Transfer pastry to pie plate. Trim pastry to ½ in. beyond edge of plate; flute edges. Line unpricked pastry with a double thickness of heavy-duty foil. Fill with dried beans, uncooked rice or pie weights.

2. Bake at 450° for 8 minutes. Remove foil and weights; bake 5-7 minutes longer or until lightly browned. Cool on a wire rack.

3. Meanwhile, in a small bowl, beat the confectioners' sugar and peanut butter until crumbly, about 2 minutes. Set aside.

4. In a large heavy saucepan, combine the sugar, cornstarch, flour and salt. Stir in milk until smooth. Cook and stir over medium-high heat until thickened and bubbly. Reduce heat; cook and stir 2 minutes longer.

5. Remove from the heat. Stir a small amount of hot mixture into egg yolks; return all to the pan, stirring constantly. Bring to a gentle boil; cook and stir 2 minutes longer. Remove from the heat. Stir in butter and vanilla.

6. Sprinkle 1 cup peanut butter mixture over crust. Pour hot filling over top.

7. In a large bowl, beat egg whites and cream of tartar on medium speed until soft peaks form. Gradually beat in sugar, 1 tablespoon at a time, on high until stiff glossy peaks form and sugar is dissolved. Spread evenly over hot filling, sealing edges to crust. Sprinkle with remaining peanut butter mixture.

8. Bake at 350° for 12-15 minutes or until the meringue is golden brown. Cool on a wire rack for 1 hour. Refrigerate for at least 4 hours before serving. Store leftovers in the refrigerator.

Editor's Note: *Let pie weights cool before storing. Beans and rice may be reused for pie weights, but not for cooking.*

Simply *Tea-licious*

BY DONNA HARDIN

The kettle's always on at our Iowa farmhouse.

At first, country life didn't seem like my cup of tea—until I found a way to brew up some excitement amid the farm fields of southern Iowa.

My family has always been city folks, so it was a real culture shock when my husband, Don, convinced me and our four children to move to the country nine years ago. Being a people person, I felt isolated at first. Every time I heard a car, I'd get all excited, hoping it was company, and then be disappointed when they'd drive right on by.

Nowadays, people flock to the our rural acres, sometimes by the busload. Our cozy tearoom has become a destination for those seeking a perfect blend of fun, friendship and comfort by the pot.

Our first winter on the cow farm was particularly frigid. So Spenser, my daughter, and I would have afternoon tea together to lift our spirits. We enjoyed it so much, we decided to hold monthly teas for area women. We were astounded by the positive response!

Our casual home business quickly evolved into Miss Spenser's Special-Teas. We hosted more than 50 tea events last year. To accommodate our growing guest list, we recently converted an attached garage into a spacious tearoom. There we welcome tour groups, social and business clubs, and people celebrating birthdays, anniversaries and other special events. Afternoon tea meals are also held a couple of times a week.

Both Spenser and I like being creative, so we develop themes and dramatic programs for many of our tea parties. They may be based on a holiday, a season, a work of literature or a famous person or event from the past.

Spenser, who's now 21, is a natural actress and often portrays a historical character in the dramas we write together. She also loves to sew and designs all the costumes we need, from Civil War-era clothing to dresses from the Victorian and Edwardian eras.

I'm an avid cook, so I research and test recipes to fit the theme and put together the menus.

Our garden tea party, for instance, showcases homegrown ingredients in dishes like gingered carrot soup, asparagus rolls, mushroom tartlets and geranium shortbread cookies. Along with the food, we serve whole-leaf teas—oolong, black, white and green.

Guests of all ages, from children to grandmothers, are steeped in the teatime experience. A local woman gave me her collection of ladies' hats for our little girls' tea parties. The funny thing is, the big girls insist on trying them on.

Of course, men are always welcome to savor our brews, and the Hardin sons—Chase, 17; Zach, 15; and Grayson, 9—are regulars in the tearoom. They're very musical and often perform with their sister in the dramas. And my husband, Don, has started assisting me with serving. He charms the ladies, who call him our butler.

Visitors often find the Hardin farm a haven from hurried urban life. By design, we have created a setting reminiscent of Grandma's house—filled with quilts, crafts, antiques, nostalgic photos and tables dressed with vintage tea sets and linens.

We want guests to feel like our family, not our customers, and to share in the unique gifts the country gives us. In fact, we plan to add a bed-and-breakfast suite above our backyard carriage house later this year.

The tearoom keeps me so busy now, there's no time to be lonely. And I no longer yearn for the big city. We've found a way to bring our friends to us!

Donna Hardin and her daughter, Spenser, gather flowers for the tearoom they run on their family farm.

from Donna's kitchen

Easy Lemon Curd Bars

A cup of tea looks lonely without something sweet beside it. These bars are a nice accompaniment. I love the combination of the nutty crust and zippy lemon curd.
—**DONNA HARDIN** NEW VIRGINIA, IOWA

PREP: 30 MINUTES **BAKE:** 20 MINUTES **MAKES:** 2 DOZEN

- 1 **cup butter, softened**
- 1 **cup sugar**
- 2 **cups all-purpose flour**
- ½ **teaspoon baking soda**
- 1 **jar (10 ounces) lemon curd**
- ⅔ **cup flaked coconut**
- ½ **cup chopped almonds, toasted**

1. In a large bowl, cream butter and sugar until light and fluffy. Combine flour and baking soda; gradually add to creamed mixture and mix well.

2. Set aside 1 cup mixture for topping; press remaining mixture onto the bottom of a greased 13-in. x 9-in. baking dish. Bake at 350° for 12-15 minutes or until edges are lightly browned. Cool for 10 minutes.

3. Spread lemon curd over crust. In a small bowl, combine the coconut, almonds and reserved topping mixture; sprinkle over lemon curd.

4. Bake for 18-22 minutes or until golden brown. Cool completely on a wire rack. Cut into bars.

Putting By

Savor the bounty of summer fruit any time of year with jewel-toned jellies and jams. Homemade sauces, pickles and butters are the perfect fix for a bumper crop of veggies and herbs. Satisfying to give and delightful to receive, the recipes that follow are sure to become perennial favorites.

Pickled Green Beans

(recipe on page 303)

"This recipe produces zippy little pickles and preserves my green beans for months to come—if they last that long. I crank up the heat a bit with cayenne pepper."

—MARISA MCCLELLAN
PHILADELPHIA, PENNSYLVANIA

Pineapple Kiwi Jam

Pineapple, kiwi and a hint of lime blend nicely in a uniquely tropical combination.

—SONDRA ROGERS COLUMBUS, INDIANA

PREP: 20 MINUTES
COOK: 15 MINUTES + STANDING
MAKES: 4 CUPS

- 4 **kiwifruit, peeled and thinly sliced**
- 3 **cups sugar**
- 1 **can (8 ounces) crushed pineapple, undrained**
- ¼ **cup lime juice**
- 1 **pouch (3 ounces) liquid fruit pectin**
- 3 **drops green food coloring, optional**

1. In a 2-qt. microwave-safe bowl, combine the first four ingredients. Microwave, uncovered, on high for 7-10 minutes or until mixture comes to a full rolling boil, stirring every 2 minutes. Stir in pectin. Add food coloring if desired.
2. Pour into jars or freezer containers and cool to room temperature, about 1 hour. Cover and let stand overnight or until set, but not longer than 24 hours. Refrigerate or freeze.

Editor's Note: *This recipe was tested in a 1,100-watt microwave.*

Raspberry-Onion Jalapeno Chutney

Sweet raspberries and spicy jalapenos come together to create a chutney that tastes terrific on top of cream cheese or over grilled chicken.

—JO-ANNE COOPER CAMROSE, ALBERTA

PREP: 45 MINUTES **PROCESS:** 15 MINUTES
MAKES: 7 HALF-PINTS

- 4 **large onions, chopped**
- 2 **large red onions, chopped**
- 1½ **cups packed brown sugar**
- 1 **cup raisins**
- 1¼ **cups cider vinegar**
- 1 **cup balsamic vinegar**
- ½ **cup sugar**
- 2 **jalapeno peppers, seeded and chopped**
- 2 **tablespoons grated orange peel**
- 2 **teaspoons canning salt**
- 4 **cups fresh raspberries**

1. In a Dutch oven, bring the first 10 ingredients to a boil. Reduce heat; simmer, uncovered, for 25-30 minutes or until thickened, stirring occasionally. Stir in raspberries; heat through.
2. Remove from the heat. Ladle hot mixture into hot half-pint jars, leaving ½-in. headspace. Remove air bubbles; wipe rims and adjust lids. Process for 15 minutes in a boiling-water canner.

Editor's Note: *When cutting hot peppers, disposable gloves are recommended. Avoid touching your face. The processing time listed is for altitudes of 1,000 feet or less. For altitudes up to 3,000 feet, add 5 minutes; 6,000 feet, add 10 minutes; 8,000 feet, add 15 minutes; 10,000 feet, add 20 minutes.*

Tri-Berry Jam

My mother-in-law and I dreamed up a recipe after we'd been picking blueberries one day. She wondered if blueberries, raspberries and strawberries would taste good together, so she made a test batch. We quickly learned that they definitely did! After some tweaking, I came up with my own version.

—KAREN MAERKLE BALTIC, CONNECTICUT

PREP: 20 MINUTES **PROCESS:** 10 MINUTES **MAKES:** ABOUT 6 PINTS

- 4 **cups fresh or frozen blueberries**
- 2½ **cups fresh or frozen red raspberries**
- 2½ **cups fresh or frozen strawberries**
- ¼ **cup lemon juice**
- 2 **packages (1¾ ounces each) powdered fruit pectin**
- 11 **cups sugar**

1. Combine the berries and lemon juice in a stockpot; crush fruit slightly. Stir in pectin. Bring to a full rolling boil over high heat, stirring constantly. Stir in sugar; return to a full rolling boil. Boil 1 minute, stirring constantly.

2. Remove from the heat; skim off any foam. Carefully ladle hot mixture into hot pint jars, leaving ¼-in. headspace. Remove air bubbles; wipe rims and adjust lids. Process for 10 minutes in a boiling-water canner.

Editor's Note: *The processing time listed is for altitudes of 1,000 feet or less. Add 1 minute to the processing time for each 1,000 feet of additional altitude.*

Strawberry Marmalade

This recipe makes ordinary orange marmalade into something really special! Sometimes I make it using strawberries that I've frozen without adding sugar or water. Thaw them in the refrigerator overnight.

—MRS. CRAIG PRESBREY
PASCOAG, RHODE ISLAND

PREP: 1 HOUR **PROCESS:** 10 MINUTES
MAKES: ABOUT 10 HALF-PINTS

- 2 **medium oranges**
- 2 **medium lemons**
- ½ **cup water**
- ⅛ **teaspoon baking soda**
- 1 **quart ripe strawberries, crushed**
- 7 **cups sugar**
- 1 **pouch liquid fruit pectin (half of a 6-ounce package)**

1. Peel outer layer of oranges and lemons; set aside. Remove the white membrane from fruit and discard. Set the fruit aside. Chop peels; place in a large saucepan. Add water and baking soda; cover and bring to a boil. Simmer for 10 minutes.

2. Meanwhile, section oranges and lemons, reserving juice. Add fruit and juice to saucepan; cover and simmer for 20 minutes. Add strawberries. Measure fruit; return 4 cups to the saucepan. (If you have more than 4 cups, discard any extra; if less, add water to equal 4 cups.) Add sugar and mix well. Boil, uncovered, for 5 minutes.

3. Remove from the heat; stir in pectin. Stir for 5 minutes to cool; skim off foam. Carefully ladle hot mixture into hot half-pint jars or freezer containers, leaving ¼-in. headspace. Remove air bubbles; wipe rips and adjust lids. Process for 10 minutes in a boiling-water canner or store in the freezer.

Editor's Note: *The processing time listed is for altitudes of 1,000 feet or less. Add 1 minute to the processing time for each 1,000 feet of additional altitude.*

Three-Hour Refrigerator Pickles

My simple recipe uses regular cucumbers and doesn't require canning. My grandkids help me make them and are proud when they take a big jar home.

—**SANDRA JONES** TROY, NORTH CAROLINA

PREP: 15 MINUTES + CHILLING
MAKES: 2½ QUARTS

- 6 **pounds cucumbers**
- 4 **medium onions**
- 4 **cups sugar**
- 4 **cups white vinegar**
- ½ **cup salt**
- 1½ **teaspoons ground turmeric**
- 1 **teaspoon celery salt**
- 1 **teaspoon mustard seed**

1. Slice the cucumbers ¼ in. thick. Slice onions ⅛ in. thick. Place both in a large nonmetallic bowl. Combine the remaining ingredients; pour over cucumber mixture. Stir well for 5 minutes.
2. Cover and refrigerate 3 hours before serving. Store in the refrigerator for up to 3 months, stirring occasionally.

Christmas Cranberries

Bourbon adds bite to this holiday standby, packed in a small heavy-duty glass storage container with a tight-fitting lid. Wrap in a vintage tea towel or cloth napkin, cinch with ribbon and adorn with small ornaments.

—**BECKY JO SMITH** KETTLE FALLS, WASHINGTON

PREP: 35 MINUTES **PROCESS:** 15 MINUTES **MAKES:** 4 HALF-PINTS

- 2 **packages (12 ounces each) fresh or frozen cranberries, thawed**
- 1½ **cups sugar**
- 1 **cup orange juice**
- ¼ **cup bourbon**
- 3 **teaspoons vanilla extract**
- 1 **teaspoon grated orange peel**

1. In a large saucepan, combine the cranberries, sugar, orange juice and bourbon. Bring to a boil. Reduce heat; simmer, uncovered, for 18-22 minutes or until berries pop and mixture has thickened.
2. Stir in vanilla and orange peel. Carefully ladle hot mixture into hot half-pint jars, leaving ¼-in. headspace. Remove air bubbles; wipe rims and adjust lids. Process for 15 minutes in a boiling-water canner.
Editor's Note: *The processing time listed is for altitudes of 1,000 feet or less. Add 1 minute to the processing time for each 1,000 feet of additional altitude.*

Pickled Peppers

I'm nearing the age of 80 and still love to can my homegrown produce. I call this recipe "Summer in a Jar." The peppers have a nice combination of tart and spicy flavors.

—EDNA CLEMENS WEST BRANCH, MICHIGAN

PREP: 30 MINUTES **PROCESS:** 15 MINUTES **MAKES:** 4 PINTS

 4 to 6 large sweet red peppers, cut into strips
 12 banana peppers, halved and seeded
 1 medium onion, thinly sliced
 8 garlic cloves, peeled
 4 teaspoons canola oil
 2½ cups water
 2½ cups white vinegar
 1¼ cups sugar
 2 teaspoons canning salt

1. Pack red and banana peppers into four hot 1-pint jars to within ½ in. of the top. Divide the onion, garlic and oil among jars.

2. In a large saucepan, bring the water, vinegar, sugar and salt to a boil.

3. Carefully ladle hot mixture into the hot jars, leaving ½-in. headspace. Remove air bubbles; wipe rims and adjust lids. Process for 15 minutes in a boiling-water canner.

Editor's Note: *The processing time listed is for altitudes of 1,000 feet or less. For altitudes up to 3,000 feet, add 5 minutes; 6,000 feet, add 10 minutes; 8,000 feet, add 15 minutes; 10,000 feet, add 20 minutes.*

Orange Rhubarb Spread

This tangy spread is easy to make and tastes especially good on hot buttered cinnamon toast. The recipe makes enough to have on hand well beyond the growing season.

—BETTY NYENHUIS OOSTBURG, WISCONSIN

PREP: 5 MINUTES **COOK:** 20 MINUTES + STANDING **MAKES:** 5 HALF-PINTS

- 4 **cups diced fresh or frozen rhubarb**
- 2 **cups water**
- 1 **can (6 ounces) frozen orange juice concentrate, thawed**
- 1 **package (1¾ ounces) powdered fruit pectin**
- 4 **cups sugar**

1. In a large saucepan, bring rhubarb and water to a boil. Reduce heat; simmer, uncovered, for 7-8 minutes or until rhubarb is tender. Drain and reserve cooking liquid. Cool rhubarb and liquid to room temperature.

2. Place the rhubarb in a blender; cover and process until pureed. Transfer to a 4-cup measuring cup; add enough reserved cooking liquid to measure 2⅓ cups. Return to the saucepan.

3. Add orange juice concentrate and pectin; bring to a full rolling boil, stirring constantly. Stir in sugar. Return to a full rolling boil; boil and stir for 1 minute. Remove from the heat; skim off foam.

4. Pour into jars or freezer containers; cool to room temperature, about 1 hour. Cover and let stand overnight or until set, but not longer than 24 hours. Refrigerate or freeze. Refrigerate for up to 3 weeks or freeze for up to 12 months.

Homemade Canned Spaghetti Sauce

Savory canned spaghetti sauce is a tomato-grower's dream come true! Use up your garden bounty and enjoy it later in the year.

—TONYA BRANHAM MT. OLIVE, ALABAMA

PREP: 1½ HOURS + SIMMERING **PROCESS:** 40 MINUTES **MAKES:** 9 QUARTS

- 25 **pounds tomatoes**
- 4 **large green peppers, seeded**
- 4 **large onions, cut into wedges**
- 4 **cans (6 ounces each) tomato paste**
- 1 **cup canola oil**
- ⅔ **cup sugar**
- ¼ **cup salt**
- 8 **garlic cloves, minced**
- 4 **teaspoons dried oregano**
- 2 **teaspoons dried parsley flakes**
- 2 **teaspoons dried basil**
- 2 **teaspoons crushed red pepper flakes**
- 2 **teaspoons Worcestershire sauce**
- 2 **bay leaves**
- 1 **cup plus 2 tablespoons bottled lemon juice**

1. In a Dutch oven, bring 8 cups water to a boil. Using a slotted spoon, place tomatoes, one at a time, in boiling water for 30-60 seconds. Remove each tomato and immediately plunge in ice water. Peel and quarter tomatoes.

2. In a food processor, cover and process the green peppers and onions in batches until finely chopped.

3. In a stockpot, combine the tomatoes, green pepper mixture, tomato paste, oil, sugar, salt, garlic, oregano, parsley, basil, pepper flakes, Worcestershire sauce and bay leaves. Bring to a boil. Reduce heat; simmer, uncovered, for 4-5 hours, stirring occasionally. Discard bay leaves.

4. Add lemon juice to nine hot quart jars, 2 tablespoons in each. Ladle hot mixture into jars, leaving ½-in. headspace. Remove air bubbles; wipe rims and adjust lids. Process for 40 minutes in a boiling-water canner.

Editor's Note: *The processing time listed is for altitudes of 1,000 feet or less. For altitudes up to 3,000 feet, add 5 minutes; 6,000 feet, add 10 minutes; 8,000 feet, add 15 minutes; 10,000 feet, add 20 minutes.*

Strawberry Freezer Jam

A dear friend shared her delightful strawberry jam recipe with me when we lived in Germany. It's lovely on ice cream, too!

—MARY JEAN ELLIS INDIANAPOLIS, INDIANA

PREP: 40 MINUTES + FREEZING **MAKES:** 4½ PINTS

- 2 **quarts fresh strawberries**
- 5½ **cups sugar**
- 1 **cup light corn syrup**
- ¼ **cup lemon juice**
- ¾ **cup water**
- 1 **package (1¾ ounces) powdered fruit pectin**

1. Wash and mash the berries, measuring out enough mashed berries to make 4 cups; place in a large bowl. Stir in the sugar, corn syrup and lemon juice. Let stand for 10 minutes.

2. In a Dutch oven, combine strawberry mixture and water. Stir in pectin. Bring to a full rolling boil over high heat, stirring constantly. Boil for 1 minute, stirring constantly. Remove from the heat; skim off foam.

3. Pour into jars or freezer containers, leaving ½-in. headspace. Cover and let stand overnight or until set, but not longer than 24 hours. Refrigerate for up to 3 weeks or freeze for up to 12 months.

Freeze scoops or rosettes of flavored butter on a parchment paper-lined baking sheet. Once frozen, arrange the butter portions on layers of paper in a freezer container. Remove the desired number of portions from the freezer when needed. Melt over steaks or broiled fish for a tasty treat.

Tarragon Butter

Tarragon is a native herb of central Asia and was brought to Spain by the Moors. It has been an important ingredient in French cuisine since the 16th century.

—TASTE OF HOME TEST KITCHEN

PREP: 5 MINUTES + CHILLING
MAKES: ½ CUP

- ½ cup butter, softened
- ¼ cup minced fresh tarragon
- ⅛ teaspoon lemon juice
  Dash salt and pepper

1. In a small bowl, beat all ingredients with a fork or whisk until well blended. Shape into a log; wrap in plastic wrap. Refrigerate for a week or freeze for several months. Slice and use on fish, poultry, vegetables, pasta and bread.

Basil Butter

Make a tasty basil butter during the growing season and freeze it for later use. When veggies are sauteed in the butter, they taste as fresh as the herbs do when they come out of the garden.
—EMILY CHANEY PENOBSCOT, MAINE

YIELD: 4 DOZEN BUTTER BALLS.

- 1-½ cups loosely packed fresh basil leaves
- ½ pound butter, softened
- 1 teaspoon lemon juice
- 1 teaspoon seasoned pepper
- ½ teaspoon garlic salt

1. In a food processor, chop basil. Add the butter, lemon juice and pepper and garlic salt; blend until smooth. Drop by half-tablespoons onto a baking sheet; freeze. Remove from baking sheet and store in freezer bags. Use to flavor chicken, fish or vegetables.

Chunky Peach Spread

This fruity spread captures the taste of summer! Low in sugar, it's not overly sweet... and the fresh peach flavor really comes through. You'll want to try it on everything from bagels to waffles.

—**REBECCA BAIRD** SALT LAKE CITY, UTAH

PREP: 20 MINUTES **COOK:** 10 MINUTES + COOLING **MAKES:** ABOUT 3½ CUPS

- 7 medium peaches (2 to 2½ pounds)
- ⅓ cup sugar
- 1 tablespoon lemon juice
- 1 envelope unflavored gelatin
- ¼ cup cold water

1. Drop peaches in boiling water for 1 minute or until peel has softened. Immediately dip fruit in ice water. Peel and chop peaches. In a large saucepan, combine the peaches, sugar and lemon juice. Bring to a boil. Mash peaches. Reduce heat; simmer, uncovered, for 5 minutes.

2. Meanwhile, in a small bowl, sprinkle gelatin over cold water; let stand for 2 minutes. Remove peach mixture from the heat; stir in gelatin mixture until dissolved. Cool for 10 minutes. Pour into jars. Refrigerate for up to 3 weeks.

Spicy Mustard

When I make mustard, I like to use fresh horseradish from our garden and vinegar seasoned with homegrown tarragon. Mustard adds zip to burgers and cold deli sandwiches.

—**JOYCE LONSDALE**
UNIONVILLE, PENNSYLVANIA

PREP: 15 MINUTES
COOK: 5 MINUTES + STANDING
MAKES: 1½ CUPS

- ½ cup tarragon or cider vinegar
- ½ cup water
- ¼ cup olive oil
- 2 tablespoons prepared horseradish
- ½ teaspoon lemon juice
- 1 cup ground mustard
- ½ cup sugar
- ½ teaspoon salt

1. In a blender or food processor, combine all ingredients; cover and process for 1 minute. Scrape down the sides of the container and process for 30 seconds.

2. Transfer to a small saucepan and let stand for 10 minutes. Cook over low heat until bubbly, stirring constantly. Cool completely. If a thinner mustard is desired, stir in an additional 1-2 tablespoons water. Pour into small containers with tight-fitting lids. Store in the refrigerator.

Home Style COOKING NOTES

Zucchini Pickles

Here's a great way to put your garden bounty to use! Turn that ripe zucchini into a crunchy, flavorful burger topping.

—**ROMAINE WETZEL** RONKS, PENNSYLVANIA

PREP: 35 MINUTES + STANDING
PROCESS: 10 MINUTES
MAKES: 5 PINTS

- 8 **cups sliced zucchini**
- 4 **large onions, sliced**
- 1 **large green pepper, sliced**
- 3 **tablespoons canning salt**
- 1 **quart white vinegar**
- 2 **cups sugar**
- 2 **teaspoons celery salt**
- 2 **teaspoons ground turmeric**
- 1 **teaspoon ground mustard**

1. In a large bowl, combine the zucchini, onions and green pepper; sprinkle with canning salt and cover with cold water. Let stand for 2 hours; rinse and drain.
2. In a large saucepan, bring the remaining ingredients to a boil. Pour over zucchini mixture; cover and let stand for 2 hours.
3. Transfer to a stockpot. Bring to a boil. Reduce heat; simmer, uncovered, for 5 minutes. Carefully ladle hot mixture into hot 1-pint jars, leaving ½-in. headspace. Remove air bubbles; wipe rims and adjust lids. Process for 10 minutes in a boiling-water canner.

Editor's Note: *The processing time listed is for altitudes of 1,000 feet or less. For altitudes up to 3,000 feet, add 5 minutes; 6,000 feet, add 10 minutes; 8,000 feet, add 15 minutes; 10,000 feet, add 20 minutes.*

Blueberry Jelly

My mother brought this old family recipe with her when she moved here from Scotland. My children and husband especially love spreading the jelly on slices of homemade bread.

—**ELAINE SOPER** TRINITY BAY, NEWFOUNDLAND AND LABRADOR

PREP: 1¼ HOURS **PROCESS:** 5 MINUTES **MAKES:** 6 PINTS

- 2 **quarts fresh or frozen blueberries**
- 4 **cups water**
- 12 **cups sugar**
- 2 **pouches (3 ounces each) liquid fruit pectin**

1. Place blueberries in a Dutch oven and crush slightly. Add water; bring to a boil. Reduce heat to medium; cook, uncovered, for 45 minutes. Line a strainer with four layers of cheesecloth and place over a bowl. Place berry mixture in strainer; cover with edges of cheesecloth. Let stand for 30 minutes or until liquid measures 6 cups.
2. Pour juice back into Dutch oven; gradually stir in sugar until it dissolves. Bring to a boil over high heat, stirring constantly. Add pectin; bring to a full rolling boil. Boil for 1 minute, stirring constantly.
3. Remove from the heat. Skim any foam. Carefully ladle hot mixture into sterilized hot pint jars, leaving ¼-in. headspace. Remove air bubbles; wipe rims and adjust lids. Process for 5 minutes in a boiling-water canner.

Editor's Note: *The processing time listed is for altitudes of 1,000 feet or less. Add 1 minute to the processing time for each 1,000 feet of additional altitude.*

Spicy Pickled Garlic

Here's a delicious condiment for the garlic lover on your list. You'll be pleasantly surprised how pickling mellows out the garlic, making it a tasty sandwich topper.

—TASTE OF HOME TEST KITCHEN

PREP: 20 MINUTES **PROCESS:** 10 MINUTES **MAKES:** 3 HALF-PINTS

2	**quarts water**
3	**cups garlic cloves**
12	**coriander seeds**
6	**whole peppercorns**
3	**dried hot chilies, split**
3	**whole allspice**
1	**bay leaf, torn into three pieces**
1½	**cups white wine vinegar or distilled white vinegar**
1	**tablespoon sugar**
1½	**teaspoons canning salt**

1. In a large saucepan, bring water to a boil. Add garlic and boil for 1 minute. Meanwhile, divide the coriander, peppercorns, chilies, allspice and bay leaf among three hot half-pint jars. Drain garlic and pack into jars to within ½ in. of the top.

2. In a small saucepan, combine the vinegar, sugar and salt. Bring to a boil, stirring constantly. Carefully ladle hot liquid over garlic, leaving ½-in. headspace. Remove air bubbles; wipe rims and adjust lids. Process for 10 minutes in a boiling-water canner.

Editor's Note: *The processing time listed is for altitudes of 1,000 feet or less. For altitudes up to 3,000 feet, add 5 minutes; 6,000 feet, add 10 minutes; 8,000 feet, add 15 minutes; 10,000 feet, add 20 minutes.*

Grandma's Dill Pickles

Treasured family recipes such as this one become like old friends. Crispy pickle spears have a slightly salty, tart flavor with a good balance of dill, garlic and peppers.

—BETTY KAY SITZMAN WRAY, COLORADO

PREP: 50 MINUTES **PROCESS:** 15 MINUTES **MAKES:** 9 QUARTS

- **11 cups water**
- **5 cups white vinegar**
- **1 cup canning salt**
- **12 pounds pickling cucumbers, quartered or halved lengthwise**
- **9 dill sprigs or heads**
- **18 garlic cloves**
- **18 dried hot chilies**

1. In a stockpot, bring the water, vinegar and salt to a boil; boil for 10 minutes. Pack cucumbers into hot quart jars within ½ in. of top. Place one dill head, two garlic cloves and two peppers in each jar.

2. Carefully ladle hot mixture into jars, leaving ½-in. headspace. Remove air bubbles, wipe rims and adjust lids. Process for 15 minutes in a boiling-water canner.

Editor's Note: *The processing time listed is for altitudes of 1,000 feet or less. For altitudes up to 3,000 feet, add 5 minutes; 6,000 feet, add 10 minutes; 8,000 feet, add 15 minutes; 10,000 feet, add 20 minutes.*

Chunky Salsa

My fresh-tasting salsa is wonderfully chunky. If you like it hotter, add more habanero peppers; if you prefer a mild salsa, add fewer.

—**DANA HAYES** CANTON, OHIO

PREP: 45 MINUTES **PROCESS:** 15 MINUTES **MAKES:** 7 PINTS

- 5 **pounds tomatoes**
- 4 **large green peppers, chopped**
- 3 **large onions, chopped**
- 2 **large sweet red peppers, chopped**
- 2 **habanero peppers, seeded and finely chopped**
- 1 **cup white vinegar**
- 1 **can (6 ounces) tomato paste**
- 3 **teaspoons salt**

1. Fill a Dutch oven two-thirds with water; bring to a boil. Score an "X" on the bottom of each tomato. Using a slotted spoon, place tomatoes, one at a time, in boiling water for 30-60 seconds. Remove tomatoes and immediately plunge in ice water. Discard peel; chop tomatoes.

2. In a stockpot, combine the remaining ingredients. Stir in tomatoes. Bring to a boil over medium-high heat. Reduce heat; simmer, uncovered, for 15-20 minutes or until desired thickness.

3. Carefully ladle hot mixture into hot 1-pint jars, leaving ½-in. headspace. Remove air bubbles; wipe rims and adjust lids. Process for 15 minutes in a boiling-water canner.

Editor's Note: *We recommend wearing disposable gloves when cutting hot peppers. Avoid touching your face. The processing time listed is for altitudes of 1,000 feet or less. For altitudes up to 3,000 feet, add 5 minutes; 6,000 feet, add 10 minutes; 8,000 feet, add 15 minutes; 10,000 feet, add 20 minutes.*

Violet Jelly

For a beautiful jelly to give as gifts, this one can't be beat. Not only is it delicious, it's guaranteed to impress all recipients!

—**BERNARD BELLIN** FRANKLIN, WISCONSIN

PREP: 40 MINUTES + STANDING
PROCESS: 5 MINUTES
MAKES: ABOUT 5 HALF-PINTS

- 8 **cups fresh violet blossoms**
- 3½ **cups boiling water**
- 1 **package (1¾ ounces) powdered fruit pectin**
- ½ **cup lemon juice**
- 4 **cups sugar**

1. Rinse and drain blossoms; place in a large heat-resistant glass bowl. Pour boiling water over the blossoms and let stand for 2 hours, stirring occasionally.

2. Strain and reserve violet liquid, pressing with a spatula to extract all possible color. Discard blossoms.

3. Measure violet liquid; add enough water to measure 3½ cups (liquid will be blue-green). Stir in pectin, lemon juice and sugar (the liquid will turn a violet color).

4. Pour into a large stainless steel saucepan; bring to a rolling boil, stirring constantly. Boil 1 minute.

5. Remove from the heat; skim off foam. Carefully ladle hot liquid into hot sterilized half-pint jars, leaving ¼-in. headspace. Remove air bubbles; wipe rims and adjust lids. Process for 5 minutes in a boiling-water canner.

Editor's Note: *Only pick flowers from chemical-free woods or lawns. Also, be sure your blossoms come from the common wild violet, not the African violet houseplant, which is inedible. The processing time listed is for altitudes of 1,000 feet or less. Add 1 minute to the processing time for each 1,000 feet of additional altitude.*

Jalapeno Pepper Jelly

My family loves jalapeno jelly served with meat or spread over crackers with cream cheese. It's in hot demand as a gift.

—BEV ELLIOTT PEOTONE, ILLINOIS

PREP: 30 MINUTES **PROCESS:** 10 MINUTES
MAKES: ABOUT 5 HALF-PINTS

- 5 **cups sugar**
- 2 **medium tart apples, peeled and coarsely chopped**
- 1½ **cups cider vinegar**
- ¾ **cup finely chopped green pepper**
- 8 **to 10 jalapeno peppers, seeded and chopped**
- ¼ **cup water**
- 6 **to 8 drops green food coloring**
- 2 **pouches (3 ounces each) liquid fruit pectin**
  Cream cheese and assorted crackers

1. In a large saucepan, combine the sugar, apples, vinegar, green pepper, jalapenos and water. Bring to a boil. Reduce heat; simmer, uncovered, for 10 minutes. Strain mixture and return to pan. Stir in food coloring. Return to a rolling boil over high heat. Stir in pectin; boil for 2 minutes, stirring constantly.

2. Remove from the heat; skim off foam. Pour hot liquid into hot half-pint jars, leaving ¼-in. headspace. Adjust caps. Process for 10 minutes in a boiling-water canner. Serve with cream cheese on crackers.

Editor's Note: *Wear disposable gloves when cutting hot peppers; the oils can burn skin. Avoid touching your face. The processing time listed is for altitudes of 1,000 feet or less. Add 1 minute to the processing time for each 1,000 feet of additional altitude.*

Gingered Carrot Chutney

Tangy and bright, this tasty chutney can top cheese spread on crackers or accompany any type of meat on your plate.

—DEB DARR FALLS CITY, OREGON

PREP: 1 HOUR **PROCESS:** 10 MINUTES
MAKES: 9 HALF-PINTS

- 4 **pounds carrots, sliced**
- 2 **medium oranges**

- 1 **medium lemon**
- 2 **tablespoons mixed pickling spices**
- 2½ **cups sugar**
- 1⅓ **cups cider vinegar**
- 1 **cup flaked coconut**
- 1 **tablespoon minced fresh gingerroot**
- ½ **teaspoon hot pepper sauce**

1. Place carrots in a Dutch oven and cover with water. Bring to a boil. Reduce heat; cover and cook for 20-25 minutes or until very tender. Drain carrots; puree in a food processor.

2. Using a vegetable peeler, remove peel from oranges and half of the lemon; cut peel into long narrow strips. Remove remaining peel from lemon and the white pith from lemon and oranges; thinly slice fruit, discarding seeds.

3. Place pickling spices on a double thickness of cheesecloth; bring up corners of cloth and tie with string to form a bag. Place in a Dutch oven. Add the sugar, vinegar and citrus peels; bring to a boil.

4. Reduce heat; simmer, uncovered, for 5 minutes. Stir in carrots and sliced fruit. Return to a boil. Reduce heat; simmer, uncovered, for 30 minutes, stirring frequently. Discard spice bag. Stir in the coconut, ginger and pepper sauce.

5. Carefully ladle hot chutney into hot half-pint jars, leaving ½-in. headspace. Remove air bubbles; wipe rims and adjust lids. Process for 10 minutes in a boiling-water canner.

Editor's Note: *The processing time listed is for altitudes of 1,000 feet or less. For altitudes up to 3,000 feet, add 5 minutes; 6,000 feet, add 10 minutes; 8,000 feet, add 15 minutes; 10,000 feet, add 20 minutes.*

Pineapple Salsa

Here's a sweet and spicy twist on salsa. Served with chips, it's an excellent party starter. It also adds a refreshing touch to grilled fish or meat.

—ANGELA LONGTIN CAVALIER, NORTH DAKOTA

PREP: 50 MINUTES **PROCESS:** 15 MINUTES **MAKES:** 7 PINT JARS

- 12 **medium tomatoes (about 4 pounds)**
- 2 **large red onions, chopped**
- 2 **medium green peppers, chopped**
- 2 **cans (8 ounces each) unsweetened crushed pineapple, drained**
- 1 **can (15 ounces) tomato sauce**
- 1 **can (12 ounces) tomato paste**
- 3 **cans (4 ounces each) chopped green chilies**
- 2 **cans (4 ounces each) diced jalapeno peppers, drained**
- ⅓ **cup white vinegar**
- 2 **tablespoons salt**
- 6 **garlic cloves, minced**
- 2 **teaspoons ground cumin**
- 1 **teaspoon pepper**

1. In a large saucepan, bring 8 cups water to a boil. Add tomatoes, a few at a time; boil for 30 seconds. Drain and immediately place tomatoes in ice water. Drain and pat dry; peel and chop.

2. In a stockpot, combine the remaining ingredients. Stir in tomatoes. Bring to a boil over medium-high heat. Reduce heat; simmer, uncovered, for 15-20 minutes or to desired thickness.

3. Carefully ladle hot mixture into hot 1-pint jars, leaving ½-in. headspace. Remove air bubbles; wipe rims and adjust lids. Process for 15 minutes in a boiling-water canner.

Editor's Note: *The processing time listed is for altitudes of 1,000 feet or less. For altitudes up to 3,000 feet, add 5 minutes; 6,000 feet, add 10 minutes; 8,000 feet, add 15 minutes; 10,000 feet, add 20 minutes.*

Mint Jelly

Here's a classic condiment to go with roasted lamb. With its bright green tone, the jelly is a striking addition to the holiday buffet table.

—NAOMI GIDDIS TWO BUTTES, COLORADO

PREP: 15 MINUTES + STANDING
PROCESS: 10 MINUTES
MAKES: 11 HALF-PINTS

- 4½ **cups water**
- 3 **cups packed fresh mint, crushed**
- 7 **cups sugar**
- ¼ **cup lemon juice**
- 2 **to 4 drops green food coloring**
- 2 **pouches (3 ounces each) liquid pectin**

1. In a large saucepan, bring water and mint to a boil. Remove from the heat; cover and let stand for 15 minutes. Strain, reserving 3⅓ cups liquid (discard remaining liquid).

2. In a Dutch oven, combine the sugar, lemon juice, food coloring and reserved liquid. Bring to a boil; cover and stir for 1 minute. Add pectin; return to a boil. Cook and stir for 1 minute. Remove from the heat; let stand for 5 minutes.

3. Skim off foam. Pour the hot liquid into hot sterilized half-pint jars, leaving ¼-in. headspace. Adjust caps.

4. Process for 10 minutes in a boiling-water canner.

Editor's Note: *The processing time listed is for altitudes of 1,000 feet or less. Add 1 minute to the processing time for each 1,000 feet of additional altitude.*

Homemade Pizza Sauce

For years, I had trouble finding a pizza my family likes. So I started making my own. The evening I served it to company and they asked for my recipe, I thought, "I finally got it right!" When I prepare my sauce, I usually fix enough for three to four pizzas and freeze it. Feel free to spice up my sauce to suit your family's preferences.

—CHERYL KRAVIK
SPANAWAY, WASHINGTON

PREP: 10 MINUTES
COOK: 70 MINUTES
MAKES: ABOUT 4 CUPS

- 2 **cans (15 ounces each) tomato sauce**
- 1 **can (12 ounces) tomato paste**
- 1 **tablespoon Italian seasoning**
- 1 **tablespoon dried oregano**
- 1 **to 2 teaspoons fennel seed, crushed**
- 1 **teaspoon onion powder**
- 1 **teaspoon garlic powder**
- ½ **teaspoon salt**

1. In a large saucepan over medium heat, combine tomato sauce and paste. Add remaining ingredients; mix well. Bring to a boil, stirring constantly. Reduce heat; cover and simmer for 1 hour, stirring occasionally. Cool.
2. Pour into freezer containers, leaving ½-in. headspace. Freeze for up to 12 months.
Editor's Note: *Use the sauce with crust and toppings of your choice to make a pizza; 1⅓ cups of sauce will cover a crust in a 15-in. x 10-in. x 1-in. pan.*

Home Style COOKING NOTES

Raspberry Peach Jam

While my jam won a first-place ribbon at our local county fair, that may not be the highest compliment it's received. Two girlfriends I share it with tell me if they don't hide the jam from their husbands and children, they'll devour an entire jarful in just one sitting!

—PATRICIA LARSEN LESLIEVILLE, ALBERTA

PREP: 35 MINUTES **PROCESS:** 15 MINUTES **MAKES:** 5 HALF-PINTS

- 2⅔ **cups finely chopped peeled peaches**
- 1½ **cups crushed raspberries**
- 3 **cups sugar**
- 1½ **teaspoons lemon juice**

1. In a Dutch oven, combine all ingredients. Cook over low heat, stirring occasionally, until sugar is dissolved and mixture is bubbly, about 10 minutes. Bring to a full rolling boil; boil for 15 minutes, stirring constantly. Remove from the heat; skim off foam.
2. Carefully ladle hot mixture into hot half-pint jars, leaving ¼-in. headspace. Remove air bubbles, wipe rims and adjust lids. Process for 15 minutes in a boiling-water canner.
Editor's Note: *The processing time listed is for altitudes of 1,000 feet or less. Add 1 minute to the processing time for each 1,000 feet of additional altitude.*

Pickled Beets

With sweet, tangy and spiced flavors, these pickled beets are so good, they'll convert any naysayers!

—EDNA HOFFMAN HEBRON, INDIANA

PREP: 1¼ HOURS **PROCESS:** 35 MINUTES **MAKES:** 4 PINTS

- **3 pounds small fresh beets**
- **2 cups sugar**
- **2 cups water**
- **2 cups cider vinegar**
- **2 cinnamon sticks (3 inches)**
- **1 teaspoon whole cloves**
- **1 teaspoon whole allspice**

1. Scrub beets and trim tops to 1 in. Place in a Dutch oven and cover with water. Bring to a boil. Reduce heat; cover and simmer for 25-35 minutes or until tender. Remove from the water; cool. Peel beets and cut into fourths.

2. Place beets in a Dutch oven. Add the sugar, water and vinegar. Place spices on a double thickness of cheesecloth; bring up corners of cloth and tie with string to form a bag. Add to the beet mixture. Bring to a boil. Reduce heat; cover and simmer for 10 minutes. Discard spice bag.

3. Carefully pack beets into hot 1-pint jars to within ½ in. of the top. Carefully ladle hot liquid over beets, leaving ½-in. headspace. Remove air bubbles; wipe rims and adjust lids. Process for 35 minutes in a boiling-water canner.

Editor's Note: *The processing time listed is for altitudes of 1,000 feet or less. For altitudes up to 3,000 feet, add 5 minutes; 6,000 feet, add 10 minutes; 8,000 feet, add 15 minutes; 10,000 feet, add 20 minutes.*

Pear Tomato Preserves

I have lived on a farm all my life, so I have always had a garden. I can a lot of my garden-grown fruits and veggies, and I make these wonderful preserves every year.

—EVELYN STEARNS ALTO PASS, ILLINOIS

PREP: 1¼ HOURS **PROCESS:** 20 MINUTES **MAKES:** 5 HALF-PINTS

- 4 **cups sugar**
- 1 **tablespoon ground cinnamon**
- 2 **teaspoons ground cloves**
- 1 **teaspoon ground ginger**
- 2 **medium lemons, chopped**
- 1 **cup water**
- 2 **pounds yellow pear tomatoes, chopped**

1. In a Dutch oven, combine sugar, cinnamon, cloves, ginger, lemons and water. Cook over medium heat for 15 minutes, stirring occasionally. Add the tomatoes. Reduce heat to low; continue cooking for 45-60 minutes or until tomatoes become transparent, stirring frequently.

2. Carefully ladle hot mixture into hot half-pint jars, leaving ¼-in. headspace. Remove air bubbles, wipe rims and adjust lids. Process for 20 minutes in a boiling-water canner.

Editor's Note: *The processing time listed is for altitudes of 1,000 feet or less. Add 1 minute to the processing time for each 1,000 feet of additional altitude.*

Freezer Cucumber Pickles

When I first saw this recipe, I couldn't imagine that freezing cucumbers would work. But to my surprise, they came out perfectly! Now I take them to picnics and give them to friends and neighbors.
—**CONNIE GOENSE** PEMBROKE PINE, FLORIDA

PREP: 20 MINUTES + STANDING
MAKES: 10 PINTS

- 4   pounds pickling cucumbers, sliced
- 8   cups thinly sliced onions
- ¼   cup salt
- ¾   cup water
- 4   cups sugar
- 2   cups cider vinegar

1. In two large bowls, combine the cucumbers, onions, salt and water. Let stand at room temperature for 2 hours. Do not drain.
2. Add sugar and vinegar; stir until sugar dissolves. Pack into 1-pint freezer containers, leaving 1-in. headspace. Cover and freeze for up to 6 weeks.
3. Thaw at room temperature for 4 hours before serving.

Orange Pineapple Marmalade

Here's a sweet and citrusy marmalade that's perfect for spreading on English muffins or biscuits. It also makes a delicious housewarming or hostess gift.
—**STEPHANIE HEISE** ROCHESTER, NEW YORK

PREP: 20 MINUTES **COOK:** 10 MINUTES + STANDING **MAKES:** 4 CUPS

- 2   medium oranges
- 2   cans (8 ounces each) crushed pineapple, drained
- 4   cups sugar
- 2   tablespoons lemon juice

1. Grate outer peel from oranges and set aside. Peel off and discard white membrane from oranges and section the fruit; discard any seeds. In a food processor, combine orange peel and orange sections; cover and process until orange is in small pieces.
2. In a wide-bottomed microwave-safe 2½-qt. bowl, combine the pineapple, sugar, lemon juice and orange mixture. Microwave, uncovered, on high for 2 to 2½ minutes; stir. Heat 2 minutes longer (edges will be bubbly); stir. Microwave for 1½ to 2 minutes or until mixture is bubbly in center; stir. Heat 2 minutes longer; stir. Cool for 10 minutes.
3. Carefully pour into jars or freezer containers; cool to room temperature, about 1 hour.
4. Cover and let stand at room temperature for 4 hours. Refrigerate for up to 3 weeks or freeze for up to 1 year.
Editor's Note: *This recipe does not use pectin. This recipe was tested in a 1,100-watt microwave.*

Home Style COOKING NOTES

Freezer Salsa Jam

This is a great addition to any Mexican dish. You can adjust the heat by reducing the amount of hot peppers and hot sauce.
—**ELLEN KATZKE** DELAVAN, MINNESOTA

PREP: 30 MINUTES
COOK: 10 MINUTES + STANDING
MAKES: 4½ CUPS

- 2 **cups finely chopped plum tomatoes (6 to 7)**
- ½ **cup finely chopped onion**
- 1 **can (8 ounces) tomato sauce**
- ¼ **cup chopped fresh cilantro**
- ¼ **cup finely chopped fresh or canned jalapeno peppers**
- 2 **tablespoons lime juice**
- 1 **teaspoon grated lime peel**
- ¼ **teaspoon hot pepper sauce**
- 1½ **cups sugar**
- 1 **package (1¾ ounces) pectin for lower sugar recipes**
- ¼ **cup water**

1. In a large bowl, combine the tomatoes, onion, tomato sauce, cilantro, peppers, lime juice, peel and hot pepper sauce; set aside.

2. In a large saucepan, combine sugar and pectin; stir in water. Bring to a boil; boil and stir for 1 minute. Remove from the heat. Stir in tomato mixture; continue to stir until well combined.

3. Pour into jars or plastic containers. Cover and let stand overnight or until set, but not longer than 24 hours. Refrigerate for up to 3 weeks or freeze for up to 1 year.

Editor's Note: *Wear disposable gloves when cutting hot peppers; the oils can burn skin. Avoid touching your face.*

Home Style COOKING NOTES

Easy Apricot Jam

Here's the best, most delightfully fruity topping for English muffins or toast. It's so simple to make my homemade jam, you'll want to share it with all your friends.
—**GERI DAVIS** PRESCOTT, ARIZONA

PREP: 5 MINUTES **COOK:** 30 MINUTES + CHILLING **MAKES:** 4 CUPS

- 16 **ounces dried apricots**
- 2½ **cups orange juice**
- ¾ **cup sugar**
- 1 **tablespoon lemon juice**
- ½ **teaspoon ground cinnamon**
- ¼ **teaspoon ground ginger**

1. In a large kettle, combine the apricots, orange juice and sugar; bring to a boil. Reduce heat; cover and simmer for 30 minutes. Stir in the lemon juice, cinnamon and ginger. Remove from the heat and cool to room temperature.

2. Puree in a food processor or blender until smooth. Spoon into jars or freezer containers, leaving ½-in. headspace. Refrigerate for up to 3 weeks or freeze for up to 1 year.

Candy Apple Jelly

With a hint of apple and cinnamon, this jelly spreads holiday cheer on everything from breads to bagels and muffins. Its rosy pink color looks lovely blushing through the clear jars I decorate with fabric-covered lids.

—BETSY PORTER BISMARCK, NORTH DAKOTA

PREP: 10 MINUTES **PROCESS:** 5 MINUTES **MAKES:** ABOUT 6 HALF-PINTS

    4 cups apple juice
    ½ cup red-hot candies
    1 package (1¾ ounces) powdered fruit pectin
    4½ cups sugar

1. In a large saucepan, combine the apple juice, candies and pectin. Bring to a full rolling boil over high heat, stirring constantly. Stir in sugar; return to a full rolling boil. Boil for 2 minutes, stirring constantly.

2. Remove from the heat; skim off any foam and discard any undissolved candies. Carefully ladle hot mixture into hot sterilized half-pint jars, leaving ¼-in. headspace. Remove air bubbles, wipe rims and adjust lids. Process for 5 minutes in a boiling-water canner.

Editor's Note: *The processing time listed is for altitudes of 1,000 feet or less. Add 1 minute to the processing time for each 1,000 feet of additional altitude.*

Rhubarb Jelly

To be honest, I don't especially like cooking. My husband, however, loves it! Now that he's retired, Bob's taken up making jelly. I help him prepare this one because it's my favorite.

—JEAN COLEMAN OTTAWA, ONTARIO

PREP: 20 MINUTES
PROCESS: 10 MINUTES
MAKES: 8 HALF-PINTS

    4½ to 5 pounds rhubarb (4½ to 5
        quarts), cut into 1-inch pieces
    7 cups sugar
    1 to 2 drops red food coloring,
        optional
    2 pouches (3 ounces each) liquid fruit
        pectin

1. Grind the rhubarb in a food processor or grinder. Line a strainer with four layers of cheesecloth and place over a bowl. Place rhubarb in strainer; cover with edges of cheesecloth. Let stand for 30 minutes or until liquid measures 3½ cups. Pour juice into a Dutch oven; add sugar and food coloring if desired.

2. Bring to a boil over high heat, stirring constantly. Add pectin; bring to a full rolling boil. Boil for 1 minute, stirring constantly. Remove from the heat; let stand a few minutes. Skim off foam. Carefully ladle hot mixture into hot half-pint jars, leaving ¼-in. headspace. Remove air bubbles; wipe rims and adjust lids. Process for 10 minutes in a boiling-water canner.

Editor's Note: *The processing time listed is for altitudes of 1,000 feet or less. Add 1 minute to the processing time for each 1,000 feet of additional altitude.*

Amaretto-Peach Preserves

Chock-full of peaches, raisins and pecans, these special preserves enhance ordinary slices of toast.

—REDAWNA KALYNCHUK SEXSMITH, ALBERTA

PREP: 1¼ HOURS **PROCESS:** 10 MINUTES
MAKES: 5 HALF-PINTS

- 1 **cup golden raisins**
- ¾ **cup boiling water**
- 2 **pounds peaches, peeled and chopped**
- 4 **teaspoons grated orange peel**
- ⅓ **cup orange juice**
- 2 **tablespoons lemon juice**
- 3 **cups sugar**
- ½ **cup chopped pecans**
- 3 **tablespoons Amaretto**

1. Place raisins in a small bowl. Cover with boiling water; let stand for 5 minutes. Place raisins with liquid in a large saucepan. Add peaches and orange peel. Bring to a boil. Reduce heat; cover and simmer for 10-15 minutes or until peaches are tender.
2. Stir in orange and lemon juices; return to a boil. Add sugar. Cook, uncovered, over medium heat for 25-30 minutes or until thickened, stirring occasionally. Add pecans; cook 5 minutes longer. Remove from the heat; stir in Amaretto.
3. Carefully ladle hot mixture into hot sterilized half-pint jars, leaving ¼-in. headspace. Remove air bubbles; wipe rims and adjust lids. Process in a boiling-water canner for 5 minutes.

Editor's Note: *The processing time listed is for altitudes of 1,000 feet or less. Add 1 minute to the processing time for each 1,000 feet of additional altitude.*

Home Style COOKING NOTES

Apple Pie Filling

My family is always ecstatic when they see an oven-fresh apple pie cooling on the counter. What a convenience it is to have jars of homemade pie filling on hand so I can treat them to pies year-round.

—LAURIE MACE LOS OSOS, CALIFORNIA

PREP: 35 MINUTES **COOK:** 20 MINUTES + COOLING
MAKES: 5½ QUARTS (ENOUGH FOR ABOUT FIVE 9-INCH PIES)

- 18 **cups sliced peeled tart apples (about 6 pounds)**
- 3 **tablespoons bottled lemon juice**
- 4½ **cups sugar**
- 1 **cup cornstarch**
- 2 **teaspoons ground cinnamon**
- 1 **teaspoon salt**
- ¼ **teaspoon ground nutmeg**
- 10 **cups water**

1. In a large bowl, toss apples with lemon juice; set aside. In a Dutch oven over medium heat, combine the sugar, cornstarch, cinnamon, salt and nutmeg. Add water; bring to a boil. Boil for 2 minutes, stirring constantly. Add apples; return to a boil. Reduce heat; cover and simmer until the apples are tender, about 6-8 minutes. Cool for 30 minutes.
2. Ladle into freezer containers, leaving ½-in. headspace. Cool at room temperature no longer than 1½ hours. Seal and freeze; store up to 12 months.

Tomato Lemon Marmalade

I make this unique marmalade for our church bazaar every fall. It sells out in no time at all! The colors are so attractive.

—HELEN WITT MINNEAPOLIS, MINNESOTA

PREP: 1¼ HOURS **PROCESS:** 10 MINUTES **MAKES:** 9 HALF-PINTS

- 5 **medium ripe tomatoes**
- 4 **cups chopped peeled tart apples (about 4 large)**
- 2 **medium lemons, seeded and finely chopped**
- 6 **cups sugar**
- 2¼ **teaspoons ground ginger**
- 8 **whole cloves**

1. Peel, quarter and chop the tomatoes; place in a colander to drain. Transfer to a Dutch oven; add apples and lemons. Cook and stir over medium heat for 15 minutes. Add sugar and ginger. Tie cloves in a cheesecloth bag; add to the pot. Bring to a boil, stirring occasionally, and cook until sugar is dissolved. Reduce heat; simmer for 40 minutes, stirring frequently.

2. Remove spice bag. Carefully ladle hot mixture into hot half-pint jars, leaving ¼-in. headspace. Remove air bubbles, wipe rims and adjust lids. Process for 10 minutes in a boiling-water canner.

Editor's Note: *The processing time listed is for altitudes of 1,000 feet or less. Add 1 minute to the processing time for each 1,000 feet of additional altitude.*

Jalapeno Bread & Butter Pickles

Even the heat-shy will want to dip into bread and butter pickles with a surprise flavor kick. Ay caramba! They're great!

—KAREN OWEN RISING SUN, INDIANA

PREP: 45 MINUTES +STANDING **PROCESS:** 15 MINUTES **MAKES:** 7 PINTS

- 4 **pounds cucumbers, sliced**
- 5 **small onions, sliced**
- 4 **jalapeno peppers, sliced and seeded**
- ½ **cup canning salt**
- 5 **cups sugar**
- 4 **cups white vinegar**
- 2 **tablespoons mustard seed**
- 2 **teaspoons celery seed**
- 1½ **teaspoons ground turmeric**
- ½ **teaspoon ground cloves**

1. In a container, combine the cucumbers, onions, jalapenos and salt. Cover with crushed ice and mix well. Let stand for 3 hours. Drain; rinse and drain again.

2. In a Dutch oven, combine the sugar, vinegar and seasonings; bring to a boil. Add cucumber mixture; return to a boil. Remove from the heat.

3. Carefully ladle hot mixture into hot pint jars, leaving ½-in. headspace. Remove air bubbles; wipe rims and adjust lids. Process for 15 minutes in a boiling-water canner.

Editor's Notes: *When cutting hot peppers, disposable gloves are recommended. Avoid touching your face. The processing time listed is for altitudes of 1,000 feet or less. For altitudes up to 3,000 feet, add 5 minutes; 6,000 feet, add 10 minutes; 8,000 feet, add 15 minutes; 10,000 feet, add 20 minutes.*

Freezer Salsa

I make dozens of jars of salsa each fall to enjoy during the winter. I also give it as gifts and donate jars to school parties. It adds zip to everything from chips and fajitas to meat loaf.

—CATH McKENNA SUMMERSIDE, PRINCE EDWARD ISLAND

PREP: 25 MINUTES **COOK:** 30 MINUTES + COOLING **MAKES:** ABOUT 6 CUPS

- ¾ **cup chopped onion**
- ½ **cup finely chopped celery**
- ⅓ **cup finely chopped sweet red or green pepper**
- 1 **to 2 jalapeno peppers, seeded and finely chopped**
- 3 **garlic cloves, minced**
- ¼ **cup olive oil**

- 12 **plum tomatoes, peeled, seeded and chopped (about 6 cups)**
- 3 **cans (6 ounces each) tomato paste**
- ⅓ **cup lime juice**
- ⅓ **cup white vinegar**
- 1 **tablespoon honey**
- 1 **tablespoon sugar**
- 1½ **teaspoons salt**
- 1 **teaspoon dried basil**

1. In a large saucepan, saute the onion, celery, peppers and garlic in oil for 5 minutes or until tender.

2. Stir in the remaining ingredients; bring to a boil. Reduce heat; cover and simmer for 20 minutes, stirring occasionally. Cool completely.

3. Spoon into freezer containers. Cover and freeze for up to 3 months. Stir before serving.

Editor's Note: *Wear disposable gloves when cutting hot peppers; the oils can burn skin. Avoid touching your face.*

Pina Colada Jam

If you like pina coladas, you'll love our jam. But here's the kicker: The secret ingredient is fresh zucchini. Because this jam is so unexpectedly delicious, we challenge you to try it in a radical new way. Tell us what you think!

—TASTE OF HOME TEST KITCHEN

PREP: 15 MINUTES **COOK:** 20 MINUTES + COOLING **MAKES:** 3½ PINTS

- 6 **cups sugar**
- 6 **cups shredded peeled zucchini**
- 1 **can (8 ounces) crushed pineapple, undrained**
- ¼ **cup lime juice**
- 2 **packages (3 ounces each) pineapple gelatin**
- 1 **teaspoon rum extract**

1. In a Dutch oven, combine the sugar, zucchini, pineapple and lime juice. Bring to a boil. Boil for 10 minutes, stirring constantly. Remove from the heat; stir in gelatin and extract until gelatin is dissolved.

2. Pour into jars or freezer containers, leaving ½-in. headspace. Cool completely before covering with lids. Refrigerate for up to 3 weeks or freeze for up to 1 year.

Garden's Harvest Pickles

This recipe is like giardiniera but sweeter. I have a certain sense of pride giving jars as gifts knowing all the vegetables were raised in my own garden.

—**LINDA CHAPMAN** MERIDEN, IOWA

PREP: 1 HOUR + CHILLING
PROCESS: 20 MINUTES/BATCH **MAKES:** 11 PINTS

- 3 **large onions, cut into wedges**
- 3 **medium green peppers, cut into 1-inch pieces**
- 3 **medium sweet red peppers, cut into 1-inch pieces**
- ¼ **cup canning salt**
- 6 **celery ribs, cut into 2-inch lengths**
- 6 **medium carrots, cut into ½-inch slices**
- 3 **cups cauliflower florets**
- 3 **cups cut fresh green beans (2-inch lengths)**
- 3 **medium zucchini, cut into 1-inch slices**
- 6 **cups sugar**
- 6 **cups white vinegar**
- ¼ **cup mustard seed**
- ¼ **cup celery seed**

1. In a bowl, combine the onions, peppers and canning salt. Cover and refrigerate overnight.
2. Drain; place in a stockpot. Add the remaining ingredients. Bring to a boil. Reduce heat; simmer, uncovered, for 15-20 minutes or until tender. Carefully ladle hot mixture into hot 1-pint jars, leaving ½-in. headspace. Remove air bubbles; wipe rims and adjust lids. Process for 20 minutes in a boiling-water canner.

Editor's Note: *The processing time listed is for altitudes of 1,000 feet or less. For altitudes up to 3,000 feet, add 5 minutes; 6,000 feet, add 10 minutes; 8,000 feet, add 15 minutes; 10,000 feet, add 20 minutes.*

Home Style COOKING NOTES

Freezer Raspberry Sauce

Here's a flavorful topping for ice cream and shortcake. We even like it over waffles!
—**KATIE KOZIOLEK** HARTLAND, MINNESOTA

PREP: 20 MINUTES + STANDING **MAKES:** 4 PINTS

- 3 **cups mashed fresh raspberries**
- 3 **cups sugar**
- 1 **cup light corn syrup**
- 1 **package (3 ounces) liquid fruit pectin**
- 2 **tablespoons lemon juice**
- 4 **cups whole fresh raspberries**

1. In a large bowl, combine mashed berries, sugar and corn syrup. Let stand for 10 minutes. In small bowl, combine liquid pectin and lemon juice. Stir into fruit mixture for 3 minutes to distribute pectin evenly. Stir in whole berries.
2. Transfer to 1-pint freezer containers; seal and let stand at room temperature for 24 hours or until partially set. Store in refrigerator up to 3 weeks or freeze for up to 1 year. Thaw and stir before using. Serve over ice cream, sponge cake, shortcake, waffles or plain yogurt.

Rosemary Jelly

My deliciously different green jelly gets its flavor from an unusual source—rosemary. The herb adds a refreshing zip to the otherwise sweet spread.

—MARGARET DUMIRE CARROLL, OHIO

PREP: 35 MINUTES **PROCESS:** 10 MINUTES **MAKES:** 3½ PINTS

1¼ cups boiling water
2 tablespoons minced fresh rosemary
3 cups sugar
¼ cup cider vinegar
1 pouch (3 ounces) liquid fruit pectin
2 to 3 drops green food coloring

1. In a large saucepan, combine boiling water and rosemary; cover and let stand for 15 minutes. Strain, reserving liquid. If necessary, add water to measure 1¼ cups. Return liquid to pan; add sugar and vinegar. Bring to a full rolling boil over high heat, stirring constantly. Add pectin, stirring until mixture boils. Boil and stir for 1 minute.

2. Remove from the heat; skim off foam. Add food coloring if desired. Carefully ladle hot mixture into hot half-pint jars, leaving ¼-in. headspace. Remove air bubbles, wipe rims and adjust lids. Process for 10 minutes in a boiling-water canner.

Editor's Note: *The processing time listed is for altitudes of 1,000 feet or less. Add 1 minute to the processing time for each 1,000 feet of additional altitude.*

Garden Tomato Relish

It's so easy to have a tasty relish on hand for hot dogs, hamburgers and other dishes. Share it with a friend.

—KELLY MARTEL TILLSONBURG, ONTARIO

PREP: 1½ HOURS + SIMMERING
PROCESS: 20 MINUTES
MAKES: 10 PINTS

---

10 pounds tomatoes
3 large sweet onions, finely chopped
2 medium sweet red peppers, finely chopped
2 medium green peppers, finely chopped
2 teaspoons mustard seed
1 teaspoon celery seed
4½ cups white vinegar
2½ cups packed brown sugar
3 tablespoons canning salt
2 teaspoons ground ginger
2 teaspoons ground cinnamon
1 teaspoon ground allspice
1 teaspoon ground cloves
1 teaspoon ground nutmeg

1. In a saucepan, bring 8 cups water to a boil. Add tomatoes, a few at a time; boil for 30 seconds. Drain and immediately place tomatoes in ice water. Drain and pat dry; peel and finely chop. Place in a stockpot. Add onions and peppers.

2. Place mustard and celery seed on a double thickness of cheesecloth; bring up corners of cloth and tie with string to form a bag. Add spice bag and the remaining ingredients to the pot. Bring to a boil. Reduce heat and simmer, uncovered, for 60-75 minutes or until slightly thickened. Discard spice bag.

3. Carefully ladle relish into hot 1-pint jars, leaving ½-in. headspace. Remove air bubbles; wipe rims and adjust lids. Process in boiling-water canner for 20 minutes.

Editor's Note: *The processing time listed is for altitudes of 1,000 feet or less. For altitudes up to 3,000 feet, add 5 minutes; 6,000 feet, add 10 minutes; 8,000 feet, add 15 minutes; 10,000 feet, add 20 minutes.*

Cran-Raspberry Jam

I'm sure to pick up extra bags of cranberries in the fall so I can make this lovely jam year-round. The kids love it on peanut butter sandwiches. Jars make great gifts.

—MARJILEE BOOTH
CHINO HILLS, CALIFORNIA

PREP: 20 MINUTES
PROCESS: 10 MINUTES
MAKES: 6 HALF-PINTS

- 2 **packages (10 ounces each) frozen sweetened raspberries, thawed**
- 4 **cups fresh or frozen cranberries**
- 1 **package (1¾ ounces) powdered fruit pectin**
- 5 **cups sugar**

1. Drain raspberries, reserving juice; add enough water to juice to measure 1½ cups. Pour into a Dutch oven. Add the raspberries, cranberries and pectin; bring to a full rolling boil, stirring constantly. Stir in sugar; return to a full rolling boil. Boil for 1 minute, stirring constantly.

2. Remove from the heat; skim off foam. Carefully ladle hot mixture into hot half-pint jars, leaving ¼-in. headspace. Remove air bubbles; wipe rims and adjust lids. Process for 10 minutes in a boiling-water canner.

Editor's Note: *The processing time listed is for altitudes of 1,000 feet or less. Add 1 minute to the processing time for each 1,000 feet of additional altitude.*

Surprise Raspberry Jam

Family and friends will never guess the secret ingredient in this jam. It's tomatoes! I got the recipe from a co-worker, and it is just delicious.

—ELIZABETH BAKER BIRDSBORO, PENNSYLVANIA

PREP: 15 MINUTES **COOK:** 35 MINUTES + STANDING **MAKES:** ABOUT 5½ CUPS

- 5 **cups chopped peeled fresh tomatoes**
- 4 **cups sugar**
- 1 **tablespoon lemon juice**
- 2 **packages (3 ounces each) raspberry gelatin**

1. In a large saucepan, combine the tomatoes, sugar and lemon juice. Cook and stir over high heat until mixture comes to a boil. Reduce heat; simmer, uncovered, for 25 minutes. Remove from the heat. Skim off foam if necessary. Stir in gelatin until completely dissolved.

2. Pour into jars or containers; cool to room temperature, about 1 hour. Cover and let stand for 3 hours or until set, but not longer than 24 hours. Refrigerate for up to 3 weeks or freeze for up to 1 year.

Apricot Pineapple Jam

Dried apricots, crushed pineapple and grapefruit juice create a memorable jam. The sweet and tart juice is what makes the jam taste so good.

—CAROL RADIL NEW BRITAIN, CONNECTICUT

PREP: 10 MINUTES **COOK:** 1 HOUR 20 MINUTES + STANDING **MAKES:** 5 CUPS

- 12 **ounces dried apricots**
- 1 **cup water**
- 1 **can (20 ounces) crushed pineapple, undrained**
- ½ **cup grapefruit juice**
- 3 **cups sugar**

1. In a large saucepan, bring apricots and water to a boil. Reduce heat; cover and simmer for 15 minutes or until apricots are very tender. Mash. Add pineapple, grapefruit juice and sugar. Simmer, uncovered, for 1 hour or until thick and translucent, stirring frequently.

2. Pour into jars or freezer containers; cool to room temperature, about 1 hour.

3. Cover and let stand overnight or until set, but no longer than 24 hours. Refrigerate for up to 3 weeks or freeze for up to 1 year.

Editor's Note: *This recipe does not use pectin.*

Three-Berry Freezer Jam

Give in to temptation and buy fresh berries in bulk. You'll be glad you did when you transform those ripe little gems into a sweet spread that can also get you out of a gift-giving jam.

—SHANNON BECKER BURTON, OHIO

PREP: 20 MINUTES + STANDING **COOK:** 10 MINUTES **MAKES:** 3 PINTS

 2 **cups fresh strawberries**
 2 **cups fresh raspberries**
 2 **cups fresh blackberries**
5¼ **cups sugar**
 2 **tablespoons lemon juice**
 1 **package (1¾ ounces) powdered fruit pectin**
 ¾ **cup water**

1. In a food processor, process the berries in batches until finely chopped. Transfer to a large bowl. Stir in sugar and lemon juice. Let stand for 10 minutes, stirring occasionally.

2. In a small saucepan, combine fruit pectin and water. Bring to a boil; cook and stir for 1 minute. Add to fruit mixture; stirring constantly for 4-5 minutes or until sugar is dissolved.

3. Pour into jars or freezer containers, leaving ½-in. headspace. Cover and let stand overnight or until set, but not longer than 24 hours. Refrigerate for up to 3 weeks or freeze for up to 1 year.

Kool-Aid Pickles

Everyone will love getting into these pickles. They owe their fun color and sweet-sour taste to a long soak in fruity Kool-Aid.

—TASTE OF HOME TEST KITCHEN

PREP: 10 MINUTES + CHILLING **MAKES:** 3 CUPS

> 1 jar (32 ounces) whole dill pickles, undrained
> ⅔ cup sugar
> 1 envelope unsweetened Kool-Aid mix, flavor of your choice

1. Drain pickles, reserving juice. In a bowl, combine the reserved juice, sugar and Kool-Aid, stirring until sugar is dissolved. Set aside.

2. Slice pickles; return to jar. Pour juice mixture over pickles. Discard remaining juice. Cover and refrigerate for 1 week before serving.

CHERRY

ORANGE

LEMONADE

LIME

BLUE RASPBERRY

Home Style COOKING NOTES

Can Do!

I'm all about preserving the harvest.

BY MARISA MCCLELLAN

I'm a food writer and teacher from Philadelphia. Home canning is an all-consuming passion of mine.

Coincidentally, food preservation is making a comeback. Cooks of all ages are increasingly interested in capturing fresh flavors and doing so affordably. I want to help people let go of their fears about canning. My goal is to make it accessible and fun.

I grew up in Oregon, and I loved helping my mother transform wild berries and backyard apples into jams and sauces. Years later, in college, I picked up a nifty old pint-size Ball jar with a wire clamp closure and started a jar collection. I used them to hold everything from sugar to leftovers. In those early years, they even doubled as drinking glasses!

Then, five years ago, I went blueberry picking with friends and came home with 10 pounds of fruit and a craving for jam. I started using my jars for their intended purpose.

Now I fill hundreds of jars each season with pickled vegetables, salsa, soup stock, whole tomatoes and more.

I extended my passion to the keyboard, too. I've launched a blog, *foodinjars.com*. Aiming to open more eyes to the world of preserving, I share personal canning experiences, food photos, tutorials on proper technique and recipes for a potpourri of canned goods.

My readers are from all walks of life, from the city and country alike. Some are longtime canners excited to find kindred spirits. Others are novices ready to roll up their sleeves and try canning for the first time.

What they all share is an appreciation for the wonderful, exciting flavors of home-canned food. They like the fact that they know exactly what goes into their foods, because they put it there.

In the canning classes I teach in southeastern Pennsylvania, my students do everything from sterilizing and processing jars to setting them out to cool and listening for the musical ping, a sound that I like to call "the symphony of sealing."

Sometimes, I also serve as guest presenter at canning parties, which is a lot of fun. Friends get together, break out their canning gear and spend an afternoon "putting up" with each other.

Canning parties are a blast—and a great way to tackle a good deal of preserving. Everyone leaves the party with a feeling of accomplishment. You take home something you've made and knowledge that will help you do more of it in the future.

You don't need a huge farm-style kitchen and fancy equipment to can—just a bit of counter space, a stove, a sink and a few pots.

Nor do you need a lot of room, as my husband, Scott, can attest. In our little apartment, Scott has grown accustomed to finding my canned goods in the hall closet, our dining room cabinet and even tucked under the bedroom dresser!

Canning is a great way to feel connected and to extend the season's bounty. It's fun to spend a sunny day at a farmers market or a U-pick farm, and then preserve your harvest at home.

There's nothing like reaching into the cupboard in the dreary days of winter and pulling out a fresh, beautiful jar of summer.

Pickled Green Beans

This recipe produces zippy little pickles and preserves my green beans for months to come—if they last that long. I crank up the heat a bit with cayenne pepper.

—MARISA MCCLELLAN
PHILADELPHIA, PENNSYLVANIA

PREP: 20 MINUTES
PROCESS: 10 MINUTES **MAKES:** 4 PINTS

- 1¾ **pounds fresh green beans, trimmed**
- 1 **teaspoon cayenne pepper**
- 4 **garlic cloves, peeled**
- 4 **teaspoons dill seed or 4 fresh dill heads**
- 2½ **cups water**
- 2½ **cups white vinegar**
- ¼ **cup canning salt**

1. Pack beans into four hot 1-pint jars to within ½ in. of the top. Add the cayenne, garlic and dill seed to jars.
2. In a large saucepan, bring the water, vinegar and salt to a boil.
3. Carefully ladle hot mixture over beans, leaving ½-in. headspace. Remove air bubbles; wipe rims and adjust lids. Process for 10 minutes in a boiling-water canner.

Editor's Note: *The processing time listed is for altitudes of 1,000 feet or less. For altitudes up to 3,000 feet, add 5 minutes; 6,000 feet, add 10 minutes; 8,000 feet, add 15 minutes; 10,000 feet, add 20 minutes.*

from Marisa's kitchen

Blueberry Jam

Summer doesn't feel complete without at least one berry-picking trip and a batch of homemade blueberry jam. Eat atop fresh scones or biscuits for maximum enjoyment!

—MARISA MCCLELLAN PHILADELPHIA, PENNSYLVANIA

PREP: 35 MINUTES **PROCESS:** 10 MINUTES/BATCH **MAKES:** 9 HALF-PINTS

- 8 **cups fresh blueberries**
- 6 **cups sugar**
- 3 **tablespoons lemon juice**
- 2 **teaspoons ground cinnamon**
- 2 **teaspoons grated lemon peel**
- ½ **teaspoon ground nutmeg**
- 2 **pouches (3 ounces each) liquid fruit pectin**

1. Place blueberries in a food processor; cover and process until blended. Transfer to a stockpot. Stir in the sugar, lemon juice, cinnamon, lemon peel and nutmeg. Bring to a full rolling boil over high heat, stirring constantly. Stir in pectin. Boil for 1 minute, stirring constantly.
2. Remove from the heat; skim off foam. Ladle hot mixture into hot sterilized half-pint jars, leaving ¼-in. headspace. Remove air bubbles; wipe rims and adjust lids. Process for 10 minutes in a boiling-water canner.

Editor's Note: *The processing time listed is for altitudes of 1,000 feet or less. Add 1 minute to the processing time for each 1,000 feet of additional altitude.*

General INDEX

HOT PEPPERS
Freezer Salsa Jam, 290
Halibut Enchiladas, 191
Italian Beef Sandwiches, 137
Jalapeno Bread & Butter
  Pickles, 294
Jalapeno Pepper Jelly, 284
Pickled Peppers, 275
Pineapple Salsa, 285
Raspberry-Onion Jalapeno
  Chutney, 272
Steak with Chipotle-Lime
  Chimichurri, 192

**ICE CREAM, SHERBET
  & SORBET (also see
  Frozen Desserts)**
Cherry-Chip Ice Cream
  Sandwiches, 255
Grandma's Orange Milk
  Sherbet, 244
Lemon Sorbet Torte, 207
Rhubarb Ice Cream, 240

**JAMS, JELLIES,
  MARMALADE
  & PRESERVES**
Amaretto-Peach Preserves, 292
Apricot Pineapple Jam, 299
Blueberry Jam, 303
Blueberry Jelly, 280
Candy Apple Jelly, 291
Chunky Peach Spread, 279
Cran-Raspberry Jam, 298
Easy Apricot Jam, 290
Freezer Salsa Jam, 290
Jalapeno Pepper Jelly, 284
Mint Jelly, 285
Orange Pineapple Marmalade, 289
Orange Rhubarb Spread, 276
Pear Tomato Preserves, 288
Pina Colada Jam, 295
Pineapple Kiwi Jam, 272
Raspberry Peach Jam, 286
Rhubarb Jelly, 291
Rosemary Jelly, 297
Strawberry Freezer Jam, 277
Strawberry Marmalade, 273
Surprise Raspberry Jam, 298
Three-Berry Freezer Jam, 300
Tomato Lemon Marmalade, 293

Tri-Berry Jam, 273
Tuscan Sun-Dried Tomato Jam, 51
Violet Jelly, 283

LAMB
Roasted Leg of Lamb, 204
Scotch Broth, 89

LASAGNA
Donna Lasagna, 168
Sneaky Lasagna, 190

LEMON
Blueberry Citrus Cake, 265
Broiled Fish with
  Tarragon Sauce, 163
Easy Lemon Curd Bars, 269
Ginger Creme Sandwich
  Cookies, 256
Grilled Lemon Pork Chops, 149
Lemon Carrot Bread, 226
Lemon Easter Bread, 210
Lemon Pound Cake, 246
Lemon Snowdrops, 261
Lemon Sorbet Torte, 207
Lemon Velvet Dessert, 251
Moist Lemon Angel Cake Roll, 238
Roasted Citrus & Herb
  Turkey, 225
Shrimp Salad Lemon Baskets, 97
Sour Cream-Lemon Pie, 248
Tomato Lemon Marmalade, 293
Turkey Piccata, 131

LIME
Lime Pudding Cakes, 239
Steak with Chipotle-Lime
  Chimichurri, 192

**LONG JOHNS See
  Doughnuts & Long Johns.**

MANGO
Curried Tropical Nut Mix, 46
Mango Chicken Wraps, 70

MAPLE
Maple Chicken 'n' Ribs, 193
Maple-Glazed Acorn Squash, 100
Maple-Pecan Snack Mix, 45
Maple Pork Chops, 143

MARSHMALLOWS
Caramel Heavenlies, 254
Crispy Star Pops, 213
Easter Fruit Salad, 229
Marshmallow Easter Eggs, 230

**MEAT LOAVES &
  MEATBALLS**
Applesauce Meatballs, 170
Meatball Stew, 181
Meatballs Stroganoff, 194
Mom's Meat Loaf, 155
Stroganoff-Style Spaghetti
  'n' Meatballs, 140
Turkey Meat Loaf, 166

MEAT PIES
Chicken Potpie, 177
Hearty Shepherd's Pie, 183
Herbed Beef Stew with
  Puff Pastry, 173
Tater Crust Tuna Pie, 132
Tourtiere, 198
Turkey Potpies, 197

MEATLESS See Vegetarian.

MELON
Honey-Lime Melon Salad, 107
Summertime Melon Salad, 108

MINT
Mint Jelly, 285
Peppermint Stick Cookies, 218

MUSHROOMS
Artichoke & Mushroom Toasts, 49
Country Chuck Roast with
  Mushroom Gravy, 169
Crab-Stuffed Mushrooms, 40
Fines Herbes & Mushroom
  Omelets Deluxe, 8
Mashed Potato Sausage Bake, 171
Mushroom-Spinach Bake, 19
Turkey Potpies, 197

NOODLES (also see Pasta)
Beef and Noodle Casserole, 142
Cream of Chicken Noodle Soup, 64
Sausage-Corn Bake, 145

Alphabetical INDEX